Y0-ADZ-658

# ZIONISM
*without* ZION

# ZIONISM
## *without* ZION

The Jewish Territorial Organization
and Its Conflict with the Zionist Organization

### GUR ALROEY

Wayne State University Press | Detroit

© 2016 by Wayne State University Press, Detroit, Michigan 48201.
All rights reserved. No part of this book may be
reproduced without formal permission.
Manufactured in the United States of America.

20 19 18 17 16     5 4 3 2 1

ISBN 978-0-8143-4206-0 (cloth)
ISBN 978-0-8143-4207-7 (e-book)

Library of Congress Control Number: 2015953523

∞

*Designed and typeset by Bryce Schimanski*
*Composed in Adobe Caslon Pro*

# Contents

*Preface* vii

Introduction: A Shared Ancestry 1

1. The Big Bang 15
2. A Land Ablaze 73
3. A Land for a People, Not a People for a Land 123
4. The Territorialist Movement in Palestine 172
5. The Search for a Homeland 202
6. Swan Song 254

Conclusion: Zionism Without Zion? 295

*Notes* 305
*Bibliography* 333
*Index* 343

# Preface

*Zionism Without Zion: The Jewish Territorial Organization and Its Conflict with the Zionist Organization*, completes a triptych begun with two of my earlier books: *An Unpromising Land: Jewish Migration to Palestine in the Early Twentieth Century* and *The Quiet Revolution: Jewish Emigration from Imperial Russia, 1875–1924* (in Hebrew). These three books—each from a different perspective—deal with Eastern European Jewry in the late nineteenth and early twentieth centuries and with the various alternatives proposed to resolve their distress and poverty. The question "Wohin?" (whither), which was a key concern in those years, is the connecting thread that runs through all three volumes.

In the first two books I examined the large wave of Jewish migration from Eastern Europe to Palestine and America from the viewpoint of the ordinary Jewish migrant who sought to escape the privations of daily existence and begin a new life across the sea. Both books describe how the decision to emigrate was reached, the perilous journey until the destination was reached, and the difficulties of absorption into the new society. On the other hand, *Zionism Without Zion* deals with the territorialist ideology, which was a political reflection of the mass migration, pogroms, and sufferings of the Jews in Eastern Europe. Historians of Jewish nationalism have written little about Territorialism. There is not even a single book about the Jewish Territorial Organization (ITO), established as a result of the crisis of ideology and principles that beset the Zionist Organization. I hope that this book will fill the gap and shed light on a political movement that had power and influence over the Jewish people at the beginning of the twentieth century but has vanished into the sea of (historical) oblivion.

The Territorialists had a pessimistic worldview and foresaw a dire fate for the Jews in Eastern Europe. Their fear that the Jews could not wait

# PREFACE

for the Zionist Organization to establish a state for the Jewish people in Palestine led them to favor a solution "here and now"—and not only in the Land of Israel.

During the four years I spent in my research on the territorialist movement, I discovered by chance (or perhaps not by chance) a copy of *Medinot la-yehudim* (States for the Jews), which Eliyahu Benyamini, the author, dedicated to a respected professor and scholar at an Israeli university: "To my neighbor, Prof. . . .: *Oy mit rahmones!* In friendship, E. Binyamini." The deeper I delved into the territorialist ideology and the more I came to understand its character and the reasons for its emergence, the louder these words rang in my mind. What did he mean, "Have mercy"? Was he asking the stern professor to treat him gently while reading the book? Or was this a cry of despair provoked by his study of the territorialist idea? I believe that intelligent readers will find an answer to this question after reading *Zionism Without Zion*.

The ITO collection in the Central Zionist Archives in Jerusalem made it possible for me to trace the history of the organization from its founding until its disbanding in 1925. Although the Territorialists seceded from the Zionist Organization after the Uganda controversy and set up an alternative organization, throughout their activities they regarded themselves as Zionists in every sense of the word and as continuing the historical path laid out by Leon Pinsker and Theodor Herzl. The fact that ITO documents in the Central Zionist Archives lie alongside those of Herzl, Menahem Mendel Ussishkin (the Territorialists' most bitter antagonist), and the institutions of the Zionist Organization is a kind of poetic justice.

*Zionism Without Zion* would not have been completed without the kind and devoted assistance of the staff of the Central Zionist Archives: Rachel Rubinstein, Batia Leshem, Simone Schleichter, and Anat Banin. Thanks are also due to the staff of the YIVO, especially librarian Yeshaya Metal, as well as Gunnar Berg and Jesse Cohen, who devoted much effort to locating the relevant files and publications concerning the Territorialists. Finally, I wish to express my thanks to the team at Wayne State University Press, especially the Editor-in-Chief, Kathryn Wildfong, for her patience, good will, and good advice; and Mimi Braverman for her professional copyediting.

# Introduction

## A Shared Ancestry

The ideologies of Territorialism and Zionism were born at the same time. "The goal of our present endeavors must be not the Holy Land, but a land of our own," wrote Leon Pinsker in *Auto-Emancipation*.[1] There were those in Jewish society who adhered to the idea of "a land of our own" and sought to establish a state, or an autonomous entity, outside the Land of Israel.

Pinsker was not the first to conceive of the idea to settle Jews in various territories around the world. The idea had been raised many years earlier by Jewish leaders who were seeking creative solutions to the Jewish question. These proposals were usually local initiatives by individuals and vanished soon after they were raised, without leaving any traces behind. From the second half of the seventeenth century until the 1880s, a variety of ideas kept springing up to settle Jews in places such as Curaçao in the West Indies; Suriname; Cayenne (French Guiana); Novorossiya; the Crimea; Buffalo, New York; Texas; broad tracts along the Tennessee, Mississippi, and Missouri rivers; Illinois, Ohio, Nebraska, or Kansas; and Cyprus.[2] None of these initiatives were connected with territorialist ideology, which was spawned by the Zionist movement in the early twentieth century.

The term ideology, as used here, is based on the definition proposed by historian Gideon Shimoni in his book *Zionist Ideology*: a system of ideas that require action. Shimoni differentiates between the basic concept ("fundamental ideology") and its execution ("operative ideology"). Fundamental ideology constitutes the substantive claims inherent in a system of ideas that require action and shape the ideology and its ultimate goals. Operative ideology, on the other hand, constitutes the strategy and tactics that are applied in service of the basic ideas.[3] In this book I use Shimoni's definition to examine the components of the

## INTRODUCTION

territorialist ideology and the core principles of territorialist thinking. I also try to trace the actual hunt for some territory for the Jewish people and the political activities of Territorialists in Jewish society.

However, in this book I do not cover any of the specific attempts at settlement (of which there were many) by individual Jews outside Palestine. I also do not review such initiatives in earlier or later periods of Jewish history. Rather, I examine the political expression of the idea and its crystallization into an organized and compelling doctrine known as Territorialism. The process began in the early 1880s but did not mature into an autonomous ideology until the establishment of the Jewish Territorial Organization (ITO) in August 1905.[4] Thus here I attempt to understand Jewish Territorialism, how the Territorialists wanted to ease the hardship of Eastern European Jewry in the early twentieth century, and their competition with their colleagues in the Zionist movement.

The use of the term Zionist colleague and not rival is intentional. The Territorialists were legitimate children of the Zionist movement; many of them saw themselves as full-fledged Zionists. They participated in its establishment, and some even implemented their Zionism by immigrating to Palestine. In contrast with the opponents of Zionism—both on the right and on the left—the Territorialists never denied the Zionist idea or rejected its legitimacy. On the contrary, they considered themselves the true Zionists, the followers of the historical path laid down by Pinsker and Theodor Herzl, and supported Jewish sovereignty anywhere in the world, even outside the Land of Israel. It was actually their conceptual closeness and common parentage with the Zionists that made the struggle between the two groups so emotional and even violent at times. The exchange of ideas between the Zionists and the Territorialists was imbalanced: The Zionists categorically rejected territorialist ideology, whereas the Territorialists believed that the two doctrines could exist side by side.

History proves that the Zionist path eventually led to the establishment of a Jewish state in Palestine, whereas the Territorialists failed in their attempt to find a territory to settle. Nevertheless, in this study I refrain from referring to "Zionist success" and "Territorialist failure" for several reasons. First, there is no place for judgmental terminology in historical scholarship. The territorialist ideology must be understood first and foremost from a contemporary perspective and not from our own. The pogroms of 1903–1906, the westward migration of hundreds of thousands of Jews at the beginning of the twentieth century, the poverty in Eastern European Jewish society, and the limited ability of Palestine to absorb masses of migrants—these were the main factors behind the emergence of Territorialism. So dire and dreadful were the burning issues of that time that some Jews feared that the timetable for the realization of Zionism would not provide a suitable solution for the Jews' distress and that it was therefore necessary to act expeditiously and establish a homeland for the Jewish people wherever possible, particularly for the poor, the emigrants, and the refugees from the pogroms. Second, 130 years of Zionist activity does not guarantee that the idea will remain successful. Zionism has indeed defeated all its opponents, but this statement should be qualified with the words "thus far." The future of the Zionist enterprise in Palestine, like the future of any individual or group, is veiled in fog and uncertainty. If the prophecies of the territorialist movement are realized one day, the historical perspective will change and the Zionists' brilliant victory will be reinterpreted as a bitter defeat. At the beginning of the twentieth century, the Territorialists argued that 600,000 Arabs would not let the Jews have any peace if they attempted to settle in Palestine, that the resulting conflict would be insoluble and would drag on for many years, that it was not right to put all the Jews' eggs in one basket, and that their concentration in a single territory would not only not provide any benefit to the Jewish people but would also endanger it. Any of these arguments might still turn out to be expressions of a sober view of reality; the Territorialists' apocalyptic vision might still, God forbid, come true. In light of the need to avoid anachronisms and in the absence of a sufficiently long perspective, I limit this study to the past and attempt to understand territorialist ideology as it was then, without trying to justify or refute it.

Historians have paid scant attention to the territorialist ideology. Compared with the wealth of research published about the Zionist movement, little or nothing has been written about Territorialism. Michael Astour, in his comprehensive *Geshikhte fun di Frayland Lige*, deplored the banishing (rather than vanishing) of Territorialism from historiography and the one-dimensional and unsatisfactory manner in which contemporary Jewish history tends to be presented: "The lives of Jews in the last eighty years, with all their multifaceted trends and processes, so complex and full of contradictions, with their ramified and fragmented spiritual world have been reduced to a naïve and childish 'happy end'—the establishment of the State of Israel. In the historiography of the Jewish people (especially in English), the 'Bund' is not mentioned even once. Very rarely one may find a reference to the old territorialist organization of Zangwill. The new Territorialism, the Freeland League, has disappeared as though it never existed."[5] Even if some may disagree with Astour's interpretation and the reasons he offers for the disappearance of Territorialism, it is absolutely clear that his claims are factually justified. Although Territorialism is as old as Zionism, it has rarely been studied objectively and in depth. The ITO is usually mentioned in the literature only incidentally and relegated to a footnote, but it is not treated as a subject in its own right. Astour's book, which was written in Yiddish and published in the 1960s, is the most comprehensive study of the territorialist ideology of the 1930s. Astour, like his father, was a Territorialist, and his book seeks to redress a historiographic wrong and present the doctrine of Territorialism and its place among the Jewish people.

Eliyahu Benyamini's *Medinot la-yehudim* (States for the Jews) is the only book in Hebrew that deals with Territorialism and the attempts to set up self-governing colonies for Jews in thirty-four different countries. This pioneering study was the first to expose Israeli readers to the various territorialist initiatives of the first half of the twentieth century. Benyamini reviewed plans to settle Jews in nearly every corner of the globe and assessed their nature and the reasons for their failure. Because the book contains a large number of documents related to Territorialism, it is more of an anthology than a research work. Yitzhak Marmur, David Vital, and Haim Avni have also addressed the territorialist movement, but their studies leave one hungry for more and certainly do not exhaust the topic.[6] There is no doubt that a comprehensive study of Territorialism in general and of the ITO in particular is necessary to fill the historiographic lacuna and shed light on an ideology that was fairly widespread in the Jewish world a hundred years ago.

The territorialist ideology has been covered in several important and illuminating studies that deal with Israel Zangwill's literary and political career and in studies of the Yishuv in Palestine in the last years of the Ottoman era. Although Territorialism was not the main focus of these works, they can certainly help us understand its ideas. In *A Jew in the Public Arena: The Career of Israel Zangwill*, Meri-Jane Rochelson

# INTRODUCTION

looks at various facets of Zangwill's public life, including his territorialist preoccupation. Arieh Bruce Saposnik, in *Becoming Hebrew: The Creation of a Jewish National Culture in Ottoman Palestine*, on the emergence of Hebrew culture in Palestine, considers the Uganda episode as it relates to the Yishuv. Adam Rovner's book *In the Shadow of Zion: Promised Lands Before Israel*, brings to life six visions of a Jewish national home outside Israel. Jonathan Frankel, in his monumental *Prophecy and Politics*, about the growth and evolution of Jewish nationalism, discusses Territorialism in the Russian Empire during the early twentieth century. In recent years several alternative history novels have been based on the idea that a Jewish state has been established in a place other than the Middle East. The most prominent among them are Michael Chabon's *The Yiddish Policemen's Union*, about the Jewish territory in Alaska, and Nava Semel's Hebrew *IsraIsland*, about an overcrowded Jewish settlement on an island near Niagara Falls.

The present study asserts its fidelity to the historical discipline and has no pretensions of dealing with what-ifs. Historians may not engage in vain imaginings or ask questions whose answers are not firmly rooted in the real world. My goal here is twofold. On the one hand, I want to understand the territorialist ideology and the solutions it proposed to alleviate the hardship of Eastern European Jews in the first half of the twentieth century. On the other hand, I also want to use Territorialism to cast a critical eye on Zionism and the challenges it faced at the start of that century. The quest for some territory that was not Palestine and, in particular, the Zionists' relentless war against the ITO, place the Zionist movement in an unfamiliar and much more critical light than is usual among historians.

The territorialist ideology became a political power with the establishment of the ITO after the Seventh Zionist Congress, but the territorialist idea was part of the discourse of Eastern European Jewry long before then. Pinsker was the first to give it significance and depth. In Auto-Emancipation Pinsker asserted that the spiritual essence of the Jewish people was more important than territory; hence the Jewish homeland could be established anywhere, not just in the Land of Israel. What was important about that country was not its geographic location but its symbolic import for the Jewish people. To whatever territory was chosen, Pinsker wrote, "We shall take with us the most sacred possessions that we have saved from the shipwreck of our ancient fatherland, the God-idea, and the Bible. It is only these which have made our old fatherland the Holy Land, not the city of Jerusalem nor the Jordan River themselves."[7] The effort to obtain a territory might be complicated; hence we need not "attach ourselves to the place where our political life was once violently interrupted and destroyed.... We need nothing but a large piece of land ... which shall remain our property, from which no foreign master can expel us."[8] Palestine was apparently unobtainable, so Pinsker was prepared to accept other territories that could provide a safe and undisputed haven that could sustain the Jews.

Pinsker adhered to this view until the end of his life. One month after the Kattowitz conference (1884), Yehiel Tchlenov, then head of the Jewish student union in Moscow, suggested to Pinsker that he change the end of *Auto-Emancipation* to conform to the "spirit of the Zionist idea."[9] Moshe Leib Lilienblum, who served as secretary of the Hibbat Zion movement, answered in Pinsker's name and explained to the young student that the author would not retreat from the position he had formulated in 1882.

> Although the author [Pinsker] of the above pamphlet [Auto-Emancipation] is now engaged in matters concerning the settlement of Palestine, not only has there been no change in his view regarding the choice of a location for Jewish settlement—he is still working on the plan he formulated for himself. But the matter is as follows: Because the author did not regard the choice of a place as being subject to the authority of any one person, he left the decision, if it may be said, to all Jewry, and he hoped that a congress of their representatives will express its final decision in favor of one country or another.[10]

In *Mi-Katovich ad Basel* (From Kattowitz to Basel) Joseph Klausner relates that in 1887—three years after the Kattowitz conference—Pinsker was asked to authorize the translation of *Auto-Emancipation* into Russian and, at the same time, to insert a correction that the Land of Israel was the only land of refuge. Pinsker refused the request.[11] In 1892, shortly before he died, Pinsker wrote in his will that he would not retract his main idea in *Auto-Emancipation* and that the national center for the Jewish people need not be established specifically in Palestine.[12] He bequeathed only

# INTRODUCTION

2 percent of his estate of 100,000 rubles to the Hibbat Zion movement, as though it was a charitable organization. Those close to him heard him say before his death, "We will have 'two national centers,' just as we have 'two Torahs' (which are one), 'two Talmuds,' 'two versions of the liturgy,' and other items in pairs that have not kept us from being 'one people.'... Because the Holy Land cannot serve as the 'physical center' for more than a small number of our brethren of Israel, it would be better to divide the work of national revival in two, with Palestine as the national (spiritual) center and Argentina as the cultural (material) center."[13]

From the moment Pinsker severed the link between a territorialist solution of the Jewish question and Palestine, he paved the way for the development and consolidation of the territorialist ideology. The Territorialists regarded him as their founding father and spiritual mentor. In arguments with their Zionist rivals, they frequently cited him as the supreme authority and quoted *Auto-Emancipation*. His assertions that a place of refuge for the Jewish people was essential, that efforts to acquire a territory should not be focused exclusively on Palestine, and that the character of the new homeland should be determined not by its geographic location but by the spiritual content that the Jews would pour into it became the cornerstones of the territorialist ideology twenty years later.

Some saw America as the answer to the central question of Pinsker's book—the Holy Land or a land of our own?—a solution that would allow for the economic development and normalization of the Jewish people. Others thought that Palestine was the solution. The establishment of both the Bilu and Am Olam movements in 1882 exemplified the territorialist dilemma that troubled various groups in Eastern European Jewish society. Am Olam was founded on the festival of Shavuot in 1881, in the wake of pogroms that had struck the Jews in southern Russia that spring.[14] Its three founders, Monye (Michael) Bokal, Moses Herder, and Shneur (Sidney) Bailey, believed it would be possible to set up agricultural colonies in America to rehabilitate the Jewish people. A study of the memoirs of Am Olam members and of the group's regulations indicates that they were pioneers whose mission was to bring about a real revolution in the lives of Jews and realize Pinsker's vision. "We are young students, the most sensitive sector of the nation, and our hearts are very bitter" about the pogroms, Bailey wrote.

# INTRODUCTION

> We have left our studies and consulted together how to help the population to extricate themselves from the state of servitude in which it has existed. "Is Israel a slave? Why is he become a prey?" [Jeremiah 2:14]. . . . We will leave Russia, the stepmother, and go to America, the land of democracy, and we shall be workers of the land, and perhaps even establish a Jewish area just like the Mormon state in Utah, and even on more humanitarian foundations than theirs.[15]

The ideological conflict between Bilu and Am Olam—America or Palestine—was in many ways a harbinger of things to come. It was the embodiment of the existential debate within the Zionist Organization, twenty years later, about the preferred territory for solving the Jewish problem.

During the first half of the 1890s, Baron Maurice de Hirsch carried out his ambitious colonization project, unprecedented in scope. He sought to acquire an entire country with all the conditions needed for successful settlement, so that the newcomers could live there as the unchallenged owners of the land. The Jews would set up an autonomous state in the district he proposed to buy, where they would be safe from economic persecution and pogroms. According to historian Haim Avni, who has studied Baron Hirsch's Argentine project in depth, it was a comprehensive plan that included the basic principles of Auto-Emancipation. The project embodied the recognition that only concentration in some territory could provide a solution to the Jewish question as well as the idea that some kind of financial institution would be needed to carry out the enterprise.[16]

The Argentina versus Palestine controversy roiled Eastern European Jewish society in the late nineteenth century. Within the Hibbat Zion movement, there was at first some opposition to the plan for colonizing Argentina, because it seemed to contradict the plan for settlement in the Land of Israel. The weekly *Hamelitz* published an article disparaging the plan: "Anyone who brings one Jew to Argentina is considered to have built an altar for a new inquisition, especially because there are no redeemers for the abject poor of Argentina. Their prophecies about the imminent salvation are vain and misleading; they have bet on a dubious enterprise."[17] However, others disagreed and claimed that settlement in Argentina was not meant to come at the expense of settlement in Palestine. They argued that Palestine could not support the masses of Jewish migrants being

# INTRODUCTION

forced to leave Russia and that, furthermore, the Ottoman government was creating obstacles for the immigrants. Therefore, asserted Yitzhak Leib Katzenelson ("Buki ben Yogli"), "Argentina will not harass Judah and Judah will not envy Argentina. I too, dear sir [addressing the editor of *Hamelitz*], believe it or not, am a lover of Zion with all my heart, but I will be very happy if our wandering people find rest for their feet in Argentina. I love Zion but I love my people more."[18] In subsequent years Katzenelson's claim that the people were more important than the land became a key element of the territorialist ideology and was frequently wielded in arguments with the Zionists. Indeed, many Hovevei Zion (as the members of Hibbat Zion were known) supported Katzenelson's views and extended a helping hand to Baron Hirsch's Jewish Colonization Association (ICA) committees that were established in the Pale of Settlement.[19] The Argentine-Palestine debate is important and interesting because it took place within the movement, among activists who regarded themselves as Zionists in every respect, unlike the dispute between the Bilu and Am Olam movements, which took place outside the Hibbat Zion movement. Within Hibbat Zion, there was growing support for the territorialist idea that the final destination need not necessarily be Palestine.

Herzl's *Jewish State*, published four years after Pinsker's death, was another important step in the consolidation of the territorialist ideology, reinforcing the ideological current within the Zionist movement for which Palestine was a possible but not necessary destination. Like *Auto-Emancipation* before it, *The Jewish State* made no conclusive pronouncement on the territorial issue. Instead of "a land of our own" and "Holy Land," Herzl wavered between Palestine and Argentina. His vacillation is particularly interesting in light of the fact that, unlike Pinsker, Zionism had been active for fourteen years before Herzl wrote *The Jewish State*. By then, twenty colonies of Jewish farmers in Palestine were already cultivating its soil. This was no longer the infancy of the Hibbat Zion movement, and the colonies, despite all the difficulties, were already an integral part of the country's landscape. But despite the settlers' achievements and the changes in the Hibbat Zion movement, Palestine was not seen as the only solution to the problem of the Jewish people. In his book Herzl made the issue more acute, because he wanted diplomatic activity to precede settlement and was against any possibility of preemptive and unplanned settlement in the Land of Israel.

## INTRODUCTION

> Should the powers show themselves willing to grant us sovereignty over a neutral land, then the Society will enter into negotiations for the possession of this land. Here two regions come to mind: Palestine and Argentina. Significant experiments in colonization have been made in both countries, though on the mistaken principle of gradual infiltration of Jews. Infiltration is bound to end badly.[20]

The resonance of Herzl's book and his magnetic power over all those around him turned the question of a territory (other than Palestine) into one of the most rancorous issues dividing the Zionist camp. Herzl was a charismatic leader who placed the Jewish question on the international agenda and worked a serious revolution in the movement's organizational structure. But it was he who also submitted a controversial proposal to the Sixth Zionist Congress, which led to a split in the Zionist ranks and the founding of the ITO. The Jewish State became a formative document, and Herzl became the prophet of the Jewish state. The Zionist movement regarded him as one of its founders; when Israel was established, his remains were brought to the country and reburied on the hill in Jerusalem that bears his name. But the Territorialists also saw Herzl as a mythological figure and, like the Zionists, regarded him as the founder of the territorialist idea and themselves as his followers.

The question of whether Herzl was a true Judenstaatler (i.e., someone whose goal was to set up a sovereign Jewish state under the patronage of a world power, wherever that might be possible) or whether his territorialist ideas were merely a bargaining chip in his quest to raise the Jewish question is one of the most challenging issues in the historiography of the Jewish national movement. Historians of Zionism are divided on this matter. Some stress Herzl's loyalty to the Land of Israel and describe his diplomatic efforts as a "magnificent failure" that eventually led to the Balfour Declaration and the UN Partition Resolution of November 29, 1947.[21] Alex Bein, author of the first comprehensive biography of Herzl, wrote that the Land of Israel never left Herzl's mind, even when he was negotiating over Uganda.[22] Yeshayahu Friedman also held that Herzl never saw the Uganda plan and other ideas for settlement outside Palestine as practical alternatives. He agreed to the allocation of a district in East Africa for Jewish settlement because he realized that he could not

# INTRODUCTION

reject an offer by the British colonial secretary, Joseph Chamberlain. He wanted to accept Chamberlain's offer pro forma but rejected it as soon as it became politic to do so. In other words, the Uganda plan was not a carefully thought-out idea but an off-the-cuff reaction to the British colonial secretary's offer.[23]

Other scholars have criticized Herzl's conduct. David Vital blames him for the crisis that struck the Zionist movement during the controversy;[24] Michael Heymann claims that Herzl was serious about the Uganda plan and that the opposition to it was justified.[25] Yossi Goldstein asserts that Herzl's support for settlement in East Africa was a continuation of the territorialist line that Herzl advanced in The Jewish State, the El-Arish plan in the Sinai Peninsula in 1902 that he tried to promote the previous year, and other proposals of roughly the same vintage.[26]

The Territorialists thought that the Uganda plan was not a diplomatic ploy and that Herzl had seriously considered setting up the Jewish state in East Africa. These claims were made by Herzl's close friends and political associates, who knew him intimately and were convinced that he never altered the basic position he expressed in The Jewish State. They venerated him as a leader and drew on his legacy as the basis for their political survival. They hung his picture at their conferences, quoted him at length in their writings, and saw their opponents in the Zionist Organization as "former Zionists" who had deviated from the true path.

It seems to me that it is impossible to reach a definitive conclusion about Herzl's loyalty to the Land of Israel. He died before it was decided whether to accept or reject the British offer. We will never know whether he would have voted for the original Basel plan (a home for the Jewish people in the Land of Israel secured under public law) or opposed it and worked to set up a Jewish state in East Africa. A study of his letters, diaries, and behavior turns up many comments and statements in favor of Palestine alongside despairing thoughts about the diplomatic process, concern for the welfare of the Jewish people, and support for various territorialist initiatives, such as the El-Arish, Cyprus, Mozambique, and Uganda plans. Zionist historiography, which has crowned Herzl the prophet of the state, downplays the importance of his territorialist arguments and regards his territorialist initiatives as attempts to find a temporary solution to the problem of the Jewish people, even as he continued to see Palestine as the ultimate goal. The Territorialists chose to

# INTRODUCTION

emphasize every statement and idea of Herzl's that gave off the slightest whiff of Territorialism, as did the Zionists, albeit for opposite reasons. One of the aims of this book is to understand how the Territorialists interpreted Herzl, an interpretation that in many respects is an interesting and challenging inversion of the Zionist ideology. In other words, the territorialist ideology is the Zionist movement's alter ego, not only because it emerged from and was an integral part of Zionist thought but also, and more important, because an analysis of its actions, dilemmas, mishaps, and failures can help give us a better grasp of the travails of the Zionist movement and the Jewish people.

Thus the idea for Jewish settlement outside Palestine as a general solution to the Jewish problem was an inseparable part of Zionist politics from Pinsker to Herzl. Many Zionists saw no contradiction between their membership in the Zionist movement and their desire to set up a state for the Jews outside Palestine. The El-Arish plan (1902) and the Uganda plan (1903) showed that the Basel plan was mutable and that there was a sizable group in the Zionist movement that was prepared to sacrifice the Land of Israel to achieve a broad and immediate solution for the Jewish people. Herzl died at the height of the crisis, before the question of the territory was resolved and the final location of the Jewish state was decided on. His departure left a leadership vacuum and spawned an ideological crisis, leading to the schism in the Zionist movement and the establishment of the ITO.

The Territorialism of the early twentieth century was sustained by two phenomena integral to Eastern European Jewish society in those years: pogroms and emigration. For the Territorialists the pogroms were proof that the Jews had no future in Eastern Europe and that if no territory was found in the near future—in Palestine or elsewhere—there would be fateful repercussions for the Jewish people. The emigration of 1.5 million Jews in the first decade of the twentieth century was an expression of their suffering and distress, both physical and existential. The Territorialists feared that the unending stream would cause the migrants' countries of destination to close their gates, leaving hundreds of thousands of Jews trapped in their native countries. Their hope was that once a suitable territory was found and a Jewish state established, the masses would emigrate there. A minority would do so by choice, but the

# INTRODUCTION

majority would do so for lack of a better alternative—because only the Jewish state would be willing to admit them.

The Territorialists' sensitivity to the Jews' suffering and distress shaped their outlook, which was simultaneously optimistic and pessimistic. On the one hand, they had dark forebodings about the Jews of Eastern Europe and saw no possibility that they could be assimilated into the host societies. On the other hand, they were optimistic that the appropriate territory would be found soon and that they would be able to set up a Jewish state. The demographer and economist Jacob Lestschinsky, who ranged between Zionism and Territorialism throughout his life, gave a good description of territorialist ideology from the perspective of six decades later.

> It was an unfortunate and tragic movement that was brimming with both Diaspora pessimism and optimism concerning the Redemption. Even Zionism did not reject the Diaspora as much as it rejected the authentic young Socialist-Territorialist movement; even Zionism could not foresee the abyss opening for the Jewish people. It is only in Herzl's diary that one can find pages that reflect the hopelessness and despair with Diaspora life that was felt by the Socialist-Territorialists. But it was also the most optimistic movement of the previous generation. It believed in the people's strength and creative powers, in its ability to build Jewish life anywhere in the world.[27]

In this book I focus on Herzl's associates who broke away from the Zionist Organization after his death and set up a new organization in what they saw as the true spirit of Herzlian Zionism. I examine this group's unique worldview, its struggle with the Zionist movement, its Zionist rivals' response, and its diplomatic efforts to obtain a territory for the Jewish people in the first decade of the twentieth century.

This book is divided into six chapters. The first chapter focuses on the Uganda plan and the crisis in the Zionist movement and Jewish society from 1903 to 1905. I begin with the British colonial secretary's proposal to grant the Jewish people a district to colonize in East Africa and then describe the heated controversy in the Jewish world in the wake of Herzl's submission of the Uganda plan to the Sixth Zionist Congress. Finally, I

# INTRODUCTION

discuss how the plan was struck from the Zionist agenda at the seventh congress—the first after Herzl's death. The Uganda plan was the big bang that turned the territorialist alternative into the territorialist movement and set the stage for its transformation into an important political force in the Jewish world. The second chapter tracks the establishment of the ITO and how the young organization coped with the tempestuous events of the early twentieth century. During these years, the earth was burning under the feet of Eastern European Jews, many of whom were massacred in pogroms or sought to flee across the ocean. The third chapter deals with the elements of territorialist ideology and the reaction in the Zionist movement. The fourth chapter discusses the history of Territorialism in Palestine and tries to understand why many sectors of the Yishuv, mainly the colonists, became enthusiastic proponents of the Uganda plan and then of Israel Zangwill and his territorialist ideas. The fifth chapter focuses on the diplomatic efforts and the desperate search for a suitable territory, which never bore fruit. I examine only those countries that were the subject of formal negotiations conducted by the Territorialists with various governments and do not address settlement proposals that were not followed up by diplomatic contacts. The sixth and last chapter attempts to understand the reasons for the ITO's dissolution after the Balfour Declaration, the revival of Territorialism in the 1930s and 1940s, and the similarities and differences between the movement then and its earlier avatar.

I

# The Big Bang

The Uganda plan that Herzl submitted to the Sixth Zionist Congress was the catalyst for the establishment of the Jewish Territorial Organization (ITO) in August 1905. The proposal deepened and sharpened the differences within the Zionist Organization between the political Zionists, who supported Herzl, and the Palestine loyalists. The proposal fomented debate and split the Zionist movement in two. The supporters and opponents of the plan argued for two years. Zionist meetings were tense; the Jewish press published scores of articles and reports in favor of the Uganda plan; both open and covert meetings were held to either promote or frustrate Herzl's plan. The Uganda plan was the big bang of the Zionist movement and led to many resignations from the fledgling Zionist Organization.

The Uganda affair can be divided into four stages. In the first stage, from December 1902 to August 1903, British colonial secretary Joseph Chamberlain offered Uganda to Herzl and negotiations over the proposal began. The second stage ran from August 1903, when the Sixth Zionist Congress discussed the proposal and Jewish society was rent by controversy, until December 1904, when a Zionist organization set out to explore the district in question. The third stage extended from January to June 1905, that is, from the delegation's departure until the publication of its findings. During this period, the plan's supporters and opponents waited impatiently for the delegation's conclusions and prepared themselves for the final and decisive struggle that would occur at the Seventh Zionist Congress. The fourth stage, in July and August 1905, was the meeting of the Seventh Zionist Congress, at which the Uganda plan was removed from the Zionist agenda and the ITO was established.

In this chapter I trace these four stages of the Uganda affair, which, taken together, laid the groundwork for the establishment of the ITO in the summer of 1905. They also turned the question of territory and the Jewish state into a central issue of Jewish society and an inseparable part of its discourse.

## BACKGROUND OF THE UGANDA PLAN

On December 20, 1901, construction was completed on the Uganda Railway, which connected the port of Mombasa on the Indian Ocean with Lake Victoria. The work, deep in the heart of Africa, had begun five and a half years earlier, on May 30, 1896. This was an imperialistic and ambitious initiative aimed at strengthening Britain's hold over Africa and its control of the sources of the Nile. More than £5 million was invested to lay the 576 miles (920 kilometers) of track between Mombasa and Lake Victoria, with 43 stations and 1,200 bridges. Thousands of laborers were required; the British imported many Indian workers to East Africa and also employed local Africans. The natives paid a heavy price for these imperialistic ambitions. Many died of illness or accidents or were devoured by lions.[1]

The railway was an extraordinary engineering achievement for the British, but it did not yield any profit. The local population did not avail itself of the train, and Europeans hardly ever traveled to East Africa, let alone to Lake Victoria. To cover their growing losses and maintain their hold on the area, the British decided to settle white European colonists in the area between Lake Victoria and Ethiopia.[2] At the end of 1902, Chamberlain toured the British East Africa Protectorate. It was probably then that the idea of settling Jews in Kenya was first raised. Chamberlain was impressed by the region and recognized it as suitable for settlement by Europeans.[3] After his return to England, he met with Leopold Greenberg, Herzl's representative in England, and officially offered the district for Jewish colonization. This was the beginning of intensive negotiations, during which the British government recognized an autonomous Jewish colony in East Africa.

On April 24, 1903, Herzl and Chamberlain met to advance the plan. It was agreed that, in light of the conclusions of the mission that had

# THE BIG BANG

surveyed El-Arish, it would not be possible to set up a large Jewish colony in the Sinai and that other alternatives should be considered. As recorded in Herzl's diary, the colonial secretary told Herzl that "I have seen a land for you on my travels . . . , and that's Uganda. It's hot on the coast, but farther inland the climate becomes excellent, even for Europeans. You can raise sugar and cotton there. And I thought to myself, that would be a land for Dr. Herzl. But of course he wants to go only to Palestine or its vicinity."[4] This was true—Herzl had at first thought that the Jews must settle in Palestine or a neighboring land or region. But following the failure of the El-Arish plan and the realization that a Jewish territory could not be established in Sinai, he accepted Chamberlain's proposal. This is the first reference to Uganda in his diary, even though the territory Chamberlain had in mind was actually in what later became Kenya. "Uganda Controversy" was Chamberlain's misnomer, but the name stuck.

The idea began to take shape after this meeting. In late April 1903, Greenberg started work on a plan for Jewish settlement in East Africa. He submitted a detailed text to the British government (the "Jewish Colonization Scheme"), comprising an introduction and seven sections with many subsections. The plan precisely defined the Jewish colony in the region and—fourteen years before the Balfour Declaration—asked that the British government officially recognize the Jewish people as a nation with a right to an autonomous territory of their own.[5]

According to the Zionist plan, the Jews would settle in East Africa in two stages. In the first stage the British government would authorize Jewish settlement in the territory, and in the second stage the management would be transferred to the Jewish Colonial Trust founded by the Zionist Organization.

> Immediately upon the approval of the said territory by his Majesty's Government as being suitable and proper for the said settlement the entire management and control of the lands of the crown in the said territory and of the proceeds of the sale letting and disposing thereof including all royalties mines and minerals shall be vested until the 31st December 1909 in the Concessionaires and thereafter in the administrators of the said territory formed in accordance with the constitution hereinafter referred to.[6]

# CHAPTER 1

The constitutional clauses can be divided into those concerning the structure and function of the government in the East African territory and those concerning the relationship between the Jewish colonists and the local population. The section on the nature of the Jewish colony in East Africa affirms that the territory intended for colonization will be Jewish and that the king will appoint a Jewish governor to rule it. It further stipulates that the colonists will be granted the authority to enact laws and regulations for self-government to foster their well-being and public order and to levy taxes for various purposes, such as maintaining a police force and a school system. Judges and law enforcement officers will be appointed and civil and criminal courts instituted. The colony would be named "New Palestine" or "such other name as may be approved from time to time with the consent of His Majesty's Secretary of State."[7] According to another important article that was to be included in the constitution, the Jewish colonists would have the right to expand the territory required for colonization:

> For acquisition with the consent of his Majesty's Secretary of State of any other lands and premises in British East Africa and elsewhere, whether abutting upon or contiguous to the said territory or not, and the enlargement of the boundaries of the said territory and the extension to any new or additional lands of the right powers and privileges vested in or exercised by the settlement.[8]

This subsection was of great significance for the supporters of the East Africa scheme, because the purpose of the Jewish colony was to provide the speediest possible refuge for the hundreds of thousands of Eastern European Jews who had begun migrating westward. If Jewish migration was to be channeled to the African continent instead of North America, an additional reserve of land had to be secured. As we will see, the East Africa colonization scheme extended beyond the boundaries of the area covered by the Zionist Organization's survey mission. This is why the terms of the concession included a clear and explicit reference to the local population and their rights: "All settlers in and inhabitants of the territory ... shall be free from molestation in respect to their persons and property and under the protection and control of his Majesty's Government," so long as they complied with the provisions and terms of the concession. These terms, as stated in Greenberg's plan, granted the Jewish settlers the right to banish anyone who was likely to express opposition to the colony or violate its laws.

> For granting to the settlement power to exclude from the said territory any person or persons proposing to enter or settle in the same, who shall or may be deemed to be opposed to the interests of the settlement or the government thereof, or the dignity of his Majesty the King, and the power, with the previous consent of His Majesty's Secretary of State, to expel from the territory without being liable for compensation or otherwise any person not fully and completely abiding by the ordinances, rules, and regulations for the time being in force in the territory or committing or conniving at a breach of the Constitution of the settlement.[9]

Cecil Hurst, the legal adviser in the Foreign Office, received the Zionists' proposal with much suspicion. In a letter to Chamberlain dated July 13, 1903, Hurst wrote that the Zionist plan went far beyond the Jews' needs. His greatest fear was that the plan would lead to the establishment of an autonomous protectorate with more privileges than those enjoyed anywhere else in the empire. He asked Chamberlain to weigh carefully the Zionists' request concerning the name of the territory, the acquisition of land, and the plans for future expansion. Hurst was also opposed to the subsection that authorized the colony to expel anyone liable to pose a threat to it. There were legal grounds for banishing those disloyal to the crown, but the expulsion of people who opposed the settlers was problematic. This clause, he asserted, would grant the Jews too much power, and the British Empire should not do so.[10]

What was the territory the British offered Herzl, and where exactly was it located? The original suggestion of this region for Jewish settlement was made by the British governor in East Africa, Charles Eliot. In a letter to Foreign Secretary Lord Lansdowne in early November 1903, Eliot proposed the Guas Ngishu plateau in northwest Kenya as a potential region for Jewish settlement. During his visit there two months earlier, Eliot had gained firsthand acquaintance with the district. Eliot wrote to the foreign secretary:

## CHAPTER 1

> I need here only repeat, that it [Guas Ngishu] is a grassy plain, well-watered and possessing a temperate climate. In August, I myself found it disagreeably cold, but this objection would doubtless not be felt by Jews from Eastern Europe. The plain is surrounded by forests which yield good timber, and is practically uninhabited, owing . . . to tribal wars, not to any defect. The position is sufficiently isolated to protect the Jews from any hostile demonstrations of other races.[11]

The region in question was bounded by the equator in the south, by the Elgeyo Escarpment in the east, by Mt. Elgon and the Kabras Escarpment in the west, and by an imaginary line running from Mt. Elgon eastward in the north.[12] Its total area was 16,000 square kilometers (slightly less than the area allotted to the Jewish state by the UN Partition Plan), with the possibility of expansion northward toward the desert region of Lake Turkana.

Charles Eliot was not the first to visit and be impressed by the Guas Ngishu plateau. He was preceded by Harry Johnston, the famous British explorer and governor of Uganda who conducted a comprehensive survey of the living conditions in the area in 1901 and 1902.[13] Johnston concluded that the Guas Ngishu plateau was suitable for settlement by Europeans because the area was completely uninhabited, had adequate precipitation and abundant vegetation, and was free of diseases that might endanger the settlers. Johnston, who toured many parts of Africa in general and of East Africa in particular, wrote that the Guas Ngishu plateau was one of the most beautiful regions in the protectorate.[14] By all accounts, it was the best and most fertile area the British government could offer for colonization in East Africa.

On September 15, 1903, Herzl recorded in his diary that "on the basis of the literature and of the government reports, this much is already certain: this territory is fertile and well suited for the settlement of Europeans. It may therefore be assumed that the long-sought place of refuge for the most unfortunate among our fellow Jews, who are suffering material distress and roaming about homeless, has been found—although, as I remarked in my opening address, 'it is not Zion and never can be.'"[15] At this stage Herzl did not yet know the exact location of the territory proposed for Jewish settlement in East Africa. In 1902 districts that had been part of the British Protectorate of Uganda were transferred to the

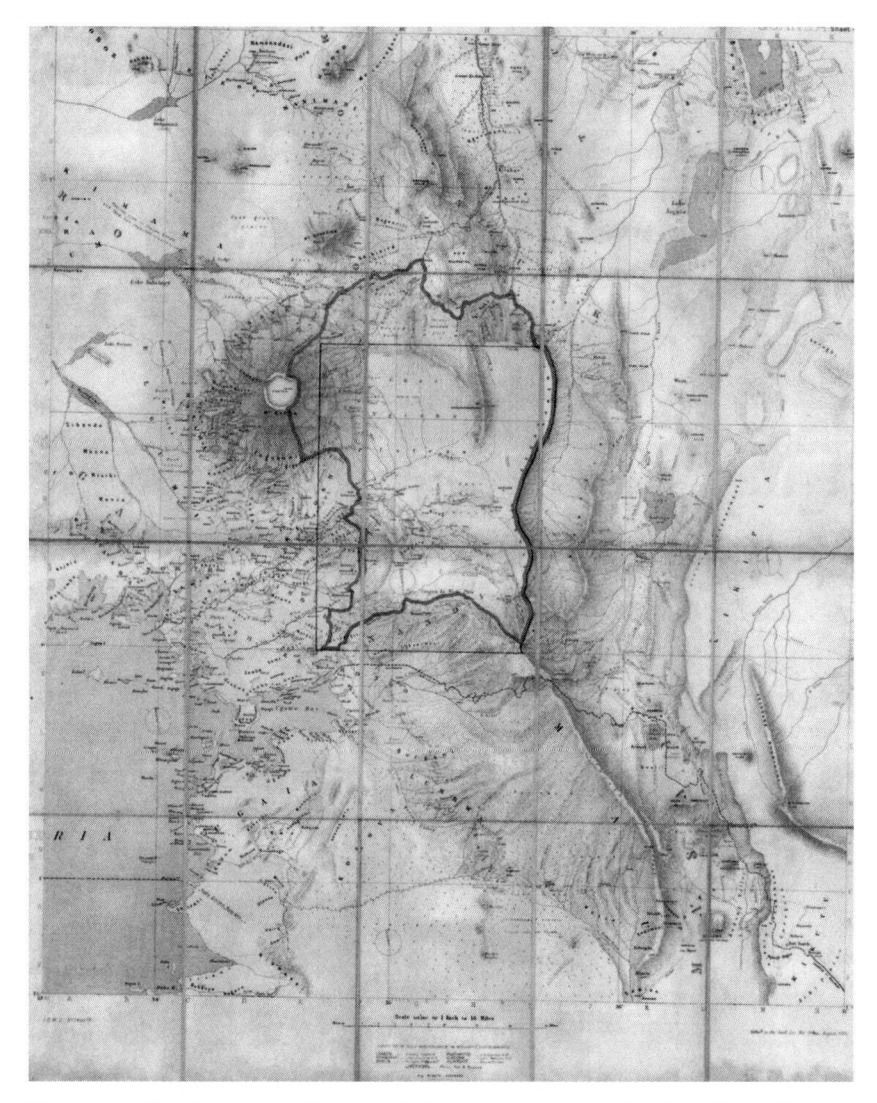

The strip of land between Kenya and Uganda that was offered to Herzl. The map served Nachum Wilbuschewitz (Wilbush) during his exploration in the region and can be found in his personal archive. (Central Zionist Archives)

East Africa Protectorate. On August 6, 1903, the British discussed the proposal with Greenberg. It was apparently only then that they told him the exact location of the proposed territory. Greenberg and the Foreign Office legal adviser tried to reach agreement on the terms of the concession. Greenberg demonstrated considerable flexibility with

## CHAPTER 1

regard to Hurst's reservations but expressed his concern that the Zionist Congress, which would convene in Basel at the end of the month, would discuss a plan that the British government had not yet authorized. During the short interval before the opening of the congress, Greenberg wanted to reach an agreement in principle between the Zionist movement and the British government. He emphasized that he had no doubt that if the British government formally announced the granting of the territory for Jewish settlement, the Zionist congress would gladly approve the offer.

On August 14, 1903, just two weeks before the opening of the Sixth Zionist Congress, Clement Hill, the head of the Protectorate Department in the Foreign Office, sent a written commitment by the British government to establish a Jewish colony in East Africa. "Sir," wrote Hill to Greenberg, "Mr. Chamberlain communicated to the Marquess of Lansdowne the letter which you addressed to him on the 13th ult. containing the form of an agreement which Dr. Herzl proposes should be entered into between [His Majesty's Government] and the Jewish Colonial Trust Ltd. for establishment of a Jewish settlement in East Africa."[16] The congress was fast approaching, and an agreement in principle needed to be reached. Accordingly, Hill noted in his letter that the foreign secretary did not have sufficient time to thoroughly review all the details of the plan or to discuss it with His Majesty's commissioner in the protectorate in East Africa. He therefore expressed his regrets that he could not express a clear opinion on this subject. He did, however, approve the dispatch of a Jewish Colonial Trust delegation to the East Africa Protectorate to determine whether or not a suitable territory was available. If so, the foreign secretary would be glad to make every accommodation to enable them to discuss the proposal. Given Lord Lansdowne's agreement in principle, it followed that if the Zionist survey team found a suitable territory,

> Lord Lansdowne will be prepared to entertain favourably proposals for the establishment of a Jewish Colony or settlement, on conditions which will enable the members to observe their National customs. For this purpose he would be prepared to discuss ... the details of a scheme comprising as its main features: the grant of a considerable area of land, the appointment of a Jewish Official as chief of local administration, and permission to

the Colony to have a free hand in regard to municipal legislation and as to the management of religious and purely domestic matters, such Local Autonomy being conditional upon the right of His Majesty's Government to exercise a general control.[17]

Herzl arrived at the Sixth Zionist Congress with this proposal in hand. From his point of view, it was an extraordinary diplomatic achievement that could alleviate the distress of the Jews, even if only as a temporary measure. Herzl's sense that the British proposal had come at the right time for the Jewish people was confirmed by the Kishinev pogrom and the hostile attitude of Vyacheslav Plehve, the Russian minister of the interior, toward the Zionist movement. Several weeks earlier, in June 1903, Plehve had sent a confidential note to all district governors, mayors, and police chiefs with detailed instructions on how the Zionist movement should be treated. He banned Zionist propaganda in public places, sought to shut Zionist institutions, restricted the movement of Zionist activists, and instituted economic controls over the movement's revenues in Russia.[18] Herzl sensed the danger looming over the Zionist movement in Russia and requested a meeting with Plehve. He was castigated for agreeing to meet the man whom many held responsible for the Kishinev pogrom, but the two met twice anyway. Against this political and diplomatic background, it is easy to understand why Herzl brought the controversial British proposal to the Sixth Zionist Congress. It may not have been the charter for the Land of Israel that Herzl had hoped to obtain, but it was a formal recognition by the British government of the Jewish people's right to establish a Jewish national colony in East Africa.

## THE SIXTH ZIONIST CONGRESS

Herzl first revealed this diplomatic achievement at the meeting of the Greater Actions Committee on August 8, 1903—two weeks before the opening of the Sixth Zionist Congress.[19] Three days before the congress, Herzl again presented the plan to the committee, this time in greater detail, including a report on the results of his visit to Russia and his meetings with Plehve. Herzl told those present that he regretted his failure to reverse the ban on Zionist activity in Russia but that he had been promised that the restrictions would be eased and eventually revoked. Herzl tried to explain the reasons for the tsarist government's

## CHAPTER 1

hostility toward Zionism and relayed Plehve's statement that the Russian government had no problem with the Zionist movement's aspirations to establish a Jewish state in Palestine, so long as they did so without also trying to run the lives of the Jews in Russia. Herzl maintained that if the Zionists returned to their former goal, they would be shown greater tolerance by the tsar's government and perhaps even enjoy its diplomatic support in Constantinople.[20] In the second part of his diplomatic survey, Herzl reported on the failure of the El-Arish plan and the difficulty of conveying water from the Nile to the arid Sinai Peninsula. Only then did he tell the committee of the British government's new offer, received only two weeks earlier, of a territory for an autonomous Jewish settlement in East Africa.[21]

The response of the Greater Actions Committee to Herzl's diplomatic survey focused mainly on Plehve's empty promises to Herzl, but it also contained a hint of what was to come. Jacob Bernstein-Kogan, whose home in Kishinev had been ransacked during the pogrom, said, "In the current situation, the Russian Jews are prepared to go anywhere, even Hell." Attorney Israel Jasinowski of Warsaw agreed with him. Max Bodenheimer, representing the German Zionists, suggested that the current circumstances warranted modifying the Basel plan "such that not only Palestine but other countries too can be considered for the establishment of a homeland secured under international law." Israel Zangwill, the British delegate, supported the idea and was the first to assert "that if Africa cannot serve as a means to reach Palestine from the geographical perspective, it could do so from the political perspective." Later at the meeting, he said that no man loved Zion as strongly and passionately as he did but that he, unlike others, had in mind the Zion of the tradition, the Zion of legend, the heavenly Zion.[22] The Russian Yehiel Tchlenov and Austrian Oscar Marmorek strongly opposed the plan and thought that it would deal a death blow to Zionism. They believed that the issue was of sufficient weight to warrant convening the Greater Actions Committee and that every member should express his basic stance.[23] Despite the differences of opinion within the Greater Actions Committee, the plan's opponents came away with the impression that it would not be approved when it was put to a vote at the congress.[24]

The Sixth Zionist Congress was gaveled into session in Basel on Sunday morning, August 23, 1903, at 11 o'clock. It was the largest Zionist congress until the establishment of the State of Israel. Six hundred eleven delegates and about 700 guests arrived to participate in the Zionist movement's gala event. None of those present could have imagined that this congress would go down in history as one of the stormiest the movement would ever know. At 1 o'clock in the afternoon, Herzl mounted the podium and delivered his speech. He focused on three issues: the Kishinev pogrom and its implications, the El-Arish plan, and the British proposal for a Jewish colony in East Africa.

The Kishinev pogrom influenced Herzl's approach and led him to conclude that the search for a solution to the Jewish problem had to be sped up. He described the situation and how it had worsened over the past year as well as the immediate need to begin a political course of action and not be content with the philanthropy of generous individuals. Philanthropy, he claimed, silences the conscience and creates a fleeting illusion that the problem has been handled but in fact weakens those looking for a radical, comprehensive, and profound response to the Jewish question.

> Money does not restore life to the dead, health to the maimed, parents to the orphaned. And how can alms relieve the fear of those who, although they themselves have not been the victims of assault, continue to live in the selfsame circumstances? Their turn may come at any moment.... The bloody days of the Bessarabian city must not cause us to forget that there are yet other Kishinevs, not alone in Russia. Kishinev exists wherever Jews undergo bodily or spiritual tortures, wherever their self-respect is wounded and their possessions are damaged because they are Jews. Let us save those who can still be saved! It is high time.[25]

Herzl did not consider the Jews' westward migration an effective solution either. He warned his listeners that the countries accepting immigrants would follow England and eventually close their gates. This would leave the Jews in an unbearable situation. They would want to emigrate but would have nowhere to go.

Thus, Herzl argued, there was no alternative to continuing the diplomatic efforts to obtain a charter from one of the European powers. He surveyed the failure of the negotiations with the sultan, a failure that left him no choice but to begin searching for other ways to solve the Jewish question: "Therefore last October I entered into communication with several members of the British Cabinet, and made them the proposition that they grant our people a concession on the Sinai Peninsula for colonization purposes." He reviewed at length the sequence of his negotiations with the British government and the decision "to send a commission composed of experts to the tract of land in question with a view to examining its fitness for colonization purposes and its possibilities."[26] The commission's conclusions were disappointing; because it would be impossible to make this district habitable for Jewish settlement, the idea should be dropped.

Then Herzl revealed the new British proposal, for the first time, to the congress delegates. "When the officials of the British government with whom I had previously been in touch learned of the expert opinion which had been expressed to the Egyptian government and of the decision which had been necessary in consequence, they immediately made me the proposition of ceding another tract of land for Jewish colonization purposes." Concerned about the way his new proposal would be received, Herzl introduced it by saying, "This territory has not the historic, traditional and Zionist significance of the Sinai Peninsula." However, he had no doubt whatsoever that the new proposal would meet with the delegates' full approval: "But I do not doubt that the Congress, acting as the representative of the Jewish people as a whole, will consider this new offer with the warmest gratitude. The proposition relates to an autonomous Jewish settlement in East Africa, with a Jewish administration, Jewish local government and a Jewish official at its head, under the suzerainty, I need not add, of Great Britain."[27]

We have insufficient sources about the reaction of Herzl's audience when they heard about the East Africa plan for the first time. Other than Zangwill who, according to the minutes, shouted out "Three cheers for England!" three times in the middle of the speech, we have no other evidence about the reactions of either the supporters or the opponents of the plan.[28] To help them digest his statement, Herzl added, "Zion it is not and can never be. It is merely an expedient for colonization purposes, but, be it well understood, an expedient founded upon a national and political basis."[29] It was an emergency measure, Herzl argued; there was no alternative to taking it, in view of the failure of philanthropic projects and of the worsening situation of the Jews in their countries of residence. The session adjourned after Herzl's speech, and the delegates began to digest the shocking news they had just heard from the president of the Zionist Organization.

Herzl's proposal and his support for the East Africa settlement plan stirred up a storm. Two camps of congress delegates formed quickly: those who wanted to accept the plan and those who did all in their power to torpedo it. The arguments became part of the delegates' daily routine and threw off the schedule that had been prepared long in advance. The first to attack the British proposal was David Trietsch, who had worked hard to promote Jewish settlement in places adjacent to Palestine.[30] Speaking at the first day's second session, Trietsch voiced his disapproval of the East Africa scheme. He was repeatedly interrupted by catcalls from the plan's supporters, indicating the depth of the divisions among the delegates.[31] Herzl's reply to Trietsch soon followed, and, according to the minutes, was met with "loud cheers and applause, which went on and on in the hall and in the galleries." If the delegates' reaction to the speeches can be taken as an indicator of the congress's position on this issue, they would seem to have supported Herzl and his controversial plan.

The second day of the congress was also marked by disputes. The opening address was given by Max Nordau, who conveyed a message to calm the plan's opponents. He stressed that the territory in question was merely a *Nachtasyl*, a shelter for the night, albeit of a unique kind, one that not only would provide shelter and food but would also offer those reaching it with the "means for political and social education—educational means that would get the Jews and the world used to the idea ... that we Jews are one people—talented, willing, and ready to fulfill the functions of a cultured and autonomous people."[32] This was followed by speeches for and against the proposal. The debate continued unabated and spilled over into the third day of the congress. It seemed that the two camps were evenly matched and that the scales would be tipped by the members of the Mizrachi Party, led by Rabbi Isaac Jacob (Yitzhak Yaakov) Reines. The Mizrachi Party decided to support Herzl and his proposal.

On the fourth day of the congress (August 26), after countless speeches and endless arguments, the delegates were asked to vote on the East Africa settlement plan. Shortly before the vote, Greenberg reported on the negotiations with the British government and read out the letter he had received from Clement Hill, head of the Protectorate Department at the British Foreign Office. The resolution to be voted on by the congress delegates was worded as follows: "In order to examine the question of settlement in the territory which the English government has considered with great generosity, the Congress resolves to appoint a committee." This committee would serve the Inner Actions Committee "only in an advisory capacity regarding the dispatch of a commission to the territories to be investigated." In addition, "It was agreed that the commission's expenditures would not be covered by the Jewish Colonial Bank, the Anglo-Palestine Company, or the Jewish National Fund." The decision about settlement in East Africa would be deferred to the next congress, which would be devoted entirely to this issue.[33]

The vote to dispatch the investigating committee was conducted in two stages. First came an alphabetical roll-call vote in which each delegate responded yea or nay (ja or nein in German). Here is Tchlenov's description of the scene:

> The Congress Hall was packed and the galleries overcrowded. Everywhere there was an ominous silence, nothing moved, everything was silent as if before a storm. Some of the delegates were trying to raise questions and comments about the vote and its formulation, but Herzl put a stop to this and rejected it all fiercely: "Wir sind in der Abstimmung" [We are voting]. Reich called each delegate by name and ja, nein, ja, nein were heard alternately all over the hall. The vote went on for two hours. It is very rare for a roll-call vote to be taken in a parliament with so many delegates—around 500! The entire hall followed the course of the voting with concentration. Many jotted down and counted the votes. I admit I was stunned to hear how often the word nein was heard. I think that the presence of 178 nay-sayers in the hall, in such conditions, would have been difficult to anticipate. But the outcome of the vote was never in doubt, of course.[34]

In the second stage, meant to confirm the results of the roll-call vote, ballots were deposited in two baskets, marked ja or nein. The slips were counted without delay. The wording of the resolution and the voting procedure were translated into French, Russian, English, and Yiddish to avoid misunderstandings and doubts about the legitimacy of the process. The final tally was 292 in favor of sending a delegation and 176 against, with 143 abstentions. At Herzl's instructions, 34 delegates abstained; 109 others abstained of their own volition.[35]

David Vital analyzed the vote and reached an interesting conclusion about the voters' profile. The proportions of Western Europeans and Eastern Europeans were almost equal in all the leadership institutions of the Zionist movement except for the highest ranking, where Western European Jews were in the majority. Younger delegates supported Herzl less than older ones did. The lion's share of the Western European delegates of all levels voted yes. But among those from Eastern Europe, the senior representatives tended to vote no; the rank and file were equally divided.[36]

When the results were announced, the tension reached its peak. The members of the Greater Actions Committee demonstratively left the stage where they had been sitting all the while and walked out of the hall. Herzl mounted the podium to deliver a speech. He made it plain to the delegates that "the acceptance of this proposal means only that we shall examine the proposal we were offered with the respect that it deserves and the seriousness that is due it." Because no decision in principle had yet been made, Herzl found it difficult to understand the behavior of the secessionists, who, according to eyewitness accounts, wept over the Zionist Organization's loss of direction. Despite their fury and frustration, many of the opponents began working to revoke the resolution that had just been passed. They viewed it as a deviation from the original Basel plan and a decision that must not be accepted and should be stricken from the Zionist movement's agenda.

A split in the Zionist movement was unavoidable. The Russian delegates convened an urgent meeting in one of the hotel ballrooms and discussed their next moves. Herzl, wishing to calm the tensions, thought it best to meet with the group to discuss the decision. When his request was not immediately granted, he waited outside in the corridor until it was resolved to hear him out. The discussion with Herzl focused on the Basel plan and whether the resolution deviated from it. "Have I undermined the Basel Plan?" Herzl asked his opponents. "No! It was not I, but others who have harmed it a hundred times over, when they opposed having separate factions with very different aims." Feeling betrayed, Herzl voiced the idea of resigning from the presidency of the Zionist Organization: "You can remove me if you wish; I shall retire without a murmur, believe me, to the longed-for repose of my private life." He concluded by saying that he wished them one thing: "May no person be entitled later to say that you misjudged my intentions and treated me with ingratitude."[37]

Herzl's anguish over the way in which the Sixth Zionist Congress ended and his thoughts about resigning the leadership of the movement were expressed in his diary as well. Throughout his Zionist activities he had always attempted to achieve consensus and did all in his power to avoid bringing controversial decisions up for discussion in the congress and the Greater Actions Committee, until he deviated from this approach at the Sixth Zionist Congress. He does not seem to have correctly estimated the proposal's impact and divisiveness. On August 31 he wrote in his diary:

> When, completely worn out, I had returned from the Congress building, after the final session, with my friends Zangwill, Nordau, and Cowen, and we sat in Cowen's room around a bottle of mineral water, I said to them:
>
> "I will now tell you the speech I am going to make at the Seventh Congress—that is, if I live to see it.
>
> "By then I shall either have obtained Palestine or realized the complete futility of any further efforts.
>
> "In the latter case, my speech will be as follows:
>
> "'It was not possible. The ultimate goal has not been reached, and will not be reached within a foreseeable time. But a temporary result is at hand: this land in which we can settle our suffering masses on a national basis and with the right of self-government. I do not believe that for the sake of a beautiful dream or of a legitimistic banner we have a right to withhold this relief from the unfortunate.
>
> "'But I recognize that this has produced a decisive split in our movement, and this rift is centered about my own person. Although I was originally only a Jewish State man [Judenstaatler]—n'importe où [no matter where]—, later I did lift up the flag of Zion and became myself a Lover of Zion [in English in the original]. Palestine is the only land where our people can come to rest. But hundreds of thousands need immediate help.

"'There is only one way to solve this conflict: I must resign my leadership. I shall, if you wish, conduct the negotiations of this Congress for you, and at its conclusion you will elect two Executive Committees, one for East Africa and one for Palestine. I shall accept election to neither. But I shall never deny my counsel to those who devote themselves to the work if they request it. And my best wishes will be with those who work for the fulfilment of the beautiful dream.

"'By what I have done I have not made Zionism poorer, but Jewry richer.

"'Farewell!'"[38]

It is unlikely that Herzl ever truly considered resigning and leaving everything. These were simply moments of human weakness for an overburdened leader who was in a state of constant tension. But the importance of this "future speech" was not the seriousness of his intentions but the way Israel Zangwill, who heard it and later became the president of the ITO, interpreted these words and how he used them to advance his own political agenda.

## THE UGANDA CONTROVERSY

After the Sixth Zionist Congress adjourned, the plan's opponents and supporters began their political and public preparation for the decisive Seventh Zionist Congress. The controversy split the Zionist movement and became one of the main issues on the agenda of Eastern European Jewish society. The evolution of the Uganda controversy was conducted along two interconnected channels. The first struggle was waged within institutions of the Zionist movement—the assemblies of Russian Zionists, the conference in Kharkov, and the reconciliation convention held several months before Herzl's death.[39] The second played out in the Jewish street and was naturally influenced by the outcome of the encounters between the supporters and opponents of the Uganda plan. The struggle "above" trickled down to Jewish society and influenced the local activists of both camps. Although the leaders of the Zionist movement tried their best to maintain decorum and follow the rules of the game (though not always successfully), for the younger members of both camps the controversy was particularly charged and violent.

## CHAPTER 1

The battle against Herzl and the Uganda plan was led by Menahem Mendel Ussishkin, one of the most prominent leaders of the Russian Zionists. In an open letter to the president of the Zionist Organization, dated October 27, 1903, Ussishkin wrote that he was glad to have had the honor of membership in the Zionist Inner Actions Committee and considered himself committed to the movement's decisions. However, "with regard to the Congress's decision to send a delegation to East Africa, I do not consider myself obligated by this resolution."[40] In fact, Ussishkin's refusal to accept the majority decision violated the rules of the game and significantly increased the tension between the two camps. Instead of dealing with the issue at hand—settlement in East Africa—he diverted the discussion to a much more important and fundamental question: To what extent is the minority bound by a majority decision taken democratically by the Zionist movement's institutions? In his reply to Ussishkin, Herzl honed in on this point. He asserted that Ussishkin must accept not only the privileges of serving on the Actions Committee but also its obligations. "He may defend his views within the Committee," but he was obligated to "accept the views of the majority just as we all do, without exception." If he was not prepared to do so, "He is legally bound to resign his position."[41] Herzl's reply to Ussishkin and the call for his resignation deepened the rift between the two camps. The feeling was that the day was imminent when the Zionist Organization would break up.

Saul Phinehas Rabbinowitz ("Shepher"), one of the founders of the Hibbat Zion Association in Warsaw and the translator of Graetz's Geschichte der Juden into Hebrew, collaborated with Isaac Nissenbaum, a leading Zionist in the Pale of Settlement, on a letter to Ussishkin. They asked him to carefully consider his actions before he replied to Herzl. It was precisely because of their opposition to the Uganda plan that they thought it necessary to soften their language rather than broaden the rift. "Our obligation to our common idea spurs us to tell you what we think." They continued:

> When we read your letter, published in Hazofeh, we anticipated that this letter would lead to an uproar in our camp; although we agree with your views on the African proposal, we were not happy with the style of the letter, which is liable to lead to an untimely split in our camp. And now, when we read Herzl's

reply to you in Die Welt, a reply that we regard as tantamount to informing against the organization in Palestine and which includes many statements that are not at all befitting of the person who said them, we realized how far things have gone. We believe that if you respond to him in kind, a fierce war will break out between the two of you, and also between the Hovevei Zion and the Zionists. This war will lead to the organization's collapse. We therefore appeal to you, dear friend, and request that you do not allow strict justice to govern you this time and that you be very careful in your reply to him.[42]

It was clear to Rabbinowitz and Nissenbaum that an exchange of charges and countercharges between Herzl and Ussishkin would lead to an explosion and real damage that might leave the Zionist Organization wounded beyond recovery. But neither did they spare Herzl, faulting him for accusing Ussishkin of holding a secret parley in Zichron Yaakov, a meeting liable to imperil the Jews in Palestine. They thought that the way the president of the Zionist Organization described the meeting was reprehensible; the Ottoman government might interpret the gathering as subversive and restrict Zionist activities in the country. In the conceptual world of the Jews in the Pale of Settlement, "informing" was unforgivable and the derogatory term informant was applied to Jews who collaborated with the tsarist government and betrayed political activists to the secret police. It was a harsh and unprecedented accusation to level against Herzl.

Ussishkin made no public response to Herzl's letter. But in late October, shortly after its publication, the Zionist district leaders in Russia convened an emergency conference in Kharkov to map out their strategy for opposing the Uganda plan. The conference was a turning point in the controversy and further deepened the rift between its supporters and opponents. The conference was devoted entirely to the Uganda crisis; its decisions were especially fierce and extreme. The minutes of the conference show that those present were eager to do battle against Herzl's unilateral diplomatic activities and revoke the plan, which they saw as a danger to Zionism and a deviation from the original Basel plan.[43] It was in this spirit that resolutions were passed regarding the Actions Committee's modus operandi, the East Africa scheme, the roles of the financial center, and budgetary matters related to the Zionist shekel (the membership dues that entitled one to vote for delegates to the Zionist congresses). It was also decided to send two members of the Inner Actions Committee to confront Herzl with the district leaders' demands and to refrain from all propaganda and political activities until the two emissaries returned.

These decisions were meant to reduce Herzl's influence in the Actions Committee and to limit its power. One resolution, for instance, noted that Herzl, as a member of the Greater Actions Committee and its chair, was bound to comply with the majority view and must not make unilateral decisions. In addition, every significant proposal with implications for the character of the Zionist movement should be discussed first by the Greater Actions Committee no later than a month before a congress convened.[44] The resolutions related to the Uganda plan were much more extreme. It was decided, by a vote of 13 to 2 (Max Mandelstamm and Israel Jasinowski), that Herzl should promise to never again submit a proposal for a settlement plan outside Palestine and that the East Africa scheme should be removed from the Zionist movement's agenda no later than the Seventh Zionist Congress.[45] The assembled district leaders also resolved that the Actions Committee should convene before the survey commission's departure to East Africa; that the delegation should not depart before the adoption of an amendment to the bylaws of the Jewish Colonial Trust that would state explicitly that it would fund only activities in Syria and Palestine; and that the Zionist Organization should engage in practical work in Palestine, in the spirit of the decisions made in the Second Zionist Congress, and begin purchasing land and establishing colonies there.[46]

Not all the members of the emergency conference chaired by Ussishkin agreed with its decisions. Mandelstamm and Jasinowski walked out and established the Committee of Defenders of the Zionist Organization (Va'ad Meginei Hahistadrut) as a way to prevent Ussishkin from undermining Herzl's authority.[47] Their departure was exploited to transfer the finance office and administration of the Zionist shekel, which had been overseen by Mandelstamm, from Kiev to Vilna. This was an attempt to put pressure on and weaken the district leaders in Russia who supported Herzl and to strengthen the naysayers in advance of the Seventh Zionist Congress.

The conference sent Grigori (Zevi) Belkowsky and Semyon Rosenbaum to confer with Herzl. They arrived in Vienna on December

31, 1903, and requested a meeting with Herzl to present the decisions of the Kharkov conference. Herzl refused to meet them as members of a delegation representing the Russian district leaders, but he agreed to meet each of them individually and even invited them to sit in on the discussions of the Inner Actions Committee. By treating them as visitors rather than as members of a delegation conveying the decisions of the Kharkov conference, he made their journey irrelevant and the resolutions meaningless. This is how Rosenbaum understood Herzl's move; he recognized that the Zionist leader was not interested in what they had to say and, as he summarized in a note to Herzl, that "your views on the Zionist idea differ from ours, and that you want to work for Palestine as only one of a number of possibilities."[48] Yet it was clear to Herzl that the rift in the Zionist movement was deepening and that every effort had to be made to resolve the differences between the supporters and opponents of the Uganda proposal. The Actions Committee meeting on April 11, 1904, was a good opportunity to do so.

In his speech to the committee members, Herzl explained his fundamental stance and his motives for submitting the controversial proposal to the Sixth Zionist Congress. His harsh criticism of Ussishkin and remarks about the methods used by his opponents show that Herzl had no intention of retreating from his original plan. From his point of view, and as president of the Zionist Organization, he could not ignore the British proposal; it was his duty to present it to the congress as a solution (even if temporary) for the persecuted Jews of Russia. But his speech to the Greater Actions Committee suggests that it was not the question of establishing Jewish sovereignty in Uganda that was at the heart of the debate between the yea-sayers and the naysayers but the sovereignty of the Zionist Organization to make democratic decisions and the minority's obligation to accept the decisions passed by the majority. This was, according to Herzl, a question of principle that had to be clarified, and on this matter he was not prepared to yield to Ussishkin and his associates.

> Fight as much as you wish. Try to win a majority in the Congress. But not by using the means of the movement against the movement, only by your personal qualities. If you rally most of the votes against me, a party, I will be grateful to you but only

on condition that you obtain the majority, because if not, I will only feel distressed. But I advise you to be quiet and accept the authority of the Congress resolutions, as all the other gentlemen must do.[49]

The meeting of the Actions Committee ended with a feeling of cautious optimism in both camps and a sense that it would be possible to end the struggle that had agitated and split the Zionist movement. However, the decisions of the Sixth Zionist Congress remained valid and binding, and the participants of the Kharkov conference were unable to have them annulled.

Historians treat this session of the Actions Committee as one of reconciliation, a meeting at which the two sides recognized that they had more that united them than divided them; however, this was not really so. The Jewish street was immersed in fierce and bitter arguments and continued to rage and seethe. The debate lasted until the Seventh Zionist Congress in August 1905. Before then, however, the Zionist movement had to deal with Herzl's sudden death on June 4, 1904. The departure of the revered leader was a painful blow to the young movement, which had drawn its strength from its charismatic leader's dynamic energy. Herzl's disappearance from the diplomatic arena caused a dramatic reversal in the balance of power between the supporters and opponents of the Uganda plan. Without Herzl's leadership it was difficult for his supporters to continue their efforts on behalf of the East Africa scheme. Nevertheless, they continued to promote it and insisted that the Actions Committee implement all the decisions of the Sixth Zionist Congress.

The Uganda controversy had another aspect that has barely been discussed by historians: the reaction of the Jewish street and grassroots activists, both the Ugandists and the Zionists, to the question. How did the fierce and at times vitriolic argument between Herzl and Ussishkin affect local activists, and how was it manifested in daily life? The debate within the leadership trickled down and influenced the attitudes of those in the rival camps. Each stage in the controversy received great attention and stoked emotions on both sides. Open letters for or against the plan, opinion pieces in the press, and garbled quotations relating to the controversy were often taken out of context; at times these misunderstandings even led to violence. The arguments in the local chapters of the Zionist movement all over the Pale of Settlement became ever more intense.

The Weizmann family is a good example of the extent to which the controversy seeped downward and influenced Zionists in the Pale of Settlement. In her memoirs, Chaya Weizmann-Lichtenstein relates that at the end of the Sixth Zionist Congress, the members of the family who had been there returned home with mixed feelings about the Uganda plan. Chaya's father was among the supporters and regarded the plan as a suitable solution for the Jews' distress. Her brother Samuel, who was not a delegate but watched from the galleries, became an active Territorialist and convinced others to adopt the idea. But her brother Chaim was opposed to it. "When all the members of our family returned from the Congress, the atmosphere in the house became somewhat uncomfortable. There was great respect for Father, but Zionism is not determined by the precept to honor one's father."[50] Chaya's father, Chaim Weizmann, later retracted his support for the Uganda plan, but Samuel remained adamantly in favor and "used to go from place to place and school to school, full of rebellious energy," to speak in favor of the territorialist idea. "When he came home the walls of the house would shake from the arguments." Chaya's mother was the family peacemaker. "Don't quarrel, children!" she would tell the debaters. "Please God, Chaimke, Chaya, and Moshe—we will be in Palestine; and if you win, Shmulke, we'll be . . . but where? Make a decision already!"[51] This is how their mother expressed her position, but at the same time defended her children without taking an explicit stance. According to Jehuda Reinharz, Chaim Weizmann initially supported the East Africa scheme and changed his position later for political rather than ideological reasons. Weizmann sought to raise his luster among the Russian Zionists by standing up to Herzl.[52] Even if Weizmann-Lichtenstein's memoirs are not historically accurate, they still demonstrate that different views about the Uganda plan could exist even within one family.

The Gepsteins were another family divided between supporters and opponents. They were a well-known Jewish family whose home served as a center for the Jewish intelligentsia in Ukraine in general and in Odessa in particular. The eldest son, who was among the elite of Russian Zionism, went to Palestine, where he eventually became one of the leaders of the Herut movement. His brothers, David and Moses, also part of the intelligentsia, were strong advocates of the Uganda plan.

David was one of the founders of the ITO; Moses was a cofounder of the Zionist Socialist Workers' Party. All three Gepstein brothers attended Russian universities, and they were all imbued with a strong spirit of Jewish nationalism; but the Uganda question divided them.[53]

Ya'akov Hazan's father supported the territorialist idea,[54] but his mother and grandmother were loyal to the Land of Israel. To preserve marital harmony, his mother chose not to quarrel with her husband, but his grandmother could not bear to hear his opinions and did not accept his territorialist deviancy. "'This will pass,' she used to say. '*S'iz da nor eyn Erets Yisroel*' (There is only one Land of Israel). My mother, who was also a devoted Zionist, listened and kept silent. She was ready to follow my father blindly to wherever he might lead her."[55] Nevertheless, the tension built up. Hazan's grandmother made up her mind to immigrate to Palestine and, not wanting to hear any more of her son's territorialist speeches, decided to attend a different synagogue in the meantime: "To hear him inspires the soul, but his words are not for me." As Hazan put it, "Thus, true to herself and steadfast in her opinion, she left all of us, and her beloved son, and immigrated to Palestine."[56]

After the Sixth Zionist Congress, the rival factions launched extensive propaganda efforts to persuade as many people as possible to adopt their position. They understood the need to build up a bloc of supporters for the crucial vote at the next congress. Letters were sent to supporters, leaflets were distributed, meetings were held, and lectures were delivered for the general public. Contrary to the opposition of the Russian members of the Greater Actions Committee, the Jewish street was generally in favor of Herzl's diplomatic course. This was the impression gained by Shmaryahu Levin, a leading Russian Zionist and Zionei Zion (Zionist of Zion), when he toured the Pale of Settlement and observed the campaign for Jewish public opinion. In a letter to Ussishkin, Levin wrote, "During my travels I met with nearly all the old *Hovevei Ziyyon* and discussed the situation and the winds that are currently blowing in our world. Many of them are in a state of total despair and predict that Herzl will be the sole ruler at the Seventh Congress and that Territorialism will inherit the place of Zionism in the presence of all the Congress delegates."[57]

The correspondence between Ber Borochov and Ussishkin reflects a similar situation: that the Jewish street was moving toward Territorialism even after Herzl's death. "They are putting great pressure on me to come

# THE BIG BANG

to Zhitomir, where the Territorialists are flourishing, and where Mr. Sheinkin promised to send a propagandist," wrote Borochov to Ussishkin in mid-February 1905.⁵⁸ In another letter that same month, Ussishkin wrote from Odessa that the "Ugandists are very strong here and we have to fight them. It is a pity that time is so short; ... the work is overwhelming. This is why I have no chance to write. My throat is already dry today after three meetings; towards the end of the debate with the Territorialists I became completely hoarse."⁵⁹ Borochov's letters to Ussishkin provide a rare glimpse into the struggle for public opinion that was taking place in the Jewish street. The crowded meetings were loud and passionate; sometimes violence broke out and required intervention by the local police. "Rabbinowitz and I stayed in Vilna for two weeks without doing anything," wrote Borochov to Ussishkin.

> While you were there we had two public meetings. On Sunday, after you left, there was a meeting at the synagogue with 500 to 600 people. Rabbinowitz spoke against Territorialism and against Uganda. They argued with him and employed personal attacks, especially against you. After this I spoke in vulgar Yiddish, to dead silence, before I made a new argument against the opponent. Everything was going well, until the third person who opposed me began with the claim: "The 'Palestinians' are not Zionists at all." This comment sparked a scandal and fierce storm—synagogue windows were smashed, fistfights broke out, and so forth.⁶⁰

The situation described in Borochov's letter is fascinating: speeches in vulgar Yiddish, a meeting of roughly 600 people, yelling, curses, smashed windows, and exchanges of blows. The friction in the upper levels of the Zionist Organization had trickled down and assumed an aggressive character. This violent meeting at the synagogue took place about six weeks after the attempted assassination of Max Nordau by 27-year-old Haim Zelig Luban—additional evidence of the extent to which the Jewish masses were passionately involved in this issue.

The turning point in public opinion came after the Kharkov conference. Many Zionists, even those who opposed the Uganda plan, came out against its decisions and rejected Ussishkin's belligerent methods. Like Herzl, many Zionist associations thought that the democratic principle of respecting the majority decision was more important than the resolution passed by the Sixth Zionist Congress. Many letters of protest against Ussishkin were sent to the editor of *Die Welt*, blasting the conference and its decisions.[61] For example: "We the undersigned, the Ozrei Zion Association of Kishinev, have read with pain in our hearts about the secret meeting of the district leaders in Kharkov and their decisions. We strongly protest against the district leaders who have overstepped the rights granted to them by the Congress."[62] The members of the Or Zion Association in Bialystok wrote a letter in a similar vein.

> We were taken aback when we read the decisions of the district leaders in Kharkov, which have been published in the press and have not yet been officially denied by the district leaders themselves. We therefore decided, at our last general meeting, to authorize the members of our board to express our strong protest if they really passed such resolutions, which are contrary to the rules of the Zionist Organization.[63]

The members of the Zionist Association in Sakiai (Shaki) wrote that they were "incurably depressed by the terrible act perpetrated by those who convened in Kharkov" and expressed their unconditional trust "in our eminent leader and president, Dr. Theodor Herzl."[64]

Protest letters were sent not only to Die Welt but also to Ussishkin, who even received occasional threatening letters from his opponents.

> Dear Menahem Mendel Ussishkin!
>
> In order to express my disgust for you regarding the subversive uprooting of . . . the one spark of hope we have in our bitter exile, while our lives are at every moment hanging in the balance, I say to you: Scoundrel, from now on may you be seen by the oppressed people in the same company as the villain Akiva of Poltava. [Signed] A Zionist.[65]

The rift in the Zionist movement that split the Zionist Organization and led to the establishment of the ITO did not pass over the Zionist-Socialist camp. Some of its adherents opposed the Uganda plan, whereas others believed that they could keep waiting for a charter for Palestine and supported Herzl's proposal. Nachman Syrkin was a prominent supporter of the Uganda plan. He told the Sixth Zionist Congress, "I gladly accept the idea of an autonomous Jewish settlement in East Africa. If you understand the scope of this idea, this Congress can be a turning point in Jewish history."[66] After the Sixth Zionist Congress, those members of Po'alei Zion who regarded Palestine as the sole solution for the Jewish people came into conflict with those who were in favor of setting up an autonomous entity anywhere, not necessarily in the Land of Israel.

Evidence of the prevailing mood among the workers during these years can be found in the letter from Shmaryahu Levin to Ussishkin (mentioned earlier), in which he notes that "there is utter confusion in the Po'alei Zion camp. If we only had gifted and capable propagandists we would easily succeed in attracting the workers to Zion and keeping them far away from the dangerous path that *many* of them are now following" (emphasis in original).[67]

Levin's pressure on Ussishkin to recruit propagandists indicates that he was unaware of the connection between Ussishkin and Borochov, whom he selected to spread anti-Uganda propaganda in the Pale of Settlement. As we will see in greater detail in Chapter 3, Borochov traveled through the Pale and gave speeches against the Ugandists and the Territorialists. Benzion Dinur set down his impressions of the debate that pitted Samuel Niger and Jacob Latzky-Bertholdi, representing the Ugandists, against Borochov, Ussishkin's advocate, which lasted for two days straight.[68] In 1904 these stormy debates gave birth to the Zionist Socialist Workers' Party, the first organization to openly and proudly profess the territorialist idea.[69]

The split in the Zionist-Socialist camp at the beginning of 1905 was a harbinger of things to come. Initially, the new party regarded itself as an integral part of the Zionist Organization and even hoped that it would be able to persuade the delegates to the Seventh Zionist Congress to support the territorialist idea. At the congress Syrkin was the main speaker for the Zionist-Socialists. Along with Grigori Abramowitz ("Zevi Avrahami"), Moshe Litvakov ("Nitzotz"), Jacob Lestschinsky, Samuel Niger, and Jacob Latzky-Bertholdi, Syrkin headed the supporters of the Uganda proposal who seceded from the Zionist Organization to set up an alternative organization.

The Uganda controversy did not spare the press. Editors were constantly lambasted for taking one side or the other. *Ha-zeman*, for example, was attacked for its sympathy for the territorialist idea. One of Ussishkin's correspondents asserted that the new periodical was causing great damage to the anti-Ugandists: "Its line is radical Territorialism and attracts all of the Territorialists. . . . What a terrible pity that, at present, the Land of our Forefathers is out of luck."[70] On the other hand, *Ha-zofeh* was perceived as reflecting the views of the anti-Ugandists. *Ha-zefirah* did not take either side.[71] Ben-Yehuda, in his newspaper *Hashkafah*, also tried to map out the various periodicals' editorial positions: "Among the Jewish newspapers in Russia, only *Ha-zefirah* openly favors a Jewish state outside Palestine in general terms. . . . *Der Fraynd*, once among the most ardent opponents, has cooled down a bit in its opposition. . . . *Ha-melitz* gives a platform to both sides. But the most zealous and absolute opponent of all is *Ha-zofeh*."[72] The debate between Nahum Sokolow, the editor of *Ha-zefirah*, and Judah Haim Hazan exemplifies the involvement of the Jewish press in the controversy.

In January 1905, Sokolow published a two-part article in *Ha-zefirah*, titled "To Restore the Old Vigor of Zionism: Against Territorialism." Taking up the entire front page, the article advanced strong arguments against the territorialist idea. "Territorialism is the utter antithesis of Zionism," wrote Sokolow. "It is also the total opposite of its own name. It champions a territory but hovers in the air."[73] Sokolow claimed that the Territorialists were fantasizing and could be compared to someone who shatters the cask but also tries to save the wine. He countered the Territorialists' claim that they were realists with political wisdom, whereas the Zionists were dreamers detached from reality, time, and space. The Zionists "have already reached the level of recognizing the obstacles; we know who we are dealing with." Hence the Zionists possess the tools and ability to overcome the anticipated obstacles. "The Territorialists have not even reached this understanding, because Territorialism is not a program but a farce. . . . You can't even criticize Territorialism. Because when the Territorialists say, some government will be found that will give us a country, it is impossible to prove otherwise."[74]

Judah Hazan wanted to respond to Sokolow from the pages of *Ha-zefirah*, but when he submitted his carefully argued reply, Sokolow chose not to publish it. His articles lay "in the editorial office of *Ha-zefirah* for many days and its editor neither answered nor published it, putting off its author with various justifications and promises."[75] Hazan was a prominent Territorialist in Warsaw and an enthusiastic promoter of the Uganda plan. After the split in the Zionist Organization, he worked to consolidate the new ITO, which he helped found. Tragically, Hazan contracted septicemia after having a tooth extracted and died three months after the Seventh Zionist Congress, at age 32, leaving behind a young wife and a small child with no means of support. Leading Territorialists assumed the mission of commemorating him and providing for his family. They published his letters and disseminated his doctrine among the supporters of the territorialist idea. The profits from the publication were assigned to his family to help alleviate their economic distress.[76]

Hazan's book, *Jewish Writers and Territorialism*, published shortly after his death, contained his essays against Sokolow. According to its introduction, "In the days before the Seventh Congress, when the deceased [Judah Hazan] was deeply involved in the party's matters, he was unable to deal with publishing [the book]. It was only after his return from the Congress that he submitted it to the press." Because of his untimely death, Hazan never saw his book on the controversy in print. The work, written at the height of the debate, allows us to trace the Ugandists' arguments during the period between the Sixth and Seventh Zionist Congresses. Hazan drew his readers' attention to the fact that Sokolow, in the vote on Uganda, had remained silent "for about two months after that Congress, while the war for and against Uganda had already begun to rage in the press and in Zionist life." Although this silence was, in Hazan's opinion, "completely his private affair," it reflected Sokolow's lack of consistency on the Uganda question. To Sokolow's assertion that the Territorialists had a weak grasp of reality, Hazan responded that precisely during the present age of colonialism, when the Great Powers wanted their overseas possessions to be developed economically, it was certainly possible to obtain a territory for Jewish settlement, because the powers needed "migrants from other peoples" to come and settle these uninhabited regions.[77] Hazan's arguments in favor of Territorialism and his criticism of Sokolow are interesting and allow us to trace the intricacies of territorialist thinking, but they are not the focus of this chapter (see Chapter 3). Of interest here is that the ideological rivalry between the two men caused Sokolow not to publish Hazan's response to his articles, thereby turning *Ha-zefirah* into a party in the debate.

Given the tension in the Jewish street over the East Africa scheme and given Herzl's sudden death in June 1904, a split in the Zionist Organization appeared to be unavoidable. The Seventh Zionist Congress, scheduled for August 1904, was postponed for a year, and with it the decision on accepting or rejecting the British offer. In the meantime, the Actions Committee had to determine the composition of the survey commission, define its aims, and send it to East Africa so it could bring back a detailed report as the basis for the congress to decide for or against settlement there.

## THE EAST AFRICA SURVEY COMMISSION

The departure of the East Africa survey commission created expectations in the Jewish world in general and among Zionists in particular. In his memoirs, Trial and Error, Chaim Weizmann relates that at that particular time it was difficult to recruit English Jewry for Zionist activity because so many were waiting "for the report on the proposed territory that was certain to be a positive one since otherwise they would not have offered it to us." He felt "helpless in the face of this naïveté."[78] It was clear that a positive report could significantly strengthen the political faction in the Zionist Organization and that a negative conclusion would lead to the idea being shelved, as had happened with the El-Arish plan after the survey team determined unequivocally that the area was unsuitable for Jewish settlement because of the shortage of water.

The East Africa survey commission set out sixteen months after the Sixth Zionist Congress and only seven months before the Seventh Zionist Congress. The timing was of great importance for the success or failure of the plan. Their report, which was to be published shortly before the seventh congress—the first without Herzl's unifying leadership—would either energize the scheme or remove it from the Zionist agenda. Herzl's original plan was that two delegations would explore the Guas Ngishu plateau. A scientific expedition would examine the soil conditions and climate, and the other group would focus on its potential for Jewish settlement. According to Herzl's diary, "Since here an area even remoter from civilization [than El-Arish] is involved, and since, utilizing the two dry seasons, two expeditions will probably have to be sent out—first a predominantly scientific one, then a predominantly practical one—the expenses are likely to be substantially higher."[79]

Funding the expedition was the main problem that Herzl and the supporters of the settlement plan in East Africa faced. According to the decision of the Sixth Zionist Congress, the survey was to be funded by outside sources and not by the Zionist Organization. For this reason, in September 1903 Herzl applied to the Jewish Colonization Association (ICA) and asked it to cover the delegation's expenses. "Perhaps I may assume that you have followed the deliberations of the Sixth Zionist Congress at Basel," wrote Herzl to its directors.

> The way things are at present, and without encroaching in any way upon the political decision of our next Congress, I believe that I am acting in the spirit of the purely philanthropic cause that you serve when I ask you whether you would care to participate in raising the funds for the expedition.... The various funds of our organization must not be drawn on to defray the expenses of this expedition, since no Palestinian territory is involved....
>
> Therefore I envision the contribution of the I.C.A., which I budget at about £8000, as a deposit on the separate account of the East African Expedition at the Jewish Colonial Trust in London.[80]

The ICA did not approve Herzl's request. Its condition for funding the commission was that the colony in East Africa "have no political character," and Herzl could not agree to this.[81] A short while after the ICA declined to participate in the East African venture, several Zionists in South Africa offered Herzl their assistance. The first to come forward was Max Langermann, who later became prominent in the ITO. He agreed to fund the delegation on condition that he be appointed as its head. Herzl was willing to take Langermann's money but refused to include him in the expedition, because he thought that the choice of its members should be based on their expertise and not on their wealth.[82] Herzl received a similar offer from Aharon Benzion and Samuel Goldreich (president of the South African Zionist Federation).[83] Herzl rejected this offer as well, because of disagreements about the delegation's composition.

As time passed, it became clear that raising the necessary funds for the survey commission was a genuine problem. Its departure was delayed, and there was great concern that the British government would retract its offer. A surprising and unexpected solution arrived after Herzl's death from Mrs. E. A. Gordon, a British Christian who was sympathetic to the Zionist idea. She agreed to finance the commission on condition that her benefaction remain anonymous and that her money be returned should the delegation fail to set out, for whatever reason.[84] In her meeting with Greenberg, Gordon agreed to contribute £2,000. This sufficed for the expedition to leave for East Africa but did not cover a serious and comprehensive survey of the designated territory. Herzl had calculated the expenses of the El-Arish commission at roughly £4,000 and estimated that the East Africa party would cost at least double that amount.

As soon as the funds became available, the Inner Actions Committee, now headed by the German botanist Otto Warburg, began putting together the East Africa delegation. The commission chair was Major Alfred St. Hill Gibbons, a veteran explorer and scientist who had published several books about his travels on the African continent. He was joined by Alfred Kaiser, a Swiss Christian botanist who had done research in the Sinai Desert and even converted to Islam to facilitate his work. The third member of the scientific team was Nahum Wilbush (Wilbuschewitz), a young mechanical engineer.[85] His qualifications did not really match the delegation's mission, and his selection was somewhat coincidental. As a matter of public relations, Warburg could not dispatch a scientific expedition on behalf of the Zionist Organization that did not include an identifying Zionist. Wilbush happened to arrive in Berlin just as the final preparations for the African adventure were being made. In his memoirs, Wilbush recounts, "Professor Warburg was then engaged with the Uganda delegation and proposed that I join it to study the possibility for industry in the Guas Ngishu region. Because I did not have to return to Palestine until the next Passover, I accepted his proposal."[86] On December 25, 1904, the three men met in Basel with Leopold Greenberg, who told them Herzl's four essential conditions for acceptance of the British proposal by the Actions Committee.

> The territory had to be sufficiently extensive to admit of an immigration of such a character as should be eventually a

material relief to the pressure which to-day exists in Eastern Jewry; it follows that the territory has to be one colonizable by such people as ours; the Concession has to be invested with such autonomous rights as would ensure the Jewish character of the settlement; perhaps governing all, the enthusiasm of our own people in respect to the offer has to be of such a nature as will overcome all the obvious difficulties which under most favourable conditions will be bound to arise in the creation of the settlement.[87]

Warburg signed a contract with the members of the expedition and arranged the financial terms. It was decided that the commission would submit a preliminary report three months after its arrival in Mombasa and a final report by April 3, 1905. They were instructed to study the region's geography and physical conditions, its natural resources, the political aspects, the native population's attitude toward the proposed settlement, and the possibility of industrialization and economic development.[88] The head of the delegation would be paid £750; Kaiser, 600 marks. Wilbush would not receive any compensation.

The next day, December 26, 1904, the three expeditioners left Basel en route to Africa.[89] Two days later, in Trieste, they boarded the SS *Africa*, of the Austrian Lloyds shipping company; on January 13, 1905, the three men disembarked in the Indian Ocean port of Mombasa. The next day they hired guides and porters and boarded the train to Nairobi. Gibbons and Kaiser were intimately familiar with Africa and spoke the local dialect, but for Wilbush this was his first visit to the continent. His encounter with the natives and their way of life left a deep impression. In his memoirs Wilbush wrote that "the local blacks [in Mombasa] are of the Swahili tribe and are the most developed of the natives. They wear clothes and will work at any menial job. But the natives in the interior of the country are quite uncivilized. They walk around without clothes, are not suited for any labor, do not know the value of money, and are not interesting in receiving it."[90]

The expedition members arrived in Nairobi on January 15 and proceeded to equip themselves for the journey to their destination. The next day, Wilbush and Kaiser met Mr. Marcus, the head of the local Jewish community, who had lived in India for eighteen years before arriving in

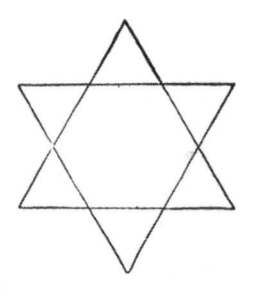

"ZIONISM STRIVES TO OBTAIN FOR THE JEWISH PEOPLE A PUBLICLY RECOGNISED, LEGALLY SECURED HOME IN PALESTINE."

# REPORT

ON THE

## WORK OF THE COMMISSION

SENT OUT BY THE ZIONIST ORGANIZATION

## TO EXAMINE THE TERRITORY OFFERED BY H.M. GOVERNMENT TO THE ORGANIZATION

FOR THE PURPOSES OF

## A JEWISH SETTLEMENT IN BRITISH EAST AFRICA.

Major A. St. HILL GIBBONS.
ALFRED KAISER.
N. WILBUSCH.

May, 1905.
Iyar, 5665.

The first page of the report of the expedition to East Africa led by Alfred St. Hill Gibbons (1905).

Nairobi in 1899. In their conversation, Marcus described the conditions in the colony and the agricultural, economic, and political situation in the region. From his survey it appeared that conditions were generally pleasant; several Jewish families had even settled in the region, and their business affairs were developing not badly. "I was very excited to find Jewish settlers in this place," wrote Wilbush.

> In virgin forests, among savage Negroes and ferocious animals, Jews are living in primitive conditions in clay huts and planning to settle down here and create a new life and remake the primordial landscape. I envied them, and thought that such pioneers should come settle in Palestine and fill the ranks of the Biluim, who have dwindled away; [they should] lift the depleted spirits of the colonists, who have been infected by materialistic aspirations and territorialist ideas. Of course, because of my role I could not say this.[91]

Clearly Wilbush's worldview was in total opposition to the political Zionism that lay behind the East Africa scheme. His outlook, which set Palestine at the center of the Zionist enterprise, would provide the basis for the negative report on the Guas Ngishu plateau, which he composed at the end of the expedition.

Gibbons, Kaiser, and Wilbush stayed only two days in Nairobi before continuing by rail to Nakuru, the jumping-off point for their journey on foot to Guas Ngishu. Here the three men wasted precious time, because most of their scientific equipment was still in Nairobi and arrived four days later. It was only on January 23, ten days after they had reached Mombasa, that the members of the survey commission, accompanied by several dozen porters and guides, set off on foot. It was nearly 100 kilometers from Nakuru to Guas Ngishu. After a vigorous journey, the expedition reached the Ravine station, perched on a small and steep hill 6 kilometers north of the equator and 13 kilometers from their destination.[92] They stayed in Ravine for several days to allow Gibbons to complete the final arrangements for the journey.

On January 29, 1905, sixteen days after their arrival in Mombasa, the expedition reached Guas Ngishu. Because so much time had been wasted on hiring porters, waiting for the scientific equipment that had been

# CHAPTER 1

forgotten in Nairobi, and attending to the various other arrangements necessary to penetrate the region, Gibbons decided that the commission would split up. Wilbush was sent west, with nine porters, to explore for a week, after which he would join up with Kaiser in the Sirgoi region. Kaiser was sent north to Sirgoi to set up the main camp; then he would proceed to the northern part of the territory, as far as the base of Mt. Elgon. Gibbons himself set off for the eastern sector, planning to continue north as far as possible, in hope of reaching the Chipchangane Mountains.[93] The separate journeys ultimately led to three different reports, which were submitted to Leopold Greenberg in May 1905.

## MAJOR GIBBONS'S CONCLUSIONS

Gibbons divided his report into five sections: climate, land, water sources, accessibility, and the native population. He had a positive general impression of the climate. Minimum temperatures in the region ranged from 6°C in the early morning to 26°C in the afternoon. To a great extent, the weather was similar to that in Europe during the summer months.[94] "The soil of the plateau is mostly rich," Gibbons noted. There was abundant grass in certain areas, which would be suitable for raising sheep and goats. In addition, most European fruit trees would grow in Guas Ngishu without any problem. The region had abundant water sources that were certainly sufficient for settlement. One advantage of the region was that it did not have any marshes, which meant that there would be no problems with mosquito-borne illnesses. In addition, the region was almost uninhabited except for a few places along its periphery (between Mt. Elgon and the Chipchangane Mountains). The most convenient point of entry into the territory was from the Ravine station, along the route taken by the survey commission.

Thus Gibbons's report on the territory he surveyed was fairly positive. His conclusion was that in the course of time and under certain conditions, it would be possible to prepare the land to receive Jewish migrants. Given that there was no precedent for bringing a large number of settlers to the region, he suggested that a pilot settlement with a small number of inhabitants be set up first.

> To supply a test sufficiently authoritative to justify the expenditure necessary for so extensive a colonizing scheme as the one proposed,

it seems to me there is but one feasible method. An agricultural expert should be sent out with a small staff of intelligent farmers—say, ten. This staff should then be selected, and for experimental purposes a farmer should be in charge of each district, and under his superintendence and direction ten peasants should be each allotted a small piece of land. The second year would give a very good idea of the possibilities of the larger scheme.[95]

## ALFRED KAISER'S CONCLUSIONS

Kaiser's report opened with a general survey of the borders of the territory and its characteristics, the trade situation in the region (there was none), accessibility to rail lines, infrastructure, roads (mainly narrow footpaths used by the natives), and the local population (most of the region was uninhabited).[96] Kaiser's temperature measurements were similar to those made by Gibbons. Kaiser also noted the relative humidity: 74% in the morning and 33% in the evening. As for health, Guas Ngishu was a disease-free region without epidemics and thus "a healthy place for people only." On the other hand, cattle were exposed to many disease vectors (such as the tsetse fly). Therefore "with regards for the sanitary conditions for cattle-breeding, it cannot be said to be of greater value than other parts of the African continent."[97] There were also many agricultural pests in the area: "On the Guas Ngishu plateau one should take into account the many field pests which are a serious impediment and considerable disruption to agriculture." There were also concerns about the "voracious wandering locusts that frequent here and often cover the ground for many square miles; they offer an ever-ready feast to thousands of raptors for weeks on end."[98] As for the feasibility of the Jewish settlement plan in Guas Ngishu, Kaiser thought they should rely on the experience of Marcus, the Jewish colonial in Nairobi. He knew the weaknesses and advantages of the region and could be of much help in the matter. However, a problem might arise with the non-Jewish white colonists. According to Kaiser, some of them were anti-Semitic, adamantly opposed to the plan, and deeply concerned about the prospect of Jews coming to Kenya in general and to Guas Ngishu in particular.[99] In his summary Kaiser rendered a negative verdict on the Guas Ngishu plateau. There was no doubt that Jews could establish a settlement there, wrote Kaiser on the last page of his report, if they were able to carefully select the persons who would carry out their scheme of immigration..., and I even believe that they could once more become a real pastoral people, as the Dutch, the Germans and the French have done. However, economic conditions on the Guas Ngishu Plateau are so unfavourable that a portion of the immigrants would certainly leave the country again, and there would thus never be a real colonizing association which could work successfully. The immigration would cost millions, and the actual usefulness of the whole scheme would be totally out of proportion to the labour expended. I consider the territory extremely unsuitable for a purely Jewish settlement, be it carried on by a co-operative association or through private enterprise, and equally unsuitable for a mixed settlement administered through a chartered company. If Jewish capital, Jewish labour and Jewish blood are to serve the Zionist idea, a more promising country must be found, not a land that is so remote from all communication with the rest of the world, that makes such heavy demands on the settlers, and is so little fitted to consolidate the bonds uniting Jews.[100]

## NAHUM WILBUSH'S CONCLUSIONS

Before I commence my report I should like to point out that it is absolutely impossible to explore a whole country in just four weeks, and to arrive at any definite conclusion, and only in an extreme case, such as if the country were either notably fertile or absolutely unfertile, would it be possible to arrive at an immediate decision in regard to its suitability or non-suitability for emigration purposes.[101]

This is how Nahum Wilbush began his report, which was much more negative than the other two. He focused on the land's poor quality and inability to absorb Jewish immigrants. The report is especially interesting because, unlike his two colleagues, Wilbush knew Palestine well and had a comparative perspective. From his report it appears that the soil was unsuited for agriculture; there were large diurnal temperature fluctuations; the winds were strong; the rivers did not contain sufficient water; there was a shortage of trees in general and of firewood in particular; Jewish settlers would be too dependent on the natives, who, unlike the white settlers, could work under the burning sun; and transportation was problematic. Wilbush stressed two main deficiencies in his report. The first was the lack of a basic infrastructure for the development of suitable industry in the region. The second, which Wilbush viewed as more critical, was that every Jewish immigrant who wished to settle successfully would have to invest a large amount of money. According to his calculations, every settler would need an initial capital outlay of £1,800.[102] His conclusion was clear and unambiguous: "Where nothing exists, nothing can be done."[103]

In response to Kaiser's and Wilbush's negative conclusions, the head of the survey commission, Gibbons, attached an appendix to his report in which he harshly criticized their work methods. Drawing on his rich experience and his many travels in Africa, Gibbons attempted to undermine their conclusions. His main argument against Kaiser was that he had examined the country from the viewpoint of a scientist and not from that of a potential settler: "The man of science devotes most of his energy to the mysteries of Nature."[104] Because of Kaiser's flawed methodology, his conclusions were unacceptable. To strengthen his position, Gibbons cited several regions in Africa, primarily in South Africa, that were similar in climate and geology to East Africa, and where white settlement had succeeded and agriculture had developed. Not only was Kaiser's research method problematic, but he also failed to follow his explicit instructions. For example, Kaiser set up the main camp in Sirgoi in a streambed that was hard to locate. This made it difficult for Wilbush and Gibbons to rendezvous and wasted precious research time. Kaiser's departure for the Mt. Elgon region was delayed by a week, and he was left without enough time to carry out his mission properly.[105]

Gibbons's strictures against Wilbush were even sharper. In his view, Wilbush's conclusions should be regarded as the "crude conjectures of a very limited and unmethodised experience, and cannot recommend that it be taken into serious consideration."[106] Wilbush's lack of experience in exploration in general and in Africa in particular led him to erroneous conclusions. For example, he did not know that he had arrived in East Africa at the end of the dry season, so the grass was yellow and the water level in the streams relatively low. Had he known that there are only two seasons in equatorial regions, rainy and dry, he would have understood

# CHAPTER 1

that what he was looking at was typical of large parts of Africa and not only the Guas Ngishu plateau. Moreover, Wilbush had gotten lost and had spent most of his time searching for Kaiser's hidden camp. In his memoirs, Wilbush himself describes his own "muddling around" and panic when he failed to find Kaiser. He lost his compass, had an unpleasant encounter with two Boers who had settled in the area, and ran low on food. Wilbush spent six days, February 5 to 11, looking for Kaiser and his porters.

> Rescue came the next day. On February 11, the twelfth day of my solo trek, about an hour before noon, a convoy of eleven porters appeared, coming from the south with a load of rice for the main camp north of Sirgoi. We stopped them and took some phuthu [a kind of cornmeal mush]. Finally my men have food. Three hours later the Masai returned with the porter and brought rice sent by Mr. Kaiser. I also received two letters from home, the first after seven weeks of separation, as well as a friendly note from Mr. Kaiser expressing his joy that I had finally turned up and saying that he is waiting for me so that we can go on together to Mount Elgon. I was happy that day.[107]

From the time that Wilbush joined up with Kaiser until the expedition left Guas Ngishu, he stayed in the main camp in Sirgoi and did not leave it for two weeks. He spent his time writing the report and reading *The Uganda Protectorate* by Harry Johnston. From his report it appears that Wilbush toured and inspected the intended district for only seven days out of the four weeks he was on the plateau.[108] The Territorialists, as we will see, did not overlook this fact. However, Gibbons's principal criticism of Wilbush was not the short time he spent in exploration but his inexperience and the preconceptions he brought with him to Africa. "It is unnecessary to reproduce more of the many inaccuracies and faulty conclusions with which Mr. Wilbush's report abounds."

> All things seem to have been looked on with the eyes of the son of a Russian landowner. The writer seems to have expected a Volga or Danube on a plateau six to nine thousand feet above

sea-level, and to have considered everything from the standard of a developed country. He cannot conceive that future transport and economic conditions will alter with economic and industrial progress. His final maxim—"where nothing exists, nothing can be done"—supplies a keynote to the whole report, the existence of undeveloped land does not enter into his consideration, nor does he realize that the existence of raw material is to some extent dependent on the hand of man.[109]

On February 28, 1905, the expedition wound up its survey and left Guas Ngishu for Nairobi. Kaiser and Gibbons stayed in the city for several days, and Wilbush continued directly to Mombasa and from there to Palestine.

In May 1905, two months before the Seventh Zionist Congress, Gibbons submitted his report to Greenberg. The commission had spent four weeks and three days in Guas Ngishu (January 29–February 28, 1905). The report's conclusions about the prospects for Jewish settlement in East Africa were not uniform. Kaiser and Wilbush stated emphatically that the country was unsuitable for settlement, whereas Gibbons took the opposite stance and asserted that although the land was undeveloped, it certainly had the potential for settlement. Of the three opinions, Gibbons's seems to have been the most serious and profound, for several reasons.

1. The Guas Ngishu plateau was first surveyed in a serious and comprehensive manner by the British governor of East Africa, Harry Johnston, in 1902. His maps and conclusions were at the disposal of the expedition. Among Nahum Wilbush's documents in the Central Zionist Archives are copies of the maps sketched by Johnston during his visit to Guas Ngishu.[110] They give a clear picture of the region's immense potential. Johnston measured the precipitation and found it to be suitable. He found a wide variety of flora from grassy plains to virgin forests. The district had no endemic diseases—"perfectly healthy," as he put it. Finally, it was uninhabited. Johnston's conclusions and general impressions were in line with Gibbons's and with those of Charles Eliot, the governor of East Africa at the time of the survey commission's tour.[111]

CHAPTER 1

2. The British had designated the Guas Ngishu plateau for white settlement—initially for Jews and then, after the proposal was rejected by the Zionist Organization, for non-Jews. The white colonists in Kenya were well aware of the area's advantages, which was why they feared Jewish settlement there. Had the Guas Ngishu plateau indeed been a place "where nothing exists [and] nothing can be done," it is doubtful that there would have been any opposition to the settlement of Jews in Kenya, and certainly no white colonists would have taken up residence there.

3. Gibbons was the only one of the three who made good use of his time. As mentioned, Wilbush explored for only one week, muddled through another week, and spent two weeks in camp, whereas Kaiser and Gibbons fulfilled their assignment. Kaiser himself was delayed, not by his own fault, but because of Wilbush, because his instructions were to wait for him and then travel north together in the direction of Mt. Elgon.

4. The advantages of the region were well-known to the leaders of the Zionist Organization. As noted, Herzl wrote in his diary that "this territory is fertile and well suited for the settlement of Europeans."[112] In early 1907, David Wolffsohn, Herzl's successor as president of the Zionist Organization, visited Jerusalem. In a conversation with the educator Ephraim Cohn-Reiss he mentioned that he visited Guas Ngishu on his way from South Africa to Palestine. Recalling this meeting in his memoirs, Cohn-Reiss wrote that Wolffsohn "saw the land and it was not at all a 'land that consumes its inhabitants,' as many said about it because of their love of Zion.... The phrase 'flowing with milk and honey' is more suited to it, but one should not speak of this in public," Wolffsohn had told him.[113] But it was only in 1933, twenty-eight years after their meeting, that Cohn-Reiss made the details of his conversation with Wolffsohn public.

5. On January 15, 1906, Gibbons presented his findings to the Royal Geographical Society in London. Although he had been sent out by the Zionist Organization, the members of the society wanted to hear his impressions of the Guas Ngishu plateau. Nine months after submitting his official report to the Zionist Inner Actions Committee, Gibbons continued to hold that the territory was suitable for settlement and had great potential. He told the society that two men had accompanied him: Alfred Kaiser, whom he defined as a scientist with knowledge and experience in explora-

The map drawn by Nahum Wilbush during his travels through the area designated for Jewish settlement between January 28 and February 6, 1905. The many erasures and arrows in the map indicate to some extent what Wilbush experienced during the course of the expedition.

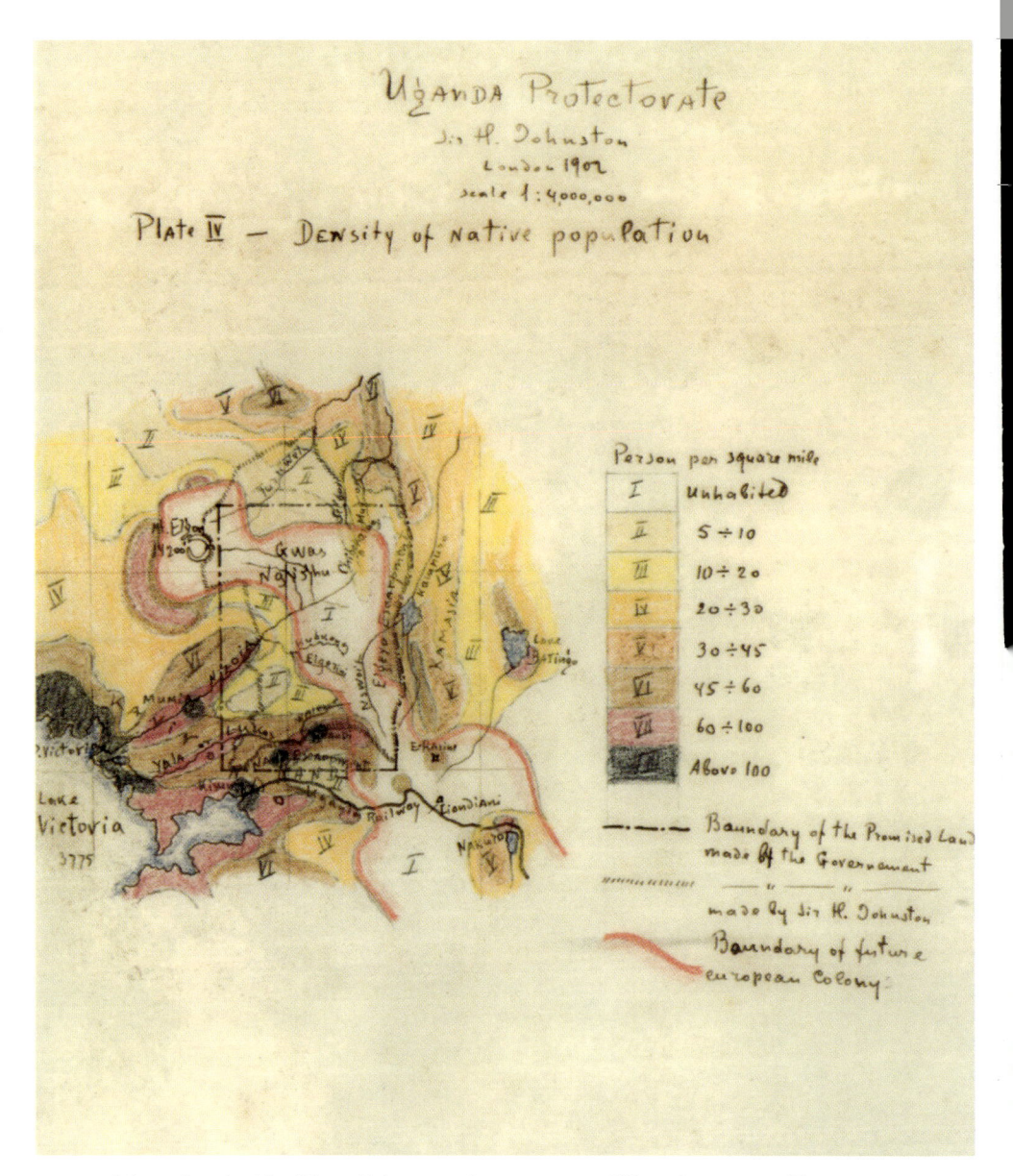

Maps sketched by Harry Johnston, the governor of Uganda, in 1902. The inherent potentialities of this strip of land and the extent of its suitability for settlement can be derived from these three maps. The maps can be found in the personal archive of Nahum Wilbush (Wilbuschewitz) and contradict his conclusions about this designated land area. (Central Zionist Archives)

The Uganda Protectorate
Sir H. Johnston
London 1902
Scale 1:4,000,000

Plate VI — Distribution of Rainfall

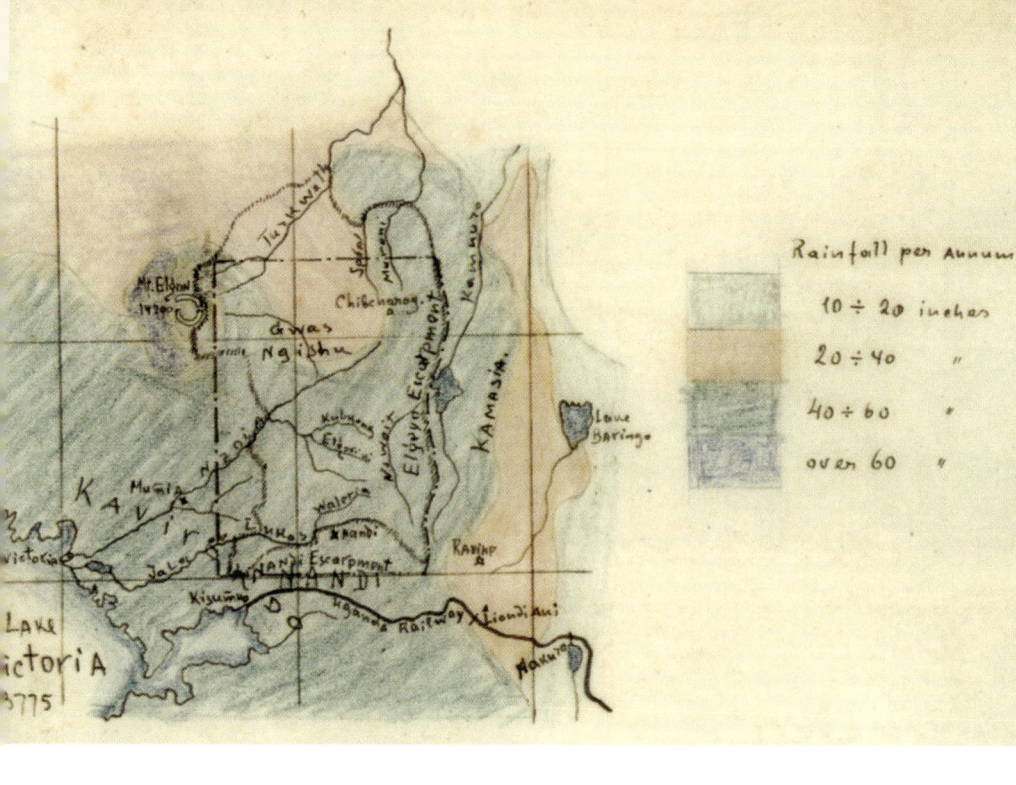

Rainfall per Annum
10 ÷ 20 inches
20 ÷ 40 "
40 ÷ 60 "
over 60 "

The Uganda Protectorate
Sir H. Johnston
London 1902 — Scale 1:4,000,000

Plate VII General distribution and range of Vegetation.

Steppe, poor vegetation, Scrub a few Thorn Trees
Grass, cultivated soil, Savanah, Parklike Scenery, occasional shade Trees.
Tropical Forest, Rubber-producing Trees, and Vines
Conifers, dense Forest with Trees & Flowers of C. o Good Hope & European affinities.
Alpine

tion, and another man, whom Gibbons chose not to name and who had never been to Africa before.[114] His decision to leave Wilbush anonymous reveals Gibbons's scorn and lack of esteem for the young man. In a scholarly and well-organized lecture, the head of the survey commission stressed the economic potential of this tract of land: dense vegetation that could become the basis for a lumber industry, land suitable for field crops (and not plantations), and broad pastures for cattle. He had no doubt that white settlers would bring prosperity to the region and that, after transportation was developed, it would take on great strategic importance for the British Empire.[115] Gibbons, we see, had not changed his position. His report was written without fear or bias and was much more professional and accurate than that produced by Wilbush.

6. If we compare the situation in Palestine in those years with that in the region surveyed by the commission, Guas Ngishu was not a place "where nothing exists [and] nothing can be done," as Wilbush described it. Had a similar expedition been sent in December 1904 to the Lower and Upper Galilee, to the Jezreel Valley, or to the sand dunes north of Jaffa on which the city of Tel Aviv would soon be built, the scene before their eyes would have been much less attractive than what the commission saw on the Guas Ngishu plateau. Because these areas of Palestine were full of swamps, infested with malaria, and home to an indigenous population, the report would certainly have been negative.

Still, although Gibbons's report was more reliable, the impression received at the time was that the Guas Ngishu plateau was unsuited for Jewish settlement. Gibbons's conclusions were played down, and the negative parts of the report were given greater prominence, to ensure that the plan would be shelved once and for all. This was the brilliant political ploy of Ussishkin and the pro-Palestine faction, who understood that it would be difficult to defeat the Uganda plan merely by alleging its contradiction of the original Basel plan.

The commission's official report was published in installments in Die Welt—the Zionist Organization's official mouthpiece. It printed the conclusions of all three men, along with Gibbons's harsh criticism of Wilbush.[116] The last installment was published only a week before the Seventh Zionist Congress convened, and the delegates had little time to study the report and determine how each of the commission members had reached their conclusions. Although it seemed on the surface that the delegates had everything they needed to determine whether the Guas Ngishu plateau was suitable for settlement, this was not, in fact, the case. For example, the expedition's travel log was not published, leaving the readers of Die Welt with the impression that its three members had inspected the territory with equal vigor but arrived at different conclusions. Unless they had access to the original report, readers had no idea that Wilbush had gotten lost and had not performed a proper investigation. They took his pithy "where nothing exists, nothing can be done" as equal in value to Gibbons's conclusion. When Wilbush returned to Palestine from Africa and was asked about the survey commission's work and its conclusions, he declined to comment.[117] It is hard to determine why he did not answer the questions and retreated into silence. Perhaps he did not feel comfortable relating his experiences in Africa, or he may simply have wanted to wait until the report was published in full.

## THE SEVENTH ZIONIST CONGRESS, JULY–AUGUST 1905

On July 27, 1905, the Seventh Zionist Congress opened in Basel. More than 600 delegates and about 700 guests and curious onlookers turned out for this crucial moment in the Zionist movement's history. It was the first congress without Herzl. In his keynote address, Nordau praised the venerated leader who had passed away too soon. At the second session Nordau was elected president of the Zionist Congress, but the choice of vice-presidents became heated when Ussishkin presented his candidacy. Ussishkin was controversial because of his quarrel with Herzl. He was disliked by some of the delegates and was even blamed for Herzl's death. His candidacy created uneasiness in the hall. The Ha-zefirah reporter noted that there was "much grumbling and fierce protests against the proposal to name Ussishkin one of the six vice-presidents."[118] This protest was a foretaste of what could be expected later in the congress, when the East Africa scheme would be brought up for discussion.

The debate began on the second day of the congress. Warburg ascended the podium and read the summary of the report submitted to him by the members of the survey commission. He reviewed the commission's goals for the delegates and noted that Wilbush and the head of the commission, Gibbons, disagreed in their assessments of the territory but that this did not undermine the report as a whole.[119] Warburg's statement was inaccurate, to say the least. Not only did it gloss over the disagreement between Gibbons and Wilbush, but it also concealed from the delegates that Wilbush had not really surveyed the district and was concerned mainly with surviving the adventure.

Greenberg spoke next and sought to rectify Warburg's statement. He noted that the differences between the two members of the commission were fundamental and essential.

> Three parts of it [the report] include the reports by the three participants of the commission (each one separately) and the fourth one is a summary by Gibbons, the head of the commission, of the other two reports. . . . Wilbush's report is negative from every aspect. He expresses a negative opinion and indicates that the territory is worthless and suited only for the local inhabitants and for wild animals. Gibbons, on his part, harshly criticizes Wilbush's report and asserts that it is invalid.[120]

In view of Greenberg's remarks, Wilbush requested the floor to explain his criticism of Gibbons and what he meant when he wrote in the report that "where nothing exists, nothing can be done."[121] The chairman refused the request, on the grounds that only the impressions were germane and that Gibbons was not present to respond.[122]

Then the congress delegates began their debate of the Uganda plan, with its opponents and proponents presenting their views. The minutes of the congress reveal that the sessions were stormy and emotionally charged. The recording secretary's annotations include "loud applause," "thunderous applause," "whistles were heard again," "catcalls," "general pandemonium," "loud laughter," "speak to the point," "get down," "hats and scarves were waved," and similar statements. This indicates that the speeches were accompanied by much heckling and that the rival sides kept interrupting each other. After Warburg and Greenberg spoke, Nordau, as president of the congress, set the agenda for the discussion. It was decided to draw up two lists of speakers, one composed of opponents of the Uganda plan and one composed of supporters. Representatives from the yea-saying and the naysaying camps alternated on the podium.

One of the first speakers was Israel Zangwill. He spoke in English, and Dr. Judah Magnes translated his words into German. Because Zangwill expected his remarks to elicit a stormy reaction, he first urged the delegates to listen quietly and patiently to his words, not out of respect for him but out of respect for the British government.[123] He tried to draw the delegates' attention to the political implications of rejecting the British offer, asserting that it would endanger the Jews' freedom and their right of refuge in England. Zangwill explained that those who were currently trying to restrict Jewish immigration to England would claim that the Jews had been offered an expansive and fertile territory; if they refused to accept it, they could "go to the devil."[124] Zangwill claimed that to just say no without a reason was unacceptable; the Zionist movement should at least ask the British government for an alternative territory for Jewish settlement in order not to throw away the diplomatic coup that Herzl had brought to the Sixth Zionist Congress. He warned the opponents of Uganda that if

Max Nordau eulogizes Theodor Herzl at the Seventh Zionist Congress in Basel, 1905. (Central Zionist Archives)

דער זיעבעטער

ציוניסטען-קאנגרעס

אין באזעל.

פערלאג
בוכהאנדלונג "הצפירה" ווארשא
נאלעווקי 24.

ווארשא. תרס"ה.
דרוק "הצפירה", מאריאנסקא 2.

СЕДЬМОЙ КОНГРЕССЪ СІОНИСТОВЪ.

ВАРШАВА 1905.

Въ типографіи "Гацефира", Маріанская 2.

Program cover for the Seventh Zionist Congress.

# CHAPTER 1

the congress rejected the plan, the members would feel that they had pulled out a rotten tooth but would soon realize that this was, in fact, their only tooth.[125]

Another argument raised by Zangwill did not relate to the Zionist Organization's obligation to the British government but to the Zionist movement's historical mission of saving Jews, even if this meant relinquishing Palestine and setting up a Jewish state in some other territory. He maintained that the people had to establish the state, and not the other way around. A Jewish state in East Africa could save tens of thousands, perhaps hundreds of thousands of migrant Jews. Although the district in question was not developed, it could be made to flourish. The migration of the Jews was a fact, he said. A hundred thousand Jews were leaving Russia every year. Why should the Jews be dispersed and become assimilated into foreign cultures, losing their identity? Zangwill noted that Kaiser and Wilbush had admitted that the Jews, like every other people, were capable of running an independent and flourishing state; the Jews were no less talented than those who made the marshes of Venice, the deserts of Australia, or the colonies of New England flourish.[126]

In the wake of the pogroms that had struck the Jews in the Pale of Settlement, Zangwill told the delegates that the Zionist Organization was not just the parliament of the Zionist movement but represented Jews from twenty-three countries all over the world. He asserted that the congress had a duty not only to the Zionist movement but also to the entire Jewish people and that it should save Jews, even against their will and whether or not they were Zionists.[127]

Zangwill expropriated the Zionist movement from the Zionists and saw it as a movement that ought to be concerned about all Jews. He beseeched the delegates to reconsider before they rejected this favorable opportunity, the best offer made to the Jews in the last 1,880 years. He asked them to also keep in mind that many devoted and faithful Zionists had been forced to stay home to protect their families, because they were afraid of pogroms. He added that the congress must recognize its responsibility toward the Jewish masses; otherwise, it would be guilty of bloodshed.[128]

To persuade the congress delegates, Zangwill, in a trembling voice, related that, right after the close of the Sixth Zionist Congress, Herzl had rehearsed for him his final speech at the Seventh Zionist Congress should he fail to obtain a charter for Palestine by then. Herzl said he would resign as president of the congress and had told him about his desire to continue his diplomatic efforts to obtain a charter for some territory other than Palestine. Zangwill's emotional story was interrupted, according to the *Ha-zefirah* reporter, "by protests and indications of agreement."[129] It can be assumed that many of those seated in the congress hall did not believe Zangwill's story about Herzl's plans for a territory after the Seventh Zionist Congress. But because Herzl had written down the future speech in his diary, it seems that Zangwill was telling the truth about what he heard in Cowen's room at the conclusion of the sixth congress.

Zangwill offered six reasons that the delegates should support the Uganda proposal:

1. The creation of an autonomous colony was half of the Basel plan and was of great importance.
2. An autonomous colony would intensify Jewish national feeling, which was a component of the Basel plan.
3. The proposal would save tens of thousands and perhaps hundreds of thousands of Jewish migrants from assimilating into foreign cultures.
4. In a Jewish state it would be easier to take action on behalf of Palestine.
5. Repeated declarations that Palestine is the Zionists' sole aim make its attainment more distant, because it increases the sultan's price.
6. Uganda was being offered to them, and Palestine was not.[130]

Because it was not clear to Zangwill whether the Guas Ngishu plateau was suitable for settlement, he proposed the following resolution:

The Congress decides to accept with gratitude the generous offer of the Government of His Majesty, the King of Great Britain, to give the Jewish people a large and fertile territory with the rights of self-government under British protection, with the hope that the proposal of the Guas Ngishu plateau which was originally mentioned be extended or replaced by another proposal, since our survey commission has reached the conclusion that this plateau is not in conformity with the intention of the British

Government to allow large numbers of Jews to settle in a British colony.[131]

His motion was translated into Russian by Chaim Weizmann and into German by Magnes. Then the delegates were asked to vote on it when the time came.

After Zangwill, other speakers rose to argue about accepting the British proposal. The arguments repeated themselves and the speakers did not present any new reasons—with the exception of M. Shire, a British delegate, who not only responded to Zangwill's speech but also touched on several points that highlighted the main elements of the dispute between the Ugandist-territorialists and the "Palestinians." Shire utterly rejected Zangwill's assertion that the congress was a parliament representing Jews from twenty-three countries all over the world. Rather, the Zionist congress was meant to serve the Zionists alone; it was not concerned with all Jews in the world and those who had not paid dues to the Zionist Organization.[132] Shire's stand shows that the Territorialists' perspective on the problems of Jewish people was much broader than that of the advocates of Palestine only. Zangwill and his supporters wanted to use the Uganda plan to solve every facet of the Jewish question, whereas Shire, as one of the anti-Uganda speakers, thought that the Zionist movement should solve only the Zionists' problems.

Another speaker who referred to this problem was Judah Hazan, who, as already noted, was one of the most energetic and enthusiastic proponents of the territorialist idea in Warsaw. His speech, which lasted for more than an hour, was polemic and interrupted by many hecklers. Its importance did not lie in the arguments he brought in favor of Uganda but in its exposition of the essential principles of Territorialism. The Territorialists, according to him, were not opposed to Palestine but just to the principle of "only Palestine." From his point of view, Zionism's primary goal was to liberate world Jewry from poverty, deprivation, and suffering. The Jews' suffering was not that Palestine wasn't theirs but mainly that they had no state of their own. Only the establishment of a sovereign Jewish state, no matter where it was located, would solve the Jewish question and rehabilitate the Jewish people: "The starting point of Zionism is the suffering and pain of the Jewish people, and the only answer that Zionism offers is to establish a free state."[133]

In his speech Hazan attacked the anti-Ugandists' single-minded focus on Palestine, which was, in his view, unsuitable for Jewish settlement: "I claim that none of those sitting here can prove that Palestine is the only place to create a new Jewish center. Let us assume for a moment that we had sent a commission to Palestine and it had reported that it was a territory with an area of no more than 10,000 square kilometers, with a population of 600,000, and that it had no sources of water."[134] At this point the anti-Ugandists lost their patience and did not let Hazan continue with his speech. As long as he had been speaking about the Zionist principle, he was heckled by delegates who did not agree with his views; but when he began to disparage Palestine and assert that it was unsuitable for settlement, the pandemonium was such that the presiding officer, Oscar Marmorek, lost control. "Gentlemen," Marmorek shouted, "Mr. Hazan is of the opinion that Palestine is not a suitable place. Let us allow him to hold his opinion and we will hold ours. I ask for quiet, and ask Mr. Hazan to continue." Marmorek's pleas had no effect and, according to the minutes, the tumult persisted. Only after the commotion had subsided somewhat did Hazan continue with his address and try to reach the necessary conclusion.

> Because realization of the Zionist idea in Palestine is hopeless, Zionism must detach itself from Palestine on principle. We are being accused of betraying Palestine, but no, we are not betrayers. But if you [the anti-Ugandists] say that only in Palestine is it possible to establish a homeland for the Jews—a place where this is difficult and nearly impossible to achieve—you are the betrayers of both the people and the land.... I am convinced that if we propose to the British that Jews settle in one of its colonies, there is no doubt that we shall be answered positively. We are not beggars going from door to door and asking for charity. Zionism's point of departure was that Jewry wanted a land for itself, and not the Land.[135]

Hazan went on to refer to the survey commission that had investigated the Guas Ngishu plateau. His was one of the few speeches that stressed not only the commission's conclusions but also its methods. Hazan expressed his doubts about the report's credibility and claimed that the Actions

# CHAPTER 1

Committee had not acted in good faith when it dispatched the survey commission to East Africa. He raised several reservations and asserted that the report's conclusions should be treated with great skepticism. Hazan recalled that the congress decided not to finance the commission from the Zionist Organization but to solicit contributions from interested parties. Somehow, though, the Greater Actions Committee never went to the trouble of publishing notices in Die Welt to raise funds for the survey commission. Moreover, "Prof. Warburg declared in our presence that a group of professional experts was being sent; yet when I read the report of the commission, it mentioned that Gibbons, the head of the commission, said that one of the members, Mr. Wilbuschewitz [Wilbush], had only minimal abilities and that it was not he who led but it was necessary to lead him."[136] Hazan also cast doubt on the commission's scientific abilities, because the time at its disposal was insufficient.

> Major Gibbons admits that the commission remained in Uganda for only four to five weeks and that in this short period of time it was not possible to survey the territory. The honorable members of the Constitutional Committee hastened to convene a congress at which they could read out Mr. Ussishkin's conclusions. Uganda is suited to serve the Jews as the site of a free society. . . . My brothers! For two thousand years we have been dragging our sufferings like beggars from one country to another. We have just heard that a territory exists for which there is no need to bargain with the vizier or the Sultan. We regard the question of Uganda as a rare chance to realize Zionism and therefore we shall not treat it as a jest. We say this: Based on the conclusions of a commission that had a three-week "pleasure jaunt" and wrote us a feuilleton, we cannot reject the project. I would like to sum up: I am not trying to make light of the movement's value. While those sitting to my left who are called Territorialists number about fifty people in this hall, behind them stand hundreds of thousands of Jews.[137]

The attempt to cast aspersions on the survey commission's work proved unsuccessful. Many delegates spoke for and against the Uganda plan. The sessions were long and continued into the night. The closer they came to the vote, the harsher the arguments expressed by the rival camps. On behalf of his colleagues, Dr. Menachem Stein, a veteran of the Bilu pioneers and one of the leading advocates of the territorialist idea, who represented Palestine at the congress, read a statement that a majority of the delegates to the present congress were there illegally because of irregularities in the election of the Russian district leaders. Therefore he and his colleagues announced that the congress was not authorized or entitled to make any decisions on the question of East Africa. He also lambasted Ussishkin for not rejecting any means to forge a majority against the plan in the Actions Committee. Dr. Stein's claims were rejected, which infuriated the Territorialists.

Leib Jaffe, who was present, described the Territorialists' reaction to the Actions Committee's decision.

> The critical moment arrived. But the minority, which does not want there to be a vote on the Uganda question, begins a new obstruction. There are scenes that far exceed anything that has taken place until then—both in the Congress and at the Russian conference. On the Left benches they are beating with sticks, knocking on chairs, stamping with their feet, screaming until their throats are hoarse. The Ugandists and the Territorialists are jumping up on chairs, shouting furiously at the President; their faces are distorted and they threaten with fists and sticks. The President does not stop pounding his gavel on the table and ringing the bell, but to no avail. . . . Some of the audience in the galleries burst into the hall and join the agitators. . . . The President leaves his place and the electric lights in the hall are turned off. The pro-Zionists seized control of the podium, which the Left factions wanted to take by storm. The noise and tumult continue for a long time in the dark hall. Only at four in the morning, as dawn breaks, does everyone begin to disperse.[138]

Utter chaos. The tension reached its peak, and after many hours of speeches, arguments, and yelling, it was time to reach a decision. The next morning, Nordau read out the resolution that was to be voted on and that had been formulated by the members of the Greater Actions Committee. The resolution stated:

> The Zionist organization stands firmly by the fundamental principle of the Basel program, namely: "The establishment of a legally-secured, publicly recognized home for the Jewish people in Palestine," and it rejects either as an end or as a means all colonizing activity outside Palestine and its adjacent lands.
>
> The Congress resolves to thank the British Government for its offer of a territory in British East Africa, for the purpose of establishing there a Jewish settlement with autonomous rights. A Commission having been sent out to examine the territory, and having reported thereon, the Congress resolves that the Zionist organization shall not engage further with the proposal. The Congress records with satisfaction the recognition accorded by the British Government to the Zionist organization in its desire to bring about a solution of the Jewish problem, and expresses the sincere hope that it may be accorded the further good offices of the British Government where available in any matter it may undertake in accordance with the Basel program.[139]

The resolution was translated into Russian and English. It passed by a majority. The Territorialists protested the decision. Nachman Syrkin announced, in the name of twenty-eight members of the Zionist Socialist Workers' Party, that he was leaving the congress, because the resolution that had just passed did not conform with either the spirit of Zionism or its aims. Syrkin was followed out of the hall by political Zionists and Territorialists who were not affiliated with the Zionist Socialist Workers' Party. After this exodus, someone was heard to proclaim, "From now on there are no more Zion-Zionists—but only Zionists." The split in the Zionist Organization was final.

On August 8, Greenberg sent an official letter to the colonial secretary, Alfred Lyttelton, informing him that the Zionist Organization had declined to accept the British proposal.

> Sir—I am directed by the chief Actions Committee of the Zionist Organization to inform you that at the recent Zionist Congress held at Basel it was resolved that having sent out the Commission to examine the Territory in the East Africa Protectorate which was offered by His Majesty's Government to the Organization

for the purpose of a Jewish Settlement and received its Report, not to proceed further with the matter. At the same time I am to convey to you the sincerest appreciation of the Congress for the offer that was made, evidencing, as it did, the very high and noble sentiments of the Government towards the Jews, and to express the hope that we may rely upon the continued goodwill of the British Government in any effort which the Zionists may make in endeavouring to ameliorate the condition and raise the status of the Jewish people.[140]

Lyttelton's secretary replied to Greenberg on August 25 to confirm receipt of the letter. He added that any initiative intended to assist the Jewish people would be received with "sympathy and good will by the British Government."[141] This was the official quietus of the Uganda proposal. Nevertheless, as we will see in Chapter 5, the Territorialists tried to revive the proposal and continue diplomatic negotiations with Lyttelton (and later with Lord Elgin).

―

The Sixth Zionist Congress was the first meeting at which the delegates had to wrestle with one of the basic questions that had engaged the Zionist Organization since its inception: Does Zionism aspire to Jewish sovereignty in any territory, or is the Land of Israel its sole final objective and the only path to be pursued until its realization? The controversy illustrates that the Zionist movement was not a homogeneous group but consisted of two rival camps that interpreted the Basel plan differently.

During the controversy, the Ugandists, who derived their strength from Herzl's unquestioned leadership, seemed to be in the majority. At the turn of the twentieth century, the territorialist idea seemed more practical than the Zionist idea. In those days, Palestine was a distant province on the edge of the Ottoman Empire, where broad tracts were infested with malaria and other diseases. The Ugandists, who were ready to accept British protection fourteen years before the Balfour Declaration, wanted to establish a state for the Jews in a region with better conditions than those in Palestine and at a much lower price than that paid by settlers of the First Aliyah. Many thought that, in the era of colonialism, it would be easier to coordinate the interests of the Zionists searching for a territory with those of one of the Great Powers seeking to expand its control over territories it held overseas.

Those who opposed the Uganda plan realized the weakness of the territorialist arguments and understood that simply brandishing the historical right of the Jewish people to the Land of Israel was not enough. For this reason they stressed Wilbush's negative conclusions and ignored Gibbons's optimism. In view of the approach they adopted, the question is why the anti-Ugandists were not content with the moral assertion that even if the Guas Ngishu plateau was suitable for Jewish settlement and the climate was better, Palestine, despite its disadvantages, was still the land of the Jewish people and the focal point of all its hopes and yearnings over thousands of years? Why did the opponents choose to emphasize Wilbush's problematic report and disregard Gibbons's optimistic report? Wasn't the moral argument sufficient to strike the plan from the agenda and persuade the congress delegates that only Palestine could fulfill the Jewish people's aspirations? Why was it necessary to create the illusion that Uganda was unsuitable for Jewish settlement but Palestine was?

The emphasis on Wilbush's problematic report and the obfuscation of Gibbons's conclusions is first and foremost an indication of how much the anti-Ugandists feared the territorialist camp in the Zionist Organization. As the Jews' situation in Eastern Europe deteriorated and emigration to countries overseas increased by leaps and bounds, the territorialist idea grew ever deeper roots among Eastern European Jewry. It was clear to both sides that a positive report meant the revival of the plan for settlement in East Africa together with the weakening of Jewish settlement in Palestine. The protection that the British government would give to the settlement enterprise on the Guas Ngishu plateau and the territory's geographic advantages significantly buttressed the political Zionists. Even Nordau was aware of the implications of a positive report. In an interview with a London journalist in early 1905, several months before the publication of the survey commission report, he said that a positive report would lead to acceptance of the British proposal.

> The urgent question that disturbs us today is East Africa. The commission has just departed on its way and will return in March. Its report will be discussed in the next Congress, and if it is positive, it will be our duty to agree to the British proposal. It

seems to me that the way we shall have to go is definitely clear. We shall have to accept a charter from the British Government in the name of the Jewish Colonial Trust.[142]

The anti-Ugandists emphasized Wilbush's unprofessional and negative report rather than Gibbons's report because they thought this was the best tactic to defeat the plan. Any vacillation or hesitation in their opposition to the East Africa scheme would win it overwhelming support. In this situation the opponents of the Uganda plan were compelled to stress Wilbush's section of the commission report, even though his conclusions were neither professional nor reliable. This made the Territorialists' single argument, that a land suitable for absorbing masses of Jewish migrants had been located, irrelevant. The Uganda plan was dropped from the Zionist agenda, along with any future proposal for settlement outside Palestine.

During the debate at the Seventh Zionist Congress, the Territorialists expressed their resentment that the Greater Actions Committee had not discussed the plan for settlement in East Africa with due seriousness and that, in their view, it had been struck from the Zionist agenda without serious and in-depth consideration. The Territorialists' resentment increased in the months after the Seventh Zionist Congress, when they had time to read the report more carefully and understood that it was far more complex than Wilbush's simplistic statement that "where nothing exists, nothing can be done." From their point of view, this was a misleading and fraudulent action that justified their secession from the Zionist Organization and the establishment of the Jewish Territorial Organization in August 1905. The Territorialists' frustration was manifested at the ITO's second congress, held in London in 1906. A year had passed since the split, but the Uganda controversy was still hanging over the participants like a heavy cloud. Their intense anger with the Zionists had not abated, and severe charges were leveled against those who had rejected the British government's generous offer. For the Territorialists the Seventh Zionist Congress was based on deception—the survey commission's report was simply untrue.

> The Zionist Actions Committee's report on East Africa was an out-and-out fraud. England's offer was, as we all know, not Uganda but a large part of East Africa that is noted for its

excellent climate and where millions of people can be settled. The Zionist scoundrels who wanted to bury the plan from the very start asked the British Government after Herzl's death to indicate a small territory in East Africa to which the commission would be sent. This is how the East Africa proposal became the Uganda Plan. It is now clear that Boers and English settlers are living in the part of Uganda about which the Zionist commission submitted a poor recommendation.[143]

This was Nachman Syrkin's summary of the issue when he reviewed the ITO first congress in his newspaper *Der Nayer Veg*, a year after the political Zionists had left the Zionist Organization.

The ITO was conceived in the Uganda storm. In its early years it was the Zionist Organization's bitter and staunch rival. The savage pogroms that occurred after Kishinev and the mass emigration of Jews to the United States strengthened the ITO's position in Jewish society, and many people joined its ranks. However, in contrast to the Zionist movement, whose institutions remained in place after the controversy, the Territorialists had to set up a new organization from scratch in the hope that it would continue on Herzl's political path, a path they believed had been abandoned by the Zionist Organization at the Seventh Zionist Congress.

2

# A Land Ablaze

As soon as the Seventh Zionist Congress ended, those seceding from it gathered in one of the halls of the hotel in Basel and held a stormy discussion on their future in the Zionist Organization. A majority voted to resign from the organization and set up an alternative group to find a place for Jews outside Palestine. The background for this decision was not merely the Uganda affair, as is usually thought, but stemmed first and foremost from the socioeconomic condition of Jewish life in Eastern Europe, which had taken an extreme turn for the worse in 1904–1905. Between the Sixth and Seventh Zionist Congresses, the severe distress of Jewish society increased significantly. The economic situation worsened, a wave of pogroms swept over the southern part of the Pale of Settlement, and the westward migration of Jews swelled alarmingly. Although the Uganda affair had been the big bang, the worsening of the situation among the Jewish population hardened the positions of those who had supported the Uganda plan and led to their resignation from the Zionist Organization and the establishment of a new group as an alternative to it. In this chapter I examine the broader historical context of the reasons for setting up the Jewish Territorial Organization (ITO) and its activities on the Jewish street during the first years of its establishment.

## ESTABLISHMENT OF THE JEWISH TERRITORIAL ORGANIZATION

The first congress of the ITO was held from July 30 to August 1, 1905, in the hall of the Safran Hotel in Basel. About sixty participants laid out the

## CHAPTER 2

plan of action for the organization and its position in principle relative to the Zionist Organization. The group that gathered was not uniform in composition. It included political Zionists, Herzl supporters, members of the Zionist Socialist Workers' Party, and Ugandists. What was common to all of them was their adamant and aggressive opposition to Ussishkin's policies, particularly their opposition to the prohibition on any proposals or plans for settlement outside Palestine, including nearby territories, for discussion at future Zionist congresses. After their vociferous secession from the Seventh Zionist Congress, they did not know what their next step would be, but it was clear to them that they would have to rethink the situation together and that they could not accept the existing balance of forces in the Zionist Organization. Historiography assigns the idea of seceding from the congress and establishing the ITO to Israel Zangwill, but a study of the protocol of the first ITO congress and the memoirs of its participants indicates that Zangwill was dragged into the matter by the secessionists. He was not fully in accord with the decision to secede and hesitated to accept the role of president of the new organization. Zangwill was one of the most fascinating and controversial figures in the Zionist Organization; he was a shaper of territorialist ideology and the person who led the ITO from its founding to its dissolution.

Zangwill was born in London on January 21, 1864, to a poor Jewish family that had immigrated from Russia to England. His father, Moshe Zangwill, was a Cantonist who escaped by the skin of his teeth from the tsarist army and arrived in England in 1848. His mother, Ellen-Hannah Marks, was the daughter of a miller from a small town in Poland; she apparently emigrated with her cousin at about the same time to join her relatives in London. Zangwill's parents were married in a Jewish wedding in 1861, and their first son, Israel, was born three years later. Zangwill's brother, Lewis, was born in 1869. The Zangwill brothers grew up in an Orthodox home and were educated in Jewish schools in Plymouth, Bristol, and the Jews' Free School in London, where they were exposed to the poverty of the Jewish migrant community in the East End.[1] Israel Zangwill's daily contact with this community and his intimate familiarity with the poverty of the Jews were the key factors that informed his spiritual world, his political Zionist outlook, and, later, his territorialist affiliation. This is well reflected in his plays and novels, such as *Children of the Ghetto* (1892) and *Dreamers of the Ghetto* (1898), the two works most strongly identified with the Jewish immigrant experience in London, and *The Melting Pot* (1909), which deals with Jewish immigrants to the United States. In his descriptions of the suffering and poverty of Jewish immigrants in England, Zangwill exposed the English reader to the backyard of Jewish society. Like Mendele Mocher Sforim, Sholem Asch, and Sholem Aleichem, he became a well-known writer who focused on the "ordinary" Jews of his time, men and women who bore the sufferings of the Jewish people on their narrow shoulders.[2]

The first encounter between Herzl and Zangwill took place in this sociohistorical context. It was Max Nordau who recommended that Herzl meet with the Anglo-Jewish writer and gain his assistance in promoting the interests of the Zionist Organization in London. The first meeting was held in November 1895 at the Zangwills' home and, their communication difficulties notwithstanding, the two men reached an understanding. Herzl described the meeting in his diary.

> Israel Zangwill is of the long-nosed Negroid type, with very woolly deep-black hair, parted in the middle; his clean-shaven face displays the steely haughtiness of an honest ambitious man who has made his way after bitter struggles....
>
> Our conversation is laborious. We speak in French, his command of which is inadequate. I don't even know whether he understands me. Still, we agree on major points. He, too, is in favor of our territorial independence.[3]

The meeting led to a firm friendship and cooperation that continued until Herzl's death. Zangwill was Herzl's contact person in England, and his role was to introduce him to people with power and influence and to present him and his ideas to the Jewish community in England. He was one of Herzl's loyal supporters and was among those closest to him throughout his diplomatic efforts and desperate attempts to receive a charter for Palestine. Zangwill adopted Herzlian Zionism literally and regarded The Jewish State as the embodiment of the Zionist idea. In his eulogy for Herzl, Zangwill said, "There are not two Zionisms; there is only Zionism, the Zionism that was laid down in Herzl's Judenstaat—the Jewish national idea, associated, indeed, with Palestine by history and tradition and the hope of generations, but even greater than Palestine itself, since Palestine without Jewish rights would be the Goluth, the exile, in its most mocking form."[4] This text already contains the seeds of the territorialist idea, which later matured into a real political force that could compete with the Zionist movement and provide an ideological alternative.

Herzl, Nordau, and Zangwill were the three tenors of the Zionist Organization in the late nineteenth and early twentieth centuries. Herzl died before his time, after having spent a lifetime establishing and shaping the Zionist Organization and its political path. Nordau was the first to join forces with Herzl and his idea of the Jewish state, and he followed the Zionist movement until his death in 1923. His great contribution was in exposing the Zionist idea to world public opinion. "If I am the hand of the Congress," wrote Herzl to Nordau, "you are its voice that speaks to Europe."[5] Compared to Herzl and Nordau, it seems as though Zangwill's contribution to the Zionist movement was marginal and insignificant. Few today are aware that Zangwill was one of the prominent leaders of the Zionist movement and one of those closest to Herzl. His territorialist activities and his return to the Zionist movement with reservations after the Balfour Declaration overshadowed his activities and his contribution to the Zionist movement.

One of the few historians who recognized Zangwill's importance is Benzion Netanyahu. In his Founding Fathers of Zionism, he lists Zangwill alongside Pinsker, Herzl, Nordau, and Ze'ev Jabotinsky. The chapter on Zangwill was initially published as an introduction to Zangwill's works, which had been translated into Hebrew by Israel Yeivin and A. S. Orlans and published in Ha-derech La-atsma'ut (The Road to Independence) in 1938. Netanyahu notes that Zangwill's main contribution was to pave the way for British recognition of the Zionist idea. He was the first to speak in favor of the idea to an audience of well-known figures with influence on British politics. In a 1901 speech at the Article Club, Zangwill spoke to senior British officials who had shaped the British Empire's policies in its overseas colonies and influenced the future of Palestine from a Zionist perspective. According to Netanyahu, this was the first time that the Jewish question began to receive not only public but also government support. It was Zangwill who smoothed the way for Herzl to make contact between the Zionist movement and the British government, which eventually led to the Balfour Declaration in 1917.[6]

Yet, despite Zangwill's contribution to the promotion of the Zionist idea during the period in which its institutional framework was being shaped and Zionist diplomacy was being consolidated, Netanyahu wrongs Zangwill by highlighting only one side of his complex and many-sided personality. A collection of Zangwill's writings translated into Hebrew, edited by Netanyahu and published on the eve of World War II, includes only articles that emphasize his attachment to the Land of Israel, his support for the idea of "transfer," and his abhorrence of the Arabs of Palestine. His many articles in favor of the territorialist idea and his criticism of Zionism, which he often expressed, were not made available to the Hebrew reader. Moreover, those of Zangwill's works that were translated into Hebrew were carefully selected from among his writings, lectures, articles, and letters and published by Morris Simon in 1937. Netanyahu discards the chapter that was dedicated to Territorialism as though Territorialism was a marginal part of Zangwill's public activities.

Zangwill had a capacity for complex thought, and he analyzed the Jewish question in a pragmatic manner. Unlike some of his colleagues in the Zionist Organization, who thought that the solution to the Jewish question was settlement and concentration of Jews in Palestine, Zangwill believed that the problem was far more complex. In an 1899 speech in Philadelphia, Zangwill said, "Even a Jewish state will not heal the sores of the Jewish people. Only a conceited person can deceive himself and others by saying there is one simple remedy to cure an ancient disease which is more complex than any other." Four years before the Uganda proposal and six years before the founding of the ITO, Zangwill was already asserting that the solution to the Jewish question would involve a multifaceted strategy:

> Of the three remedies, . . . the revival of the nation, the revival of the spirit, and assimilation among the nations, I am prepared to accept all three in order to provide a triple solution to the age old melancholy drama of Jewish history. Those who think that the isolation of the Jewish people and its separation from other nations is a vain belief that is corrupt and harmful, let them become assimilated among the people amongst which they are living. Those who think that the Jewish people can fulfill its destiny in a more sublime way by being scattered and isolated among nations rather than living securely in its own land and under its own government, let them make centers of justice and

uprightness in all the countries in which they dwell and disseminate publicly, not only for themselves, their good doctrines, laws, and religion that affect the lives of the private citizen and the life of the nation. For the many Jews who preserve their religion and doctrines and are persecuted in many countries, a Jewish state will be a good gift.[7]

In addition to these three avenues for a solution to the Jewish question—national rebirth, spiritual revival, and assimilation—Zangwill proposed a fourth: that "there is no remedy." He explained, "Even if this was not a unique kind of despair . . . that the sufferings of the Jews are merely part of all human suffering . . . there is still hope that at the final end, when civilization will slowly spread and broaden in the countries of darkness, that they will cease to persecute the Jew and he will be freed from his troubles that they have unjustly placed upon him."[8] Zangwill depicted the solution through assimilation in his hit play The Melting Pot, first staged in Washington, DC, in 1908. The play was the fruit of Zangwill's involvement in Jewish immigration from Eastern Europe to the West and the Galveston plan, discussed in Chapter 5. But it was clear that the idea of assimilation, which had matured years earlier, was part of the solution to the Jewish problem because the condition for its realization was the establishment of a state for the Jews. If Jews had a state, some would come and settle in it, whereas others would prefer to remain in their current countries of residence and integrate into the general population rather than face the accusation of dual loyalties. According to this perspective, the territorialist solution would be beneficial not only to the members of the ITO but to the entire Jewish people, because it would allow Jews in the Diaspora to determine their identity and their level of affiliation with their countries of origin: "And when the Jew receives political rights as everyone else, his destiny will be one of these two, he will either become assimilated among the nations and the memory of the Jewish people will be wiped off the face of the earth, or the Jew will revive once again his religion and his beliefs."[9]

In 1903 Zangwill was one of the energetic supporters of the Uganda plan and, after Herzl's death, he became the most prominent political Zionist in the Zionist Organization. For him, the establishment of the ITO was not a matter of crossing the lines and betraying the Zionist idea but a continuation of the political line Herzl had laid out. However, although Zangwill was one of the Uganda plan's most prominent supporters and one of Herzl's strongest backers, the secessionists were led by Russian and Polish delegates to the Seventh Zionist Congress. It was they who conducted a spirited struggle for the Uganda plan in the months that preceded the Seventh Zionist Congress. In Bialystok, for example, leaflets were distributed on the eve of the seventh congress to influence public opinion and persuade the Russian delegates to support the Uganda plan.

> The Seventh Congress is drawing close; the moment is arriving when we will need to decide the question of Uganda; the moment when, after two thousand years of bitter and harsh exile, after two thousand years of being repressed and beaten down, physically, materially and spiritually, we have the opportunity to receive our own territory, to stem the tide of Jewish migration, and to create there, in time, an independent Jewish society with the freedom to develop in political, economic, and national terms.[10]

The rhetoric of this leaflet's authors contains a clear recognition of the fatefulness of the hour and the unique opportunity that had come their way, which must not be squandered. "To work, brothers!" the authors exclaimed. "With united forces! We will outvote the Zion-Zionists through the large majority we will send to the Congress."[11]

Similar leaflets were issued in Warsaw, and Joseph Kruk even noted in his memoirs that it was the Zionists of Warsaw who led the secession in the congress.[12] The calls for a struggle against the Zion-Zionists in the days preceding the Seventh Zionist Congress created exaggerated expectations that a majority supported the Uganda plan, but the high hopes led to deep disappointment, which ultimately led to secession. Whether the group who led the protest and left the congress hall in demonstrative style was from Bialystok or Warsaw, it was clear that Zangwill did not initiate the secession. The protocol of the first congress of the territorialist secessionists shows that Zangwill did not even participate in the discussion. He was engaged at the time in attempts to mediate between Marmorek and Nordau and to prevent resignation from the Zionist Organization, even after the decision was passed.[13]

Zangwill did not take part in the discussion on whether in principle the Territorialists should remain in the Zionist Organization or resign from it. Nachman Syrkin regarded secession as a revival of political Zionism and said, "Today, the dreamer's Zionism was defeated and practical Zionism has begun. Its basis is the question of leaving [the Diaspora]. Had we begun this twenty-five years ago, we would already have a large country."[14]

During the discussion, important decisions were made that would continue to affect the ITO until it was disbanded in 1925. The subjects on the agenda for the meeting were the idea of a mass concentration of Jews in an autonomous territory outside Palestine, the establishment of an organization to achieve this aim, the composition of a memorandum to the British Government, the transmission of notices to the press on what took place at the congress, the establishment of a subsidiary party in the Zionist Organization affiliated with the new organization, and the selection of a central committee for this party.[15]

Because of a lack of time, not all the issues were raised for discussion, but it was clear to most of the participants that a new organization had to be established immediately to replace the old Zionist one. Judah Hazan, who presided over this measure, maintained that "it is impossible to remain in the old organization. A new organization should be established that will aspire to create a haven for Jews who cannot or do not want to remain where they are now living." His proposal was accepted by most of those present. Thus ended the historic first day of the newly born organization.

On the following day, July 31, the elected committee read out the main points of the new organization's plan to the audience in the hall. This was the Territorialists' Basel plan, which was not essentially different from the original Basel plan, except that it did not designate Palestine as the final objective. The name of the new organization was decided upon: JTVO—Jüden Territorial Volks Organization—the Popular Jewish Territorial Organization. It set out its aims as follows:

1. The JTVO aims to obtain an autonomous territory for those Jews who cannot or do not want to remain in their places of residence.
2. In order to achieve this aim, which was defined in Paragraph 1, the organization seeks to bring together Jews who agree with its aims; to conduct negotiations with governments and with

public and private organizations; to establish the financial institutions and information bureaus necessary to carry out its aims.[16]

The second day of the congress was marked by a discussion about the attitude of the JTVO toward the Zionist Organization. Most of those present accepted the position of attorney Israel Jasinowski, a leader of Hovevei Zion in Warsaw and a Herzl loyalist. He claimed that the JTVO was a separate body independent of the Zionist Organization but that any member could belong to both organizations at the same time if he so wished. If circumstances made it possible to obtain Palestine and if a territorialist solution were to be found there, the members of the JTVO would support it, and there was therefore no reason to mention this explicitly in the plan that was taking shape. Rubinchek, the Po'alei Zion leader in Minsk added that the new organization did not have to take a stand with respect to the existing Zionist Organization and that every member of the JTVO had the right to determine their attitude toward the Zionist Organization.[17] Both proposals were unanimously accepted. As we will see, this decision would greatly influence the complex relations between the Territorialists and the Zionist Organization.

On August 1, at 5 o'clock in the afternoon, Zangwill arrived with his wife at the final session of the congress. He was received with tumultuous applause and delivered a pragmatic but enthusiastic speech in favor of the territorialist idea, but he hesitated to accept the presidency. He sought to convey the main points of his political plan to those in the hall. If it was accepted, avenues for cooperation could be discussed. Zangwill also said that only after the congress expressed support for the plan would they address the question of cooperation between them and the Zionist Organization. At first, Zangwill attempted to make it clear that it was forbidden to exclude Palestine from the territorialist program. It was a good land, and if everyone agreed to give it to the Jews, it would be gladly accepted. However, he said, the Zionist congress was wrong to reject the British proposal to establish a Jewish settlement in East Africa. Furthermore, Zangwill suggested changing the name of the organization that had been chosen the previous day to drop the word Volks. The new name, he maintained, should encompass the entire Jewish people, including the rich and affluent. The term Volks was liable to alienate the bourgeois Jews from political activism; this group was not to be disregarded.[18] By making this statement, Zangwill seemed to be trying to distinguish himself and the new organization from the socialist line led by Po'alei Zion and the Zionist-Socialists. For this reason, Zangwill suggested the name Jüdische Landorganisation, or the Jewish Territorial Organization. Shmuel Weizmann proposed another name: Jewish-Popular Territorialist Organization. After consultations, the decision was reached: The new territorialist organization would be called the Jewish Territorial Organization (ITO).

Even after the congress accepted Zangwill's proposal, he was uncertain about accepting the ITO presidency. "You want me to accept the leadership, but there is neither need nor possibility," he explained to the participants. "My health is weak, I do not speak German, and I know no Russian." Because most of the Jewish people were concentrated in Russia, he maintained, it would be better for the leader to be chosen from the Jewish society of Eastern Europe, some young and energetic man who would be a fair match for Ussishkin. "Our opponents defeated us because they had Ussishkin, whom they all obeyed. We need a leader like him, one we can rely on and obey as long as he heads the organization."[19]

Despite his hesitancy and his suggestion that the first president of the new organization be a Russian Jew, the honesty of Zangwill's declarations is dubious. The aim of his statement seems to have been to hint to his supporters what he expected from them. Without saying so explicitly, he made it clear that loyalty and obedience—of the kind Ussishkin had won for himself—were the necessary conditions for the chosen leader's success. In his memoirs, Kruk relates that once Zangwill believed that his audience wanted him take the reins of leadership, he declared that he wanted to consult with his wife, Edith Ayrton Zangwill, a determined and independent woman who was active in the suffragette movement in England. Acceptance of the presidency required a complete change in lifestyle and devotion of significant time to realize the ideals, and Israel Zangwill could not make such a crucial decision without his wife's blessing. Another reason for consulting her was Zangwill's desire to avoid the turbid relations that Herzl had with his wife, a relationship that embittered his life and burdened his political work heavily. Thus Zangwill thought it wise to consult his wife before accepting the demanding position.[20]

Israel Zangwill and his wife, Edith Ayrton, in Basel, 1905, on the eve of his resignation from the Zionist Organization. (Central Zionist Archives)

The ITO was established after three days of intensive discussion. From then on, the members had to spread the message of Territorialism throughout the Pale of Settlement and to recruit as many activists as possible to their struggle. The Zionist Organization saw the ITO as a real and present danger to its stability. In the future the two organizations would compete for Jewish support and sympathy through propaganda, political commentary, and the press.

By the time the first ITO manifesto was published in October 1905 in Vilna, Kovno, and Grodno, three main patterns of activity had already been set out: propaganda, organization, and fundraising.

> 1. Propaganda: The ITO must be a popular movement. Its plan is not for a specific class among the Jews, but for all Jewry, without class distinction, who feel the troubles of exile. Therefore it is necessary to conduct widespread propaganda among all the Jews. 2. Organization: In every country with a large number of

members, sub-organizations of two to fifteen members must be set up. These organizations will receive circulars from the head organization about all ITO activities. Each organization will send the head organization a monthly account [of its activities]. 3. Fundraising: Every ITO member, whether or not he belongs to any other organization, must pay 50 kopecks per year. Shekalim can be obtained from the head organization. In addition, collection drives should be held on various occasions for the benefit of the organization.[21]

## STRUCTURE OF THE ITO AND ORGANIZATIONAL BASIS

The structure of the ITO was hierarchical. The organization was managed by the International Council, which was composed of representatives of the Sectional Councils, which were spread throughout the Jewish Diaspora (Europe, America, Australia, and South Africa). The main office was directed by the British Sectional Council, which also functioned, effectively, as the Executive Committee.[22] According to the constitution of the ITO, anyone, regardless of race or religion, could join its ranks and become a member so long as he or she paid the membership dues. It was decided that the number of members in the ITO branches in Austria, France, Germany, England, Russia, Switzerland, and the United States would not exceed thirty; in South Africa, no more than twenty; and the number of members in the other countries would be determined by the International Council of the ITO. Because the territorialist movement was in the stages of being built, it was decided that the members in the local Sectional Councils would elect the president of the ITO. Only a year after its establishment, that is, on August 1, 1906, would the ITO begin holding democratic elections to determine the composition of the smaller bodies. In addition to the local Sectional Councils and their representatives in the International Council, a Geographical Committee was set up. Its members were charged with locating a designated territory, learning about it, and bringing their decision for confirmation by the appropriate bodies in the ITO. The ITO headquarters was in London, and office services were provided by the British Sectional Council.[23] The constitution stated that the president would be chosen by the International

Council with a two-thirds majority of the votes of the Sectional Councils participating in the elections. A meeting of the International Council would be held at the request of at least three Sectional Councils and at least twenty members of the British Sectional Council.

The Sectional Councils were composed of the branches that were scattered among the Jewish towns in the Pale of Settlement. These branches played an important role in disseminating the territorialist doctrine and recruiting members for the movement. The members of the branches were those who were in contact with the Jewish population and intimately familiar with its distress. They publicized the ITO's political and practical activities for the Jewish people in general and for Eastern European Jewry in particular. Every branch was subordinate to the Sectional Council, but the local branches were permitted to coalesce, cooperate among themselves, and set up federations of several branches. In the various federations, representatives were chosen for the Sectional Councils; some of them were also members of the International Council.[24] Besides sending representatives to the International Council, the Sectional Councils also had the important task of searching for a designated territory for Jewish settlement. Although negotiations for the designated territory were placed solely in the hands of the ITO president and the Geographical Committee, the Sectional Councils were charged with examining possible territories, making initial contact with the local governments, and mediating between them and the ITO president.

At the end of the preparatory committee in Basel, the delegates returned home and began building up the organization and establishing its institutions. It was clear that without branches in the towns and cities of the Pale of Settlement, the territorialist idea would not get off the ground. The main difficulty for the Territorialists in Russia was obtaining legal recognition from the Russian authorities for the new organization. Without freedom of action, no public activities could be conducted. This difficulty had also faced the Zionist Organization in its early days. Until 1890 it was an illegal organization in the tsarist empire, and the authorities frequently persecuted Zionist activists, closed printing houses, and arrested those who posted notices. When the Zionists were granted license to act in April 1890, they were able to gather openly and found the Society for the Support of Jewish Laborers and Craftsmen in Syria and Palestine in Odessa, otherwise known as the Odessa Committee.[25]

ITO members understood that the success of the organization depended first and foremost on receiving approval from the authorities so that they could act without fear of persecution. This issue was brought up for discussion at the second ITO congress in London in early January 1906, and it was decided that vigorous efforts must be made to obtain the desired license. Because it was difficult to receive a license that would cover all ITO activities throughout the Russian Empire, it was decided that every branch would apply to the mayor of its city and obtain authorization for its local activities. The territorialist activists received quite a detailed explanation of how to apply. They were told to attach two copies of the ITO constitution to their letter of request; to include 5 rubles, in accordance with the temporary legal regulations on publicizing the establishment of a new organization in the press; to indicate the names of the members (at least five), their titles, family names, and places of residence; and to have the signatures on the application notarized and the completed documents sent to the mayor.[26]

The first to receive the desired license were the Territorialists in Yelizabetgrad. They defined the three aims of the organization as (1) studying the possible countries outside Europe and conditions for settlement there, (2) finding out how the governments in those places felt toward settlement and the immigration of Jews; and (3) providing monetary assistance and information to migrants who wanted to leave Russia, especially those who were interested in joining agricultural colonies outside Europe. Nothing was written in the organization's constitution about the ITO's aspirations to set up an autonomous Jewish settlement for Jews who could not or did not want to remain in their countries of origin, because the insertion of such a paragraph into the constitution of a local association would present difficulties in receiving a license and would delay territorialist activities. After the Yelizabetgrad association received the official license, the activists could hold public meetings and make the public aware of the ITO's aims.[27]

The receipt of local permits from city mayors made it easier for the territorialist activists to work with and reach the Jewish masses. The Pale of Settlement was divided into areas of activity, each with one ITO representative who supervised the members' work. A branch in Warsaw was established to coordinate all the work in Poland and in the Grodno District; the branch in Yelizabetgrad, in the Kherson District, supervised the branches in Poltava, Kharkov, and Yekaterinoslav; the main branch for southern Russia was in Odessa, and it was responsible for the branches in Podolia, Bessarabia, and Taurida; the branch in Kovno supported the branches in Vilna, Minsk, Mogilev, and Vitebsk; and the branch in Kiev oversaw the branches in Volyn and Tchernigov. There were also territorialist branches in the Caucasus (Baku) and in the interior districts of Russia.[28] In view of the Russian bureaucratic difficulties, the establishment of these branches was an impressive achievement. Within a relatively short time, the ITO managed to set up a broad organizational infrastructure in Eastern Europe and throughout the Jewish Diaspora. This infrastructure made it possible for the leaders of the ITO to disseminate their ideological doctrine, to begin their struggle over the Jewish street, and to try to win as much support as possible among Eastern European Jewry.

## THE STRUGGLE FOR THE JEWISH STREET

The ITO began its activities during a fateful period for the Jews in the Russian Empire. In 1905–1906, there were 657 pogroms in the Pale of Settlement, in which more than 3,000 Jews were murdered. The district of Tchernigov alone saw 251 pogroms, with 76 Jews killed. Kherson and Bessarabia had 153 pogroms, fewer than Tchernigov but much more violent, with 1,300 Jews murdered. In Yekaterinoslav, 285 Jews were killed in 41 pogroms, and in Grodno, 356 Jews were killed in only 10 pogroms.[29] The pogroms had a clear regional pattern. More than 87 percent of the acts (575) of murder, robbery, and plunder took place in the southern provinces of the Pale of Settlement (Tchernigov, Poltava, Yekaterinoslav, Kherson, Podolia, Kiev, and Bessarabia). A quarter of those murdered were women. The number of orphans came to about 1,500. Eight hundred children lost one parent, 2,000 were badly injured, and 15,000 were lightly to moderately wounded. Property damage was estimated at between 57 million and 84 million rubles. Fires were the main cause of property loss. Towns, synagogues, factories, and stores were set ablaze, and many Jews had their sources of livelihood severed.[30] The Kishinev pogrom, it seems, was no exception, and the pogroms that followed left a deep impact on Jewish society, arousing doubt as to the readiness of Russian society to accept the presence of Jews within it.

CHAPTER 2

Jews standing around the bodies of the victims of the Yekaterinoslav pogrom.

The political expression of the influence of the pogroms was the strengthening of the ITO. In view of the acts of murder and plunder, many of the Jews in the Pale of Settlement placed their hopes on Zangwill and the speedy solution to the Jewish question he proposed. From the towns ravaged by pogroms came leaflets, manifestos, and public letters begging Jews to support the ITO. Kiev, for example, stood out among the cities in the Pale of Settlement for the extent to which the territorialist movement set down roots there. The 1897 census reported the city's population as 246,000, including 31,800 Jews (13 percent). From 1905 to 1906, Kiev saw 41 pogroms, which led to the murder of 167 Jews.[31] In her memoirs, Marie Waife-Goldberg, Sholem Aleichem's daughter, described the pogrom that was engraved in her childhood memories.

> The very next morning we were awakened by a terrifying noise, a confused racket of clatters and crashes of loud shouts and shrill cries. We ran from our beds to the windows on the streets and looked down on a scene of brutality and murder—a gang of hoodlums beating a poor young Jew with heavy sticks; blood was running over the face of the young man, who was vainly

shrieking for aid. A policeman stood nearby, casually looking on not moving a finger. Our mother quickly pulled the shade down, sent us back to bed and ordered us never again to go near the window. But what we had seen was enough to give us nightmares for weeks to come.[32]

The pogrom in Kiev raged for three days. "Three days and nights of terror," Waife-Goldberg wrote in her memoirs, "in which we were incapable of eating or sleeping, walking around quietly, scared, in case our fortress, 'The Imperial,' would fall at any moment."[33]

Moshe Rosenblatt, one of the main public activists in Kiev and a member of the Mizrachi Party, wrote a letter to Zangwill that bluntly described the pogrom in Kiev and its implications for the city's Jewish community.[34] The letter was written as the events were taking place, and the voices emerging from his letter are testimony to the atmosphere of apprehension and terror that prevailed in the city during the pogrom. The author's emotional turmoil is tangible, such that readers feel as though they are standing near the writer's desk and looking out the window of his home at the city streets awash with Jewish blood. "Not in ink but in blood and tears are we composing these words to you! The hand trembles, the eyes shed tears," Rosenblatt wrote to Zangwill.

> A shout [is heard] in the streets of Kiev. The soldiers, Cossacks, and police are slaughtering our brothers and sisters in the company of hooligans, and there is no one to protect them. The defense societies have become disheartened; they cannot stand up against the battle-hardened armies with their amazing tactics. Shouts outside, screams in the homes, in the basements, in the attics, in the caves. The screams of children and infants, the sound of women fainting, the groans of the dying, and the breaking of the bones of old people thrown from the upper floors deafen the air of Kiev! Infants and children are being torn up, ripped in half, and thrown to the dogs! They are slicing open the stomachs of pregnant women, cutting out organs from healthy people, and flaying them with iron combs. If the heavens don't explode at the sound of the cries, they must be made of iron and brass! If the

earth doesn't shudder at the sound of the wails, then it is a bloody earth, a wasteland full of the fire of the inferno![35]

Following this description of murder and abuse, Rosenblatt detailed the economic situation that prevailed in the city after the plunder. "All the merchants and shopkeepers in the city have been left naked and destitute, with only their shirts on their backs." Food was scarce and a famine fell upon Kiev.

> We are all dying of hunger, including our infants and children! Thousands of people are crying out for bread but there is none. The children are fainting from hunger. The committee distributes loaves of bread and herring every day, and like locusts they all fall upon the distributors, pushing and shoving, shouting and weeping loudly, "Give me! Give me bread! Give me herring!" Like predatory wolves they fight over a loaf of bread and grab the herring away from each other![36]

To escape the rioters' claws and find some help, the Jews assembled in the city's public buildings. "The theaters and community centers are crammed like [chicken] coops with men, women, and children, ill and wounded, heads bandaged, screaming in pain! Every day, many of them die horrible deaths in terrible agony!!!" According to Rosenblatt, about 700 families (some 3,500 people) found themselves without a roof, and "beset at all times by fear of death." In view of this grim reality, Rosenblatt asked Zangwill to publish in England the account of the massacre of Jews and to pressure the government to give the Jews a territory that would provide a refuge for their distress.

> Our purpose in writing this letter is as follows: Please, honorable President! Please, crown of Israel! Print our words in the English newspapers! We ask and plead that the great Jews in England approach the King of England and the ministers, with you, Mr. Zangwill, our president, at the head of the deputation, and ask them to give us Uganda immediately, because the entire Jewish nation wants Uganda. The "Zionists of Zion" turned down the offer on their own initiative without consulting their people. . . .

> We all want to escape from the bloody land! We are not secure in our lives! Please, great Jews in England, please, Mr. Greenberg, return to Territorialism for the sake of the spilled blood of your brothers and sisters.[37]

A month later, on December 6, Rosenblatt wrote Zangwill another letter containing further descriptions of the horrors and cries for help. Rosenblatt noted that the number of victims had risen in the city, and a great flight in the wake of the pogroms had emptied the city of its inhabitants. Only the poor remained, he reported, along with those who had died of hunger.

> In brief, Mr. President, we are like a sheep among seventy wolves. We dwell among scorpions! In this letter I speak on behalf of thousands of Jewish families among whom I live. They have charged me with appealing to you and beseeching you to ring the bells in England, move heaven and earth in the London newspapers, beat the great drum and call for assistance, help the nation of six million who are in terrible distress, in life-threatening danger![38]

Rosenblatt repeatedly urged Zangwill to find "some territory that will be a cause for celebration, a holiday of redemption and salvation, a day of deliverance and reprieve!" He also noted that he had met with Sholem Aleichem, who had made him enthusiastic about the territorialist idea. He explained that a personality like Sholem Aleichem could help spread territorialist ideology and could exert a considerable influence on the Jews.

> Finally, I have some advice: "Sholem Aleichem," the popular author known for his great talent, lives in our city. He is the storyteller of the ghetto, a writer who sketches and depicts all the slight movements of Jewish life in exile. This author's every artery and drop of blood are of ghetto life. The nation loves him for his wit and style, and he has tremendous authority. I recently converted him into a Territorialist, and I tried to convince him to go to Brussels, because I know that when Sholem Aleichem speaks onstage, even the walls will have

ears. The walls of the building will be moved by his voice, and his authority will have an enormous amount of influence on the nation. He promised me, but nevertheless, to reinforce the matter, I recommend that he be sent an invitation from ITO headquarters in London, which is under your jurisdiction, honorable President. Then I am sure that we'll catch this big fish. Don't make light of it.[39]

Rosenblatt's claims that Sholem Aleichem had become a Territorialist were exaggerated and far from the truth. Although Sholem Aleichem had visited Zangwill's summer home near London in 1906, it had been merely a courtesy visit. The disparity between Zangwill, who had grown up in the poor neighborhood of Whitechapel in London and had worked his way up the socioeconomic ladder to become an English gentleman, and Sholem Aleichem, who had left behind an affluent life to live among his fellow Jews in Eastern Europe, was too great a gap to bridge. Sholem Aleichem did not feel comfortable in the company of the English writer and did not show any interest in the territorialist idea.[40]

Nevertheless, Rosenblatt's description of the pogrom and the terrifying anguish of the Jews of Kiev conform with other sources that described and documented the acts of murder and pillage. Following the violence of October 1905, the Zionist Organization commissioned Leo Motzkin to write a comprehensive summary of the pogroms. The aim of the book, which was financed by the Zionist Aid Fund in London, was to compose a complete survey of the carnage that had struck the Jews in the districts of the Pale of Settlement. To write such a survey, Motzkin printed detailed questionnaires and had twenty assistants distribute them in eighty-five towns and cities in the Pale of Settlement that had been under barbarous attack. At the same time, Motzkin examined the newspapers of that period and verified the testimonies against his supplementary sources. He found a resemblance between the pogroms of 1905 and those of the 1880s and therefore decided to broaden the subject of his research. The result was a thick volume with more than 900 pages of testimonies and other material about the pogroms.[41] A comparison between Rosenblatt's letters and the testimonies and official reports in Motzkin's book, Die Judenpogrome in Russland, shows that his descriptions were not exaggerated. The testimonies that Motzkin collected match Rosenblatt's letters, and the pogroms had a profound impact on all those who experienced them.[42]

Zangwill also received letters of grief and lamentation like Rosenblatt's from small towns in the Pale of Settlement that had also experienced the terror of the pogroms. In Calarasi (Kalarash, Bessarabia), a "Committee for the Support of Pogrom Victims" was set up to provide support and assistance to the afflicted Jewish community. In that small town of less than 1,000 people, a cruel pogrom occurred on October 23–24, 1905; more than sixty Jews were shot, killed, or burned alive. In a booklet published shortly after the pogroms, Yakov Tsippeleshter, one of its residents, described the acts of plunder, rape, and murder of his neighbors.

> In the courtyard of one of the houses, there were 18 dead bodies, most of them burned alive. The owner of the courtyard, a widow, and her granddaughter, age 13 or 14, collected a bag of silver objects. As soon as the pogrom began, they began running through the courtyard to find a place to hide. The Christian neighbor noticed them and met them with an axe. First he took the bag of silver from them, and then killed them both. When the fires broke out, he threw them into the flames; apparently they weren't dead yet. The next day, they were found among the smoldering brands locked in an embrace and with bruise marks on their bodies.[43]

When the extent of ruin and destruction in Calarasi became clear, the community notables issued an emotional call for assistance and rehabilitation for the community. The committee published a call for help, which was posted on synagogues and Torah academies and distributed throughout the Pale of Settlement. A few copies even reached Zangwill in London: "The small town of Calarasi has perhaps 1,000 families and 600 houses, 300 of which have been consumed by fire. Not a stone remains, all the shops in the city have been razed to the ground.... 500 families consisting of 2,000 people are roaming outside without a place to sleep."[44] The committee appealed to Zangwill, who "would find it easy to gather certain sums to sustain the thousands who are starving" by virtue of his position and status.[45]

Despair took hold of some sections of the Jewish population in the wake of the wave of violence; the 3,000 murdered, the thousands wounded, and the plunder and general destruction suffered by the Jews in the Pale of Settlement made them more amenable to a speedy territorialist solution that aimed to find a territory "here and now" for Jewish settlement and strengthen the territorialist movement. This support was not the product of opposition in principle to the Zionist idea and the return to the Land of Israel but of the realization that the Jews did not have sufficient time to wait until conditions were ripe and Palestine became able to absorb immigrants. Unlike the rabbis (who regarded the Zionists as illegitimate), the Communists, and the Bundists, the Jewish victims of the pogroms sought a radical solution to their distress. In many ways, Territorialism offered a solution to their needs. Russian Jews found themselves helpless against the wave of hatred from Russian society and the severe economic hardship brought on by the pogroms. In this bleak situation the territorialist idea could put down roots in a wounded and divided Jewish society. Many hung their hopes on Zangwill's diplomatic efforts and censured the Zionist movement for giving preference to "the good of the land" over "the good of the people."

The writer Yosef Haim Brenner expressed similar criticism of the Zionist movement and maintained that the territorialist idea could provide an expeditious solution to the Jewish question. Although Brenner was living in London at the time and was not himself exposed to the pogroms, he had lost a close friend, Haya Wolfson, in the pogrom in Bialystok. In his article "Mikhtav arokh" (A Long Letter), he aptly expressed the feelings of many Jews in the Pale of Settlement: "What do we care about the fatherland? What is the Promised Land to us when it cannot be reached? What is the use of our past if the past is gone, if we have no past and no future, but only disaster upon disaster—as though we are in the Middle Ages?! A cave, we need a cave for the refugee.... Bring us a cave where we can hide."[46] Brenner's call for a cave was not unlike the call from Rosenblatt in a December 1906 letter to Zangwill: "We yearn for redemption—anything to escape this bitter exile! We yearn also for the Mountains of Darkness, to be in the coal mines, the salt mines, in a land whose soil is iron and brass—as long as we can breathe air, sleep in peace, eat dry bread without harassment, and not have our flesh pierced by knives and axes and our blood spilled like water!!!"[47]

Brenner's and Rosenblatt's modest request for a cave was not only an expression of the desire of the Jews in the Pale of Settlement for security and a normal life but also a criticism of the Zionist movement. Unlike the recently established ITO, the Zionist idea had been ingrained in Eastern European Jewish society for twenty-five years. In the half-century since Pinsker's teachings had heralded the Zionist message, not only had the desired change failed to materialize, but also the situation had become more severe. The pogroms of 1903–1905 were more violent than those of 1881–1882, the poverty had grown worse, and Jewish emigration had reached proportions heretofore unknown. Brenner's statement in "Mikhtav arokh"—"The carnage has come, my brothers, it has come! It didn't come as a surprise, brothers. No. It developed, it developed gradually, it developed according to scientific laws"—was largely an indictment against the Zionist movement for its failure to bring about the desired breakthrough in all the years of its existence. The writing was on the wall, and the Zionist movement had shown itself to be powerless.

For the Territorialists this dark, violent situation substantiated their basic claim that the land was ablaze and that finding an immediate solution for hundreds of thousands of Jews was of the utmost urgency. However, the young organization was not yet prepared to cope with the extent and consequences of the crisis. An open letter distributed by the Territorialists in Kiev mentioned that "the pogroms and riots interrupted us in our worldly activities, because at a time when we must be helping our thousands of brothers who are suffering hunger, when everything is paralyzed by the post office strike and of the railway lines and general economy, it is not possible to maintain any kind of routine."[48] The Territorialists' work was disrupted not only by the difficulties in mobility and communication but also by the heavy pressure of the masses that they fulfill their promise to find a land for settlement.

> And what a tragic jest the present times have played upon us. Thousands upon thousands of our suffering brethren demand assistance with force and pathetic cries. They call out: "Where is the land to which you said you would bring us? Give us a land wherever it may be, as long as we can be safe from slaughter, as long as our children will not be torn to pieces and our sisters and daughters not be raped." In view of the fact that the Territorialist Organization is only a few months old, nothing much can be done in the diplomatic sphere to advance the idea of a charter. Their

inability to provide the desired solution for the needy masses has caused frustration among the local activists: "And what can we answer them in this hour? Are we like God to command the wings of the eagles to lift up all the people from the valley of death and carry them to a good and spacious land?"[49]

The Territorialists wanted to use this hostile situation and the ensuing distress and fear to advance the territorialist idea and broaden the circle of support among all the ranks of Jewish society: "Now our brothers believe that you have an important duty to gather a majority of the people under the flag of the Jewish Territorial Organization and to work on behalf of those still remaining before it is too late, and to save them before disaster comes upon us, God forbid."[50] Petitions of support for the ITO were distributed throughout the Pale of Settlement, and Jews were asked to sign them and express their support for the organization. "We need to begin the work immediately, even before the fears and panic subside. We cannot wait for the days of peace to arrive." The Territorialists were charged with "reading the petition before the people" to obtain "the signatures of all Jews who are in agreement with our idea" and to send the petitions "directly to London to our President, Israel Zangwill."[51]

Indeed, the declarations were sent to the Jewish towns in the Pale of Settlement to recruit popular support for the ITO. Thousands of Jews signed them and urged Zangwill to find the desired land as soon as possible.

> We, the undersigned residents of [name of the town] are convinced that the only meaningful way to save the existence of the Jewish people and to escape our tragic and unnatural situation is to have a land of our own, a free place in which we can live independently without constant fear of Russian hooligans and European anti-Semitism, a place that we can naturally develop our economic and intellectual powers and be who we really are, both men and women. We are convinced that all philanthropies and ideologies will only lengthen and confound our tragic situation and distract our attention from the only true solution. In this declaration, we appeal to you with the request to continue your work to acquire a territory on an autonomous basis for the Jewish people. Declare

in our name to the civilized world that this is the only solution to the Jewish question.[52]

The response was greater than anticipated. Thousands of Jews signed the petition and authorized Zangwill to search for a suitable land for Jewish settlement. A look at the towns mentioned in the petitions reveals that support for the ITO came mainly from regions that had suffered pogroms in the Pale of Settlement.

This mass cooperation of Jews with the Territorialists does not necessarily prove that they had abandoned or become alienated from the Zionist idea. Many had indeed changed their position in principle from "only the Land of Israel" to "not exclusively the Land of Israel," but not because of alienation from Zionism. The city of Kiev became the stronghold of the territorialist movement in the Pale of Settlement and the bridgehead between London and the Jewish population in Eastern Europe. The person who supervised the work was Max Emmanuel Mandelstamm, Zangwill's loyal right-hand man and his senior representative in Eastern Europe.[53] More than anything, Mandelstamm's path to Territorialism and to the position of second in command in the ITO shows how close the Territorialists were to Zionist ideology and that they differed in only one thing: their pessimistic approach to the fate of the Jews in the Russian Empire and their desire to find a territory for the Jewish people as quickly as possible, before it was too late.

## MAX EMMANUEL MANDELSTAMM

Mandelstamm was one of the most interesting figures in the ITO and one of its prominent activists in the Russian Empire. He was born in 1838, in the small town of Zagare on the Courland border.[54] His father, Ezekiel, was a highly educated merchant who engaged in biblical research and wrote in Hebrew. He gave his children a general education and taught them German and French but also nurtured a Jewish consciousness in them.[55] Yiddish was not spoken in the house. In his memoirs, Mandelstamm wrote that his mother used to read "Robinson Crusoe [to him and his brothers], and taught us to recite the narrative poems of Schiller by heart; these captured my mind."[56] He mentioned his studies in the heder and wrote that "its poetic qualities and shortcomings" were engraved on his memory. When he was 12 years old, his family moved to Vilna and he began studying at the local high school. This period left a deep impression on him, shaped his worldview, and sharpened his Jewish identity and his views of Russian society. There were nine other Jewish students at the school, and all were "targets for the canes of the Christian pupils who beat them mercilessly. We did not hear any other terms of endearment except 'cursed Jew!' We were always the insulted and they were the assailants."[57] This humiliation shaped his Jewish identity and attracted him to the Zionist idea many years later. In a brief essay he published in Hashiloah titled "Why Am I a Zionist?" Mandelstamm noted the persecution he suffered from his schoolmates as the events that gave shape to both his Jewish identity and his nationalist identity. "I am therefore a Zionist from the first moment that a Christian boy lifted his hand against me for being a Jew."[58] After four years at the school, Mandelstamm enrolled to study medicine at the University of Dorpat in Estonia. He considered that time the happiest and most beautiful years of his life. Dorpat was known as an important center of learning in Germany, and as a student there, Mandelstamm had access to famous lecturers in the field of medicine. But a downturn in his family's finances made it difficult for his father to pay for his studies, and Mandelstamm was forced to return to live with his parents, who were about to immigrate to Kharkov. The transition from a leading university to a mediocre one made it difficult for Mandelstamm to continue his studies, but he overcame the hardships and completed his courses. In 1860, at the young age of 21, he received his doctor's certificate.

After completing his studies, Mandelstamm opened a small clinic. He used his scant savings to travel to Berlin for advanced training and later to Heidelberg. When he returned to Russia, he settled in Kiev, where he founded a hospital for eye diseases. This work exposed him to the troubles of Russian society in general and Jewish society in particular. During the pogroms of 1881, Mandelstamm devoted all his energies to helping the injured and afflicted. He headed a support committee that solicited and received a large amount of money from the Jews of Western Europe and America and even participated in conferences held by assimilated Jews in St. Petersburg to discuss the issue of emigration from Russia. Contrary to the majority position, Mandelstamm was in favor of immigration as a solution for the Jews in the Pale of Settlement. He was

Max Mandelstamm, 1838-1912. (Central Zionist Archives)

in complete agreement with Pinsker and defended the positions in Auto-Emancipation. From that moment, Mandelstamm notes in his memoirs, "My heart and soul were given devotedly to the sorrow and distress of my people. Who will put a limit to this anguish and who can envision its final end?" Even though he began defining himself as a Zionist "on the day my Gentile friend lifted his cane to strike me because I was a Jew," Mandelstamm headed the Am Olam movement in Kiev, which encouraged migration to the United States instead of Palestine.[59] But in 1899, when his autobiography was published in the Ahiasaf Literary Almanac, Mandelstamm noted that he believed in the return of the Jews to their country and that only on their free land would they be able to become "an exemplary people and a light to the nations." In that year, he wrote in Hashiloah that "Palestine is the country of the future. According to knowledgeable sources, it can be turned by willing hands and hard work into a flower garden; Palestine and Syria can provide food for thousands upon thousands of people, but at present they are uninhabited wastelands."[60]

Mandelstamm's encounter with Herzl was a turning point in his Zionist career. He was impressed by Herzl's personality and ability and became his aide and loyal partner in his political effort. Mandelstamm participated in the First Zionist Congress and was chosen to be one of the four representatives of Russian Jewry to the Zionist Executive Committee.[61] On his return to Kiev, Mandelstamm was charged with setting up the financial center of the Zionist Organization in Russia, and his home became the central meeting place of the leaders and activists of the movement. Mandelstamm was an active Zionist; his work in building up the young Zionist organization during the Herzl period, marshalling the Jewish intelligentsia in support of the Zionist idea, and raising funds from the richer residents of the Pale of Settlement were of major importance. Besides his public activities, Mandelstamm also made some cogitative contributions that apparently disappeared from Zionist historiography when he joined the ITO and became one of the leading figures in formulating territorialist ideology.

In 1900, Mandelstamm published Mahut Hatsiyonut: Michtav Le-viti (The Essence of Zionism: A Zionist's Letter to His Daughter), in which he explained the importance of the Zionist idea for the Jewish people and for human culture as a whole. This essay was written after his daughter distanced herself from her Jewish identity and drew closer to the cosmopolitan ideas circulating in tsarist Russia at the time. His fear that she follow her uncles and assimilate into Russian society led him to write this open letter in defense of Jewish nationalism. Mandelstamm remonstrated against Jewish youth who were trying to assimilate into Russian society without understanding the real implications of their actions. "The cosmopolitan dream and the desire that nations will live side by side in peace and amity are not a new phenomenon," he wrote to his daughter, and he quoted Isaiah 11:6: "And the wolf shall dwell with the lamb, and the leopard lie down with the kid."[62] This, he explained, was a worldview that had emerged from the suffering of the world and from a natural instinct in mankind, an outlook held by those who cannot look indifferently at human evil and at man's hatred of his fellows. Yet the conclusion that there was no place in our world for national movements (including the Zionist movement), and the assignment of blame on the division of humankind into peoples and races was erroneous and baseless. He tried to explain that there was no contradiction between belonging to humanity and to a nation. When a person lives and acts within a certain social framework and feels that he or she is part of a certain collective, that person contributes greatly to humanity as well. People cannot deny their national characteristics. Artists and writers such as "Shakespeare, Schiller, Tolstoy, Heine and Yehuda Halevy flourished within their nations and influenced all human thought."[63] To be a citizen of the world, Mandelstamm held, was "to support the freedom of the individual, to uphold the idea of equality before the law, to respect the views and beliefs of others, and not necessarily to lose national identity." A cosmopolitanism that aimed to mingle all the nations "into a socialist porridge will not only fail to advance humanity but will take it one step backwards."[64] Thus those who tried to alienate themselves from the Jewish people and to assimilate were sinning not only against themselves but also against humanity as a whole, even if they did succeed in preserving their existence in an unprecedented way. They were eliminating "the healthy sprouts that, when developed and nurtured, can be of benefit to human culture and civilization as a whole." For this reason, Mandelstamm believed that Zionism would benefit not only the Jewish people but all humanity; he compared it to the work of an artist who wanted to mend "a good and superior kind of musical instrument that had broken down and was left in an abandoned attic, an instrument that was necessary for the entire human orchestra, just as a violin, cello or flute were necessary for an ensemble."[65]

As a well-known ophthalmologist of some status, Mandelstamm was in close touch with the Jewish intelligentsia and the circles that advanced the idea of Russification. In an article he wrote in 1898 and published eight years later, when he had already become a Territorialist, he decried the assimilated members of the Jewish intelligentsia and called on them to join the Zionist movement. He related that upon his return from the Basel congress, he gave a lecture at his home on Zionism and the decisive role it played in the lives of the Jewish people. The lecture was attended by a distinguished Jewish audience composed of doctors, lawyers, factory owners, bankers, and rich merchants. From the applause he received, "I drew the conclusion that Zionism had won and that those present were in support of it. But when I asked an intelligent woman whether she had become a Zionist, she told me: God forbid! Your lecture was very interesting, but Zionism is total folly."[66] This rich and comfortable group of Jews, he explained in his article, regarded Jews with pity and was prepared to contribute to their welfare but not to recognize them as a nation. It viewed Jews as a religious community that needed to cultivate a love of productivity and be supported financially. "Under these conditions, assimilation with the local population will occur and the Jewish question will resolve itself."[67]

Mandelstamm also maintained that the assimilated Jewish intelligentsia in Russia was greatly influenced by French philosopher Ernest Renan, whose various works negated the very existence of the Jewish people. Renan's lecture "Jews as a Religion and Race," delivered in the early 1890s, was translated into Russian and was widely read among the assimilated intelligentsia. Renan's assertion that the Jews (in his time) no longer belonged to the Semitic race and were not the descendants of the early Hebrews was positively received. Thus Renan broke the tie that linked the Jewish race (in the sense of a people or an ethnic group) with the Jewish religion and paved the way for the full integration of Jews into the surrounding society.

Mandelstamm was completely opposed to this worldview. Even though he was a member of the Jewish intelligentsia and an esteemed doctor, he did not forget that he had been persecuted and abused as a pupil at the Russian high school and denied admission to the University of Kiev because of his Jewishness. He refused to accept the assimilationists' argument that the Jews shared a common religion but were not members of a nation. Nor did he share their opinion that the Talmud was the main factor that impeded and continued to impede their integration into the surrounding society. In his worldview the Jews had all the necessary components to define themselves as a nation: a common past, language, and territory. Although Yiddish was not spoken in his home, he recognized it as the language of the Jewish people. Seven million of the 9 million Jews in the world spoke and wrote in it, and it reflected the spirit of the people. In his article "Zionism—Territorialism," he wrote that Hebrew had also made an important contribution to the experience of the Jewish people. Throughout the period of exile, not only had an immense and important body of "philosophical literature been composed in this language, it was also the language of prayer for Jewish liturgy."[68] Mandelstamm regarded the Talmud as a literary creation that served as "a mobile spiritual homeland, thanks to which the Jews survived."[69] He also rejected Renan's assertion that the Jewish race was nonexistent and held that "the Jews—except for the assimilationists—have never ceased to believe that they were a people, even a chosen people. Although it was chosen for affliction and suffering, it nevertheless continued to believe in national revival and the return to the homeland."[70] Mandelstamm rejected the possibility of integration into the surrounding society and stressed again and again the hatred of the Russian people for the Jews. Thus, in his view, the only solution to the Jewish question was the development of a national consciousness and the acquisition of a land of their own where Jews could live their lives without fear.[71]

Mandelstamm was a political Zionist in the fullest sense, and the Uganda controversy was a good opportunity for him to prove to Herzl that he could be regarded as a faithful ally. He supported the Uganda plan and urged Herzl not to give in to the pressure of the naysayers. He waged a stubborn war against his opponents, especially Ussishkin, and dubbed him the "Cossack of the Hibbat Zion Movement." In *An ofener brief tsu di rusishe tsiyonisten* (An Open Letter to the Russian Zionists), composed after Herzl's death, he wrote:

> Only this remains after the emptiness. Even before Herzl's death, the mayhem began against the East Africa plan. In this mayhem, the well-known manipulator of Hibbat Zion stood out for his excellence as a real Cossack. He acted in every possible way, with disgusting tricks and threats, which is the duty of every Zionist who respects himself to keep away from him in revulsion, to gird himself with infinite patience so he may be satisfied with the expression "May God forgive him."[72]

In his open letter Mandelstamm wrote that everyone agreed that Zionism had set itself the goal of strengthening and saving the Jewish people.

To achieve this objective, Jews had to obtain an autonomous territory in which the follow conditions existed:

> That there would not be people of a different culture or that they would be few in number, so that their proximity would not lead the Jews to become assimilated; secondly, that the country be politically free, so that the people may develop their latent physical and spiritual powers and will once more be a civilized and free nation.[73]

According to Mandelstamm, Palestine met the first condition but not the second, whereas Uganda met both.

Mandelstamm was one of the prominent supporters of the plan for settlement in East Africa. After the Kharkov conference, he and Jasinowski set up the Committee of Defenders of the Zionist Organization. Mandelstamm regarded Ussishkin's activities as subversive and a threat to the democratic foundations of the Zionist Organization. Yehudah Slutzky later explained his unbounded support for Herzl, his conversion into a Territorialist, and his decision to join the ITO under Zangwill as the natural process of a Jew raised in an assimilated home. In his article "Dr. Max Mandelstamm in the Period of Political Zionism," written as a seminar paper in Benzion Dinur's course on Herzl and his contemporaries, Slutzky claimed that Mandelstamm was a person of "gentle sensibility, but three generations of Enlightenment education and assimilation separated him from the ardent love of Zion that was deeply embedded in the blood of his opponents."[74] In view of Mandelstamm's writings and his public activities during and after Herzl's presidency, it seems that Slutzky's claims are baseless and completely unfounded.

Although Mandelstamm tried to integrate into general society, his fight against the assimilated intelligentsia is clear proof that he was far removed from their worldview. His support for Uganda and his desire for a quick solution to the Jewish question did not result from a lack of love for Zion but from his sensitivity to the suffering of the Jews in the Pale of Settlement. In his speech at the first general meeting of the Territorialists in Odessa, Mandelstamm explained the reasons that caused him—and other Zionist activists like him—to leave the Zionist Organization and join the ITO.

> It may seem strange to you that I come today as one of the representatives of the Territorialists when, not too long ago, I was a Zionist leader; but I hope that you will not consider this contradiction a sign of my argumentative weakness if I inform you that Territorialism and Zionism are, for me, two separate concepts. Zion is the flag under which the Jewish people must march to preserve its free national position, its national form. On this flag is written: "A free Jewish territory." Although Palestine is a territory, our dearest and most desirable territory, and although we are bound to it with thousands of memories and traditions, it is not free, and for the present it is not obtainable. I am very afraid that by the time it becomes a free land that is open to us, there will no longer be any Jews left to settle it.[75]

As an eye doctor, Mandelstamm treated hundreds of Jewish emigrants who passed through his clinic before leaving for America, and he became familiar with their distress. It was not assimilation that distanced him from the love of Zion but his intimate familiarity with Jewish suffering and his desire to find a swift solution. In 1900 he published *How Jews Live: A Report upon the Physical Condition of Jews*, in which he claimed that the poverty and studious lifestyle prevalent among Jews were poorly affecting their health. Children were sent at an early age to study in a narrow, unventilated, foul-smelling room, and this influenced their growth. At the age of 10 or 11, they were sent to the yeshiva and exposed to the glories of the Talmud. At this age, Dr. Mandelstamm claimed, their tender minds were not sufficiently mature to cope with the wisdom of the Talmud and the study "seriously overburdened their brain."

> Their miserable lives begin in their fifth or sixth year when the boys are sent to the heder where there is a melamed with unlimited authority. Imagine those young children, locked in a small narrow room without ventilation and with bad odors. There they sit on benches in crooked postures while reading or writing. The hours of study are from nine in the morning until nine at night, and only one hour for rest. All this is enough to destroy the delicate body of those poor creatures. The studies are generally left in the hands of half-starved ignorant teachers. The

numerous repetitions of Hebrew biblical texts, without dealing with the rules of grammar or syntax, which the teachers hardly knew themselves, with a few exceptions, was certainly a burden on these young minds. If we also add to all this the insensitive and cruel way in which those teachers used to punish the pupils for lack of discipline or misunderstanding, you may draw the conclusions about the bitter outcome.[76]

The Jews of the ghetto, Mandelstamm explained in his lecture, lived a life of extreme poverty in harsh conditions. To back up his claim, he cited Andrei Subbotin's study of the Pale of Settlement and his bleak descriptions of the material and physical situation of Russian Jewry.

When we approached a dwelling of this kind for the first time, we had no idea about its nature. We saw before us a large hole covered partly by rotten boards of wood. Scattered around this pit were various kinds of refuse, fish bones, rags, etc. At first we regarded this as a cesspit, but at a closer and more precise look, it was possible to discern that this was a human residence. In order to enter it we had to crouch low down, and after descending about twenty dirty and befouled steps, we found ourselves in a kind of cave, four meters long and two and a half wide, illuminated by an opening like a chimney that rose up to ground level.... This place was rented by a Jewish woman for the price of 50 rubles a year, and she sublet it to five other families, each paying ten rubles. One of them held a husky-looking child completely unlike his surroundings. The other half of the dwelling was leased by three subtenants and inhabited by six people. On one bed, there was a day laborer with his wife. On the other bed was a beggar with his wife. And on the third bed, an adult woman with her son.[77]

As he saw it, these conditions naturally influenced the Jews' physical state. Measurements of their height showed that Jews were shorter than the general population. The average height of a non-Jewish man was 165–170 centimeters, whereas that of a Jewish man was, on average, 162 centimeters.[78] Jews were not engaged in physical work, their muscles were weak and undeveloped, and their chests were narrow. Among the

4,372 Jewish recruits who were medically examined, 589 (13.5 percent) were afflicted with various lung diseases, and 172 of them suffered from chronic pulmonary inflammations.[79] Given the dismal state of the ghetto Jew, Mandelstamm claimed, the only way to revive the Jewish people and improve their conditions was the physical and economic rehabilitation of Jewish society. In his opinion, this could not be done on European soil, only on a land owned by the Jews. "Therefore we have to return to our homeland, to the only country in the world where we can be free and renew our strength by moral and physical reform."[80]

Another example of how Mandelstamm's work as a doctor influenced his nationalistic views was the fear that the United States would close its doors and not allow the multitudes of Jewish migrants to enter. The Jewish masses would then find themselves trapped on the European continent without being able to migrate to a land of refuge. The American government's meticulous eye examinations performed on the immigrants on Ellis Island increased his anxiety. In his article "Trachoma and Migration to America," he wrote that because the immigration authorities were unable to prevent the entry of poor immigrants into their country, trachoma was an excuse to send them back to the place from which they had come.[81] He believed it was necessary to quickly find a land to absorb the thousands of persecuted Jews before the largest country for immigration closed its gates to them and they were blocked from pursuing other possibilities. He saw the murderous pogroms of 1905–1906 as proof of his predictions about the future of Eastern European Jewry.

Mandelstamm's activities to help the Jews in Eastern Europe were the reason that the leaders of the ITO chose him as their representative to the Brussels conference. There, he gave his pessimistic speech "Finis Judaeae" (The End of Jewry), in which he urged those attending the conference to find a land for the persecuted Jews as quickly as possible.

## THE BRUSSELS CONFERENCE

The Zionist Organization reacted with increasing discomfort to the accelerated activities of the ITO and the expanding support for the territorialist idea in Jewish society. The Zionist leadership headed by David Wolffsohn was well aware of the broad support that the Uganda

## CHAPTER 2

plan acquired after the Kishinev pogrom, and it feared that the 1905 pogroms would bring additional plans for settlement to the Zionist public agenda. Only half a year had passed since the stormy debate at the Seventh Zionist Congress split the Zionist Organization, and the wounds had not yet healed. The pogroms were proof of the Territorialists' claim that the Zionist movement did not have enough time to set up a homeland for the Jews in Palestine and that it was necessary to act as soon as possible to find, as Brenner and Rosenblatt had said, the desired cave for refuge. These fears led Wolffsohn to hold a general Jewish conference in Brussels to discuss how to assist the oppressed Jews of Russia.

On January 29, 1906, eighty people gathered in Brussels, most of them members of the Zionist movement and the ITO but some of them members of the Anglo-Jewish Association (AJA) and the Hilfsverein der Deutschen Juden.[82] Wolffsohn's call to bring together the largest number of non-Zionist organizations and community leaders under one roof was met with suspicion. The invitation to the conference made clear that this was not a Zionist assembly but a Zionist initiative to discuss the distress of Russian Jewry. Nonetheless, important Jewish organizations refused to cooperate with the Zionist Organization and did not attend. On the other hand, this was an excellent opportunity for the Territorialists to present their positions publicly only half a year after their resignation from the Zionist Organization.

When it was advertised in Die Welt that a world Jewish conference would be held in Brussels, the territorialist activists began to prepare for it. In late December 1905, a letter was sent to Zangwill informing him that the Jews of Kiev had decided "to send a number of delegates to the conference to raise the matter of acquiring a territory for the Jewish people, who were being killed, massacred, plundered, robbed, and starved to death." In their estimate, they wrote, "Representatives from Odessa, Kishinev, Zhitomir, Hammel, Yelizavetgrad, Minsk, Warsaw, Bialystok, Vilna, and others were coming to the conference in Brussels, hundreds and thousands of people."[83] The letter to Zangwill shows that the Territorialists were the first to inform Zangwill of their wish to attend the conference and to exert their influence. This initiative came from the Jewish street and worked its way up even before Zangwill made his position known. "We still do not know your opinion, our great and honored president, about this conference!" they wrote him.

> We are waiting anxiously for your letter and your response: Do we have any attitude towards this conference? Can we participate, can we influence the conference as part of the presidium and of equal status to Zionei Zion? Can both of you, Wolffsohn and yourself, come together and conduct the conference on an equal basis, as two presidents of two different organizations, with neither having any advantage over the other? These things have to be clarified as early as possible, since the time is very near and the work is immeasurably great! We are now counting the number of hours, not days, from the time this letter is sent for your reply or the reply of your secretary, to clarify everything to everyone! Our personal view is that we should ascend the ramparts, that you should send out a circular to the agents around the world and urge them to get their city associations to choose the representatives and delegates as soon as possible, and to send a large number of them to Brussels.[84]

To spur Zangwill to make a decision, further petitions were sent to the ITO in London, signed by thousands of Jews in the Pale of Settlement. The signatories begged and urged him and the Jews in Western Europe to participate in the conference and persuade those attending of the urgency of the territorialist solution: "Our brothers, the people of Israel, hear the words of your brethren who are drowning in the sea of sorrow and are now coming to the podium of the Jews to pour out their bitterness, to recount the distress and burden on their souls, to open their hearts, to open the dried-up fountain of their tears. Hear how they beg their faithful brothers to join us in making heaven and earth tremble with their clamor." Once more, the intensity of the pogroms and the gruesome acts of the hooligans against the Jewish population were stressed: "We, the Jews in the Pale of Settlement, and even more so those in the outlying cities, are well aware of the nature of the people among whom we dwell; we know very clearly that we are living among scorpions, savages, louts, muzhiks, a special type of humanity whose nature no one can understand." Because of this gloomy and dangerous situation, "We have ended, loyal brethren, because there is no longer any good advice or remedy for our bruises that is better than asking for a special territory for our people, based on broad autonomous rights under the protection of a mighty and enlightened empire."[85]

## CHAPTER 2

The petition contained not only a proposal for an immediate solution but also criticism of the Jews of Western Europe who did not come to the aid of their brethren until after the catastrophe. "If you had risen up to help Israel at the beginning of the 1880s, we would not have reached the days of Kishinev. And if you had not been satisfied after Kishinev with merely cries and protests, our brothers would not have suffered the terrible destruction of seventy-three cities. And if you do not wake up now and put an end once and for all to the troubles of Israel, who knows what will happen to us." This claim, which will be discussed in Chapter 3, was one of the main claims of the ITO against the Zionist movement. The ITO saw the pogroms of the early twentieth century as the beginning of violent acts that in the future would become even harsher and more cruel. As a preventive measure, the ITO sought autonomy anywhere on the globe it could be found. Those who signed the petitions did not ask for money, contributions, or philanthropic acts but for a general effort to find a permanent solution for the anguish of the Jews. The Brussels conference was an opportunity for them to raise the issue of their distress after the massacres in their regions.

The Brussels petition, like the petition for ITO support, also received the signatures of thousands of Jews. In Bessarabia, for example, 1,092 people from six towns (Briceni, Yedintsy, Sakirani, Rashkanvki, Novoselitsa, and Staraya Ushitsa) signed the petition and sent it to Moshe Rosenblatt in Kiev. Many of the signatories were members of the Zionist movement who were drawn to the Territorialists by the acts of violence. In the town of Briceni, Bessarabia, the initiators of the petition were members of the First Briceni Zionist Association. The town's population was 7,500, including 7,200 Jews (96 percent).[86] Of the 1,500 families in the town, 256 people signed the petition (17 percent). This percentage was high and indicative of the degree of support for the ITO among the Jews of the Pale of Settlement in the organization's early years.

Israel Zangwill recognized the importance of the conference but also harbored suspicions about the hidden intentions of its initiators. The ITO was in its infancy, merely 6 months old, and the necessary internal mechanisms had not yet been established. Only a short while had passed since the Territorialists' break from the Zionist Organization. Thus it was decided that Max Mandelstamm would be the senior territorialist representative. He was sent to the conference with ITO members in

Russia and was among its prominent speakers. This was the first time since the riotous resignation from the Zionist Organization in August 1905 that the Territorialists had the opportunity to voice their views and propose their solution for the distress of the Jews suffering from the pogroms and the increasing stream of emigration westward.

The Brussels conference opened on Monday, January 29, 1906. Eighty delegates attended, mostly Zionists and Territorialists, and some activists in the Hilfsverein and the AJA. The Jewish Colonization Association (ICA) and the Alliance Israélite Française did not send any delegates, fearing that the discussions would focus on the question of nationalism and a territorial solution. The conference was opened by David Wolffsohn, who expressed the hope that a common ground could be found among the participants and that it would be possible to translate this into help and support for the Jews of Eastern Europe. He believed that "only on the land of Palestine would the Jewish question be resolved." However, he also told the delegates that he had set up the conference not to advance the Zionist idea but to lay "a cornerstone for general work and the unification of all the Jewish forces" in the Jewish world. It was necessary to create the necessary means "to save us from the troubles of today and the dangers of tomorrow."[87]

At the end of Wolffsohn's speech, the presidium members went up to the podium: Paul Nathan; Dr. Hirsch Hildesheimer, of the Hilfsverein; Professor Simmons, of the AJA; Frederick Hermann Kisch, of the London AJA; Mandelstamm, the Territorialist; and Jaccob Cohen-Bernstein, the Zionist. The first to speak was Paul Nathan, who said, "Each of the organizations and parties can solve the Jewish question according to its program, but it is certainly possible to work together to relieve the sorrowful situation without letting partisan motives interfere."[88] After this, Mandelstamm gave a belligerent speech that ruptured the unity of the conference. He presented his territorialist doctrine to the delegates and criticized the objectives of the Zionist movement and the activities of the philanthropic organizations.

Mandelstamm's speech in Brussels against Zionism and for Territorialism was the first public confrontation between the Zionists and the Territorialists after the Seventh Zionist Congress. It was published in full in the daily newspaper *Ha-zeman*, under the heading "On the Situation of the Jews in Russia." At the start of his speech, Mandelstamm explained his reason for coming to Brussels, which differed, as it turned out, from that of the conference planners.

> I shall not describe to you the terrible scenes that we experienced in October and the poison cup we drank to its dregs. Nor have I come here ... to tell you the painful aftermath of the endless pogroms against the Jews. After all, poverty and sorrow are not new to the ghetto; what happened in October only made the situation more terrible and bitter. I came here only to encourage you to take action, not only to help alleviate the current situation, if that is even possible, but also to open the way toward a solution of the Jewish question in Russia, which is the core of the Jewish question. I urge you to work toward a radical solution that, even if it takes a long while, will at last resolve this question, and will do so in the relatively near future.[89]

Unlike the official and formal declarations by Wolffsohn and Nathan on the need to rise above political dispute and try to unify all the forces for the sake of Eastern European Jewry, Mandelstamm chose to stress the unique value of Territorialism as the only solution to the Jewish question. In his speech he divided Jewish society in Russia into four groups. The first group was the assimilated Jews who, like those in Western Europe, maintained that "the ultimate resolution of the Jewish question in Russia had to be in Russia itself." This group included, for the most part, those "in a fairly good economic situation, as well as many of the intellectuals." This group "regards the Jewish question as part of the general Russian question." The second group consisted of Jews who belonged to the socialist revolutionary parties that were struggling against the regime for a just society. "With a courageous spirit, without fear or dread of the Siberian wilderness, the prisons, or even the scaffold, with bombs and rifles, they are trying to bring to autocratic Russia, and to the ghetto dying under its oppression, the kind of social order that even social democracies in more civilized countries has not been able to establish." Mandelstamm regarded most of the members of the Social Revisionists, the Social Democrats, and especially the Bundists as "still immature and yet to receive a political education."[90] The third group was the wandering Jews, "who distance themselves from poverty, oppression, hunger, and the danger of being beaten and robbed." Knowing "instinctively that they cannot hope for anything from their precious homeland," this group chooses to immigrate across the ocean. They include hundreds of thousands of Jewish migrants who, in their great despair, have begun moving from Eastern Europe to the American continent.[91] The fourth and largest group, and the most problematic, was the "class of indigents and beggars, the Luftmenschen, [whose number] is gradually growing within the ghetto population." A suitable and considered solution must be offered for their plight.

After he had schematically divided Jewish society into four groups, Mandelstamm asserted that the fourth group required immediate assistance. The only movement in Jewish society that had taken up the cause of assistance to the "indigents and beggars" was the Zionist movement "among whose members I am honored to count myself," he explained. The Zionists, he added, were the only group that did not believe in the integration of Jews into the surrounding society, neither through reliance on philanthropic support nor through identification with socialist ideas. "They don't lull themselves to sleep with lullabies or with the vague illusion of equal rights at the end of time, [nor] with cosmopolitan dreams." Although he had resigned from the Zionist Organization and become a senior member of the ITO, Mandelstamm still saw himself as a political Zionist in all respects: "Zionism has never had, in the broadest sense of the word, a right to exist as it has in these very days."[92]

The violent pogroms and the impoverishment of Eastern European Jewry had aggravated the Jews' condition, and it was therefore necessary to find a quick solution to the distress of the Jews in the Pale of Settlement. It was to this cause that Mandelstamm enlisted Herzl, who had not spent all his energies on Palestine during the period of his diplomacy: "This synthesis: an uninhabited land but fruitful even though it is abandoned, an autonomous territory, and the land that had once been the homeland to which the Jewish people are connected through thousands of traditional ties—seemed to Herzl the best territory for the ultimate solution of the Jewish question. Another reason for this choice was that 25 years after the pogroms of the 1880s, the first attempts at settlement were made there." Mandelstamm held that because Herzl had unfortunately failed to achieve the desired outcome in all his years of

Zionist activity, he wanted "to obtain the other half of that synthesis—a free territory." This was why he tried to acquire the Sinai Peninsula and failed, because "Lord Cromer, the English representative, refused to allow watering these lands with the waters of the Nile." Later, Herzl brought Uganda into the discussion. Mandelstamm did not want to reopen the discussion around this painful affair and therefore noted, "He passes in silence over the matter of Uganda, which continued for two years and cost a lot of blood." At the end of this affair, a minority broke away to continue on Herzl's political path and pursue the negotiations with the British government.[93]

From this stage onward, Mandelstamm spoke about the territorialist idea as the solution that could properly resolve the current situation. "The approach of the ITO is no pipe dream, but is extremely realistic and practical. The troubles of the Jews became a burning question not only for the Jews of the East, but for their co-religionists in the West, who are suffering from the burdensome transit of Jews fleeing from Russia."[94] If a free territory could be found for the wandering Jews, masses of people could be taken there to create for themselves a "city of refuge—a home—to which even those who remain in the countries of their birth will turn their eyes."[95] The program would require a large amount of money to be launched, which the Jewish philanthropic societies would have to obtain. To strengthen his position, Mandelstamm used New Zealand as an example of a state that had been founded and established in accordance with the Territorialists' idea.

> I am not speaking here about uprooting mountains or leading a hundred thousand people at once to a new land. Rather, I am talking about pioneering work that is thought-out ahead of time and conducted with human resources that are appropriate and sufficient for the work. This is the kind of work that was done in New Zealand, which was populated 50 years ago by cannibals who would gladly have eaten their enemies. Today, it has a population of nearly a million people who have already achieved the highest political and social freedom—and this, too, took place under British rule. Those cannibals, the Maoris, and their wives are now participating in parliamentary negotiations and exercising their right to express their opinions.[96]

Mandelstamm regarded New Zealand as a suitable model for the Jewish people. From his viewpoint the British rule over New Zealand since the beginning of the twentieth century was not a colonial regime forced on the Maoris. But he did not note that in the second half of the nineteenth century a cruel and bitter war over control of the island territory had broken out between the white population and the Maori tribes and that the natives did not receive the invaders with open arms. Mandelstamm stated that once a territory was found, he was sure that "if we could bring [2,000 families] in the first five years" to the intended country, the Jewish question will have been solved and the government under whose protection these families were found would enable many others to follow them. But Mandelstamm warned the conference delegates:

> If this final attempt should also fail, if it should have no more success than today's attempts to rehabilitate destroyed families, only to have them destroyed again ... then the Jewish question can be considered as in the Torah, in its manner, and we will then have to say *Finis Judaeae*! We will then return to the theories of our rabbis who think that we are destined to be constant wanderers over the earth and the gatherers of moral concepts that others use ... on which the tree of freedom will flourish for all the world but not for the Jews. But I hope that this will not come to pass and that our unfortunate and oppressed people will finally find a safe haven.[97]

Mandelstamm's speech aroused anger among the conference participants, who were trying to focus on the immediate distress of the Jews in the Pale of Settlement and trying to avoid a fundamental discussion of the issue of Jewish nationalism and refrain from ideological polemics on the Jewish question. To placate them, Wolffsohn noted that Mandelstamm had only expressed his personal view and that the presidium was opposed to the suggested solution. The Zionists refrained from open confrontation with the Territorialists, and the conference ended with a whimper. This outcome was completely unexpected for the Territorialists, who had hoped that the conference would serve as a platform for a public discussion of the territorialist solution. The petitions with thousands of signatures on them that had been sent to Zangwill seemed to have had no effect on the content and depth of the discussion, and the decisions that were made bore no glad tidings for the bruised and beaten Jews of Eastern Europe.

Tragically, even the Zionist movement, which had initiated the Brussels conference, failed to achieve anything substantial for the suffering Jewish population in Eastern Europe. In the face of the ITO's strengthened position, the pogroms, the waves of emigration, and the harsh economic situation of the Jewish community, the Zionists could not stand idly by. Throughout the conference they tried to prove that Zionist activity was not just focused on Palestine, that it was concerned with Eastern European Jewry as a whole. Nevertheless, the decisions made at the conference attested to the movement's weakness and perhaps also to its lack of sensitivity to the hardships of daily life for the Jews in the Russian Empire. For example, Dr. Hirsch Hildesheimer, one of the representatives of Ezra at the conference, raised the proposal "to limit the emigration of poor Jews" entering Germany on their way to the United States. He claimed that "the Jews of the West have already become reluctant to bear the heavy burden of emigration. The number of emigrants is increasing daily while the coffers of the charitable associations are gradually emptying out." Therefore, "It is necessary to take all possible measures to limit and lessen the emigration before it is too late, for the sake of the emigrants themselves."[98] In the vote that was conducted, his proposal was accepted with a small majority: "The Conference has noted the remarks of the Jewish aid associations, according to which emigration assistance should not be given to those without means.... The Conference thinks it necessary that this notification be published among the Russian Jews."[99]

Hildesheimer's proposal provoked a great storm. The idea of curbing the emigration of poor Jews totally contradicted the main purpose of the conference. For the Territorialists this was proof that the Zionist movement had abandoned the Jews of Eastern Europe to their fate. The conference not only failed to find an answer to the Jewish problem, but it also made decisions that actually worsened the situation, especially for the poor Jews who did not have the means to escape the Russian Empire.

In the early twentieth century the Territorialists saw themselves as primarily a movement for the rescue of the Jewish people, unlike the Zionists. The Zionist movement concentrated its efforts only on the Palestine arena, with hardly any heed to the existential distress of Eastern

European Jewry. The ITO, on the other hand, thought that in addition to searching for a territory suitable for permanent settlement, Jewish organizations should also work to find immediate relief for the daily hardships of the "ghetto Jew" in the Pale of Settlement. Thus emigration became the central issue on the territorialist agenda.

After the Brussels conference and as a challenge to the decisions taken there, the ITO began setting up a mechanism with the sole aim of helping the wanderers (the immigrants) implement their decision. In early 1907 the Yudishe Emigratsyone Gezelshaft (Jewish Emigration Association) was founded. It worked out of Kiev, provided valuable information to the Jewish emigrants on the process of immigration to various countries, and helped them to cross the ocean and safely reach their destination.

## THE JEWISH EMIGRATION ASSOCIATION

One of the burning issues in Jewish society in Eastern Europe at the turn of the twentieth century was emigration. From 1904 to 1914, 2 million Jews moved to countries on the other side of the Atlantic Ocean. Most went to the United States, but smaller groups settled in Argentina, Canada, Australia, South Africa, and Palestine.[100] The emigration of hundreds of thousands in such a short time completely changed the character of Jewish society in both the countries of origin and the destination countries and created many problems. The immigrants and their families had to cope with numerous obstacles, such as obtaining the required documents to legally emigrate, selling their businesses and homes, crossing the border, buying train tickets, traveling thousands of kilometers from their town to the port of departure, finding their way around, and buying tickets to sail to their destination. To cross the ocean and arrive safely, the emigrants had to possess an ability for improvisation and resourcefulness. For many this was the first time they had left the confines of their hometown. Coping with the unknown was beyond their capability, and they were often at a loss for direction and advice.[101]

Emigration became a profitable business, and emigrant money was a source of income for travel agents. The contemporary press was filled with stories of emigrants who sold all their possessions only to find that they did not have the means to continue their journey after their departure. Family tragedies were frequent, and heartbreaking stories were published daily in the newspapers and journals to stir up public interest and to help the Jewish emigrants reach a safe haven. In reaction to both public pressure and the concern among German Jews that other Jews in Eastern Europe would settle down in the ports of embarkation instead of crossing the ocean, a network of information bureaus was set up along the emigration routes. Their main aim was to help the emigrants realize their objectives and to find out as much information as possible about the emigration process and all that it entailed.

The Jewish Colonization Association (ICA) was the first to establish an information system for Jews who wished to emigrate to the West. The ICA information bureaus were dispersed throughout the Pale of Settlement in the tsarist empire. They provided important information on the immigration process, its dangers, and the possibilities available in the desired destinations. Within a few years information bureaus were set up in all the large cities and main centers of immigration to help Jewish migrants cross the ocean. In 1906 there were 160 ICA information bureaus in the Pale of Settlement; in 1907, 296; in 1910, 449; and in 1913, 507.[102]

The ICA bureaus invested much effort in disseminating information. Various manuals for migrants were written to enable them to plan carefully before setting out on their journey. The one most widely distributed was the *Algemayne Yedies far di vos villen forn tsu fremde lender* (General Information for Those Wishing to Immigrate to Foreign Countries). Sold by ICA agents for the nominal price of 6 kopecks, the manual contained a brief and simple explanation of important information for migrants in anticipation of their departure as well as practical advice with short descriptions of the destination countries. It recommended that emigrants not leave without a certain amount of money, and it taught them about exchange rates, border crossings, and the danger of agents. It also contained information on how to deal with seasickness, where to buy sailing tickets and the dangers of prepaid tickets, how to obtain a passport, what baggage to take, the rules of etiquette in the destination country, and brief information about those countries (the United States, Canada, South Africa, Argentina, Australia, and Palestine). The ICA published the manual in 1906. It was the first of its kind, and more than 10,000 copies were printed every year.[103]

Emigrants could obtain detailed and updated information about the countries of destination from special booklets on each country: Argentina, Australia, Canada, South Africa, Chile, and, of course, the United States. Several editions of each booklet were issued, and they were updated from time to time. They included geographic information about the country, with maps attached, and information about the climate and animal life in the region, the local population, the exchange rates and value of the local currency, the opportunities for agricultural work and other means of livelihood, the cost of food, and the cost of traveling by ship to that country. The most comprehensive booklet was the one on the United States, which contained information about each state and the possibilities of employment there. The policy of the information bureaus was to prevent the concentration of immigrants in the large cities and to encourage their dispersal among the cities of the interior. The ICA printed 6,000 copies of the U.S. booklet and updated it annually. In 1907 the ICA inaugurated the newspaper Der Jüdische Emigrant, which was devoted entirely to emigration issues. This paper appeared twice a month and contained current updates and information about various countries. Baron Ginsburg edited the paper until his death in 1910; after that it was edited by the general secretary of the ICA information bureau, Shmuel Yanovsky.

Following the conference in Brussels and the decision to limit the number of impoverished migrants passing through Germany, the ITO decided to contribute to the support for migrants and help them in their arrangements rather than focus solely on the search for a territory. The ITO saw aid to Jewish immigrants as a priority no less important and urgent than finding a land for autonomous Jewish settlement. These were difficult days for the Jews in the Pale of Settlement, and the Territorialists believed that they should extend a helping hand to those who were trying their luck in countries overseas. Assistance for the immigrants was not part of the ITO's official platform, and it could be considered an attempt to deepen the ITO's hold in Jewish society, to gain wide popular recognition, and to be portrayed as a political movement that cared for the suffering Jewish masses. ITO members also entered the field of emigration for fear that by the time a desirable land was found, the territorialist movement and its activists would have fallen into a state of inactivity, which would negatively influence the stability of the young movement. The more engaged and immersed in the troubles of the Jewish people the activists were, the easier it would be to gain their assistance at the moment of truth, once a land was found to absorb the Jewish masses. It would thus be possible to make use of the existing infrastructure to divert emigrants from the United States to the country that was found, if and when it was.

The central ITO information bureau was opened in Kiev and directed by Mandelstamm and David Jochelman. Within a short time, scores of bureaus were set up throughout the Pale of Settlement, providing emigrants with the relevant information on the process of migration. The Territorialists helped emigrants make the decision to leave and then to carry it out.[104] The regulations of the Jewish Emigration Association state that it was "founded with the aim of systematically improving and facilitating the emigrants' travel conditions, directing them not necessarily to Europe or Asia, but settling them in equal numbers in new places as artisans and farmers."[105] Out of concern that the authorities might regard the association's work as subversive and dangerous, a footnote was added: "The association will carry out its activities subject to the orders of the government; it aspires to no political or national aims, but restricts its activities to arrangements for Jewish migration. The association does not incite anyone to immigrate; it only assists those who have already decided to emigrate from Russia to other countries."[106] Although the association did not publicly declare its nationalistic aims for fear that the tsarist government would shut it down, Zangwill and Mandelstamm's objectives extended beyond local assistance to the migrant in distress.

The local agents, the ITO representatives in the information bureaus, provided verbal and written instructions on the migration routes to anyone interested, offered medical assistance to those in need, maintained contact with immigration agents in and outside Russia, helped emigrants obtain passports and exit visas from Russia, signed agreements with shipping and railway companies to reduce migration expenses, helped immigrants settle in their new countries, and published manuals. In late 1911 the Territorialist newspaper, Wohin: Organ far di interesen fun der yiddisher emigratsye un kolanizatsye, was published. The ITO method of activity was similar to the ICA's. The ICA's motives were philanthropic, whereas the ITO's were nationalistic. But the immigrants who approached the bureaus cared less about their motives than about the quality and reliability of the service they provided. Comparisons were frequently made between the services offered to the migrants by the ITO and the ICA and, in most cases the differences depended on the benevolence and personality of the local agent. The newspaper *Ha-zeman* reported, "Although the ICA dispatches Jewish immigrants to countries overseas, [it usually does so] in an extreme careless and desultory manner. Any signs of energy that it shows are expressed in an attitude of malice and cruelty towards the immigrants in need." In the ITO bureaus, by contrast, "We have become used to seeing ... a more delicate conduct in relation to the emigrant, a greater concern and higher devotion to his interests, from the moment he declares his intent to set out over the ocean waves, until he reaches his destination."[107]

Naturally it is not possible to evaluate the work of the ITO and ICA information bureaus on the basis of one report, but it is clear that they provided an important and direct contact between ITO representatives and the Jewish masses. Through them, Mandelstamm and Zangwill tried to come closer to the people and to (indirectly) spread the territorialist doctrine. Even if potential emigrants had not been exposed to territorialist propaganda, they got the chance to meet, converse, and get to know the ITO representatives. As a whole, the emigrants came to appreciate the ITO's willingness to come to their aid. After all, the Zionists—the Territorialists' main rivals—disregarded the migrants' plight and offered help only to those who wanted to go to Palestine. The Territorialists anticipated that after a suitable territory was found, Jewish society would remember their help and would migrate to the new area en masse.

※

The ITO's first years were characterized by a campaign for public support and an effort to recruit supporters and activists for the new organization. Shortly after the political Zionists seceded from the Zionist Organization, violent pogroms broke out, strengthening the Territorialists' principal claim that Eastern Europe was about to go up in flames and that the Jewish people had to find a territory as soon as possible, one not necessarily in Palestine. The murder of 3,000 Jews attracted many sectors of Jewish society to Territorialism, mainly in the areas that had suffered pogroms and needed an immediate solution to their distress. Letters by Jews in distress and petitions signed by thousands were sent to Israel Zangwill. These letters expressed support for the young organization that had arisen as an alternative to the Zionist movement. The impression in the offices of the territorialist movement in London was of wide support for the territorialist idea and for Zangwill's leadership. The Territorialists sent Max Mandelstamm to the Brussels conference, which was held under the patronage of the Zionist movement and was intended to offer solutions to the Jewish question. Mandelstamm gave a speech there against the Zionist solution and in favor of the ITO.

In short order, the ITO set up an efficient organizational infrastructure and began its work soon after the Seventh Zionist Congress. Branches were established in all parts of the Pale of Settlement and in important Jewish centers in Western Europe. First, the activists received authorization from the tsarist government to disseminate the territorialist idea. Next, they began to conduct an open information campaign in the press and published leaflets and notices. Because the Geographical Committee under Zangwill had not yet found a suitable territory for settlement, the ITO handled the arrangements for Jewish emigration and offered assistance to the large number of migrants who had begun their journey westward.

The Territorialists' immigration-related activity and the establishment of the Jewish Emigration Association were no accident. First, emigration was the burning and central question on the Jewish social agenda, and it served as a vehicle for the Territorialists' attempts to reach all levels of Jewish society. Second, if and when the desired territory was found, the Jewish Emigration Association and its branches throughout the Pale of Settlement would serve as the means to send the masses there. However, the ITO did not act in a vacuum in the Pale of Settlement; it worked alongside the Zionist movement, which saw it as a great rival and competitor. The Zionists and the Territorialists offered similar solutions to the Jewish question: the establishment of an autonomous settlement. They functioned in a situation that required them to respond to the existential questions of Jewish society in Eastern Europe, to formulate a coherent doctrine about contemporary matters, and to expand their efforts beyond the search for the desired territory.[108]

3

# A Land for a People, Not a People for a Land

The ITO was created and established first and foremost out of the distress and deep despair of the persecuted Jews, who no longer saw any future in the land of their birth. As described in chapter 2, anguish and resignation were the fate of many Jews who lived in Eastern Europe under unbearable economic, social, and political circumstances. Many people in Jewish society regarded the Zionist movement's idea as a long-term solution, but the contemporary problems of Eastern European Jewry were existential and required an immediate solution. Out of this situation the territorialist idea was born: a yearning for a safe haven, a land to which hundreds of thousands of persecuted Jews in Eastern Europe could immigrate. The search for a suitable territory for autonomous Jewish settlement outside Ottoman Palestine was not a rejection of Palestine as a solution to the Jewish problem but a reflection of a gloomy and pessimistic worldview on the fate of Jewish society in Eastern Europe.

In this chapter I outline territorialist ideology, its relations with the Zionist movement, and the Zionists' attitude toward the rival organization, which was established in August 1905 after the Uganda controversy. Obtaining a territory was one of the ITO's main goals. But alongside the search for a suitable land for settlement, the Territorialists also formulated a clear doctrine on a variety of issues concerning Jewish society in the early twentieth century. Their position in relation to the Zionist movement should also be examined, particularly because many territorialist activists saw themselves as the true Zionists and Herzl's heirs. Many of them did not reject the Zionist idea; rather, they simply did not think that Palestine was the only solution to the Jews' distress. In this chapter I focus on the ideological struggle between the two territorial worldviews: one that placed Palestine at the center of the national enterprise, and the other, which believed that the fate of the Jewish people was bound to one particular territory. I also explain the principles of territorialist thought and the Zionists' response to it.

## LAND OF REFUGE

Shortly after the official establishment of the ITO in August 1905, its bylaws and methods of activity were formulated. Its objective, according to its constitution, was simple and clear: "to procure a territory upon an autonomous basis for those Jews who cannot or will not remain in the lands where they currently live."[1] The constitution stated that to achieve its goals, the ITO would bring together all the Jews who supported its mission, make connections with governments and public and private institutions, and eventually establish the financial and other institutions necessary for realizing its goals.[2] The term autonomous basis was defined as a territory with a Jewish majority that could be obtained. This constitution was the Territorialists' Basel plan and the basis for the ITO's activities throughout its existence.

In propaganda booklets that were written in Yiddish and distributed throughout the Pale of Settlement, the Territorialists developed the ITO's objectives more fully than the constitution. In the booklet "Who We Are and What We Want" the authors formulated the principles of territorialist ideology through two questions: What are we striving for, and what could make that possible? Regarding the first question, they stated that "our people have suffered enough in its two thousand years of aimless wandering" and that they aspired to change the physical and mental situation of the Jewish people once and for all and to find a solution to the Jewish question. "We cannot continue to see Jewish blood spilled like water, our brethren a toy in the hands of the Gentiles in every generation, at the mercy of murderers and mobs. . . . Hundreds of thousands of our kith and kin are hurled from exile to exile, aimless, hopeless, knocking at every gate for admission and begging for the mere right to live."[3] In answering the second question, the Territorialists explained their spheres of activity: "We must have a land of our own, and in that land we must possess autonomy to make our own laws, so that our people may be free of economic oppression by those instruments of torture, 'exceptional laws'—a land where we shall be protected, free and able to develop our culture, our literature, and our national existence." According to the territorialist bulletin, the root of all evil, which caused this grim reality, was that the Jews were beggars and foreigners everywhere. "The sooner this situation is brought to an end, the faster the Jews' condition will improve."[4]

The Territorialists tried to use this basic standpoint to distinguish and separate themselves from the Zionists. It was not an opposition in principle to the Land of Israel that led to their secession from the Zionist Organization but the fear that the Zionist movement did not have enough time to establish a state in Palestine for the Jewish people. The Zionists held the Land of Israel as sacred and thought that a Jewish state should be established there at any cost, even if it took a long time. On the other hand, the Territorialists wanted a state for the Jews "here and now" and attributed no importance to where it would be established. The idea of the "rejection of the Exile" in its earthly and physical sense was much more central in territorialist than in Zionist thought in the early twentieth century. Other opponents to Zionism, such as the Bund and Autonomism, did not reject life in the Diaspora and believed that receiving cultural autonomy in a non-Jewish environment was all that was needed to solve the Jewish problem. By contrast, the ITO did not believe that the Jews had any future in Eastern Europe or of integrating into Russian society. This was the reason for its ceaseless attempts to find a land where Jews could settle.

> The Seventh Zionist Congress, having refused to identify itself in any way with the immediate solution to this burning question of our people's well-being, resolve to restrict its activity to Palestine. We say that the most important matter, under present circumstances, is to save and revive our people and our culture. A land exists for people and not a people for a land. It would be a sin to let our people go to the dogs while we shout "Palestine, only Palestine!" If, as it seems, we shall be unable to obtain Palestine for generations, we have no right to sit idly by and do nothing,

or to make do with slow, small-scale colonization and be content to wait and wait.[5]

The idea of rejecting the Exile in territorialist ideology was one of the controversial points that separated the Territorialists from the Zionists, but it was also one of the points of similarity between them. This paradox shows how similar the two ideologies were, despite the difference in their respective understandings of the situation. In his comprehensive book on Zionist ideology, Gideon Shimoni defined the largest common denominator in the beliefs of those who called themselves Zionists. According to his definition, Zionists rejected the Exile and thought that Jewish life in the Diaspora was incomplete, not only in the messianic sense but also, and principally, in the national one. Zionists believed that the solution lay in the return of the Jews to the Land of Israel (or in another temporary place) with sovereignty or, at least, autonomy and that the way to realize this aim was by means of settlement and political and cultural activity.[6]

A look at the ITO through the lens of Shimoni's definition reveals the extremely complex identity of those who called themselves Zionists (and Territorialists) in the early twentieth century. The Territorialists—like the Zionists and unlike the anti-Zionist currents among the Jewish people—rejected the Exile in national terms but saw the Land of Israel as merely a possible solution, not an exclusive one. According to Shimoni's definition, the solution to the Jewish problem from the territorialist perspective was the return of the Jews to the Land of Israel and/or their settlement in another territory. After the Seventh Zionist Congress, when the Zionists said "only the Land of Israel," the Territorialists continued to adhere to the views of Pinsker and Herzl and held that they were still valid. The resemblance between the Territorialists and the Zionists was so great that it could be said that they were twins who had been separated after the divisive congress and reunited after the Balfour Declaration. The difference between the two movements was not in the solutions they proposed but in their prognosis regarding the Jewish problem in Eastern Europe. The Territorialists were much more pessimistic than their Zionist brethren over the question of Jewish distress and what the future held for them in Eastern Europe. Because they predicted the worst, they wanted to hasten the redemption, even at the price of forgoing the Land of Israel. On the other hand, the Zionists thought that the plight of the Jews did not justify relinquishing their historical homeland, and therefore they wished to continue with their national endeavors.

In his article on the Exile and sovereignty Amnon Raz-Korkotzkin discusses how the term "rejection of the Exile" changed in Zionist thought over the years and traces its influence on Zionist historiography, Jewish history, and public discourse.[7] In its early usage by Pinsker and Herzl, rejection of the Exile defined the basic need for a safe haven for the Jewish people in light of the uncertainty of their existence in Europe and the dangers they faced. Later, in the years following the Seventh Zionist Congress, the Zionist movement underwent a gradual process that led to the total rejection of the legitimacy of Jewish existence outside the Land of Israel and outside the sphere of Zionist ideology. In contrast to this, no such change in the term took place in territorialist ideology, and it continued to be understood in the same way as Pinsker and Herzl defined it early on: as a safe haven. Unlike Zionism, which passed into a new period called post-Uganda, the Territorialists continued to maintain the tradition and well-known views of Zionist ideology. In their search for a land of refuge, the Territorialists rejected the Diaspora in Eastern Europe or in any other place that posed an existential danger to the Jews living there. From their viewpoint, if Jews could conduct their lives in an independent territory, even if outside the Land of Israel, the state of exile would cease to exist. This was not a total rejection of the possibility of Jewish life outside the Land of Israel but an agreement in principle that political aspirations could be realized in any territory given to the Jews. In times of peril, the Territorialists argued, a territory would have a decisive and functional role, which was to save persecuted Jews: "A land exists for a people and not a people for a land."[8] According to the territorialist doctrine, the Land of Israel was supposed to be the means and not the end. Therefore, if it could not be obtained, there was no reason not to look for another territory.

For this reason the decision of the Seventh Zionist Congress to reject the British proposal and prohibit the congress from discussing similar proposals in the future was a formative event in the history of the Zionist movement, the territorialist movement, and the Jewish people. Shabtai Beth-Zvi, for example, in his book *Ha-tsiyonut ha-post ugandit be-mashber*

# CHAPTER 3

*ha-shoah* (Post-Uganda Zionism in the Holocaust Crisis), noted the link between the way the Zionists acted at the Sixth and Seventh Zionist Congresses and during the Holocaust. The indifference to the plight of the Jewish people and the unwillingness to help Russian Jewry were already present during the Uganda controversy.[9] Beth-Zvi defined this attitude as an egocentric trait, deeply rooted and inherent in Zionism, and connected the Uganda crisis and the veto of the British plan to the murder of the 6 million during World War II. In both instances, he argued, the Zionists turned their backs on the Jewish people. Beth-Zvi also maintained that the primary aim of the Zionist movement and the Jewish Yishuv in Palestine was never to rescue the Jews.[10] I do not intend to discuss Beth-Zvi's arguments or attempt to confirm or refute them. I only note that the Territorialists made accusations against the Zionists that were similar to those mentioned in his book and blamed the Zionists for intellectual dogmatism and pointless inflexibility.

In a December 1907 speech in Manchester, England, Israel Zangwill explained the meaning of the term *territory* in territorialist thought. It did not mean the Land of Israel: "The ITO has always declared its readiness to co-operate in developing Palestine if the Zionists could guarantee the political safeguards." Because it could not provide the appropriate guarantees, the ITO could not link the destiny of the Jewish people to only one single territory that could not be securely obtained. This act would be treason against the Jewish people, who were suffering economic distress and persecution in their countries of residence. According to Zangwill, a suitable piece of land had to be uninhabited and undeveloped, with no roads, railways, shipyards, or houses, but large enough to absorb the tens of thousands who would enter its gates every year. Not a Jewish ghetto like "New York, with 400,000 sickly souls in one square mile," but a state whose "population was scattered over thousands of square miles."[11] When they arrived in the designated land, the Jews would build it up and create the groundwork to foster their successful absorption. In this context successful absorption does not entail only the cultivation of land and the return to an agricultural lifestyle; productivity in the lives of the Jewish people was of secondary importance in territorialist ideology. The Jews, as Zangwill argued, did not need to prove to the world that they could farm, nor was it necessary for them to become farmers. However, as we will see, Zangwill regarded the Jewish farmers as pioneers whose main role was to prepare the land for the masses of persecuted Jews. Agriculture, he claimed, was a means to achieving the final aim: autonomy.[12]

The Territorialists tried to persuade the European countries that it was in their immediate interest to allocate a territory to the Jews. Europe's reliance on colonialism and imperialism were the main source of their hope to receive a grant of land. In his debate with Nahum Sokolow (discussed in Chapter 1), Judah Hazan said explicitly, "Territorialism sees various possibilities to acquire free territory for the Jewish people in the colonies possessed by governments that only have an economic objective—to create new markets for metropolitan trade and industry."[13] Because these governments were unable to settle the areas under their control with their own people, they would be interested in "drawing emigrants from other peoples to their colonies": "Governments with an open manner of settling their lands have been trying to attract wandering settlers to their available territories by all kinds of discounts and privileges, and by giving them freedoms such self-rule, to a great extent." These places were the "great source of hope to obtain a territory for our people."[14]

Despite the categorical statement by Zangwill and his territorialist disciples that referred to "not only, but also, the Land of Israel," on several occasions he expressed his opposition to Palestine as an area for settlement and opined that it was an inappropriate location for a Jewish state. Although the Territorialists stressed that the element of time and the charter were vital reasons for choosing Palestine as the final objective, they also brought arguments against the Land of Israel and explained why, in their assessment, it would be difficult for the Zionist movement to reach that goal. One of the main obstacles that Zangwill foresaw for the Zionist movement was the Arab population in Palestine. As early as 1905, Zangwill recognized that the Land of Israel was populated by Arabs and that the Jews would find it difficult to attain a majority.

> There is, however, a difficulty from which a Zionist dares not avert his eyes, though he rarely likes to face it. Palestine proper has already its inhabitants, the pashalik of Jerusalem is already twice as thickly populated as the United States, having fifty-two souls to the square mile. And not 25 percent of them Jews; so we must be prepared either to drive out with the sword the tribes in possession as our forefathers did or to grapple with the

problem of a large alien population, mostly Mohammedan and accustomed for centuries to despise us.[15]

The proportion of Jews to Arabs was not the only problem facing the Zionists that Zangwill saw; he also pointed out the challenge of Arab ownership over most of Palestine. "At present we are only 12 percent of the population, and hold only 2 percent of the land. A good deal of the holy soil is in the hands of private proprietors, and would not be ours even if we got the Charter, while the Crown lands, which belong to the Sultan, and might, therefore, be negotiated for as a whole, are, unfortunately, low and swampy and fever-haunted."[16]

Hillel Zeitlin (1871–1942) also referred to the question of the Arab population of Palestine. Zeitlin grew up in a strictly Hassidic family and was exposed at an early age to Haskalah (Jewish Enlightenment) literature and was captivated by it. He abandoned the Torah and its precepts and began to study Hebrew. At the end of the nineteenth century, he published articles in Hebrew and Yiddish on various subjects in the Jewish press. He was an ardent supporter of Herzl's political Zionism and even served as a delegate of the Gomel Zionists at the Fifth Zionist Congress in 1901. Following the Uganda affair, he resigned in frustration from the Zionist Organization and joined the ITO. In 1905 he was appointed the editor of the newspaper *Ha-zeman*, which was the mouthpiece of the territorialist movement at the time.[17]

In his article "Ha-mashber: Reshimot Teritoryali" (The Crisis: Impressions of a Territorialist), Zeitlin expressed his fear about the Jewish people after the decisions made at the congress: "I am not worried about the separation, nor the rift, nor the ban, but about the destruction of the nation. Waking or dreaming, I see before me the words: 'The third destruction—the ruin of the nation.'"[18] The reason for his fear was the Zionist position, which placed all its hopes on the Land of Israel and regarded it as the only national home of the Jewish people. He pointed out in his article the intellectual failure of Zionist ideology: the disregard for the fact that Palestine was settled by the Arabs, whom he termed the "Palestinians."

> And who has given you Palestine or will give it to you? Or perhaps you are able to take Palestine? . . . I have heard your youthful

babblings, but what sane, educated man will pay attention to them? And if you were to say, for example, that you will take Germany or France, would anyone take you seriously? What all the "Palestinists" forget, whether accidentally or deliberately, is that Palestine is in the hands of others and is completely inhabited. I have as much right to dream about Palestine as I do about Paris or London.[19]

Zeitlin opposed the common Zionist argument that the Territorialists were "hovering in the air," whereas the Zionists had a defined and "known object" and were more practical. Zionism, he claimed, could not be realized because of the Arabs residing in Palestine: "And in what way will you expel half a million Arabs living in Palestine? How will you throw out the numerous Christians living there?" His questions remained unanswered. Thus Zeitlin concluded that Zionism should be regarded as a utopian movement that would find it difficult to achieve its aims. "We are optimists," Zeitlin asserted. "Until the time when our ideas are realized and the real settlement arrives ... you [the Zionists] are optimists of a totally different kind. You want something to be what it was once and can never be again. You are creating your utopia in a place that is not yours and can never be yours."[20]

The Territorialists were the first group in the Zionist Organization to claim that the Arab population in Palestine cast doubt on the success of the entire Zionist enterprise. In his 1891 article, "Emet me-Eretz Yisrael" (Truth from the Land of Israel), Ahad Ha'am was the first to refer to this issue, but he did so only incidentally. At the center of his focus were the farmers and their problematic nature, not the Arab population. He did not follow up on this reference in his later writings. As the Hebrew teacher Yitzhak Epstein put it, the Arab question was "nonexistent" in Zionist thought before the Balfour Declaration. Zangwill and his colleagues recognized it, understood the inherent danger of Jewish-Arab friction, and expressed pessimism regarding the success of the Zionist idea in Palestine.

Even in later years, when the Zionist Organization received the desired charter in the form of the Balfour Declaration and optimism prevailed, Zangwill tried to cool the Zionists' excitement. He repeated the argument he had made in 1905, albeit with slight changes, that only by expelling the Arabs from Palestine could the Jews set up a state and develop it: "It seems to me that if logic and goodwill cannot find a solution—and certainly it is necessary to first try and make use of them—a single act of enforcement would be better for both sides than would eternal friction; just like the extraction of a bad tooth would be better than a toothache that never ends."[21]

Zangwill believed that the Arabs of Palestine posed an obstacle to the realization of the Zionist dream for that country, but he did not display the same sensitivity toward the native populations of the various territories he considered for a Jewish state. The Zionist proposal submitted to the British government concerning the Guas Ngishu plateau in East Africa (discussed in Chapter 1) can instruct us about the relationship between natives and Jewish settlers that was foreseen by Territorialists in general and by Zangwill in particular. As noted, the terms of the concession, as formulated in Leopold Greenberg's document, would have allowed the Jewish settlers to expel anyone who might oppose the colony and flout its laws. Even though the concession was never granted, it reflects the position that the Zionists (and Territorialists) took regarding the natives of the designated territory and their image of the residents of East Africa.

The Jewish polity that was to be established in East Africa or somewhere else was not intended to integrate into its surroundings. Instead, the Jewish immigrants would rule over the natives and could even banish them if that proved necessary to safeguard their control.[22] As Meri-Jane Rochelson has shown, Zangwill's attitude toward nonwhites was so ambivalent as to defy understanding. On the one hand, he was one of the first Zionist leaders to realize that the movement would find it difficult to realize its objectives in Palestine because it was already home to 600,000 Arabs. On the other hand, he saw no problem in setting up a Jewish colony in Africa alongside or supplanting the natives.[23] This internal contradiction marked the ITO from its first days until its disbanding in 1925.

"A territory on an autonomous basis," as stipulated in the ITO constitution, was one of the most important and basic principles of territorialist thought. The ITO wanted to continue the path of Herzlian Zionism and to create an autonomous Jewish government under the aegis of one of the Powers. For this reason the Territorialists warned against Jewish settlement in densely populated areas where they might become a persecuted minority suffering at the hands of the majority. They claimed that it would be absurd for the old problems, which had plagued them in their own country and still prevailed there, to be reproduced in the new country. This was, in their view, the necessary condition for realizing the idea of Jewish autonomy and the goal to which they should aspire.

For certain groups among the Jews of Western and Central Europe, the possibility of an autonomous territory was sufficient reason to oppose Territorialism. Many of them had been emancipated and integrated into the majority society, and they did not conceal their fears that an independent Jewish government would injure their rights, status, and loyalty to their native countries. As an English Jew who had been born in London, Zangwill understood their innermost fears but did not agree with their fundamental opposition to the territorialist idea.

> But—would not the existence of a Jewish state, or the efforts to establish it, be liable to cast doubt on the patriotism of Jews in other countries, or even to cause their expulsion by force to the new state? No. They would not be accused of this, just as we do not accuse a German, Swede, or Italian of a lack of patriotism if he decides to emigrate to the United States; nor would we accuse the German, Swede, or Italian who is already in the United States for lack of patriotism to the United States, just as no one demands that he return to Germany, or Sweden, or Italy, and live there. The right of citizenship in the modern world is optional and not obligatory.[24]

Zangwill's assertion that the fears of Western European Jewry were unfounded did not pass the test of reality, and the issue of Jewish loyalty, which had not been relevant at the beginning of the twentieth century, became one of the most problematic issues at the time of the Balfour Declaration. The assimilated English Jews, led by Edwin Montagu, were afraid that the British government's declaration of support for a Jewish homeland in Palestine would harm their standing in their native country. Montagu's adamant opposition to Zionism led the British government to add a qualifying phrase to the Balfour Declaration: "it being clearly understood that nothing shall be done which may prejudice the civil and religious rights of existing non-Jewish communities in Palestine, or the rights and political status enjoyed by Jews in any other country."[25] In 1905, of course, Zangwill did not know about the fundamental opposition of the assimilated Jews in England, but he was certainly aware of their difficulty in recognizing Jewish autonomy. For this reason he tried to persuade them that not only had they nothing to fear but also their choice not to move to a Jewish state and to remain in their native land would testify to their loyalty to their country and would prove that "their patriotism was non-Jewish and their tie merely religious." Zangwill also wrote, "The Jews already prosperously settled in any country would have rather less to fear than nowadays." Moreover, a successful Jewish state "would drain off their surplus population and deflect the streams of impending immigration."[26]

In their demand for a territory on an autonomous basis, the Territorialists effectively came out against the practical Zionist enterprise in Palestine, which regarded the establishment of settlements and land acquisitions as their ultimate aim. In doing so, they continued the line of thought in Herzl's *Jewish State*, which he wrote in 1896, after there were more than twenty settlements in Palestine: that settlement in the Land of Israel was being done according to the "mistaken principle of the gradual infiltration of Jews. Infiltration is bound to end badly. For there comes the inevitable moment when the government in questions under pressure of native populace—which feels itself threatened—puts a stop to further influx of Jews."[27] Zangwill's *Be Fruitful and Multiply*, written in 1909, repeated Herzl's assertions almost word for word. Zangwill opposed those who thought that Turkey would not agree to Jewish settlement in Palestine on an autonomous basis, so "it would be preferable to begin with small colonization so as not to alarm her [Turkey]." This policy was faulty and dangerous, and originated from the old idea "that Turks are fools."[28]

The Territorialists believed that receipt of a charter should precede practical settlement. For this reason they also opposed the Jewish Colonization Association (ICA) settlement enterprise in the Argentinean pampas, which could not ensure autonomy of the Jewish settlers. "We cannot play with toy-colonies like the Jewish Colonization Association hitherto," Zangwill said, criticizing both the work of Baron Hirsch and the practical Zionism of Menahem Ussishkin. "Either the Turks are willing to see a publicly-recognized, legally-assured home for the Jews grow up under their flag, or they are not. If they are, we can talk business. If they are not, let us know it before we waste our time and our money."[29]

Thus territorialist doctrine abided by the plan that Herzl had presented in The Jewish State. The Territorialists were not prepared to deviate from it and adopted Herzl's vigorous assertion in full: "Let sovereignty be granted us over a portion of the globe adequate to meet our rightful national requirements; we will attend to the rest."[30] The land given to the Jews could be anywhere on the globe, so long as the Jews could establish an independent autonomy there with a Jewish majority.

> Perhaps ere long—speedily and in our days—it shall float, if not over Palestine proper, at least over a provisional Palestine, over some new Sinai, over a land where our oppressed masses shall draw free breath, where soul and body shall grow straight again ... where we shall know again what it is to love mountains and rivers that are our own; where we shall no longer need to hang up our harps because we cannot sing the song of Zion in a strange land; where we shall sing them because we remember Jerusalem. For our Passover aspiration is not only "next year may we be in the land of Israel"—it is also, and perhaps, this is not the less important half—"next year may we be Sons of Freedom."[31]

## MIGRATION

The Territorialists regarded the large emigration from Eastern Europe as the phenomenon most indicative of the harsh problems afflicting Jewish society. They considered the emigrations of the early twentieth century to be the "constant spectacle of Exile." So long as the Exile "existed, that is, so long as this abnormality exists in the lives of our people—the lack of a special country for it—the Jews will continue to wander."[32] The emigration was, for them, primarily proof that Jewish life in Europe could not continue as it was and that it was necessary to find a radical solution to their problems: Jewish autonomy. So long as "the foreign national body within which it dwells is not developed enough to carry out all the necessary economic functions and to impose its culture on all those living in its country," the Jews can live safely in their land of residence.

But when the Jewish masses are expendable and unnecessary for the people who rule the land, when the majority people begin to feel that they are sufficiently strong and developed to take control of all economic positions and to leave their unique cultural mark on all life within the country, from that moment they begin to drive out the Jewish masses. In other words, Jews will begin to emigrate and will continue to do so until the Jewish settlement becomes a significant minority in comparison with the ruling majority.[33]

To fight against the "vision of Exile" and provide a solution to the Jewish problem, the Territorialists tried to intervene in the dynamics of the emigration and change its course. Instead of immigration to the United States, hundreds of thousands would immigrate to the new land that the Territorialists would acquire for them. The Territorialists saw Jewish emigration as a tool with which to realize their aims and bring their plans from theory into practice, which was a large concentration of Jews in an autonomous entity in a land of their own. They regarded the tens of thousands of Jewish migrants as the moving force that would foster the establishment of a Jewish state, if and when that became possible. Instead of migrating to the United States and concentrating in the New York ghetto, the Jewish migrant masses would go to a designated land and build the Jewish state with their own hands. But although the Territorialists continued to search for a suitable territory, it was clear to them that the Jewish migrants could not wait until one was found and that in the meantime a solution had to be found to the distressing problems of their daily life. The Jewish Emigration Association, discussed in Chapter 2, was a kind of "work in the present" (Gegenwartsarbeit) of the ITO; the ITO activists under the leadership of Max Mandelstamm and David Jochelman did all they could to help the Jewish wanderers.

Even on this issue, some disagreements on matters of principle erupted between the ITO and the Zionist movement. The Zionism of the early twentieth century campaigned for selective immigration to Palestine and preferred the wealthy over the poorer Jews who wanted to enter. Given the choice between the good of the land and the good of the people, the leaders of the Zionist movement preferred the Land of Israel. Arthur Ruppin, the director of the Palestine Office in Jaffa, wrote explicitly in his book *The Jews of To-Day* that "the natural place for immigration is not Palestine but the United States" (i.e., not Palestine).[34] Even Menahem Sheinkin, the director of the Hibbat Zion information office in Jaffa, thought that it was necessary to first bring the rich to Palestine to establish an economic infrastructure and lay the foundation for the absorption of the Jewish masses later on.[35] In a letter to the Odessa Committee in 1909, he noted that recently, despite the "energetic change in improving the political and economic situation of Palestine, the rich have stopped coming, and only a number of youngsters and poor people arrive on every ship." Migration of this kind, he claimed, degrades "our value very much in the eyes of the local residents [who regard us] with disdain and mockery and have ceased to consider us at all." So long as capital funds do not enter the country, he strongly asserted, the future of the Jewish Yishuv was doubtful, and "if they do not begin to invest substantial sums in Palestine and a certain number of new settlers do not come, our situation here is dangerous, internally and externally. Extinction awaits us, a natural death caused by exhaustion."[36]

Sheinkin's and Ruppin's positions on the future and aims of the Yishuv were also expressed in their replies to those who sent inquiries about the possibility of immigrating to Palestine. A statistical examination of their replies shows that the more unstable the economic status of the applicant, the greater the likelihood that he would receive a response telling him not to come. The two men told 60 percent of applicants not to come to Palestine and invited 20 percent of applicants to come alone to see the country and decide for themselves. Only 20 percent of applicants—the wealthy sector—were invited to settle there.[37] Their objection to unselective mass immigration was due first and foremost to the fear that Palestine did not have the resources to absorb the Jewish masses who were trying to leave Eastern Europe. In their view, the limited economic viability of the country required that suitable immigrants be chosen with extreme care, lest they become a burden on the limited Zionist movement, with its low budget.

The ITO was totally opposed to this policy and regarded unselective mass immigration as central to the establishment of Jewish autonomy. Here, too, they adopted Herzl's position: "We must not visualize the exodus of the Jews as a sudden one. It will be gradual, proceeding over a period of decades. The poorest will go first and cultivate the soil. . . .

The Jews will soon perceive that a new and permanent frontier has been opened up for the spirit of enterprise which has heretofore brought them only hatred and obloquy."[38] The Territorialists saw mass immigration to the United States as a scandalous waste of working hands, which were building America instead of building a Jewish autonomy: "a huge snowball, which is fast melting away into general American life."[39] They believed that the encounter between the majority society and the Jewish migrants was the source of the problem in the United States and Argentina. In both of these countries the immigrants were assimilating and adopting the culture of the majority society too quickly. Only in a country of sparse population, with no majority society to engulf them, could the Jews create a new national life ex nihilo.

Zangwill also addressed the economic aspect of Jewish emigration. The movement of tens of thousands of Jews year after year meant the loss of a source of funding that could support significant progress in the designated territory. The wave of immigration in the late nineteenth and early twentieth centuries was an economic transaction in every respect. Over half a billion rubles was spent on shipping companies, trains, hotels, smugglers, restaurants, and other facilities.[40] "The immigrant who travels between the covered decks of a ship is considered a symbol of destitution and poverty," Zangwill wrote in *Be Fruitful and Multiply*. "Yet so great is the financial power of the steerage emigrant that the North German Lloyd and the Hamburg American Lines would go bankrupt without him, as was clearly shown by the balance sheet of both these great steamship lines this year, when through the financial panic in America the third-class emigration to that country fell away."[41] Although the Jewish immigrants tended to be indigent, they became a major economic power as a collective of tens of thousands. This collective had the power to bring down large, well-established shipping companies and to build up a remote land in need of working hands.

The Territorialists did not conceive of immigration solely in economic and social terms. The period of mass migration was characterized by a liberal policy that permitted every Jew (and non-Jew) to immigrate to any corner of the world without a passport or entry visa. All they had to do was demonstrate to the immigration authorities that they possessed a minimal sum of money and were in good health. The Territorialists' main fear was that the immigration of thousands every year would lead to stricter immigration policies and to the closing of the gates. In 1905 the British passed the Aliens Act, which was designed to restrict the number of immigrants entering Great Britain. Other countries seemed likely to follow by barring the entry of migrants as well. In this situation the Jews would find themselves locked into their own countries and unable to escape their plight.[42] To forestall this situation, the Territorialists sought to locate a territory to take in Jewish immigrants.

Moreover, the Territorialists were not naïve about the attraction of the designated land. It was clear to them that, given the situation in the early twentieth century, most of the immigrants would prefer the United States over any other country. They recognized the impossibility of artificially reversing the stream of immigration and inducing immigrants to prefer the ITO land over America. But if, on the one hand, immigration policy changed and the gates of the destination countries closed and if, on the other hand, the reasons to leave the countries of origin grew stronger, the Jews would have no choice but to immigrate to a land that was prepared to absorb them. The ITO state would be built over the ruins of the Jewish Diaspora and the adversities of immigration.

> But imagine an ITO land established and, say, Mesopotamia acting as a centre of refuge against the evil days that may come. There is panic in Morocco—the Jews fly to Mesopotamia. There is a pogrom in Russia—Mesopotamia receives the refugees. There is an agricultural riot in Roumania—the farmers carry their scythes to Mesopotamia. There is a threatened congestion of Jewish refugees in Paris or Berlin—no need for the police to expel them: the Jewish Committees emigrate them to Mesopotamia.[43]

Zangwill had no doubt that, had the ITO located a territory before the terrible pogroms of 1904–1905 broke out, the Jews in the Pale of Settlement would have settled there. In his speech at the annual meeting of the ITO in December 1906, Zangwill noted, "If the territory had been created seventeen months earlier," there would have been enough Jews "who could not or did not want to remain in their countries of residence. During this period 639 pogroms occurred, which led to one of the most terrible catastrophes in the history of the Russian Empire and doubled the number of people in need of a Jewish territory."[44] The ITO state could provide a safe haven for the Jews, who in times of trouble would be willing to move anywhere on Earth, so long as they and their families knew that they would come to no harm there.

## TERRITORIAL PIONEERING AND THE CHARACTERISTICS OF A JEWISH TERRITORY

In their speeches and writings the Territorialists dealt little with the character of Jewish society in the ITO land. Did the Territorialists want a Jewish state or a state for the Jews? Who would be charged with building the ITO state and leading practical Territorialism? They had a clear and unequivocal position on the subject of an autonomy for Jews who could not or did not want to remain in their countries of residence and on the short- and long-term questions of migration. But the Territorialists also tried to sketch, in broad strokes, the future Jewish state in the designated land.

The Territorialists, like the Zionist movement, saw the pioneers as a central factor in creating the conditions for the absorption of the immigrant masses in the new territory. Zangwill was totally opposed to any kind of philanthropic measures as a tool for building the Jewish state. He cast a cold eye on the ICA's assistance to the Jewish settlers in Argentina and Baron Rothschild's support for the Jewish farmers in Palestine. He saw these as acts of philanthropy with the sole aim of helping needy settlers, devoid of any higher national purpose. "Zionism is a political movement," said Zangwill to his opponents in the Zionist Organization, "and a political movement needs statesmen. We have hitherto been governed by good rabbis and kind millionaires."[45]

Zangwill recognized the importance of the farmers and regarded them as the primary factor in creating an infrastructure for absorbing the persecuted Jews who were running for their lives. In his lecture at the second ITO conference in London, Zangwill began by emphasizing that territorialist pioneering groups had already formed in Russia. These groups aimed only to come to the land that would be given to them and build it up, not for their own needs but for the benefit of all Jewish people. They wanted to immigrate at their own initiative, to gain their livelihood through their own toil. They believed that "any settlement enterprise that expected philanthropic assistance was doomed to failure, as it happened in Argentina and in Palestine."[46]

Zangwill criticized the Zionist movement's immigration policy for preferring the wealthy capitalists over the poorer masses. However, he thought that migration to the designated territory should be done in stages. This was also the position of the ITO. Zangwill was inconsistent on this issue; he wavered between support for unselective mass immigration and orderly gradual migration. In 1909, in his Be Fruitful and Multiply, he stated that the ITO state should be a land of refuge for every Jew who wanted to move there to save his life. Four years earlier, in a detailed memorandum sent at the end of 1905 to the colonial secretary, Alfred Lyttelton, Zangwill wrote that the first settlers in the designated territory would come from tsarist Russia and would be carefully screened.[47] He went on to say that contrary to the widespread claims about the Jews' physical weakness and inability to cope with difficult agricultural work, reality had demonstrated otherwise.

> In Czarist Russia the model viticulture of the Jews of Bessarabia has received the praises of the Russian Minister of Agriculture. Several hundred thousand Russian Jews have been toughened by military service, and myriads are just returning from the frosty camps of Manchuria. Of a batch of refugees that arrived in London last year, all of [them] are now at work on the Canadian Pacific Railway. . . . I have myself seen the Jewish agriculturist of Palestine, stalwart sun-browned horsemen. In the Argentine, though from lack of Jewish autonomy, it has not attracted the Jewish masses, there are several flourishing agricultural colonies.[48]

Although the Jews were essentially an urban people, history had proven that it was possible to interest them in the idea of working the land and to bring strong, determined people to build the designated country and prepare it for the absorption of the masses.[49]

A year after he submitted this memorandum to the colonial secretary, Zangwill expressed the same idea in his speech at the annual ITO conference in December 1906. He stressed the importance of the pioneering group in creating the suitable conditions for mass absorption. The farmers would come first; the Jewish masses would follow later.

What awaits us [in the new land] is paving the roads, building houses, raising bridges, forest woodcutting, draining swamps, and plowing fields. Only people who are qualified for this kind of work and know how to engage in agriculture and sheep grazing can travel to the new territory together with owners of private capital. But if the masses of Jewish tailors, cart drivers, and shopkeepers arrive suddenly in the territory they will all die of starvation. Only when the villages begin to turn into cities and industry develops can a large number of migrants be absorbed into the new state.[50]

Zangwill maintained that the territorialist pioneers would prepare the land and lay the groundwork for those who would follow. His claim that a territorialist pioneering group had been consolidated in Russia was well-founded. As the president of the ITO, Zangwill received many letters from various branches of the organization throughout the Pale of Settlement, expressing their readiness to become the vanguard pioneers of Territorialism. His diplomatic efforts inspired hope in the Jewish communities; his adherents thought that his statement that Zionism without Zion is possible was a feasible plan. For example, Territorialists from the town of Bendery in Bessarabia wrote to Zangwill, "Two years ago, we sent to Paris our representative and the rabbi of our community, Rabbi Shlomo Wertheim, to persuade the directors of the ICA association to give us a small holding in Palestine." Their proposal was accepted at first but later rejected. Instead, they were offered a chance to settle in Argentina. In the meantime, the situation of the Jews in the Pale of Settlement, and those in Bendery, worsened. They told Zangwill that "during the last two years, we have come to realize that Zionism has fallen asleep, and who knows until when and who will arouse it?" Therefore they concluded:

In vain we believed in our strength to suffer longer, but the blows on our necks were too hard and bitter. . . . So we said let us try and speak to our brother, the leader of the ITO. Perhaps he can find us a small holding in any land he chooses to cultivate and settle. We decided in our minds that we would be the first in this matter, an example to our brothers who are against the ITO.

> We will give our every last penny to your Honor, and we will pour all our strength and abilities into working our land. We are all hardworking farmers, vineyard growers, and tobacco planters, and our skills and integrity can be attested to by the rabbis of our community.... Our request is laid before your Honor to answer yes or no, at your earliest convenience.[51]

The Territorialists recognized the importance of the pioneers as a dynamic force that could prepare the land to absorb the masses that would follow. Like the Zionist movement, the ITO also included groups that subscribed to the pioneering ideology and sought to settle the land, if and when it was found, and to lead the camp of the wanderers. This outlook bears a certain resemblance to the Borochovist worldview (the therapeutic movement), which distinguished between two stages in the process of realizing the Zionist idea. In the first stage the pioneers would go to Palestine and prepare the land to absorb the immigrant masses who would arrive in the second stage.[52] But this worldview was paradoxical, because it did not conform to the catastrophic outlook and the belief that a calamity was facing the Jewish people. Dependence on pioneers meant a slow process of land cultivation, which did not indicate urgency.[53]

The settlement of a Jewish territory was based on a structured, well-organized plan. First, a financial body would be established, including several branches. Its primary goal would be to raise funds to encourage immigration and develop the designated land for Jewish settlement. The financial body would conduct a comprehensive survey, and the natural resources of the state would be used to develop roads, railway lines, canals, and other means of transportation. According to the plan, the Jewish immigrants would be divided into two ranks: those who came independently and invested their capital and those who came after careful selection. The latter group could be subdivided further into two groups: those who were able to finance the expenses of their journey and provide for their own needs and those who would need assistance with their travel expenses and their acclimation to the new country. The immigrants from both subgroups would receive vocational training before their arrival and would work in whatever jobs the administrators assigned them. Members of the second subgroup would work for a few hours every day without pay to repay their travel expenses to the designated territory.[54]

In a comprehensive interview with the *Sydney Daily Telegraph* in October 1910, Zangwill laid out his territorialist worldview of how the Jewish autonomy would be built. He told the interviewer that the Territorialists wanted to obtain a piece of land extensive enough to eliminate the need for small, scattered settlements that were distant from each other. In addition, "We should ask [for] the right to say what Jews should and should not enter our territory" and to determine the laws of immigration ourselves. To the reporter's question as to what would happen if, after the Jews were settled, they decided to leave their land and settle in already inhabited areas, Zangwill replied that in this case the ruling government could prevent their entry into those areas. In their area Jews would be sovereign, but "do not think that we would promote the emigration of undesirables." The process of settlement would be gradual and preference would be given to farmers: "In the first year a few hundred settlers would be sent. We do not propose to flood it with paupers. This is not a charity movement. We do not propose to pay fares. The people who want out would be Russians, with enough means to pay their way and start themselves."[55]

After discussing the pioneers' contribution to building up the autonomous Jewish state, Zangwill went on to speak about the character and cultural aspect of the future country. He visualized the "State of the Jews" as a "Jewish State" that stands tall spiritually and physically. Unlike the vision Herzl laid out in *Altneuland*, Zangwill regarded religion as an important component of the ITO land's identity: "Religion preserved the national spirit for a period of nearly two thousand years, and since the national spirit has gained victory, it should repay that same power that had preserved it and discharge the debt it owes to Judaism. The national festivals cannot be other than those we celebrated during biblical times."[56] Zangwill stressed this issue in his 1910 interview with the Australian journalist and noted that the Sabbath would be observed in the designated territory. He emphasized that it was not enough merely to gather the Jews in one place; it was also important to make sure that the Jewish way of life was expressed there.[57]

Thus Zangwill envisioned the ITO state as being profoundly linked to Judaism and claimed that the two foundations for the existence of every people were "territory—preferably autonomous" and religion, "which supports and unifies it spiritually. Race unaided has no power of permanence."[58] Yet religion, in Zangwill's mind, did not imply "a seat in a synagogue and a grave in a Jewish cemetery."[59] In this spirit, Zangwill claimed, the Jewish state would become a model state of justice, morality, and equality. In his article "The East Africa Offer," written shortly after the founding of the ITO, Zangwill described in broad terms the territorialist utopia and the moral image of a Jewish society in a future ITO state.

> Let the Jews, with their genius for righteousness, establish a Jewish State in which justice shall be better done than any existing State, in which mortality stands higher and crime lower, in which social problems are better solved, in which women's rights are equal to men's, in which poverty and wealth are not so terribly divided, in which the simple life is a universal ideal; let them light this beacon fire of theirs upon Zion's hill or East Africa's plateau, and they will do more for the Jewish mission than in twenty centuries of pulpit talking.[60]

Thus Zangwill tried to impart a Jewish character to the future political entity and considered religion as central in preserving its identity. The Territorialists envisioned the society there as liberal, democratic, and, most of all, ethical, in the spirit of the prophets of Israel. On this matter, they did not follow in Herzl's path. Pinsker's position in *Auto-Emancipation* was closer: "Not the 'Holy Land,' but a land our own. . . . Thither we shall take with us the most sacred possessions which we have saved from the shipwreck of our former fatherland, the God-idea and the Bible. It is only these which have made our old fatherland the Holy Land, and not Jerusalem of the Jordan."[61]

Like Pinsker, the Territorialists thought that the establishment of a Jewish state did not need to depend on the acquisition of Palestine. The "concept of divinity" and all that it entails could be expressed in any territory, provided it contained a sufficiently large number of Jews to create a full Jewish way of life there. In his book *Jewish Writers and Territorialism* Judah Hazan addressed this issue: "The Territorialists can take another step forward and decide that all the longing and desire for Zion are not merely the trappings of money and the strong yearnings of the wretched people for a safe haven where the Jews can settle with dignity."[62] That is, the yearning for Zion is motivated not only by religious reasons but also by a deep desire for a secure and stable territory for the Jewish people. For this reason it is possible for a full and complete Jewish national life to exist outside the Land of Israel: "In any land in which a free Jewish society is established, a society in which all its members are united and attached to one another by the conditions of their social and economic lives, this collective experience will increase and deepen the knowledge of national unity within their hearts and will foster a complete and perfect national development."[63]

## THE ZIONIST REACTION

The Territorialists' secession from the Zionist Organization and establishment of a rival group forced the Zionists to face the challenge posed by the new movement and to prevent it from expanding and growing stronger in the Pale of Settlement. The relations between the two organizations were complex and fraught with tension. In many ways, their interactions resembled the relationship between a polytheist and a monotheist. Like a polytheist, who believes in multiple deities and also recognizes the existence of his neighbor's god, the Territorialist thought that the state of the Jewish people could be established anywhere, including Palestine. The Zionist, like a monotheist, regarded the Land of Israel as the one and only land of the Jews. So the relationship between them was one-sided. The Zionist Organization was not prepared to recognize the legitimacy of the ITO and refrained from cooperating with it. On the other hand, the members of the ITO were ready to cooperate with the Zionists and to recognize the existence of the Zionist movement alongside the ITO. In October 1905, only two months after the establishment of the ITO, Judah Hazan published the manifesto of the Territorialists in Warsaw, in which he defined the relations between the Territorialists and the Zionist Organization. On the one hand, as we saw in Chapter 1, many Territorialists were angry with Ussishkin and his colleagues for ejecting them from the Zionist Organization. On the other hand, the Territorialists continued to regard Palestine as the solution to the Jewish problem, but not the exclusive and immediate one.

> When the [Seventh Zionist] Congress imposed a kind of Inquisition on the way every member of the movement thought,

when it denied the more vital and fresher part of the movement the right to defend its views, the members of that group found themselves in an oppressive and distressing atmosphere, and it was clear that there was no longer any place for them. Zionism, as a movement that was to meet the real and actual interests of the people and to give a clear response to the burning demands in our economic and national lives ... has ceased to exist, and therefore they were forced to leave the organization and create ... the Jewish Territorial Organization.[64]

Despite its severe criticism of Ussishkin and the Zion-Zionists, the manifesto also stated that the new federation did not define its relationship with the Zionist movement and that "every member and group was permitted to determine their attitude toward the Zionists according to their view and outlook."[65] This tolerant position toward the Zionists was characteristic of the ITO from its inception; its members regarded themselves as the legitimate followers of the political current in the Zionist Organization.

The Territorialists were not alone in claiming that it was possible to be a Zionist and a Territorialist at the same time. Max Nordau, who was close to Herzl, supported the Uganda plan, and was a political Zionist, thought so too. In a letter to Zangwill in October 1905, he wrote, "I claim that a person can be a Territorialist and a Zionist at the same time. Territorialism seeks immediate relief to Jewish distress, while Zionism wants to solve the Jewish question altogether—which I believe it cannot accomplish anywhere outside of the Land of Israel."[66] Nordau did not regard Territorialism as a real danger to the Zionist movement and even wished Zangwill success. "I am very happy," he wrote to the ITO president, "that you are full of hope about the possibilities of Territorialism. I wish you success with all my heart. Fondly, M. Nordau."[67]

However, in the years after Herzl's death, few members of the Zionist movement were willing to support the ITO openly and publicly. Only Nordau, by virtue of his position, could do so, and he was the exception to the rule. One of the most severe Zionist critics of the territorialist movement was Ahad Ha'am. Unlike the criticism of the practicalists, who regarded working the Land of Israel as one of the conditions for the success of the Zionist idea, Ahad Ha'am opposed Territorialism because he adamantly believed that the Land of Israel was the answer to a religious issue, not a national one, a solution for Judaism and not for the Jews. Every attempt to settle Jews outside the Land of Israel was, in his view, tantamount to heresy. In his article "Ha-bochim" (The Weepers), which he wrote after the Sixth Zionist Congress, he described the Territorialists as "Sabataeans" (followers of Shabbetai Zevi). He claimed that "the yea-sayer," especially the Westerners among them, are "like matter without form, in the hands of their creator to do his will at any time. They cannot say 'nay' when he says 'yea.' It was people of this kind who followed Shabbetai Zevi and Frank, even on a road much farther than Africa, a road of no return. How can they follow Herzl to Africa only so they can return from there to Palestine?"[68] Moreover, Ahad Ha'am's criticism was directed against not only the yea-sayers but also their supporters in Eastern Europe, who felt inferior to "the pretentious manners and pompous language" of the Zionists in Western Europe "and were like grasshoppers in their own eyes."[69]

But Ahad Ha'am was wrong to define the Territorialists as "matter without form." Like them, he did not believe in Palestine's capacity to absorb all the Jews of Eastern Europe. Paradoxically, although he was one of the opponents of the Uganda plan, his own doctrine actually pushed for Territorialism in practice. Jacob Lestschinsky, one of the founders of the Zionist-Territorialist Party, mentions in his letters to Judah Sharett that "Ahad Ha'am has actually made me a Territorialist and not a Zionist." It was he who claimed that "the Land of Israel was the answer to a religious issue, not a national one." The reality in the late nineteenth and early twentieth centuries was that the situation of the Jews had worsened. Thus, "The Jewish question has increased in importance in our eyes and has taken a central position. . . . The crisis in political Zionism has decisively influenced our despair about the Land of Israel."[70]

When Zionism and Palestine could not provide a complete solution to the Jewish problem, particularly at a time of pillage and murder, there were those who found refuge in ideologies that proposed an immediate response to the predicament here and now. But although the Territorialists had accepted half of Ahad Ha'am's doctrine, they opposed the other half, which regarded a spiritual center and moral education as the solution to the Jewish problem. The Territorialists believed that the current crisis was the most urgent matter and that the Jewish people could not follow Ahad

Ha'am. Given the acts of violence and the mass exodus from Eastern Europe, the national question was more urgent than the religious one.

The most profound and best informed Zionist response to the territorialist ideology was that of Ber Borochov. In 1905 he wrote his comprehensive article "Li-she'elat Ziyyon ve-Territoriya" (The Question of Zion and Territory), in which he tried to undermine the Territorialists' basic claims. This was one of Borochov's most brilliant articles. It testifies to his analytical mind, his ability to delve into an issue deeply, to understand it thoroughly, and then finally to confront it and overthrow its very foundations. He wrote the article in 1904–1906, a time that his biographer, Matityahu Mintz, defines as one of the most intensive and fascinating periods of his life.[71] It was in this period that Borochov became the agitator of the Zion-Zionists and one of Ussishkin's close associates.[72] He traveled throughout the Pale of Settlement, speaking in favor of the Zionist idea and against Territorialism, and tried to persuade broad circles to oppose the Uganda plan and the territorialist ideology. During his travels and in between his lectures, Borochov wrote this comprehensive review. In one of his letters to Ussishkin, describing his lecture experiences, he also mentioned the article: "This will be a great work, almost comprehensive, on Territorialism. I am writing without bias, and admit the rights of the Territorialists."[73]

Borochov's essay begins by presenting the principles of Territorialism and only then comes out against them: "Our duty is to set before us the statement of our opponents in a forthright and consistent manner."[74] Only by understanding the territorialist ideology would it be possible to criticize its principles and propose the correct and relevant alternative to the Jewish problem. "Given that the Exile is a dead end, as has been scientifically proven," Borochov claimed, and given the miserable conditions of Eastern European Jewish life, "the Territorialists demand the quickest remedy for the disease." According to them, the only cure is "territorial autonomy ensured by charter."[75] They blame the Zion-Zionists "for their lack of ability to think realistically" and "boast about their own intelligence and realistic thinking." At the same time, the Territorialists see Zionism as an ideology of "complacent people who have the leisure to dwell on visions of Zion and to exalt the historical and spiritual traditions of ancient times." Although it is clear that Territorialism originated with Pinsker and Herzl, even Herzl could not have "founded a movement that broad without the aid of external constraints"—that is, the pogroms and the emigration. Territorialist ideology is not built on skepticism about the "Zionist vision" but on the complexity of the Jewish question and the desire to obtain a rapid solution.[76]

The analysis of the territorialist arguments was precise, and Borochov understood them perfectly. In a proclamation issued at the end of 1904, the Territorialists stated that "the creation of a Jewish settlement on a free and autonomous basis under British protection" is an inestimable achievement for the Zionist movement.[77] "Without a land, we are liable to lose everything," claimed the supporters of the plan for settlement in East Africa, "and by acquiring a land, we can save everything." They added, "The establishment of settlements in Palestine in the present situation without political rights and without any diplomatic security" is an irresponsible action with slight chance of success.

> It is not possible that these gentlemen [the Zionists] fail to understand that such settlement, dangling in the air, will not succeed, cannot succeed and, moreover, will not bring about the results we seek. It will do nothing but add ruin to what already exists—no more. This is because every new settlement in any country is at first in need of much support and many leniencies from the local government. In the first stage, the colonialists will be exempt from taxes and property dues. The land will be given to them without charge, or by payment in installments, and the government will try to make the immigrants' lives as easy as possible, until they acclimate and strengthen their position. At the same time, our settlement in Palestine not only lacks support from the Turkish government, but encounters difficult obstacles at every turn.[78]

The Territorialists' claim that the establishment of settlements in Palestine without the protection of an international power is an experiment with no chance of success did not differ from the position Herzl had formulated eight years earlier in The Jewish State. The territorialist political camp maintained this position even after his death, and it was at the center of their argument with the Zion-Zionists.

After Borochov explained the principles of Territorialism and before he went on to confront the Territorialists themselves, he spoke about his colleagues in the Zionist camp who were using irrelevant arguments in their debates with their territorialist rivals. According to Borochovist theory, the Zionist idea was composed of three elements: the redemption of Israel, the revival of Jewish culture, and the return to the ancient homeland. However, Borochov thought the claim that "Jewish culture cannot develop anywhere outside the Land of Israel" ought to be used with caution. The two assumptions—the expectation that Jewish culture would flourish in Uganda and the opposing concern that it would be swallowed up by British culture—were of equal weight. Moreover, "No one can guarantee us that we will be free of the pressure of some foreign culture even in the Land of Israel—after all, there was a time that the danger of Hellenization loomed even there."[79] For this reason, Borochov tried to refrain from claiming that the culture could flourish only in Palestine. "What will happen if you find that the culture can thrive even outside the Holy Land—would you not then have to stop holding the Land of Israel as your highest principle and ideal?" The main issue to consider, in his view, was the rescue and liberation of the people, if only for the reason that without the Jewish people, Zionism could not succeed. The enterprise could begin, but it could not be brought to fruition.

From this point on, Borochov attacked the Territorialists and presented arguments as to why there was no place for their ideology in the Zionist camp. He regarded them as minimalists for whom the starting point was the failure of settlement in Palestine, even before it was proven that the country was unsuitable. Borochov rejected this approach and maintained that the character and greatness of a national movement was not dependent on the size of its territory. If Zionism wanted large numbers of Jews to gravitate to its vision, it had to raise its demands to the maximum and not be satisfied with the minimum requirements, like the Territorialists were. Because "we do not tend to be spiritually impoverished voluntarily, we reject Territorialism in principle. Under no circumstances can we allow the assumption of failure to be our starting point—whether total or only partial failure is immaterial. . . . Failure, even a good failure, even the best of all failures, is nevertheless failure."[80] Borochov opposed the Territorialists because they had given up on Palestine too early, even before the possibility of setting up an autonomous and recognized Jewish settlement there had actually been examined. This was a defeatist approach that showed a poverty of spirit and will.

As long as it is not proven that the Land of Israel is unattainable for the Jews, that is to say, as long as the first of all the fateful failures we are anticipating does not come about—we will hold on to our vision to the full extent of its threefold synthetic unity. So long as the people do not find lesser opposition in some other territory, and do not go there in a powerful, unbridled force; as long, on the other hand, as our hopes for the Land of Israel will remain in effect—we will continue to be Zion-Zionists not only in our principles and ideals, but also in our practical program.[81]

Contrary to the Territorialists' arguments, Borochov asserted that the Zionists were also extremely anxious about the wretched state of the Jewish people in Eastern Europe. "In our hearts, too, the people are more precious than the Land of Israel. In Zangwill's words, we too believe that Zionism without Zion is better than Zion without Zionism." If the Territorialists were right that the Zionist program "is totally out of reach and we have no chance of carrying it out," Borochov continued, he would be ready to give up on Palestine. "With sorrow we would overcome our anguish and depart from Zion—tearing out our love for her from our hearts. We would resign ourselves to this, the way people resign themselves to a painful failure."[82] But reality teaches otherwise, Borochov insisted. Zionism can still fulfill itself in the Land of Israel and relieve the sufferings of the Jewish people.

After Borochov laid out his arguments against Territorialism and in praise of the Zionist idea, he gave free reign to his imagination and sketched out a territorialist scenario that provided the best illustration of the primary weakness of this ideology. Suppose, he wrote, that we find a colonial power in Europe that would give the Jews an autonomous territory. The Territorialists will send a fully equipped delegation to investigate this land. And let us say that the delegation even brings back information "of the most exuberant kind about the climate, the land, the hippopotamuses, and the savages."[83] As a result, a decision will be made and several thousand Jews will go there, at their own expense or that of the ICA, to settle it. The residents of the European cities will move there gradually: artisans, consumers of culture, physicians, pharmacists, engineers, the bourgeoisie, the intellectuals, proletarians, ordinary folk, and so on." Despite all this, Borochov claimed, even if it is an optimal and "peerless" territory, Jewish settlement will not last. Not only that, but it will bring many dangers both to the Jewish settlers and to the natives. Borochov divided the problems that Jewish settlement would face into four main spheres: enmity between the Jews and the native population, population density, changes in land use, and economic disparity.

The first sphere involved racial and nationalist enmity between recent immigrants and the native population. The economic relations between the Jews and the local inhabitants would lead to acts of fraud and hostility: "Even if the settlement organization centralizes all commerce with the local inhabitants and bans individual trade, . . . the savages' concept of justice differs from that of the Europeans."[84] The conflict and the hatred would be even more intense if the natives had already been converted to Christianity or Islam. Moreover, as soon as the natives understood that the Jews were trying to take control of the land, the tension would exacerbate and clashes between the two sides would break out. Borochov also raised the issue of sovereignty over the region.

> We would like to get a clear answer from the Territorialists. Uganda, for example, currently belongs to England by international treaty, but whom is the country destined for in the future? Here, there is no room for doubt—Uganda is destined not for the English but for its natives, who are even more dangerous than the Ugandists—and they are well aware of it, even if they have not yet learned sociological and legal concepts.[85]

With these prophetic words Borochov foretold what would happen to the world map after World War II. Madagascar would belong "not to the French but to the Havasu and the Sakalavasu"; and if South Africa would not belong to the Boers, it would not be because they surrendered to the English but because most of its inhabitants, "who outnumber the white by nearly tenfold—are Khaffirs, Bushmen, and Hottentots."[86] Anti-Semitism would grow among the natives, and the Jews would grow to "hate the Negroes and the Malawi." The problem of racism would plague and endanger the Jewish colony.

The second sphere was concerned with population density. Borochov thought that, following the Jews' arrival in the territory, the natives' mortality would decrease and the population density would increase. Given that no "charter would give us the right to exterminate the population," the Jews could expect to be engaged in a ceaseless struggle against the natives. In that case they would not receive support from the European powers and would find themselves isolated by the international community: "Hardly anyone has paid attention to the violent and destructive behavior of the English in Australia and Tasmania, of the Dutch in Java, of the French in the Sudan, of the Germans in Kamerun ... to this very day."[87] But in the case of the Jews, the whole world would focus on them and scrutinize their behavior toward the natives. Every unethical act would stir up public opinion about the Jewish colony and raise questions about its prospects of success. Moreover, the local inhabitants would regard the Jews as their common enemy, spurring them to unite and to develop their self-awareness and national identity.

The third source of problems would be a change in the nature of the natives' pattern of land use. Borochov expected the Jewish settlement to bring about substantial advances in farming methods and economic conditions. The lower the cultural level of the local tribes, the sooner this change would occur. A few Jewish settlers would succeed in "catalyzing progress and civilization." At the same time, the land owned by the natives would gradually be reduced, and "increasingly large areas will be transferred to the Jews." In this situation a normal way of life would not be possible, and the Jewish population would become mired in a constant struggle with the local people.

Finally, there would be intensified economic contrasts between the Jews and the local inhabitants as a result of land acquisition. Some of the locals would be dispossessed "and will join the reserve forces of the proletariat for lack of work," whereas others would become rich and gain possession of most of the land. The number of Jews in the territory would increase and a process of capitalization and alienation would begin. The proletarian class would become estranged from Jewish society (and would stop feeling they are part of it), and this would exacerbate the class struggle even more. "Where is the country," asks Borochov, "where we will have no fear not only of the entry of migrants and foreign capitalism, as we tend to fear elsewhere, but also of a foreign proletariat? Where is the country in which the proletariat consists not of strangers, but of people close to us in blood and spirit?"[88] His answer was, only in the Land of Israel, where the local population was related by blood to the Jews. In his view, the Arab *fellahin* (farmers) were the direct descendants of the Jewish agricultural and Canaanite settlement, "with a very light admixture of Arab blood." The racial kinship was so close that it was not possible to distinguish between the Sephardic porter and the *fellah*, and an external resemblance "of this kind is much more important to us" than any other aspect.

After detailing the weaknesses of territorialist ideology, Borochov explained why the Land of Israel was the only place suited for Jewish settlement. The four dangers he had warned against—racial and nationalist hatred, population density, changes in land use, and class polarization—could not be present in the Land of Israel. He noted the special qualities required for a territory designated for Jewish settlement: The power that possesses the territory should not have a developed capitalist economy; it should be politically weak; a Jewish population should already be living there; it would preferably not be situated near a capitalist settlement; it should not have any gold or diamond mines; the local population should not be subject to any civilizing influence; the racial composition of the local inhabitants should resemble that of the Jews; the land should be close to the sea. Borochov concluded that the Land of Israel was the only territory that met these conditions, and therefore the Zionist idea could succeed only in that country.

Naturally, the fact that Borochov's list of conditions conformed to the reality in Palestine was not a coincidence but a product of his own Zionist convictions. As one of Ussishkin's closest associates and a paid propagandist for the Zion-Zionists, Borochov had to provide ideological justification for the choice of Palestine over any other territory. Borochov's essay was written and put together during his travels through the Pale of Settlement and his struggles against the Territorialists. He had to present a logical and persuasive alternative to the simplicity of territorialist ideology. His arguments resemble those of the Territorialists in structure and substance; he, too, considers the choice of the territory to be of highest importance and sees it as the best solution to the Jews' plight, but he focuses these arguments on Palestine. His was the most comprehensive article that had ever been published by a Zionist who was trying to confront Territorialism through an in-depth understanding of its principles of thought.

Another attempt to justify Zionism and rebuff territorialist ideology was made by Ze'ev Jabotinsky. At the beginning of the twentieth century,

## CHAPTER 3

Jabotinsky was a young journalist in Odessa who was taking his first steps in the Zionist movement. From 1903 to 1905 he witnessed the pogroms in the Pale of Settlement and even went to Kishinev to help the grievously afflicted Jewish population. While there, he met Ussishkin, Ze'ev Tiomkin, and Chaim Nachman Bialik, and this acquaintance made him sympathetic to the Zionist idea. After this meeting, Jabotinsky translated Bialik's poem "In the City of Killing" into Russian, took part in organizing Jewish self-defense in the Pale of Settlement, and gradually became familiar with the ideas of Pinsker, Herzl, Ahad Ha'am, and Lilienblum. At the young age of 22, he served as a delegate to the Sixth Zionist Congress and was among those who voted against the Uganda plan.[89]

In 1905 Jabotinsky published two articles—"Tsiyonut ve-Eretz Israel" (Zionism and the Land of Israel) and "Al ha-territorialism" (On Territorialism). The starting point of the first article was mainly positive: Zionism could realize itself only in Palestine and the Zionists are justified in their claims to the country. The starting point of the second was negative: refuting the Territorialists' arguments and explaining why their willingness to compromise and forgo Palestine in favor of setting up a Jewish settlement elsewhere was not justified. In "Tsiyonut ve-Eretz Israel" Jabotinsky tried to understand how Diaspora Jews had managed to preserve their identity and survive as a people. "A single glance from a bird's-eye view reveals the full extent of our dispersion and makes the general picture clear at once." Everywhere "there are scattered groups of Jews surrounded by hosts of Gentiles," who actively demonstrate their hostility "and their hatred [of the Jews]. This has continued generation after generation with monotonous regularity." However, the Jews do not surrender and prefer to "suffer the ceaseless afflictions."[90] In view of this impossible situation, Jabotinsky asks, "What is the most precious thing for this group of people? What is the sacred treasure which it defends so stubbornly and with such devotion that it seems to have been the basic motivation throughout the history of this people without a country?"[91] His answer is definite: That sacred treasure is religion. "The people of Israel have fought for the Torah and suffered for the sake of the Torah.... The history of the Diaspora is a chronicle of the struggle for the faith." But after the Jewish people lost the Land of Israel and were driven into exile, its religion stopped changing and improving. "It has become frozen at the same level on which it stood at the thunderous time when the homeland was lost."[92] This process began at the moment the people of Israel became a people without a country, and it can only change if the Jews return to their country and homeland.

> Before we came to the Land of Israel, we were not a people and we did not exist. On the land of Eretz Israel we grew, and on it we became citizens; in creating the belief in one God, we breathed into ourselves the spirits of the land; in our struggle for independence and rule, the atmosphere enveloped us and the wheat that grew on the land nourished our bodies. In the Land of Israel the ideas of our prophets were developed, and in the Land of Israel the "Song of Songs" was heard for the first time. Everything that has passed through us was given to us by the Land of Israel; all the rest within us—is not Hebrew. Israel and the Land of Israel are one and the same. There we were born as a nation and there we grew up.[93]

Therefore only in the Land of Israel could the Jews return to what they once had been and revive their former life. All attempts to bring them to another country were doomed to failure. "Another climate, other flora, other mountains will surely pervert the body and soul which had been formed by the climate, vegetation, and mountains of the Land of Israel."[94] Thus loyalty to Palestine was not "a matter of blind and semi-mystical emotions" but primarily a choice based on an "impartial investigation into the very essence of our history and movement."[95]

"Al ha-territorialism" was much more militant and antiterritorialist. "Without the Land of Israel," Jabotinsky declared, "Zionism does not merely commit heresy; it simply cannot be realized." From his point of view, the main axis on which the "circle of our Exile" revolved was the Land of Israel. This axis had to move "on the same tracks as the entire historical train of the Exile had moved." A train that is derailed is doomed to be wrecked and destroyed. That was why he deemed the Uganda proposal ill-advised: "Not because what will eventually come out of it is not a Jewish state in the Land of Israel but a Jewish-Ugandan one; it is bad because in the end no state will emerge from it."[96] Jabotinsky's main argument was that neither Uganda nor any other territory could succeed in moving the masses, and therefore it was fated to wither away.

To justify his claim, he mentioned Baron Hirsch's Jewish colony in Argentina. Despite the vast sums the baron had invested in the Jewish farmers in Argentina, the Jews of Eastern Europe did not hasten there. Whereas millions immigrated to the United States, only a few chose to immigrate to Argentina.

Like Borochov, Jabotinsky tried to understand and confront territorialist ideology by first defining its objectives. The Territorialists believed that the Jewish people were suffering and could not wait any longer. Although the Land of Israel was the optimal solution to the Jewish problem, it was not attainable at this stage, so another territory could provide a viable alternative for the suffering masses. The entire burden of the Jewish people must never be thrown on the Land of Israel alone; it was necessary to compromise so that the Jewish people would not be left without a country. In Jabotinsky's analysis, the territorialist doctrine was based on two basic assumptions: "A speedy salvation is required and a territory that can be found more surely and rapidly than 'Zion'; without these two requirements Territorialism would not exist."[97] Jabotinsky came out against and tried to undermine both these ideas in "Al ha-territorialism." There could be no quick solution to the Jewish question, and the establishment of a homeland, whether in Palestine or elsewhere, would require time and patience.

> Zionism is not meant to apply an "immediate" bandage to some wound of the Exile, but to eradicate the Exile itself. This is a vast goal and therefore needs a long time. This should be admitted both by the proponents of Palestine and the Territorialists. Whatever land is finally chosen—whether Zion or (let us say for a moment) Uganda or the Congo—by doing so we are still not promising the people a "quick salvation" but only a fundamental salvation, once and for all.... Our motto is "forever," not quickly.[98]

Jabotinsky also warned against the dissonance that might arise among the Jewish people if a state was not established in the Land of Israel: "Let us assume for a moment that Uganda is available. Let us assume that at the Seventh Congress it will be found suitable in all respects." The ITO would then invest its ample funds in Uganda, begin practical work, and finish building it within fifty years. There is no doubt that in such a situation, the Jewish people, which had kept the Land of Israel on its lips throughout its Exile, would be thrown into cognitive dissonance. "The Jewish psyche was shaped in the Land of Israel"; any attempt to set up a state elsewhere would lead to a decline in morale and activity. The dissonance, according to Jabotinsky, might "weaken the tension of will and the work." It would not be possible "under such conditions, when the people will have to concentrate for decades on the systematic reconstruction of past in the Land of Israel, [for] the workers [to] not be troubled by the question: And why not in the Land of Israel? Why didn't we break that Sultan's stubborn neck? And perhaps we haven't missed our chance?" What would happen, Jabotinsky asked, if ten years after the Seventh Zionist Congress accepted Uganda, the sultan agreed to Jewish settlement? "Would we accept it or not? On one hand, it is a pity to give up the beginnings created in Uganda; but it would be impossible to prevent the solid outburst of love for the Land of Israel."[99]

Jabotinsky refuted the basic principle of territorialist doctrine—utilitarianism—and maintained that the Jewish people should not be guided by such considerations in choosing a land for settlement. If the Territorialists' standard for the choice of a designated land was the degree to which it was suitable for Jewish settlement, a problem was liable to arise to which the Territorialists had no answer. What would happen if the Germans, Italians, French, Belgians, and even Russians were to follow England's path and propose a territory for the Jews? "All these countries . . . have broad wastelands at various and strange latitudes: the concern was great and there was no one to settle them." Jabotinsky argued that Uganda was chosen for its pleasant natural environment, but another territory (if given) might have even better conditions. In that case, Jabotinsky asked, would it be worthwhile to discard the beginnings and concentrate efforts in the new country? "At the moment we endorse the principle of choosing a territory on the basis of its relative utility, there will be no further restraint: Even if they make us innumerable propositions, we must seriously examine all of them and abandon the first one without delay. . . . This is not the way to conduct a serious popular movement."[100] Thus, wrote Jabotinsky, the Jewish national movement can find its way only if the Land of Israel is its ultimate goal: "The itinerary of our wanderings in the name of the Land of Israel, the route that from the very first step to the last was entirely the worship of the Land of Israel, this route can conclude only in the Land of Israel. If we stray from this route, we will be derailed from the tracks of history, stray from the road, and lose our way with no chance of return."[101]

These arguments against Territorialism were published repeatedly in the Eastern European Jewish press. The Territorialists found themselves under attack precisely because their ideology was so close to the Zionists'. Unlike other ideologies, which fundamentally rejected Zionism, the Territorialists did not regard Palestine as an unacceptable objective that must not be pursued. Their opposition did not derive from alienation from the people and detachment from the Jewish experience; on the contrary, they were sensitive to the Jews' suffering and pain. Their main argument with the Zionists was whether the Jews had sufficient time to set up a state in Palestine before they were decimated by the pogroms. They tried to sharpen this issue time and again in their struggle against the Zionists and to draw the attention of those who were undecided and questioning. Shortly before the Seventh Zionist Congress, one Territorialist reported in the monthly *Ha-zeman*, "Already they are calling us Pappus and Tineius Rufus and accusing us of intentionally extracting one of the Jews' holiest treasures from the nation's heart."[102] But, he went on, they were afraid "that even if, while waiting in the Exile, we may one day acquire the land, what will happen to the people? The land that is destroyed can be restored by a Zerubabel and a Nehemiah, but what if the people are destroyed?!"[103] The Territorialists' metaphors came entirely from the history of the First and Second Temples of Jewish history and reveal the great similarity between their ideas and those of the Zionists. The problem was not the Land of Israel but the distress of the Jews in Eastern Europe, and that had to be solved as soon as possible.

Yosef Haim Brenner, who had veered between Zionism and Territorialism during the pogrom years, is the best personification of the dualism in each of those ideologies. In his article "Pinkas Katan" (Small Notebook), published in *Hame'orer* in the summer of 1906, he wrote that the trouble of the moment (the pogroms) was an eternal trouble that had not and never would cease. For this reason, "Zionism must be a movement that will fortify the House of Israel for its constant wanderings." Because the Territorialists, headed by Zangwill, aspired to this, they were in fact advocates of the Zionist idea. "I wonder," Brenner asks, "how we can make an enthusiastic Jew talk specifically of the Zionism of Zion, the Zionism of revival, merely of revival, and not of rescue?!"[104] Rescue must precede the revival of the people in its land, and therefore the Territorialist idea is an appropriate alternative to Zionist ideology, which is not sufficiently sensitive to the Jews' distress. Brenner's pessimism matched that of the Territorialists. Both feared the persecutions and did not regard them as a series of passing incidents that would vanish as quickly as they came.[105] Brenner's basic assumption was that one had to be ready for the next massacre and to come to the aid of future orphans. The goal that must be pursued is "a land! Any land that can be obtained, any land in which it will be possible to begin building our home; a land not for today, which is already lost, but a land for tomorrow, for the coming generations, for the orphans of Nemirov in twenty years, fifty years, a hundred years' time."[106]

One of the few members of the Zionist Organization who showed tolerance for the Territorialists was the Mizrachi leader, Rabbi Yitzhak Yaakov Reines. The Mizrachi Party was founded in early 1902 after the fierce debate over the question of cultural work by the Zionist Organization. At the end of the Fourth Zionist Congress (1901), young Zionists founded the Democratic Faction to promote cultural work by the organization. Chaim Weizmann and Leo Motzkin were the main speakers at the faction's founding conference in December 1901. They wanted the topics of national education and democratization in the Zionist Organization and cultural work to be placed on the agenda of the Fifth Zionist Congress, which was to meet at the end of that month.

Religious Zionists in the organization were strongly opposed to these demands and did all they could to undermine the initiative. They claimed that placing the issue of culture at the top of the Zionist agenda would alienate the masses of religious Jews in Russia because the Jewish people were in need of bread, not culture. They also held that the Zionist Organization's main concern was to return the Jews to the Land of Israel, not to educate them. Herzl was afraid of a cultural war and wanted to postpone the argument. He refrained from putting the issue to a vote, and the faction members left the hall in a show of protest. After the establishment of the faction and its struggle against Herzl, the religious Zionists felt threatened, and in February 1902 they established the Mizrachi Party. The founding conference of this movement in Vilna was attended by seventy-two delegates from various cities in the Pale of Settlement. They established an independent religious faction within the framework of the

## CHAPTER 3

Zionist Organization. Herzl and Rabbi Reines developed a strong political alliance, which became apparent during the Uganda controversy. Reines demonstrated his loyalty as a faithful ally of the supporters of the Uganda plan and backed Herzl's controversial views.[107]

On the eve of the Seventh Zionist Congress, Rabbi Reines published an article in *Ha-zeman* on Mizrachi's position toward the Uganda plan and Territorialism. By then, two years had passed since the Sixth Zionist Congress, Herzl's death, and the controversy that had split the Zionist camp in two. This led to a certain change in Reines's position; he seemed to have gravitated toward Ussishkin and the Zion-Zionists. He rejected Territorialism and claimed that "Mizrachi, as a party of religious Jews who see the observance of the Torah and its commandments and the aspiration to return to the Land of Israel as the vocation of the Jewish people and the condition of its existence, can never, under any circumstances, tolerate the Territorialist view, which denies the holiness of the Land of Israel and rejects the essential need to obtain and rebuild it."[108] His position toward the political Zionists was more conciliatory and much less adamant: "While the Mizrachi is in consensus on their approach toward Territorialism, Mizrachi views are divided with regard to the political Zionists who admit the Palestine principle and also try to find other autonomous centers."[109] According to Rabbi Reines, the Mizrachi Party reached no decision on whether Jewish centers established outside the Land of Israel would "strengthen and develop the national spirit and exalt with enthusiasm the love for Zion and its redemption" or whether those centers would "not only be of no benefit to Zionism, but [would] even harm it."[110] At present, Reines asserted, "It is not possible to know in which direction Mizrachi is destined to go, because not all the branches have expressed their views on this question."[111]

After the secession of the political Zionists from the Zionist Organization and the establishment of the ITO, Zangwill asked Rabbi Reines about his fundamental position on the new territorialist organization. This led to a correspondence between them, which indicates Reines's sympathy for Territorialism, despite his article in *Ha-zeman*. In contrast to his declared position on the eve of the congress, in his letters to Zangwill, Reines did not object to the existence of the ITO. In fact, he even gravitated toward the territorialist idea during the period of the pogroms. A comparison between his articles in *Ha-zeman* and his correspondence with Zangwill reveals significant differences in the rabbi's position toward the ITO. In answer to Zangwill's question about Mizrachi's position on the territorialist organization, Reines tried to clarify that "permission was granted to every Mizrachi member to express his own view—just as the opinion I have expressed here is only my own private opinion, the opinion of an ordinary Zionist Jew; it has nothing to do with the Mizrachi Party as a whole and the responsibility for it is mine alone."[112] Even though Reines noted in his letter that he was representing only himself, not the entire movement, his position had much influence, as we will see, on the other members of the movement. In his letter to Zangwill, Reines said he was aware of the dangers facing the Jewish people and recognized the need for a territory that would serve as a "land of refuge for thousands of our wandering brothers." He regarded the immigration of Jews to the United States as a danger to Judaism.[113] The multitudes of migrants arriving there were becoming assimilated "materially and spiritually," and therefore "we are forbidden to overlook this matter, which is unfolding before our very eyes." The solution was

> some land of refuge for these unfortunate people—as long as we do not have the ability to show them the way to Zion. As long as the gates of our sacred country are locked to us and we can only do work of a preparatory nature, we must obtain another land of refuge for our brethren. And my strong realization and firm faith is that this land, besides rescuing hundreds of thousands of our people from destruction and annihilation, besides giving bread to hungry multitudes, providing rest for the weary and consolation for the wretched, and leaving room for a wide range of activities for the free development flourishing of our religious, national and human sensibilities—besides all this, the land of refuge will also be the best way to achieve our ultimate objective in the Holy Land.[114]

Reines saw the designated territory as a means for obtaining the final goal, the Land of Israel. Unlike Ussishkin, Borochov, and Jabotinsky, who thought that the Territorialists' diplomatic efforts to acquire a land would weaken the chances of obtaining Palestine, Reines thought that if "a respectable number of our people were to form a free political society, healthy in body and spirit, wealthy in material assets and spiritual attainments, with recognized political authority and established economic relations—then our reputation and honor among the nations will increase, our internal strength will grow more powerful, and our efforts to obtain our holy land will look completely different."[115] In contrast to the Zionists, Reines did not object to the territorialist organization and even regarded it as vital in the advancement of Zionist aims. "I hereby accept the ITO with all my heart," he wrote to Zangwill, "and I think that any intelligent Zionist should lend a hand to the ITO." But he also stressed, "I should say openly and explicitly that despite my allegiance to the ITO and its aims, I and my colleagues cannot regard it as our final goal in our national work. None of the lands that the ITO will obtain for us will meet our national needs, which can only be met by obtaining the Land of Israel." For him, the Land of Israel was and remained the Jewish people's breath of life: "This is the land that God had destined for us when he drew the borders of the nations, this is the cradle of our birth, the graves of our forefathers, the haven of our future hopes.... Zionism is holy to us as the final aim, the ultimate and complete objective we cherish, while the ITO is the interim goal, the intermediate one, the transition to a glorious future in the Holy Land: the land of our fathers and our sons."[116]

Reines's speech was a statement of his belief that immigration to the Land of Israel was the definitive solution to the Jews' predicament; settlement in any other country was only a partial one. At the end of the letter, Reines assigned Zangwill a historical role: "And here I say to you: 'Go forward in this way and you will rescue Israel!' Rescued, but not saved, because only from Zion will true salvation come!"[117] His warm attitude toward Zangwill and the Territorialists shows how small and bridgeable the gaps were between the political Zionists of the Zionist Organization and the Territorialists of the ITO.

Shortly after he clarified his position toward the ITO to Zangwill, Reines sent him another letter to ask for help in raising funds from Jewish philanthropists for the yeshiva in Lida, which he headed. "I here take the liberty to trouble his Honor and ask for his moral help for the sake of this great institution of ours."[118] Zangwill's efforts and success strengthened the bond between them, and the rabbi continued to regard Zangwill as a "warm-hearted and hardworking Zionist." The ITO, in his view, was inseparable from the Zionist Organization, which moved the Zionist idea toward its final goal through action and initiative. The wave of pogroms that swept through the Pale of Settlement in late 1905 and the price that many Jewish communities paid in blood brought Rabbi Reines closer to the territorialist idea and even led him to consider setting up a religious territorialist organization. "I have decided," he wrote to Zangwill, "to begin working to establish a national federation of religious Jews.... I wish therefore to ask his Honor to let me know: (1) Will he be prepared to grant the religious Jews in all countries the permission to unite and form a special federation? (2) What are the obligations and rights of such a federation? (3) What are the regulations of the territorial federation? What are the arrangements for the division of labor?"[119]

Like Rosenblatt's heartbreaking pleas to Zangwill after the pogrom in Kiev, Reines's letters imploring Zangwill to speed up his efforts to solve the Jewish predicament were a clear expression of anxiety about the fate of Russian Jewry.

> The blood of our brothers that is spilling like water through the streets of Russia cries out to us. The time has come that we have had enough and can no longer endure our suffering. Thousands are dead, tens of thousands are wounded, hundreds of thousands are robbed and left penniless, and millions are frightened for their lives day and night—this is the condition of the Jewish people in Russia today. Thousands of orphans, widows, the sick and the maimed—hundreds of thousands are hungry and thirsty and millions are suspended between heaven and earth.... Every human eye can now see the future and prophesy what will come. The material and economic situation of the Jewish people in Russia will get even worse, the migration overseas will break out with vigor, the gates of other countries will close even more, and the question of "where to go?" will loom before us in all its horror and terror.[120]

Reines rejected the solution proposed by the proponents of the struggle for equal rights and for a change in the government's attitude toward the Jews. The local population's hatred was so great and deep that "we could see our future." The Jews were the scapegoats of the government, of the police, of all levels and ranks in Russian society. The pogroms, Reines wrote to Zangwill, "are a clear testimony of that hidden feeling buried in the heart of these bestial tyrants." For this reason, he wanted to rescue the Jews from Exile and bring them to a safe territory. "The Exile is our destruction, and we need a national revival in an autonomous land!"[121]

Reines's conciliatory attitude was an attempt to set aside the rivalry between the two organizations and to convene "a general meeting of Zionists and Territorialists that would certainly make peace between them. This is because I doubt that there is a single person today who denies the need for some territory. At this hour, when the Jewish people are drowning in blood, there seems to be no time for disagreements." Reines saw Zangwill as the man who could bring a rapid solution to the plight of the Jews in Eastern Europe. At the end of the letter, Reines blessed and called on him to save his Jewish brothers in Russia: "To his Honor, I say from a burning and wounded heart: 'Arise and go out bravely to help your people, and may the God of Israel be with you on the road you take. May He make your actions successful and bring relief and deliverance to your brethren who are being killed, and bring them salvation from their enemies!'"[122]

The pogrom in Bialystok was the turning point in Reines's attitude toward Zangwill and the ITO. The violence broke out in the city after four months of quiet in the Pale of Settlement. On June 14, 1906, about 200 Jews were murdered and more than 700 were wounded by the Black Hundreds, soldiers, officials, police, and government functionaries. Official government reports noted that those responsible for public order had not only refrained from preventing the pogrom but had also participated in it and acted with cruelty and brutality.[123] Eight days later, Reines sent an emotional letter not only to Israel Zangwill, "the head of the ITO devoted to his people with all his heart," but also to "the great man of many accomplishments, Mr. Lucien Wolff and other honored members of the ITO Directorate." He detailed the distress and the need for an urgent and speedy solution.

> With a bitter and battered heart, with my life's blood, I call to you now with despair as the fear of death overtakes me. This call bursts out from the throat of the six million Jews living in Russia who are standing on the brink of an abyss: Help! Here comes the spring and with it the butcher—the terrible butcher of Bialystok. A butcher who casts his fear and terror upon all the cities where the Jews live, who decreed the mayhem in Bialystok on every

side, leaving hundreds of dead and wounded.... Who cannot see what is about to befall the Jewish people in Russia? Who cannot sense the future in his heart? The danger in the air is already palpable ... six million Jews in danger—can one delay at such an hour? An entire nation on the edge of the pit—can it be left to the destroying angel?? Will our older brothers not arise and go to the governments of the powers, and bring them here to protect our lives and our honor? Can the enlightened governments stand by silently at the sight of all this blood? Where is the civilization that they glorify, where is the love of mankind, the feelings of duty and righteousness?[124]

In view of this gloomy situation, Reines urged Zangwill and the members of the ITO to make the governments of England and the United States aware of the pogroms against the Jews. They should exert international pressure and set out "against the cruel savages with a strong hand and outstretched arm" and end the violence once and for all. Even though he was a member of the Zionist Organization, Reines thought that salvation for the Jewish people would come through the Territorialists, not the Zionists. "Who among the Jews can take this great task upon themselves, if not you?" He believed that Russian Jews could not wait until the Land of Israel was ready to absorb them, and a quick and immediate solution for their problems had to be found. "Help! This is the one terrible word that the Jewish people cry out to you. Arouse yourselves and do whatever you can with your utmost strength and bring the necessary succor. Go in the name of the people and in the name of our God—and save your brethren!"[125] Reines saw the ITO (not the Zionist Organization) as the rescue organization, and in the moments of crisis and despondency, he anticipated help from the Territorialists rather than from the Zionists. This correspondence shows that although Reines did not resign from the Zionist Organization, he gravitated toward the ITO's ideas and accepted its basic argument that a territory, any territory, was necessary to save the Jews of Russia.

Reines maintained this view not only during the pogroms but also during the years that were relatively quiet. In 1908 he wrote to Zangwill that the latter's departure from the Zionist Organization and conversion to Territorialism was not due to "a deficit of love for

Zion and its holy places" but because "his practical sense told him that the Jewish people could not find what they needed in the Zionist Organization, which had become a purely spiritual movement. He sought a more practical organization that would reckon with the practical and material matters of life."[126] Even though Reines defined himself as a Zionist and never crossed the lines to the ITO, he nevertheless recognized the importance of the ITO and felt great sympathy for its activities for the Jewish people.

> I know in my soul that I am devoted with all my heart and mind to Zion and to our holy places, and I am ready at any hour to sacrifice myself for them. Yet I was one of the first to understand the practical value of the Territorialist movement and its concern for the exigencies of life and to assist it.... And because it seems to me that Territorialism is more practical and closer to real life, I have overcome my spiritual doubts and join the ranks of those who love and serve it.[127]

Reines's position toward the ITO was supportive and positive. He not only viewed the territorialist idea as important but also thought that the ITO had a place alongside the Zionist Organization. He saw them as complementary: One represented the spiritual aspect of the movement and the other the practical one. Zangwill and Reines respected each other, and even though one belonged to the Zionist camp and the other to the territorialist camp, they had more in common than not. Reines's personal and noncommittal attitude trickled down to his followers and became part of the movement's official line. On the basis of their letters to Zangwill, the members of the Mizrachi Party agreed with the rabbi's moderate and sympathetic approach toward the Territorialists. For example, as we saw in Chapter 2, Moshe Rosenblatt, a Mizrachi member in Kiev, wrote to Zangwill to request assistance. He even initiated petitions of support for the ITO, signed by hundreds of Jews, and urged the ITO president to participate in the Brussels conference.

Other members of the Mizrachi Party expressed their support for the ITO after it became clear to them that the rabbi approved of the activities of Zangwill and the Territorialists. "Let his Honor know," eleven members of Mizrachi wrote to Zangwill, "that many have gone to the door of our great rabbi, Rabbi Yitzhak Yaakov Reines, to ask his opinion of Territorialism and to hear his views, to decide whether to join its ranks or not."[128] They noted that many were afraid to participate in territorialist activities and join the ITO's ranks because they did not know their rabbi's position. But once they found out through the "newspapers in Russia about our rabbi's lecture on Territorialism in London, our joy increased." The rabbi's support for both the ITO and the Zionist Organization "whipped up excitement among broadening circles of Mizrachi members and among our other brothers who are sympathetic to Territorialism." However, the members of Mizrachi who signed the letter were aware that their rabbi had not yet crossed the lines and had not become a full participant in territorialist activity. In their letter, they urged Zangwill to persuade the rabbi to do so and promised him that such an act would greatly strengthen the territorialist camp.

> In this regard, we think it our duty to inform his Honor that if he wishes to acquire a diligent and influential worker like our rabbi, if he wants to benefit from his monumental work, which would be very productive for us—then his Honor will please rescue our rabbi from his confusion and bring him out of the terrible situation he is in. If he does so, his Honor will surely see the fruits of this action in the near future.[129]

The letter to Zangwill shows that Mizrachi members were eager to join the ITO but could not do so as long as their rabbi was a member of the Zionist Organization. Thus they wanted Zangwill to persuade their rabbi to openly join the ITO. Only then could his many followers and supporters become active participants in spreading the territorialist doctrine. "Our movement could profit very greatly," they wrote to Zangwill, if only "the rabbi [could be seen] at the head of those doing the practical work in our land." Then it "would grow and flourish into a mighty movement." The use of the first person plural—our movement—shows the Mizrachi members' deep sense of identification with the ITO and its leader, on the one hand, and their fear of committing an act that might be interpreted as insulting their rabbi, on the other. They concluded their letter: "And we ask his Honor for forgiveness and bring him the blessings of the people for his holy work. [Signed:] His respectful admirers, devoted to his cause."[130]

※

This chapter's look at the consolidation of territorialist ideology demonstrates the resemblance between the ITO and the Zionist Organization. They agreed in principle that the establishment of an independent political entity was the only solution to the Jewish problem. The main difference between them was the extent of the danger they anticipated for the Jews in the Pale of Settlement. The Territorialists were much more pessimistic and sought an immediate solution to the plight of the Jews. In contrast, the Zionists did not regard the pogroms as an existential threat and tried to conduct a balanced, responsible policy that opposed unselective migration to Palestine. The Territorialists did not negate the Zionist idea or the Land of Israel as a solution to the Jewish problem. Their main criticism resulted from their assessment of how long it would take to establish a Jewish state. The Territorialists thought that Zionism would not succeed in setting up a Jewish state before the sword held over the heads of the Jewish people would strike its blow and the Jewish people would lose their race against time.

The Territorialists also gave serious thought to the character and the image of Jewish society in the designated territory. Here they deviated from the Herzlian doctrine, as expressed in *Altneuland*, and sought to establish a Jewish state rather than a state for the Jews. Zangwill had grown up in the Jewish ghetto in London and his father had moved to Jerusalem to engage in Torah study there. As a result, he was far more suffused with Jewish culture and familiar with the classic Jewish texts than Herzl was. In his attempts to sketch out the defining features of the designated territory, he emphasized religion, the Jewish festivals, and the Hebrew language.

Just as the Territorialists wanted to move closer to the Zionist camp, the Zionists wanted to keep their distance and undermine their ideology. To that end, Menahem Ussishkin—the Territorialists' bitter rival—recruited Ber Borochov to travel throughout the Pale of Settlement and give lectures denouncing Territorialism, debate ITO members, and bring as many people as possible into the Zionist camp. In the struggle over the hearts and minds of the Jews in the Pale of Settlement, the Territorialists never found a champion to parry Borochov, who was gifted with rhetorical skills, analytical thought, and abundant charisma. At the end of his travels, during which he delivered innumerable lectures and conducted many debates, Borochov wrote his profound and comprehensive article against Territorialism. Some members of the Zionist camp accepted the ITO's existence and were not afraid to cooperate with it. After Herzl's death, Rabbi Reines did not forget the brave alliance he had forged with the political Zionists and became the only ally of the Zionist Organization who was at the same time loyal to Zangwill and the ITO.

4

# The Territorialist Movement in Palestine

The support that the territorialist idea received in the Yishuv before and after the Uganda controversy is one of the most fascinating issues concerning the ITO, the territorialist idea, and the renewal of Jewish settlement in Palestine. Contrary to what might have been expected, the Zionist Yishuv did not oppose the Uganda plan, did not fight Territorialism, and did not try to thwart the attempt to set up a Jewish state outside Palestine. On the contrary, many Yishuv residents supported the Uganda plan, and the ITO won approval among various sectors in Palestine.

Three significant works on the Uganda controversy in Palestine have been written. The first is by Haya Harel, who wrote her master's thesis on Herzl and the Zionists of the Land of Israel. The last chapter of her study focuses on the reactions to the Uganda affair in the Jewish colonies against the background of the struggle between the Committee of Zionist Associations, which was led by central figures in the colonies, and the Palestine Zionist Federation, founded by Ussishkin on his 1903 visit to the country.[1] The second study, also a master's thesis, is by Shifra Schwartz and focuses on the positions of the Yishuv in Palestine on the Uganda plan from 1903 to 1905.[2] Schwartz's research examines the background, motivations, and reactions of the Yishuv toward the Uganda proposal and "presents the positions of the prominent figures in Palestine who took part in the debate, including Eliezer Ben Yehuda, Hillel Joffe, Yehiel Michael Pines, and Rabbi Kook . . . and how they were expressed in the contemporary local Jewish press (1903–1905)."[3] The third is Arieh Saposnik's study of the echoes of the Uganda affair in the Yishuv in

Palestine as part of the construction of a Hebrew culture there at the turn of the twentieth century.[4] The decisive conclusion of the three studies is that the new Yishuv was Ugandist but not territorialist. After Herzl died and the Uganda plan was removed from the Zionist Organization's agenda, the Yishuv returned to the official party line of the Zionei Zion and refrained from supporting the ITO.

In this chapter I claim that the territorialist idea continued to exist among the Jewish inhabitants of Palestine, even after Zionei Zion had defeated the Uganda plan and the Territorialists had resigned from the Zionist Organization and established the ITO. In the years after the Seventh Zionist Congress (1905–1914), the Yishuv retained a fairly large cadre of Territorialists (not Ugandists) who openly supported Zangwill and his plan to set up an autonomous Jewish state outside Palestine. In fact, the shifts in the Yishuv's support reflect the changes in public opinion among Eastern European Jewry. During the years that Territorialism enjoyed widespread popularity, some sectors in the Yishuv even openly expressed their support. On the other hand, as Territorialism became less popular, mainly because of the difficulties in finding a suitable territory, support in Palestine declined as well. In the first part of this chapter I present evidence of the controversy aroused by the Uganda plan in the Yishuv, including expressions of support for the plan. In the second part I focus on the Yishuv's support for the ITO and the territorialist idea after the Seventh Zionist Congress removed the Uganda plan from the Zionist agenda.

## UGANDISM IN PALESTINE

When the Uganda crisis broke out in the early twentieth century, it seemed as though the Yishuv in Palestine had managed to overcome the pains of absorption experienced by the pioneers of the First Aliyah and was embarking on a promising new course. Twenty-five settlements had already been established in the country, concentrated in four regions: the Lower Galilee, the eastern part of the Upper Galilee, the southern Carmel region, and the northern Judean lowlands. Each of these regions had a cluster of settlements and large tracts of Jewish-owned land.[5] Five thousand people were living in the settlements at this time. The large ones (Zichron Yaakov, Petah Tikva, and Rishon Lezion) had 700–800 people each; the medium-sized ones (Rehovot, Metulla, and Yesud Hama'alah) had 200–300 people each; and the small ones ranged from 28 (Motza) to 152 (Hadera) residents.[6] In 1900 Baron Rothschild transferred the executive powers to the ICA, and the ownership of the settlements changed hands. This period of change led to economic recovery, and for the first time the Jewish colonists experienced success. Substantive changes also occurred in the Jewish urban communities of Palestine. Jaffa became the center of a new settlement and competed with Jerusalem for primacy. In the late 1880s Jewish neighborhoods were founded in Jaffa (Neve Tzedek and Neve Shalom). The number of Jews increased year after year, and the city gradually became the metropolis of the renewed Jewish settlement in the Land of Israel.[7]

Most of the New Yishuv was composed of Orthodox Jews from Eastern Europe with large families. Most of the colonists and some of the urban settlers (mainly in Jaffa) belonged to the Hibbat Zion movement, which had emerged after the pogroms of the early 1880s in Russia and after the publication of Pinsker's *Auto-Emancipation*. In immigrating to Palestine, they implemented the Zionist idea and also maintained contact with the leaders of the movement in Eastern Europe. The first years of Zionist settlement in Palestine were a time of crisis. The young movement was unable to support the new settlements, which bent under the burden. Baron Rothschild came to their aid and extended his patronage, supporting the settlers for eighteen years and taking care of all their needs. He bought land, developed roads leading to the settlement, built houses, set up wineries, provided agricultural training, and saw to the education of the children. The colonists paid a heavy price for his help. Instead of being proud and independent workers of the land, they became despondent, embittered hired laborers, subject to the authority of the baron's officials and their capricious ways.[8]

The colonists' dependence on Baron Rothschild and the lifestyle they adopted aroused sharp criticism. Ten years after they came to Palestine, Asher Ginsburg (Ahad Ha'am) surveyed the settlements to obtain an impression of the Zionist enterprise that had begun to take shape. In his article "Emet me-Erets Yisrael" (The Truth from the Land of Israel), published in *Hamelitz* in 1891, he leveled harsh accusations. "Is the land already fit for revival, and are the people of Israel fit to make it fruitful once again?" he asked. He replied that the land was good, but "it is not easy to find an answer regarding the people."⁹ He criticized the corrupt way of life that the farmers had adopted. His article was the beginning of the rift between the colonists and the leaders of Hibbat Zion in Eastern Europe, who found it difficult to understand the problems of the situation in Palestine. The fact that a large number of the colonists supported Herzl exposes the depth of the crisis and lack of trust that some of the people in the colonies felt toward their leaders in Russia.

Herzl's devotion to the Zionist enterprise and the establishment of the Zionist Organization in August 1897 led to a transformation in the Yishuv. The years 1901 and 1902 were marked by a flurry of Zionist activity. Zionist associations were established in the settlements and in the main cities. These included Eretz Israel and Jerusalem and Zionism in Jerusalem, Ein Hakoré in Rishon Lezion, Yavneh in Wadi Hanin, Zion in Rehovot, Mazkeret Batya in Ekron, Yehuda in Gedera, Marom Zion in Kastina, Hamizrahit and Barkai in Jaffa, Hatikva in Petah Tikva, Al Shefer in Sejera, and Yavniel in Yema. The committee wanted to set up more associations in the country, to annex them to the main committee, and to gain recognition from the Actions Committee in Vienna.[10]

Although the Hibbat Zion movement stressed the importance of practical Zionism, whereas Herzl prioritized diplomatic efforts over settlement, many inhabitants of the Yishuv supported Herzl and esteemed him highly. His 1898 visit to Palestine left a deep impression on them. He visited Mikve Yisrael and the settlements of Rishon Lezion, Nes Ziona, and Rehovot. Each settlement prepared a grand and emotional welcome. In Rishon Lezion, Herzl visited the wineries and met the settlers in the community hall (*beit ha'am*); in Nes Ziona, children sang for him and offered him bread, salt, and wine; in Rehovot he was met by a group of twenty horsemen, who galloped toward him with shouts of welcome and greeted him with a ceremonial volley, "lustily singing Hebrew songs and swarming about our carriage." The gesture of the youth of Rehovot moved him deeply: "Wolffsohn, Schnirer, Bodenheimer and I had tears in our eyes when we saw those fleet, daring horsemen."[11] The colonists' admiration for Herzl knew no bounds, and when he brought the Uganda proposal to the Sixth Zionist Congress for discussion, their representatives, the Palestine delegates, supported him and gave him their approval.

One of the interesting testimonies that we have about the support for the Uganda plan expressed by the colonists, or at least by some of them, can be found in Shlomo Zemach's memoir *Shanah rishonah* (The First Year). Zemach went to Palestine in the early days of the Second Aliyah from the city of Plonsk, Poland. When he reached the port of Jaffa, he took a diligence (carriage) to Rishon Lezion. In the chapter "The Collapse," he describes his disappointing encounter with the members of the settlement. It appears that he arrived at the settlement in late December 1904, when Feivel the cart driver "brought Ben Yehuda's [newspaper] *Hashkafah*, which published twice a week, with him from the city." The heading of the bulletin read "in large thick letters . . . that the survey team had set out."[12] Even though he stayed only one day in Palestine, Zemach felt free to criticize the colonists not only for their support of the Uganda plan but also for their lifestyle and the style of building in the settlement. "Why do they make such grand dwellings? These are not the modest farmhouses that I had hoped to see."[13] On their clothing: "His trousers are riding breeches, wide over the hips and narrow from the knees downward. They say that he intends to leave the settlement and go to Australia, and therefore has already begun to dress in English-style clothing."[14] Judging by outward appearance, the colonists' daughters looked to him like Parisian prostitutes: "The women are very important and grandly dressed, as if they were going to a ball. They are strapped into their corsets, wrapped in long dresses with many flounces, sewn according to the style of Hemda Ben Yehuda."[15] Zemach also did not hesitate to criticize the colonists' Ugandist outlook and open admiration of Zangwill, to which he was exposed for the first time at a meeting conducted on the day he arrived at the settlement.

As he was wandering through the settlement, Zemach saw a notice summoning the members to a gathering at the home of Aharon Freiman, where David Yudelovich would read a Hebrew translation of one of Zangwill's speeches. With the innocence of a new immigrant who had just arrived, Zemach was impressed by the colonists' custom of "setting aside time for study on the Sabbath eve and not wasting their time in idle carousing in taverns. I said I would go to this meeting and see what happens."[16] The comedown was even greater than his expectations. Zemach heard Yudelovich speaking and did not understand "why his eyes shone with such a strange fire as he read Zangwill's speech? What was the source of the hatred in his eyes? Yudelovich complained 'No, Zionism without Zion is better than Zion without Zionism!' in his spellbinding voice, and it seemed as though his irritated tones and his audience's ears were in agreement."[17] So great was his disappointment with the colonists of Rishon Lezion that he could not keep silent and asked for permission to speak at the meeting. He rebuked them for their fecklessness.

> I jumped up from my place and shouted that I wanted permission to speak! My demand broke into the noisy and demonstrative audience like a heavy ax from the ceiling, and split the excitement down the middle. The chairman asked me to speak, and everyone around the room turned to me with their eyes full of anger at me for coming and sitting at their meeting. . . . My thoughts were not well-ordered in my mind, and I did not want to return to this cursed affair called Uganda, whose turbid waters had already dried up. . . . In the morning, I disembarked the ship and came ashore, and in the evening, I came under the shadow of your trees with only one question: Tell me, Mother Earth, wide, full, and large, why don't you offer your breast to me, a poor and desiring soul? . . . And I lifted my fists into the air: Do not see me as an old fool, I shall fight you! And all this time they accompanied my words with waves of mighty laughter from every mouth. My Hebrew words, this garbled language of Polish Jewry, which chisels all the *o*'s and whistles all the *a*'s, with every *e* like an open *aleph* followed by a *yod*, and every *o* like a long *oy*—this garbled language was certain very ridiculous.[18]

The farmers scorned and derided Zemach's criticism: a ludicrous young man who had just arrived in the Land of Israel and dared to preach at them and decry them for their support of Zangwill. "You have only just come this morning," said one of those present at the meeting, "and you're already making speeches? We like 'young hotheads,' and we, too, were hotheaded when we were young, but what is the meaning of the word 'fever,' do you know it? . . . And do you know the meaning of eye ache?"[19]

Although Zemach's memoirs were written nearly fifty years after his visit to Palestine, they coincide with contemporary sources. In the *Rishon Lezion Jubilee Book*, Yudelovich notes that Freiman, in whose home the meeting was held, was a Territorialist in outlook and had placed "himself immediately in the ranks of the Territorialists, published some articles on this subject, and desired with all his heart to see an 'official Jewish state' authorized by the governments of the world, even if not yet in the Land of Israel."[20] Getzel Kressel noted in this connection that he interviewed Zemach for his article, "Eliezer Ben Yehuda's Uganda Vision." Zemach told him "important details about this subject that it was not appropriate to publish then, but supported what was said in 'The Collapse' a thousand times over."[21] Indeed, the Uganda controversy had not only struck Palestine but also seemed to have taken on an even more violent and mordant character in the Mediterranean climate.

This assertion contradicts Shifra Schwartz's claim that the supporters of Herzl's controversial plan took their position because of their esteem for the president of the Zionist Organization, not their support of the principles of territorialist ideology. Schwartz maintains that most of the members of the New Yishuv did not uphold Territorialism for its own sake, as confirmed by the criticism of the members of the Second Aliyah toward the farmers on the colonies. She further argues that the pioneers of the Second Aliyah, who began arriving in Palestine at that time, took advantage of the support for the Uganda plan among the colonists of the First Aliyah and used it in their struggle to create a new framework for the practical settlement activities in the country.[22] She maintains that aside from Eliezer Ben Yehuda and the settlers in Rishon Lezion, no one else in the country demonstrated support for the Uganda plan, either in Judea and the Galilee or in the towns of Jaffa, Tiberias, and Safed.[23] It therefore appears from her research that Zemach's memoirs reflect only the position of the farmers in Rishon Lezion and that this was not the position of the entire Yishuv.

In contrast to Schwartz's research, some sources indicate that a fairly large number of circles in the Yishuv in general and in Rishon Lezion in particular supported the Uganda plan and the territorialist idea. On November 1, 1903, two months before the expedition to East Africa had set out, Yudelovich, who was then in the Far East, wrote a letter to his friend Dov Lubman in Rishon Lezion, in which he referred to the Sixth Zionist Congress and the Uganda plan.

> I read in *Die Welt* nearly all the details of the Congress. . . . What can be done when our Russian brethren have instead of "wisdom and understanding," instead of "intelligence and logical

European judgment," only a sharp mind and patience. And their sharp minds push them to sit on the floor and wail over the destruction of the Temple. And instead of being happy that a fresh stretch of territory has been found where they can stand up and build, plant, rule, become somebody—they are crying . . . protesting, etc. and weeping "How Zion and Jerusalem sit in solitude!" But how can crying help? What are Rabbi Asher Ginsberg's lamentations worth? If he were to wail with all our Russian brothers from today till tomorrow and the day after, for a thousand tomorrows, and if we were to sit on the floor for another ten thousand Tisha b'Avs, would that save the miserable people? There is a good opportunity now to obtain some kind of "Jewish center" somewhere in the world, which we shall obtain. We will not stop trying to obtain the land of our inheritance, Zion and Jerusalem, at long last. But it would be foolish, childish, primitive, ignorant, and blindly fanatical to reject and oppose the acquisition of a Jewish state.[24]

Yudelovich's letter to Lubman matches Zemach's description of his views at the meeting in Rishon Lezion. It seems that this letter reflects the support of a majority of the colonists for Herzl's political line. A similar view can be found in a letter sent from Rishon Lezion to the editor of *Hashkafah*, containing further evidence of the extent of that settlement's support for the Uganda plan. A notice published in that paper under the heading "Rishon Lezion" stated that the official bulletin of the Zionist Organization, *Die Welt*, had published erroneous information on the victory of Zionei Zion over their Ugandist rivals in Palestine and "that most of the Zionists in the settlements of Rishon Lezion and Gedera, especially the farmers there, are Zionists who belong to the Vilna faction." The writer stressed that the real situation was completely different: "As a person who has been in Rishon Lezion this entire time and is quite familiar with the Zionist position here in this settlement, I wish to inform my 'colleague' that his words are not at all true." He implies that the "220 dues-paying members of the Ein Hakoré association are all political Zionists of the faction of Professor Mandelstamm and Rabbi Reines, in other words, supporters of the Kiev program. Their manifesto is public knowledge, and one of its section clearly states 'work in an autonomous territory wherever it may be.'"25

In Gedera, too, the real situation differed from what was described in *Die Welt*, even though the writer was not present at the meeting. Most of the members of the Zionist Committee in Gedera sent an "authorization to the Zionists of Rishon Lezion" asking "to be included in the cost of sending off a delegate. And this means that, like most of the Rishon Zionists, most of the Gedera Zionists are political Zionists."26

Another testimony that demonstrates the majority of the colonists' support for the Uganda plan and corroborates the report in *Hashkafah* is that of teacher Yosef Markovsky, Ussishkin's right-hand man in Palestine and one of the opponents of the Uganda plan. Like Zemach, Markovsky had high expectations of the country's inhabitants when he visited. Shortly after he arrived, he began touring the country to meet the people and get an impression of its scenery. His exchange of letters with Ussishkin describes his first impressions and provides a fascinating testimonial not only of the settlers' attitude toward the Uganda plan but also of his first encounter with the country. "In spite of my strong desire to write you, I could not do so until now," Markovsky wrote to Ussishkin. "The great happiness—being in the Land of Israel—which had suddenly fallen to my lot confused me so much that time after time I found myself unable to sit down at my desk and write." After his initial excitement had ebbed, Markovsky was exposed to the prosaic everyday routine in Palestine.

> After I had become somewhat accustomed to my new situation and began to contemplate those already so fortunate, those who had always seemed to me like heavenly angels—the inhabitants of the Land of Israel—my eyes glazed over at what I saw. Instead of happy people, I found people who saw themselves as miserable, and instead of heavenly angels I met grumblers, quarrel-mongers, protesters, people for whom it is no exaggeration to say that the very word "Zion" strikes them with horror. Imagine what impression I received from the meeting in Rishon Lezion, when only five [sic] of the thirty-six members who came to the meeting were in agreement with me: Mr. Barzilai of Jaffa, Mr. Papirmeister from Rishon, Leibovitch and Hazanov from Gedera, while almost all the rest were opposed to Zionism in Palestine. They

heartily hate the Zionist Organization, which in their hands seems to be a weapon to fight against our faithful Zionists, who are like a bone in their throats. There are some people here who expressed their wonder that I could wish to leave a land of milk and honey and come to a land that devours its inhabitants; they look at me as a crazy dreamer, they expect me also to change my views after I become a citizen in the country, and some say that I am a missionary sent by Ussishkin to spread his views here. And I shake my head and say: "Woe to me that I have regarded you as my beloved brothers! How low you have fallen, that you cannot even appreciate your situation nor sense your good fortune!"[27]

Markovsky's disappointment with the colonists was similar to Zemach's. He regarded them as an embittered community of complainers, whose love for the country was so limited that it weakened the spirit of newcomers. They openly expressed their hatred for Ussishkin and saw Markovsky as a missionary who wanted to disseminate his views. They cooled his enthusiasm with the same argument they made to Shlomo Zemach: that it was only a matter of time until he, too, would be burdened by doubts about the Zionist enterprise. Markovsky received a teaching position in Be'er Tuvia (Kastina), and only two months after his arrival, he requested permission to leave the settlement and teach at a girls' school in Jaffa. Life in the settlement became unbearable for him and his family. It seems that the colonists' prophecies were quickly realized. "I am sorry to upset you with this letter: My situation in the Land of Israel has changed, but not for the better," he wrote to Ussishkin.

> My soul is not dismayed, God forbid, with the country and my work. No! The country and my work in it are still dear to me, as are its troubles, which have crept up on me and my family, but for their sake, I must leave my position in Kastina at the beginning of next year. . . . For two months, we have been suffering from various illnesses, such as scabs on the skin, which is called *charara* (rash), malaria, and eye disease. . . . It is now three weeks since one of my daughters contracted a dangerous disease of the eyes and ever since she became ill, her eyes have been closed and she

cannot open them. We have been forced to take her to Jaffa, where my wife is staying with her.[28]

At the end of his letter, Markovsky concluded, "Ben Yehuda has gone crazy: In the articles in his rag in support of Uganda and describing the future of the Jews there, he says: 'They can even speak Hebrew there if they wish.' I will be responding to his views in the coming days, and will ask him not to disseminate them any more."[29] Markovsky left Be'er Tuvia and became a teacher in Jaffa, where he realized the extent of the opposition to Ussishkin and Zionei Zion on the eve of the Seventh Zionist Congress in Basel.

> Zionism is now banned in the Land of Israel, and this is purely a result of slander. About six weeks ago, someone sent sections of "our program" to the Pasha, denounced the Congress, the teachers' organization, and even Mr. Dizenhoff for coming here as an agent of "salvation," and the denunciations are continuing. ... And who gave them the power to denounce? Is it not the rotten element here that has destroyed the atmosphere and given birth to all kinds of vermin and noxious creatures: Territorialists, denouncers, etc.? ... And our united forces are weak and worthless against the deadly force that prevails in the country.[30]

Markovsky's description suggests that in the days preceding the Seventh Zionist Congress, a tense atmosphere prevailed in Palestine, teeming with mutual accusations. The Uganda supporters denounced their opponents and tried to have them arrested by the Turkish authorities. Ben Yehuda reported in *Hashkafah* that a meeting held by the Zionists in Jerusalem boiled over into verbal violence and almost ended in fist fights between the supporters and opponents of the Uganda plan: "In one moment, the emotions took hold on either side and impolite words were spoken—we almost had a totally 'parliamentary' argument like those in Vienna and Paris. But good men intervened and matters did not come to a head. I admit that in such matters, I join those who say 'do not follow their laws.' We have a lot more to learn about cultured behavior, and we should leave the custom of settling arguments by blows to them for now."[31] In the same article he also reported a recent act of denunciation that "regarded the Palestine Federation." Ben Yehuda condemned the act and noted that "whoever did this has done a despicable deed and is an informer.... This is a contemptible act that cannot be excused or justified."[32] Such descriptions greatly resembled those in the letter Borochov sent to Ussishkin, in which he described the violence in the Odessa synagogue between Zionists and Territorialists. The stormy debates led Markovsky to the conclusion that the Zionei Zion were a minority in Palestine and were not sufficiently united in the struggle against their opponents.

Moshe Smilansky also blamed his farmer friends for their weak pioneering spirit and their support of the territorialist idea. In 1905 he published a detailed, comprehensive article in *Hashiloah* on the situation in the renewed Yishuv in Palestine. He gave an extensive description of the lives of the vineyard growers, the colonists, and the workers and focused on their economic difficulties, the range of their agricultural products, their settlement in relation to the ICA, and their attitude toward the hired laborers who worked for them. One of the sections of the article was devoted to spiritual life in the settlements: "If the past year was difficult materially, it was far more difficult spiritually," Smilansky wrote.[33] One of the expressions of the weakness of spirit that Smilansky noted in his article was the spreading of the territorialist idea throughout the settler society: "In no other country has the Territorialist idea found so many adherents—in proportion, of course, to the number of Jews living in the country—as it has in Palestine." According to him, the Palestine Ugandists are no different from their colleagues in Eastern Europe, and both of them tend to treat "the defects of our country not through deep words of sorrow or a desire to mend, but through gleeful gloating over their 'enemies' and a desire to destroy."[34] The main reason for the increasing strength of the Ugandist idea, Smilansky maintained, was the absence of nationalistic emotions among the farmers in Palestine. If there had been such emotions among them, "Under no circumstances would a farmer who loved his land and was inherently bound to it be in favor of Uganda; he would regard it as a slap in the face of everything he held dear. In no way would a nationalistic, normal, healthy person born in the country and attached to it in such a way that he would never be able to part with it support a new country that would be created at his own country's expense."[35]

Another example of the hatred felt by certain groups in the Yishuv toward Ussishkin and his struggle against the Uganda plan was the *gabbai* (treasurer) of the Jaffa synagogue, Yaakov Zvi Zisselman. After the Kharkov conference, Zisselman expressed full confidence, on behalf of his congregants, in the "director, agent and founder" of the Zionist Organization "exalted above the people, pre-eminent among ten thousand, the rock of divine providence, may his Torah enlighten us, who stands before kings, a lover and faithful brother to the Jews and the Land of Israel, may it be rebuilt—his Excellency, Dr. Herzl." On the other hand, the *gabbai* described Ussishkin as a person who walks "in the path of Jeroboam son of Nabat, who led Israel astray from the House of David," a faithful pupil "who follows the words of his well-known master Agag of Odessa [Ahad Ha'am], the reformer— that is, the destroyer, the founder and high priest of the corrupt Bnei Moshe Society, who came up to the Land of Israel, may it be built and established, with those who do his will to undermine by their schemes and manipulations."[36]

These examples demonstrate that the Uganda controversy did not bypass Palestine and prompted a struggle there akin to that in Eastern Europe, as described in Chapter 1. Although the argument in principle centered on the place of the Land of Israel in Zionist ideology, it seems that large sections of the Yishuv did not support Ussishkin and his followers. The testimonies of Zemach, Yudelovich, Markovsky, Smilansky, and Zisselman provide a fairly reliable picture of a Yishuv divided into two polarized camps.

One of the prominent Yishuv personalities who led the fight for Uganda and against Ussishkin was Eliezer Ben Yehuda, a newspaper editor and a leader of the campaign to revive the Hebrew language. He devoted extensive space to the controversy in his paper and did not hesitate to express his adamant views in public.

## ELIEZER BEN YEHUDA AND THE UGANDA PLAN

Historians have already discussed Eliezer Ben Yehuda and his territorialist views. In the 1960s Getzel Kressel published "Eliezer Ben Yehuda and the Uganda Plan: Eighty Years from the Beginning of Ben Yehuda's Journalistic Career and Sixty Years Since the Uganda

Eliezer Ben Yehuda.

Controversy." In the early 1970s, Kressel published another, shorter article, "Eliezer Ben Yehuda's Uganda Vision."[37] Historian Yosef Lang wrote a doctoral dissertation on the positions and attitudes of Ben Yehuda's journalistic writings concerning the Yishuv and the national movement from 1885 to 1915. Naturally, the Uganda controversy received broad coverage in his research. Lang also refers to this issue in detail in his comprehensive and erudite biography of Ben Yehuda.[38]

Kressel's and Lang's work indicate that Ben Yehuda was one of the prominent supporters of the Uganda plan and the territorialist idea. His support was both active and public. He published many articles

## CHAPTER 4

on the subject in his newspaper and fiercely attacked the naysayers. Sharp denunciations were leveled at Ben Yehuda for his promotion of the controversial plan, but he responded scathingly to his castigators and criticized their claims.[39] Like many other figures in Palestine at that time, Ben Yehuda was a political Zionist, faithful to Herzl's policy, and felt great admiration and esteem for Israel Zangwill. In the spring of 1897 Zangwill visited Palestine on a tour to express the identification of Western European Jewry with the Jewish inhabitants of the country. On his visit Zangwill met his elderly father, Moshe Zangwill, who was then living in Jerusalem. He also stayed as a guest in Ben Yehuda's home.[40] From this meeting a strong friendship grew between the Zangwills and Hemda and Eliezer Ben Yehuda, which lasted for many long years. In the summer of 1898 the Ben Yehudas sailed from Palestine to Europe to allow Hemda to recover from a bout of malaria. In Paris they met Max Nordau and Israel Zangwill, who were passing through on their way home from Italy. They met again in London: "While we were still in Paris, Zangwill invited us to dinner at his home on our first Sunday in London," wrote Hemda Ben Yehuda in her memoirs.

> Zangwill was in a mood of mockery, even more than all the characters he described in *The Ghetto* and the *King of the Beggars*, and he made us laugh so much that just when we managed to take a mouthful we would burst into laughter, while he ate undisturbed.... He had a large library, and when we entered it to drink a cup of coffee, he went up on a ladder and took down a small book to show me. It was the Alharizi that I had given him as a memento when he was in Jerusalem. Then he gave us an autographed photograph of himself.[41]

Ben Yehuda's fervent support of the Uganda plan was a product of his admiration for Herzl and his meetings with the leaders of the political Zionist stream in the Zionist Organization (Nordau and Zangwill). His articles in favor of Uganda expressed the views of a sizable share of the Jews in Palestine. Moreover, his statements were an inseparable part of the controversy that swept through the entire Zionist Organization. For those who supported the Uganda plan, in Palestine and particularly in

Eastern Europe, Ben Yehuda was a source of pride, mainly as a symbol and testament to the fact that Territorialism was not a deviation from the Zionist idea. *Hashkafah* identified with this line of thought and with territorialist thinking more than any other Jewish paper published in or outside Palestine. Everything published in this paper was meant to strengthen the yea-sayers and change public opinion. A short while after the Sixth Zionist Congress, *Hashkafah* established a regular column called "The Jewish State," in which Ben Yehuda expounded on his Ugandist views, debated his rivals, and provided various kinds of information about the controversy. A collection of his articles was later published in *The Jewish State: Various Essays on the East Africa Proposal*, which appeared in early 1905 and reflected the positions of the supporters of the Uganda plan in general and, later, of Territorialism in particular. In his polished critical style Ben Yehuda attacked the plan's opponents and encouraged its supporters.

*The Jewish State* was published in Warsaw—a territorialist stronghold—by the Medina publishing house, which published extensive literature on Territorialism. The book became an integral part of the territorialist propaganda literature. Noah Finkelstein, chairman of the Territorialist Committee in Warsaw, wrote to Ben Yehuda that "in the propaganda for the dissemination of our idea, your book *The Jewish State* has made a good impression on readers, who regard it as words from a warm heart, from a man who seeks the truth in the revival of his people, who has lived in the land of our forefathers all his life and preaches from there the idea of national freedom, of obtaining a land anywhere that will be only for ourselves. We wish to express our deepest thanks to you for your spiritual participation in our national work."[42] Ben Yehuda's claims in *The Jewish State* did not differ from those of Yehuda Hazan in his *Jewish Authors and Territorialism* or those mentioned in *Konstitutsyon un teritoryalismus*.[43] Both works were published by the same publisher and appeared at about the same time as Ben Yehuda's. All three were distributed among the territorialist activists throughout the Pale of Settlement and became valuable propaganda material.

A thorough reading of *The Jewish State* shows that Ben Yehuda had adopted the principles of territorialist thought, described in the first and third chapters of the book, and used the same terminology that was characteristic of the ITO activists after the Seventh Zionist Congress.

Their slogan, "A land for a people, not a people for a land," was the central thesis of his book. He stressed that "the people, not the land, were primary." Just as the Zionists believed that the Jewish people could "return to life" in the Land of Israel, so "we too" are allowed to believe "that the people could—with difficulty, with great difficulty, but they could—create a land for itself anywhere and live there!"[44] Further on, Ben Yehuda underscores this issue: "It would be best if the people could be in the land, but if they cannot, if there is any doubt about that possibility, we shall for the present establish the people in some territory, anywhere, as long as it belongs to the people, to preclude the danger that threatens the people!"[45]

Another aspect that Ben Yehuda emphasized in his book, which also corresponded with the territorialist line of thought, was the increasing suffering of the Jews of Eastern Europe and the immediate solution that should be provided for them: "In another twenty years, another ten, perhaps even five, there will not be a single nation available on earth where our wandering people can lay its head."[46] Therefore it is necessary to quickly accept the government of England's proposal, because any hesitation could lead it to change its mind about the original plan. The element of time, which was the central focus of the territorialist argument, was given special attention in Ben Yehuda's book. He believed that it was forbidden to delay the establishment of a Jewish state; postponement of the plan was an existential danger for the survival of the Jewish people. "If we do not unite all our forces so that this very difficult endeavor can succeed, we will be the enemies of our own people, and their blood will be upon our heads."[47]

As other Territorialists had done before him, Ben Yehuda directed his attack on the opponents of the Uganda plan, primarily against Ussishkin and Nahum Sokolow, the editor of *Hazefirah*. He blamed Ussishkin for the split in the Zionist movement and for its contemptuous attitude toward the nations of the world. In his view Ussishkin's public declaration that he did not accept the majority's decision turned the Sixth Zionist Congress in Basel into "a convention of synagogue wardens from Lithuanian towns, where the pious do not pay too much attention to the decisions of the meeting." Two-thirds of the congress delegates supported Herzl's plan, and therefore any attempt to contravene the decision could bring disgrace on the Zionist Organization. Then "all the world would know what a Jewish Congress was, how worthy the Jews are of being a partner in negotiations, and the value and importance of the decisions made by their great assemblies!"[48] Ben Yehuda's criticism of Sokolow was that he did not properly understand the situation. He rejected the *Hazefirah* editor's analogy between the prospective failure of settlement in East Africa and the loss of the opportunity to settle in Argentina or Canada. The main difference between them was that the British proposal allowed the Jews to set up an independent state in a territory where they could be the majority in every respect. On the other hand, Baron Hirsch never intended "to set up a Jewish state," and therefore the settlements of Jews in Argentina did not differ "at all from the Jewish communities in the Pale of Settlement."[49]

But it seems that the main force of the book was not in its arguments for or against Uganda but in the identity of the writer: a native of the country and an integral part of the Yishuv in Palestine. The expression of support for Herzl and the East Africa plan by a famous philologist and newspaper editor who had lived in the Land of Israel for almost a generation strengthened the political Zionist camp and provided evidence that Ugandists were the real Zionists. Ben Yehuda was aware of his status and stressed it in his book: "Twenty-five years ago, when your thoughts were as far away from the Land of Israel as east is from west, when even an intellectual like Ahad Ha'am was satisfied with nationalism in the Diaspora, I issued the first call for territorial nationalism.... Twelve years ago, when the idea of the revival of the spoken language was strange to all of you, I issued the first call. And I actually began to speak the language, both in school and in my home."[50]

Ben Yehuda was among the first to recognize the importance of immigrating to Palestine in the 1880s and the need to revive the Hebrew language in order to carry out the Zionist enterprise, and thus he must also have been right about the Uganda plan. Ben Yehuda believed that if he had been right in the past, he was right now too. He therefore believed that the Zionists should accept the establishment of a Jewish state in East Africa. He rejected the opposing argument that the established state would not have a Jewish character and that its inhabitants would speak English. The character of the Jewish state would be determined not by its location but by the content that the Zionists poured into it. For that reason, Ben Yehuda wanted to make Hebrew central to the formation of the national identity. "The language gives every population its personal

## CHAPTER 4

form and makes it an entity in itself, with a special character and a special quality of its own." So long as the people speak their own language, they will own the land on which they live: "If we wish it, the new population in the barren new country, where no language dominates as yet, will speak its own language, a language which will shape it into a Hebrew population, and the state into a Jewish state. We can only do this if we want and desire it. We will not encounter any outside obstacle on our way."[51] Ben Yehuda did not see any contradiction between his philological pursuits and his support for the Uganda plan. The Hebrew language, he claimed, could be revived both in Jerusalem and in Guas Ngishu. In his view the establishment of a Jewish state in East Africa would not harm his efforts to revive Hebrew. On the contrary, it would help the language take root and spread among wider groups of the Jewish people. "The language we yearn for can exist" only in areas with a Jewish majority. In the schools, the villages, the cities, and "even in the higher academies of learning, we will have the authority to make Hebrew the main language, the language of study, . . . the official language."[52]

Ben Yehuda's uncompromising struggle against the naysayers frustrated his opponents. They found it difficult to understand how such a prominent and central personality in the Zionist experience in Palestine could hold a worldview that was contrary to Zionist ideology. Yosef Lang's biography of Ben Yehuda describes how the philologist was shunned and many people stopped visiting his home. The anger toward him was expressed in the boycott of the party organized by Hemda Ben Yehuda for her husband on the twenty-fifth anniversary of his first article, "She'elah nikhbadah" (A Weighty Question). His opponents claimed that he was one-sided and was exploiting his newspaper to fight Zionei Zion. Yehoshua Barzilai was even harsher: Given Ben Yehuda's status as a resident of the country, his support of the Uganda plan was unnatural and even sick.[53]

Ben Yehuda's enthusiastic support for the Uganda plan and territorialist outlook also dismayed historians and researchers of the Yishuv. Getzel Kressel wondered about "the surprising, dare we say, the shameful phenomenon of veteran members of the Yishuv, glorified pioneers in their various fields of activity, who supported the Uganda idea and were enthusiastic about it."[54] Yosef Lang, whose writings were less judgmental than Kressel's, also regarded Ben Yehuda's views as a deviation from the general Zionist line of the Yishuv and his struggle for Uganda as a retreat (temporarily) from his zeal for the Hebrew language.[55] I believe that these claims are disconnected from the historical context of the territorialist discussion and even anachronistic.

It seems to me that Ben Yehuda's support for the Uganda plan was not incompatible with his Zionism; he concurred with the position of many Zionists that the people's welfare preceded the good of the land. The Ugandists in Palestine (and later the Territorialists) saw themselves at the center of the Zionist consensus, not on its margins. From their viewpoint it was the Zionei Zion who were taking the Zionist movement into areas where it did not belong, and the fate of their persecuted brethren in Eastern Europe was their responsibility and that of political Zionism. Ben Yehuda expressed his concern for the welfare of Russian Jewry and his desire to find them a solution "here and now" even before the Uganda controversy began. His support was not a product of blind admiration for Herzl but of his worldview that there was no other immediate way to solve the Jewish problem. He had already expressed this outlook in his reaction to the Kishinev pogrom and the way he reviewed it for readers of his newspaper. He described the acts of murder and malevolent abuse almost obsessively and did not spare the horrifying and gruesome descriptions published in the world press.

> The following list of brutalities was published in the daily *Novosti*: (1) Sarah Fanarosh had two nails inserted in her nostrils that went through her brain. She died. (2) The hands and legs of Lis who was found at the corner of Seimshana and Gastina Streets were broken off. (3) Harotin had his lips cut and then they tore out his tongue with tongs, together with his throat. (4) Zeltzer was found in the new market with his ear cut off and twelve wounds in his head. This unfortunate person lost his mind and is now being treated at the hospital. (5) At the end of Svitashna and Seina Streets, they took a pregnant woman, placed her on a chair, and beat her stomach with a wooden rod; on Kirawaska St., they threw small children from the second floor. Besides this, we know of many cases of young girls being raped and dying in the arms of their tormentors; a child was also found torn in two.[56]

## CHAPTER 4

Ben Yehuda did not limit himself to a description of the murderous acts and the number of murdered victims. He also provided the victims' names and did not hold back in describing the cruel ways in which they were murdered. His descriptions recall Moshe Rosenblatt's letters to Zangwill at the height of the pogroms in Kiev, in October–November 1905. The abhorrent acts that Ben Yehuda described so clearly in his reports weighed on him and led him to gravitate toward the territorialist solution, which began to take shape after the Kishinev pogrom. By the time he wrote "Nehamateinu be-onyenu" (Our Consolation in Our Affliction), he had begun thinking about the idea of a land of refuge for the Jewish people, wherever one could be found.

> Ten million people choosing a life of shame and disgrace! And what do we say about it? What cause do we have for screaming at anyone but ourselves? . . . Only here does the heart tremble and the soul feel. Our brothers everywhere are coming to the realization that we need a niche—a niche that will be ours, wherever it may be found! And this recognition cries out and pierces every heart, even those that are armored with steel plates from the Krupp munitions factories, which have been split open by the axes of the murderers in Kishinev. This is our consolation in our affliction![57]

The niche that Ben Yehuda sought was Brenner's cave in the "Long Letter" and the mountains of darkness and the coal and salt mines that Rosenblatt wrote about.[58] Half a year later, Ben Yehuda expressed a similar position when the pogroms broke out in Homel: "And even more than the deeds in Kishinev, the recent actions convey, in a language that can be no clearer or more explicit, that 'my sons will find no respite among the nations,' and that they have no hope and salvation as long as they are aliens living among others, but only as citizens in their own state, wherever and whatever this state may now be!"[59] It is not surprising, therefore, that when Herzl publicized the British proposal for Jewish settlement in East Africa, Ben Yehuda supported it fervently and joined the territorialist camp in its campaign against the Zionei Zion. This was not a struggle between those who loved the Land of Israel and those who hated it but between those who sought an immediate solution to the rapidly growing distress in Eastern Europe and those who thought that only in the Land of Israel could Zionism achieve its ultimate goals and establish a state for the Jewish people.

## TERRITORIALISM IN PALESTINE

Zionist historiographers, both early and late, have hardly studied the popularity of the territorialist idea in the years following the Seventh Zionist Congress. The support given to the Uganda plan by the colonists and Eliezer Ben Yehuda is portrayed as a momentary stumble and lapse of common sense. From the moment the Uganda proposal was removed from the Zionist agenda, the Ugandists acceded to the majority decision and accepted the congress's resolution. Moreover, there is no evidence or proof that the Ugandists renounced the Land of Israel, except for the colonists' position in the Herzl-Ussishkin argument. Their opposition to the idea of the Palestine Federation and the way Ussishkin was conducting his struggle generated antagonism toward Zionei Zion, which was not necessarily motivated by ideological considerations.[60]

However, the support that the territorialist idea enjoyed in Palestine did not disappear after the Seventh Zionist Congress. Moreover, many were in favor of the new organization and Zangwill. This was not support for a "safe haven for the night" for the Jewish people but an ideological position that the Land of Israel was not the only existing territorial solution. Although the territorialist idea suffered a political defeat at the Seventh Zionist Congress, hope that a land would be found for Jews to settle en masse was still strong. Ben Yehuda expressed this feeling of alternating hope and despair in "The Sum Total," which he published after the Seventh Zionist Congress: "Territorialism fell because there is no land, and there is no land because there is no Herzl. The Zionei Zion won not in Basel, but in Kharkov!" But, he added, it would be possible to recreate Territorialism if another land could be found: "If Zangwill and his colleagues searched for and found a land that meets the requirements—in that hour, Territorialism would be born anew—real, Territorialism, not one that is abstract, theoretical, and impotent."[61]

Indeed, shortly after the establishment of the ITO, letters of congratulation and support for Zangwill and the ITO were sent out. At the beginning of September 1905, one month after the ITO was established, the Mizrachi representative in Palestine, Secretary Yitzhak Moshe

Weinberg, sent Zangwill a letter of support: "We, the committee members of the Shlomei Emunei Israel Association inform your Honor that our association of a hundred and twenty members has decided to take the same position as yours, because this was also the position of our leader Dr. Herzl, may his memory be a blessing. We protest with all our strength against the Seventh Congress that has betrayed the Basel Program and turned into the cult of Zionei Zion, who are all talk and no action."[62] The letter reflected only the position of the members of the Mizrachi Party in Palestine and certainly not that of Rabbi Reines, who had, as noted, given Zangwill his blessing but refused to officially join the ITO. It can be assumed that the letter was sent before the rabbi's followers heard about his basic stance. The representative of the association urged Zangwill to send them territorialist publications so that "we can distribute them among the Zionists, who nearly all hold the same position as your Honor."[63]

One month later, Weinberg wrote a similar letter to the president of the ITO: "We hereby congratulate you and hope you will succeed in the path you are taking." He told Zangwill that the number of members in the association was rising and that the territorialist idea was taking root in the country: "I can inform your Honor that we have acquired many members.... Almost all the Zionists in our city agree with you that we cannot acquire the Land of Israel in any way." Weinberg asked Zangwill to write a letter to the inhabitants of the country "to stir the people into action" and asked him to send them the letter "so that we can print thousands of copies here to be sent to all the cities in the Holy Land."[64]

But the broadest expression of support for the ITO in the Yishuv in the post-Ugandist period seems to be the manifesto that the Center of Territorial Associations in Palestine and Syria sent to Zangwill shortly before the Brussels conference. Upon the ITO's establishment in August 1905, a decision was made to set up branches throughout the Jewish world to promulgate territorialist doctrine. The activists had to act vigorously to receive legal permission from the Russian government to embark on the practical work of attracting followers. The pogroms that broke out in the months after the Seventh Zionist Congress deepened the hold of Territorialism in the Jewish street around the world, and a broad substantial foundation was being laid in Eastern Europe. Many of the Jews in Russia turned to Zangwill and asked him to expedite the process of finding a suitable territory. In their letters they described their fears of the surrounding population, their lack of security, and, most of all, their desire to live a peaceful, secure life in their own land.

The Zionist movement, which was afraid that the territorialist idea would catch fire, initiated an all-Jewish conference in Brussels in an attempt to propose solutions to the crisis. Many towns in the Pale of Settlement sent Zangwill manifestos and asked him to participate in the conference and promote the aims of the recently established organization. The territorialist branch in Palestine also sent a manifesto to the ITO president and urged him to join the conference. The letter was sent by the secretary of the Center of Territorial Associations in Palestine and Syria in Jerusalem, Haim Arieh Zuta, and was signed by 294 residents of the Yishuv. The Center of Territorial Associations in Palestine and Syria had developed from the Jerusalem-based Eretz Israel Association, whose members were prominent Ugandists. After a majority of the delegates to the Seventh Zionist Congress voted to reject the East Africa plan, the Ugandists in Palestine established a national center to represent the position of all its members. Their attempt to unite into a central committee was no different from the successful attempt in March 1902 to establish the Committee of United Zionist Associations in Palestine in Rishon Lezion. This was a real change in the work methods of the Territorialists in Palestine. Eretz Israel, the Jerusalem Zionist association, coordinated their activities and functioned under the title "the Center of National Associations." Its membership consisted of members of the local Zionist associations, and it was they who signed the following manifesto:

> Honored Sir! We, the undersigned, ask you to take part in the gathering in Brussels in the name of all the national associations in general, and in the name of our Eretz Israel association in particular. The terrible situation that the Jewish people are in is the truest sign that the idea of a "Jewish state" is the only solution to the "Jewish question"—and that this solution should be considered, especially by all those who are planning ways to help our oppressed people. As long as a truly safe refuge for our people—an autonomous state—is not found, we cannot be certain that the events in Russia will not be repeated in other countries, where our people are living in large numbers and being forced to participate in public life and in the ambitions of various political

parties. Only a Jewish state, wherever it may be can give refuge to the Jewish people, to their body, soul and spirit. Therefore, we beg you, Sir, as the head of the national organization: Be the messenger of the House of Israel in the gathering of the leaders of the people in Brussels, and announce, together with all who truly love our people, in the name of all the national associations and the thousands of those who are groaning under their oppression, that the eyes of Israel are lifted towards the realization of the idea of the Jewish state. In action, our people will find rest from persecution; thus, the main question to be discussed by all who love our people and truly desire its existence is how to implement this idea. With feelings of esteem and the blessings of the people.[65]

The content and the presentation of arguments in the manifesto indicate that many members of the Yishuv continued to hold territorialist positions. They authorized Zangwill to represent them at the conference and to promote the idea of a Jewish state in the name of the Jewish inhabitants of Palestine. The terminology in the letter is clearly territorialist—"autonomy," "Jewish state," "the only solution to the Jewish question"—as is its overemphasis on Jewish suffering to demonstrate the tremendous anguish and the need for an immediate solution. Compared with similar manifestos sent from Eastern Europe, the number of signatories was large. The territorialist chapter in Palestine managed to collect more signatures than any of the branches in tsarist Russia. In Palestine 294 people signed the manifesto, whereas the average number of signatories in Britchani, Yednitsi, Skirani, Rashkonvki, Novoselitsa, and old Oschitsa was 220.[66] This figure is especially interesting because there were no pogroms in Palestine and the existential crisis was not a part of daily life there. Nonetheless, a fairly large group of Territorialists arose there.

The names of the signatories also show the breadth and diversity of the sectors in Palestine society who supported Zangwill. The initiator of the manifesto was the Eretz Israel Association secretary, Haim Arieh Zuta, who came to Palestine in 1904 and was appointed a teacher in a girls' school in Jaffa. He was well-known as a notable pedagogue and was invited to teach at the Lemel School in Jerusalem. He published many articles, which were later compiled and published as the *Writings of H. A.*

# THE TERRITORIALIST MOVEMENT IN PALESTINE

*Zuta*. It should be noted that in neither his memoirs, *Bereishit darki* (My Early Path), nor his book, *Darkhei ha-limmud shel ha-tanakh* (Methods of Bible Study), did Zuta mention his activities as a Territorialist and Ugandist in Palestine. Other signatories include Hemda Ben Yehuda (but not her husband, Eliezer); Mordechai Salomon, son of Yoel Moshe Salomon; Yisrael Halevi Teller, a Hebrew teacher in Rehovot; zoologist Yisrael Aharoni, the principal of the Rehovot school, founder of the colony's first kindergarten, and a teacher in Rishon Lezion; Yaakov Goldman, secretary of the Ashkenazic community in Jaffa, one of the founders of Shaarei Zion, the city library, and a delegate to the Palestine Assembly, which met in Zichron Yaakov; chemist Yosef Goldberg, one of the first members of the Ahva association in Jerusalem and Jaffa; farmer Menahem Cohen of Be'er Tuvia and later of Rishon Lezion; Yitzhak Cohen, secretary of the Bnai Brith Shaar Zion lodge in Jaffa, the chief secretary of the main office of Bnei Moshe, and principal and teacher at the Rehovot school; Shlomo Haim (Alter) Shapira Bernstein, a guard in the settlement of Ekron (Mazkeret Batya); the physician Yisrael Meir Wallenstein; and merchant Aharon Diskin, who purchased plots of land and built houses on Yehuda Halevi Street in Tel Aviv.[67]

Right before the Jewish New Year 5667 (September 1906), nine months after the Brussels conference, fifty residents of the Yishuv, including David Yudelovich and Pesah Yafo, sent a letter of new year's greetings to the ITO president. The letter was written in a flowery style, praising the territorialist organization and its president, and wishing for him (and for the Jewish people) that the designated land would be found in the coming year.[68]

The letters of support for Zangwill, the Brussels manifesto, and the new year's letter demonstrate that even after the Seventh Zionist Congress, there was considerable support in Palestine for the territorialist idea. This was not a form of Ugandism, which saw East Africa as a refuge for the night, but a comprehensive worldview that supported the goals of the ITO and tried to advance the territorialist agenda in the Jewish world as a whole and particularly in Palestine.

As time passed and Zangwill trudged through the mud of diplomacy, support for the ITO began to wane, although there was still evidence of local adherents. In September 1911, for example, Avigdor Keleter, a resident of Jerusalem, sent Zangwill a letter on behalf of the association

## CHAPTER 4

he directed. The letter described the problem of Jewish labor in Palestine in somber terms, explaining that the colonists did not employ Jews to work in their fields, preferring to hire Arabs, who were cheaper and more obedient. The members of his association were not interested in living in the city and depending on the "schnorrer kind of distribution money." Thus they wanted to leave the country and settle wherever Zangwill believed a Jewish state could be established. At first, they suggested settling in Mesopotamia, but after Zangwill made it clear that the plan for settlement there would not be carried out, they asked him to let them immigrate to the United States as part of the Galveston plan.[69]

It is difficult to assess the range of activities of the Committee of National Associations and the other territorialist groups in Palestine. It can be assumed that their activities from the Seventh Zionist Congress to World War I were minimal and insignificant on the Palestine scene. Zangwill was otherwise occupied with trying to find a suitable country, and the Territorialists in Palestine found it difficult to determine a political agenda in his absence. Ben Yehuda's assertion after the Seventh Zionist Congress that "Territorialism fell because there was no land" proved true, and it highlighted the main source of the ITO's weakness. Even the Territorialists in Eastern Europe faced a similar problem, but, as we will see in Chapter 5, unlike Territorialists in Palestine, they invested time in organizing emigration and recruiting people for the Galveston plan, which began to take shape in 1906. These activities gave moral justification to their venture, but even this, it seemed, was insufficient. Without a territory it was just a matter of time until the territorialist idea would fade away and the territorialist activists would find themselves walking down a dead-end road.

~

The Uganda controversy, which tore apart the Jewish world, did not bypass Palestine. Yishuv society was divided between supporters and opponents of the plan, as was Jewish society in Eastern Europe. The lack of documentation makes it difficult to assess the size of the Ugandist camp, the range of its activities, and whether it outnumbered its rivals, Zionei Zion. But it is absolutely clear that the Ugandists (and later the Territorialists) of Palestine were not a marginal phenomenon and that well-known public figures openly supported the Uganda plan and later the ITO. Palestine was an interesting test case for an understanding of the Ugandist and territorialist idea, and it embodied all the elements of the controversy, as we saw in Eastern Europe, and perhaps did so even more strongly.

However, it appears that those in Palestine who supported Uganda and the ITO had a unique and unusual role to play. After all, they were veteran Zionists, living in the Land of Israel, who had realized their ideal by settling there. If the "local elite," as represented by the smallholders in the colonies and Eliezer Ben Yehuda, thought it necessary to set up a Jewish state outside Palestine, then perhaps the territorialist idea had real merit and was feasible. Their support for Uganda and the ITO had greater moral and ethical force than the support of the Territorialists in Eastern Europe, and their tenacious positions, especially Ben Yehuda's, were articulated in the Jewish Eastern European press.

One of the interesting and challenging questions that arises from the discussion in this chapter is how the Zionists of Palestine could support the territorialist idea and abandon the dream that had brought them to the Land of Israel. The consensus in the literature is that twenty years of living in Palestine left their mark on the pioneers of the First Aliyah. These daydreaming, idealistic farmers had become more sober and realistic. The daily hardships of their strenuous and exhausting labor, the patronizing attitude of the baron's officials, the harsh attitude of the ICA, and the criticism leveled against them by the members of the Second Aliyah and by high-ranking figures of the Hibbat Zion movement made them embittered, despondent, and devoid of ideological vision. But this argument is unconvincing and does the colonists an injustice. Many of the supporters of the Uganda plan and Territorialism in Palestine were public activists who were far from despondent. David Yudelovich, for example, was a teacher and educator who taught Hebrew in the kindergarten and school in Rishon Lezion, and there were other pedagogues like him, such as Yisrael Halevi Teller and Haim Zuta. Nor could Eliezer or Hemda Ben Yehuda be considered despondent. Their support of Territorialism had no connection with their experience of life in Palestine. Rather, it was a product of their concern for the persecuted and humiliated Jews of Eastern Europe. Despite their immigration to the Land of Israel, they were still an inseparable part of Jewish Eastern European society; others had even left behind their families: parents, brothers, and sisters.

# CHAPTER 4

The residents of the New Yishuv accepted the territorialist view that the welfare of the people came before the good of the land. It was the acts of murder and robbery in Eastern Europe that had attracted them to the territorialist idea. Their own familiarity with the realities of life in Palestine led them to agree with the territorialist claim that the Jews of Eastern Europe were in danger and that the Zionists did not have sufficient time to set up a state for the Jewish people in Palestine. Their support for Zangwill was not caused by a lack of devotion and love for the Land of Israel but was a product of their dread about the fate of Eastern European Jewry.

Even the claim that this group's support for the Uganda plan was a product of its scathing criticism of Ussishkin and blind esteem for Herzl cannot explain the controversy that broke out in Palestine in the early twentieth century. Most of the Ugandists in Palestine became Territorialists after the Seventh Zionist Congress. The Zionist associations in Palestine supported the new organization's goals and its president, and they functioned as territorialist branches in every respect. They asked for materials to be sent for distribution in Palestine and worked to recruit new members. It is difficult to assess the range of activity in the territorialist branches, how many participants they recruited, and how long they were active. There is some basis to assume that the territorialist idea subsided more quickly in Palestine than it did in Eastern Europe. The lack of a territory, on the one hand, and the intensive concerted Zionist activity they had to face, on the other, caused the Territorialists in Palestine to assimilate into Yishuv society and disappear as though they had never been. In Eastern Europe, however, the Territorialists kept busy with the task of making arrangements for immigration and helping the masses of immigrants who sought their assistance. They could realize the territorialist worldview through their activities on behalf of the Jewish immigrant. But, as we will see in Chapter 5, the absence of a territory made it impossible for even the Eastern European Territorialists to maintain their loyalty, and they gradually abandoned the ITO and returned to the Zionist mainstream.

When the pioneers of the First Aliyah wrote their memoirs many years after their arrival in Palestine, the Uganda affair had been forgotten, as though it had never occurred. In 1941 the *Sefer Rishon Lezion: 1882–1941* (Book of Rishon Lezion) was published. It was edited by David

# THE TERRITORIALIST MOVEMENT IN PALESTINE

Yudelovich and made no mention of the support among the colony's residents for the territorialist idea or the ITO. Mordechai Freiman, whose support for Territorialism was mentioned in the jubilee volume of the settlement in 1907, was simply not mentioned in the new edition.[70] Nor was the Bilu doctor Menachem Stein, who was one of the most devoted and fervent Territorialists in Palestine. In the debates at the Seventh Zionist Congress, Dr. Stein called the legality of the decision into question, resigned from the Zionist Organization, and even participated in the establishment of the ITO in the Safran Hotel in Basel. His activities on behalf of Territorialism are not mentioned in the book; this is no coincidence.[71] The pioneers of the First Aliyah were ashamed of their support for the Uganda plan and their territorialist activities and wanted to erase it from the historiography of the Yishuv, which began to consolidate in the 1940s and 1950s.

5

# The Search for a Homeland

Finding a territory for Jews who "cannot or do not wish to remain in the countries in which they are living at present" was the ITO's main aim and raison d'être. As mentioned, the defeat of the Uganda plan at the Seventh Zionist Congress was not the only reason that the Territorialists seceded from the Zionist Organization; of equal importance was another decision made at that time to bar members from submitting any proposal for Jewish settlement outside Palestine. The Territorialists were ready to accept the argument that Uganda was unsuitable, but under no circumstances would they agree to a decision in principle that no similar proposals could ever again be submitted to the institutions of the Zionist Organization. From the moment they walked out, the Territorialists devoted all their time and energy to searching for a land that would be suitable for Jewish settlement, with conditions that would allow the absorption of all the Jews who might wish to move there. For Israel Zangwill and his followers, Territorialism meant finding such a place. They had to prove that their secession was justified and that they had read the geopolitical map of the early twentieth century correctly.

Zangwill spent nine years looking for such a territory but never found it. He crossed continents and oceans in his search: Africa, Australia, the Americas, and Asia. He conducted negotiations with governments who filled him with hope, only to dash it with bitter disappointment. From our viewpoint in the early twenty-first century—the Zionist movement has achieved all its goals and there is a Jewish state in the Land of Israel—it might be argued that the territorialist idea had no chance of success.

The failure of territorialist diplomacy and the inability to find the sought-after territory prove this. However, the search for a suitable land should be examined from the perspective of the Territorialists at the beginning of the twentieth century; at that time, they were convinced that in their age—the heyday of colonialism—their prospects were at least as good as those of the Zionists. Their assertion that it was quite likely that some European power would be willing to give the Jews a district in one of its colonies matched the imperialist reality of that time. Zangwill thought that the British would allow the Jews to settle in one of their colonies, given the sparse population of them. He held that the countries of Europe could be persuaded that it was moral and proper to assign some district to the Jews, because no country had the right to hold underpopulated territories when other races were agonizing for lack of a place and the sun.[1]

The decision as to which territory was suitable was the province of the ITO's Geographical Committee. Its members were prominent figures in the Jewish world, including Lord Rothschild, Oscar Strauss, Daniel Guggenheim, Judge Mayer Sulzberger, Max Mandelstamm, James Simon, and Paul Nathan. The ITO constitution laid down that political negotiations be conducted by the president of the ITO,[2] who proposed to establish a Jewish state in two stages. In the first stage a large and unpopulated territory would be acquired; in the second stage, the emigrants from Eastern Europe would be directed to it and a Jewish majority would be created there.[3]

In this chapter I trace Zangwill's unremitting efforts to find a suitable territory. I focus only on the settlement plans that involved official negotiations with governments and senior officials. Details of the diplomatic efforts by members of the ITO are preserved in the ITO archives, deposited in the Central Zionist Archives in Jerusalem. The files include Zangwill's correspondence with heads of government, ministers, ambassadors, and various influential persons in the Jewish and non-Jewish worlds. These documents allow us to determine the scope and duration of each proposal and the reasons for the failure of the diplomatic efforts.

# EAST AFRICA

After the Zionist Organization rejected the Uganda plan and sent an official letter of thanks to the British government expressing its gratitude for the generous proposal while politely declining it, Zangwill renewed his contacts with the British colonial secretary, Alfred Lyttelton. This was the ITO's first diplomatic gambit. Only one month after the founding of the new organization, Zangwill wrote to Lyttelton and asked whether the offer of the Guas Ngishu plateau was still in effect; if so, the ITO would like to pursue it. He added that Lucien Wolff was going to speak with Foreign Secretary Lansdowne on his behalf to acquaint him with a new settlement plan.[4]

Lyttelton replied to Zangwill in the negative but did not slam the door in his face. As noted, his government's offer to Herzl had aroused bitter opposition among British politicians and among the white settlers in East Africa. Lyttelton wrote that he had sent a letter to the governor of East Africa, informing him that the Zionist Organization had rejected the British proposal and that the territory offered should no longer be reserved for this purpose.[5]

He also clarified that it would be difficult to accede to Zangwill's request to enter into negotiations about Guas Ngishu. He saw the ITO as a breakaway movement that sought to promote its own political ideas and lacked the backing of the Jewish people. Under these circumstances, he told Zangwill, "I feel that it is impossible for me to grant the request contained in your letter of the 8th September."[6] However, he left the door open for future negotiations by "His Majesty's Government of any well-considered proposals which you may hereafter feel yourself in a position to make."[7]

Zangwill seized on Lyttelton's concluding sentence. In his reply he told the colonial secretary that he took his offer seriously but also wished to correct his mistaken impression of the ITO.

> I note, however with gratification, that this will be no obstacle to the consideration by his Majesty's Government of further proposals for such a settlement which the new Jewish Territorial organization may submit to you. I ought to mention that you have somewhat misapprehended the nature and prospects of the Jewish Territorial Organization. Although it had its germ in the Zionist minority, it was from the start an entirely independent body, and has now taken in fresh and powerful elements from all classes of the Jewish people in every country.[8]

In an attempt to revive the plan for settlement in East Africa, Zangwill and the ITO turned to Joseph Chamberlain—who, when colonial secretary, had offered Guas Ngishu to Herzl—to ask him to try to influence the decision makers in the British government. Chamberlain wrote back that he sympathized with the suffering of the Jews in Eastern Europe and would be glad to offer any assistance required and to speak in warm support of the proposal made to Herzl when he was in office.[9] However, several years had passed and Chamberlain no longer had any influence. It seemed that the East Africa plan was defunct and that the proposal made to Herzl in 1903 would not be renewed for the Territorialists.

Zangwill hoped that two dramatic incidents in 1905 and 1906 could be exploited to revive the idea of settlement in East Africa. These were the pogroms in Russia in October–November 1905 and the Aliens Act, which took effect in Britain on January 1, 1906. Zangwill met with Lyttelton on December 4, 1905. In preparation for their discussion, Zangwill had sent him a detailed 32-page memorandum in which he described the desperate plight of Russian Jewry. A reading of this document makes plain that the agonizing letters Zangwill received from Jews in Russia stayed in his thoughts and influenced the contents of the memorandum. Zangwill included an English translation of the letter by Moshe Rosenblatt (quoted at length in Chapter 2) as an appendix to the memorandum.

The memorandum begins with a description of the brutal pogroms that struck the Jews of Russia and their implications for Europe, with vivid pictures of Jews being tortured and slaughtered. "Who could refuse entry for example to the Jewess of Tschernigoff," whose letter Zangwill quoted: "The whole town is a perfect ruin. My young brother perished in the conflagration. My sister Esther was subjected to unspeakable violence and then cut to pieces by ferocious Cossacs. My old father lies near me upon the ground and groans. His eyes have been put out with red-hot iron. God have mercy upon us!"[10]

Zangwill warned that the persecutions would produce a mass flight of Jews from Russia; even the Aliens Act would not keep the flood of refugees out of England. He therefore requested a safe territory in which Jewish policemen could defend Jewish inhabitants from those seeking to harm them. In pursuit of such a territory, he wrote, the ITO wanted to conduct negotiations with the British government, not only because

## CHAPTER 5

of the role that England had played in the Zionist movement but also primarily because England was the homeland of freedom and liberty.[11]

Zangwill realized, however, that rousing sympathy for the suffering Jews was not enough. He also had to demonstrate to the colonial secretary that the Jewish people had the ability to implement the idea: "But you will naturally ask, who will be behind such a scheme?" His answer was that the experience of the past months, since the founding of the ITO, proved that the Jewish people as a whole would yoke themselves to the task: "Zionists and Anti-Zionists alike are joining us at an unprecedented rate. And this when our programme is merely theoretical and shadowy."[12] Zangwill noted in the memorandum that ITO chapters had been set up all over the Jewish world: in London, Paris, Berlin, Vienna, Antwerp, St. Petersburg, Sofia, Warsaw, Lemberg, Johannesburg, Cape Town, New York, and Jerusalem. Scores of branches were opened in the Russian Empire. Moreover, the territorialist idea was backed by prominent Jews who had the power to promote any settlement plan that Britain found suitable and worthwhile: Lucien Wolff, Hermann Kisch, and Paul Hirsch in England; James Simon and Paul Nathan in Germany; Oscar Strauss, Judge Mayer Sulzberger, and Daniel Guggenheim in the United States; and Max Langermann in South Africa.[13] Zangwill stressed that he had no doubt that the leading Jewish philanthropists would stand behind him and help fund the plan at the moment of truth and hour of need.

In many ways the memorandum continued Herzl's line of thought, with the assumption that wealthy Jews could be persuaded to support the idea of a Jewish state. Zangwill also recognized their importance and regarded their wealth as an important factor for developing an autonomous Jewish entity. Zangwill explained to Lyttelton that the land assigned for Jewish settlement would be cultivated by Jewish farmers. A selective immigration policy would make it possible to choose those who had already demonstrated their talents wherever they had gone, whether Palestine, Argentina, Wisconsin, or New Jersey.[14]

Zangwill asserted that the proposed territory would have to be large enough to absorb the Jews who migrated there. He did not believe that the Guas Ngishu plateau, which had been offered to Herzl and the Zionist Organization, met this criterion and had vaster uninhabited districts of East Africa in mind. He petitioned Lyttelton for a territory with an area of 200,000 square miles to serve as a refuge for the persecuted

Jews: "A British Judaea self-governed as one of the free colonies of the Empire."[15] He called the colonial secretary's attention to the fact that there were many uninhabited or sparsely populated regions all over the British Empire, including Canada, Australia, and South Africa. A regular political regime had already been established in those dominions, but East Africa was still in the early stages of development and could become a favored objective both for the Jews and for the British government.

Zangwill regarded Jewish settlement in the region as part of the wide-ranging colonialist enterprise to strengthen the British hold on Africa. It was a wild and unknown district with a harsh climate: "It is a land of fierce suns and violent rains, of chills and fevers. . . . Locusts and caterpillars endanger the crops. The battle with nature has only begun. The native tribes show little capacities for development, and for the building of the railway, coolies had to be imported who returned to India. There are no mineral prospects. The land has neither gold nor coal."[16] Because budgetary and administrative considerations deterred the British government from encouraging large-scale migration to East Africa, the Jews were the best solution, inasmuch as they would constitute a "European migration" by "white settlers."[17]

In his negotiations with Lyttelton, Zangwill endeavored to emphasize the inherent deep and common interest between the aims of the ITO and England's imperialist aspirations in Africa. According to the memorandum, the ITO would become an instrument of British policy and at the same time serve the Jewish people.

Zangwill came away from their meeting on December 4 with the impression that Lyttelton was enthusiastic about the ideas he had raised and his detailed plan.[18] But the main problem in getting the British to accept the plan was its unfortunate timing. The meeting with Lyttelton had been set up at the beginning of November 1905, but by the time it took place, December 4, a new government was in the works and Lyttelton was about to leave office. A week after their meeting, he wrote to Zangwill that the plan needed much more work before it could be submitted to the British government, but because he was no longer in the cabinet, he did not intend to deal with it any longer.[19] Zangwill thanked Lyttelton politely for his help and asked whether his proposal had been transmitted to the new colonial secretary or whether he had to start all over again.[20] Evidently Lyttelton did not leave Zangwill's plan on his desk

## CHAPTER 5

for his successor. When the Liberal leader Henry Campbell-Bannerman moved into 10 Downing Street on December 5, he named Lord Elgin as colonial secretary. Unlike Balfour's Conservative government, the Liberals were not eager to promote new settlement initiatives abroad; once again Zangwill found himself at a diplomatic dead-end.

Zangwill had to start practically from scratch with the new Liberal government and devise new ways to interest the colonial secretary in his territorialist ideas for the Jewish people. As noted, Zangwill had seen the pogroms of 1905 as a good starting point for his talks with Lyttelton. When they were aborted, it was the Aliens Act, which restricted foreigners' entry into Britain, that he tried to take advantage of to advance his ideas.

The Territorialists saw the Aliens Act as a warning of what the future held in store. These were the years of mass emigration from Eastern Europe. Every month, thousands left tsarist Russia, Galicia, and Romania en route to the United States. More than 140,000 did so in 1905, and more than 170,000 did so the next year.[21] The Territorialists' great fear was that the Aliens Act might be the first sign that heralded the closing of the gates by the destination countries and that hundreds of thousands of Jews would have nowhere to go. Zangwill tried to make the new colonial secretary cognizant of the Jewish problem that might emerge if other countries followed Britain's lead, and at the same time he tried to attract Lord Elgin to the territorialist idea.

Zangwill sent two letters to the Colonial Office, on December 19 and 23, 1905, requesting an interview with the secretary to present his plan.[22] He hoped to go to the Brussels conference (discussed in Chapter 2) with a diplomatic achievement he could present to its participants. Because of time constraints, the meeting did not take place then; but on January 26, 1906, Lord Elgin's secretary dispatched an official letter on behalf of the Colonial Office, which the Territorialists viewed as a political document of the utmost importance.

Dear Sir,

Lord Elgin desires me to reply as follows to your letter of the 23rd instant. He feels very deep sympathy with the people of your race in their recent afflictions, and fully understands their desire to inhabit some land which they could enjoy safely and freedom, and would be glad if it should prove possible to find some unoccupied or undeveloped part of the British Empire where, as you desire, a Jewish colony might be planted with fair prospects of success ... and he will give his most careful and sympathetic attention to any schemes which may be brought before him.[23]

Winston Churchill, the new undersecretary in the Colonial Office, expressed enthusiastic support for the territorialist idea and for the possibility of settling persecuted Jews "under the flag of tolerance and freedom."[24] Coming on the eve of the Brussels conference, this letter had great significance. Zangwill and his followers regarded it as a political achievement and proof that the British government had not abandoned its commitment to the Jewish people.

Zangwill's enthusiasm waned after he finally met with Lord Elgin in March 1906. He told the ITO Executive Committee that Lord Elgin was not particularly interested in the territorialist settlement program. Unlike Chamberlain, who wanted to find solutions for the Jewish question and even offered the Zionists a territory, Lord Elgin was passive on the matter. Furthermore, his preferred solution was a syndicate and not an autonomous Jewish colony. Zangwill reported that Lord Elgin had shown some flexibility at their meeting by not totally rejecting the idea of a Jewish majority and self-government in one of the East African colonies. But the colonial secretary stressed that the governor would have to be British, although there was no objection to his being a British Jew (so long as he was suited to the position); the prime minister of the self-governing entity could be a Jew of any origin. But it was clear to Zangwill that these statements were merely hypothetical and that Lord Elgin would not advance any idea until he received a detailed plan that could be discussed in official channels.[25]

Lord Elgin laid out three necessary conditions for promoting a plan for Jewish settlement: (1) The proposal had to be submitted by what he called responsible people; (2) the plan had to be formulated in general outlines; and (3) there had to be sufficient proof of financial support for it.[26] In other words, the ITO needed to produce a methodical plan before the British government and the Colonial Office would consider the matter. Zangwill was confronted with an obstacle that Herzl had also encountered; it was difficult to enlist Jewish philanthropists to support the ITO before it had a territory to offer them. The Jewish magnates with whom Zangwill was in contact were willing to contribute, but only after the Territorialists received a territory suitable for Jewish settlement. Lord Rothschild, for example, was skeptical about the economic viability of the enterprise. Jacob Schiff, the American Jewish banker, asserted that the territorialist idea was impractical and preferred to solve the distress of Russian Jewry in Russia itself and not by means of migration to countries overseas.[27] Zangwill was hard put to extricate himself from the resulting vicious circle. On the one hand, the British government wanted to receive a detailed settlement with guaranteed funding before it would even look at the plan; on the other hand, rich Jewish philanthropists would not commit themselves before a territory was in hand.

Despite Lord Elgin's reservations and the obstacles he raised, Zangwill sent his friend and ally Helena (Nellie) Auerbach to East Africa to study whether large numbers of Jews could be settled there. Auerbach was the treasurer of the National Union of Women's Suffrage Societies in England, a close friend of Zangwill's suffragette wife, Edith Ayrton, and a resident of South Africa. Unlike the official Zionist delegation in early 1905, Auerbach did not go to investigate the territory itself but to gain a general impression of the place, talk with influential people, and determine whether the white settlers already there would oppose or support the arrival of hundreds of thousands of poor Jews from Eastern Europe. Zangwill asked Auerbach not to publicize his plan but requested that she try to form ties with suitable people and enlist them to offer public support for Territorialism if and when the plan became realistic.[28]

Auerbach's letters to Zangwill during her trip reveal the many problems and perhaps also the infeasibility of the East Africa settlement idea. She emphasized the fertility of the land. Refuting the assertion of Nahum Wilbush in the report submitted to the Zionist Organization that "where nothing exists, nothing can be done," Auerbach pointed out the territory's positive aspects and suitability for European agricultural colonization. There was adequate rainfall, the land was good, a significant portion could support cattle, and there were possibilities for industrial development. "I think," she wrote, "that there is no part of the globe so fertile and valuable as this where man will have fewer difficulties in subduing raw nature to the needs of civilization."[29] She noted, however, that the local population would be a problem. Asians (mainly Indians) occupied key positions in the East African economy. Rather like the Jews in Eastern Europe, they were the middlemen between the native population and the European colonists. They made their living as contractors, carpenters, foremen, tailors, cooks, and waiters; some were merchants, exporters, and importers.[30] The fear that Jewish immigration might cause a rise in the cost of living could arouse severe opposition a priori. In her meeting with Lord Delamere, an influential white colonist, Auerbach heard adamant opposition to any autonomous Jewish natural entity. Her conversations with the white settlers persuaded her that there was no chance of acquiring a territory in East Africa.[31]

Despite Auerbach's conclusion, Zangwill pursued his efforts to persuade Lord Elgin to offer the Guas Ngishu plateau to the ITO. It seems, however, that the plan was in its final death throes and the Colonial Office was no longer interested in following up on Zangwill's ideas. Even Churchill, who had shown enthusiasm for the plan when he entered office as colonial undersecretary, reneged. In a letter to Zangwill he emphasized the difficulties and limitations of the plan to settle Jews in East Africa: "The more I examine the question, the more oppressed I am by consciousness of the serious, and in some cases, growing obstacles, which stand in the path of action."[32] The Guas Ngishu plateau was no longer uninhabited, wrote Churchill, who also feared strong opposition to Jewish settlement by the white colonists.[33] The good will of Chamberlain, who had offered Guas Ngishu to Herzl in 1903, was replaced by the hesitant and even negative approach of his successors in the Colonial Office. Their request for a detailed plan and definite sources of funding and fears of the European colonists' opposition to Jewish settlement led to the Uganda plan's removal from the territorialist agenda.

But new proposals for Jewish settlement were being floated around the same time, and Zangwill and his colleagues on the Geographical Committee had to consider them. One of them referred to Canada.

# CANADA

Unlike the negotiations over East Africa, which extended over four years, the negotiations to acquire a territory in Canada were brief. At the beginning of the twentieth century, Canada was a vast but sparsely populated country.[34] To settle its uninhabited regions, in the early 1880s the Canadian government tried to attract immigrants from Europe. The

Canadian high commissioner in London, Alexander Galt, charged with implementing this policy, wanted to bring immigrants (both Jewish and non-Jewish) to northwestern Canada and turn them into farmers. Galt was especially interested in Jews from Russia who had gone to England during the 1880s. This was not necessarily because of any concern for the Jews; rather, he expected that efforts on behalf of the Jews would give him access to the Rothschild family and enable him to promote the railway line linking the Canadian interior with the Pacific Ocean.[35]

The first immigrants to reach Canada in the early 1880s were sent to southern Manitoba to settle thinly populated areas and establish agricultural settlements: near the towns of Moosomin (1884) and then (1886) Wapella. The first settlers were followed by other Jewish families, and a small Jewish community emerged in the region.[36] Difficulties in acclimation and the harsh natural conditions were part of the Jewish settlers' daily routine. Like the residents of the Jewish agricultural colonies founded in Palestine, the United States, and later in Argentina, these Jewish farmers found it hard to make ends meet without outside monetary assistance. In Palestine it was Baron Rothschild who gave his patronage to the farmers, in Argentina it was Baron Hirsch, and in Canada help was first extended by the Young Men's Hebrew Benevolent Society and later by Baron Hirsch and the Jewish Colonization Association (ICA).

The Jewish agricultural settlement in Manitoba, the immigration of about 10,000 Jews to Canada between 1880 and 1900, the allocation of land on easy and reasonable terms, and a liberal immigration policy—from the territorialist viewpoint, all these constituted a suitable basis for an autonomous Jewish colony. In the summer of 1906, after all chances of obtaining a territory in East Africa had been exhausted, Zangwill approached Lord Strathcona, the Canadian high commissioner in London, tried to interest him in the territorialist idea, and presented his request to receive an uninhabited tract of land for the Jewish people. Contact with the Canadian high commissioner did not involve any real diplomatic effort. The location of ITO headquarters, London, made it easy for Zangwill to meet with diplomats and visiting heads of state. Moreover, after a period of relative quiet, pogroms broke out in Bialystok on June 14, 1906, in which more than 200 Jews were murdered and 700 wounded.[37] A new wave of massacres and violence seemed to be erupting in tsarist Russia, increasing the urgency of finding a solution to the

# THE SEARCH FOR A HOMELAND

Jewish problem. Zangwill was afraid that the lives of Jews in Eastern Europe were suspended over an abyss. A few days after the pogrom, on June 19, he met with Lord Strathcona and asked whether his government would be willing to allocate an extensive area of undeveloped and sparsely populated land for settlement by the persecuted Jews of Russia. Zangwill stressed that the Jewish immigrants would find Canada to be a land of refuge where they could establish an autonomous Jewish district subject to the laws of the country. He noted that the territory would have to be large enough to absorb the millions of Jews who would arrive over the years. Because the Jews would provide their own capital, there would be no need for the Canadian government to invest its own resources to develop the area.[38]

The meeting between Zangwill and Lord Strathcona and the letter sent immediately afterward was the beginning of a diplomatic inquiry. In early June the ITO sent a detailed seven-paragraph memorandum to the Canadian high commissioner with explanations of how the organization wanted to solve the Jewish problem in Eastern Europe. It stressed the need for an autonomous Jewish colony that would be open to Jews of all ranks: "Families and individuals, with capital and without capital, agriculturalists, professional men, traders, artisans of every kind, and skilled labourers."[39] The ITO would handle settling Jews in the territory, supervise industrial development, the paving of roads, and the laying of railway tracks, and establish schools for the younger generation. The aim and function of the autonomous settlement were also stressed. It would be a land of refuge for the persecuted Jews. In view of the situation of East European Jewry and the Jewish migration westward, the solution to the Jewish question was not the migration of individuals to Canada but a national migration, organized and directed toward a specific territory. Moreover, Zangwill asserted, it had been shown that the non-Jewish population in Eastern Europe would not accept the Jews as a minority among them. In Russia, for example, the Jews constituted only about 4 percent of the population but were seen as a domineering minority with enormous power and influence. Zangwill expressed his fears that the arrival of Jewish immigrants in Western countries might lead to legislation against foreigners—such as the Aliens Act in England—and anti-Semitic laws that would impair the immigrants' legal and judicial status. For this reason, he told the high commissioner, it was preferable to

# CHAPTER 5

concentrate the Jews in a specific territory and not allow them to disperse throughout Canada.[40]

About a month after the memorandum was sent, Zangwill received an answer from Lord Strathcona to the effect that the minister of the interior in Ottawa had examined the plan and decided to reject it. The territorialist program that had been submitted to the minister contravened Canadian immigration policy, which was "to give the public lands in the west without reserve or discrimination to the first applicants who are willing to comply with the settlement conditions; . . . so far as [the Minister] can see, it will not be possible to alter this policy in such a way as would bring it into the line with proposition made by you on behalf of your society."[41]

The response was firm and unequivocal and left Zangwill with no opening for resuming his diplomacy. Because his colleagues regarded Canada as an ideal place for large-scale Jewish settlement, one that suited the aims of the ITO, the members of the Geographical Committee recommended that he cooperate with the Canadian government but circumvent its immigration policy. Initially immigrants would be sent on an individual basis and settle in the designated territory. Later they would prepare the ground for those who did not want or were not interested in remaining in their places of residence.[42] They viewed Alberta and Saskatchewan in western Canada as the best place for Jewish settlement. Zangwill opposed a gradual infiltration of Jewish settlers and was afraid that it could not be carried out without the support in principle of the Canadian government. He also thought that without a definite settlement plan with a national character, it would be difficult and perhaps even impossible to bring millions of Jews to Canada.

Unlike the negotiations over East Africa, which had lasted for a number of years, those regarding Canada took only a few months. However, in the beginning of May 1907, a year after his meeting with Lord Strathcona, Zangwill again attempted to arouse his interest and to persuade him to accept the ITO plan. The Canadian high commissioner suggested that Zangwill write him an official letter with details of his proposal and its advantages. In reply, Zangwill explained that the ITO was a territorialist organization that represented may Jews all over the world and that its main aim was to procure an autonomous territory for those Jews who could not or did not want to remain in their present homes.[43] "The world, as you know," wrote Zangwill, "is still empty. Outside Europe every continent contains great tracts that might shelter us, and we have now before us at least half a dozen territorial possibilities, but the majority of our headquarters council, which is situated in London, would view with sorrow the passing away of this great potentiality from the British flag."[44]

To persuade his interlocutor, Zangwill laid out the advantages that the Jews would bring to Canada: "I venture to say that the particular corner of Canada allotted to us would develop six times as fast as it will without us, and that we should bring a much more fervent and intelligent patriotism to the Empire which came to our rescue, than will be brought by the motley individual immigrants from Europe and the States, whom Canada must chiefly draw upon."[45] He expressed his hope that the Canadian prime minister, Wilfrid Laurier, would contact the former British colonial secretary, Joseph Chamberlain, and learn from him about the necessity and importance of the plan. However, Lord Strathcona filed Zangwill's proposal away and did not forward it to Ottawa.

The plan for a Jewish settlement in Canada was dropped. Soon after, Zangwill turned to an attempt to promote Jewish settlement in northern Australia.

## AUSTRALIA

### The Northern Territory

On June 29, 1906, Richard Arthur, the president of the Immigration League of Australia, published an article in the *Hebrew Standard* (Sydney) titled "Australia to the ITO." In it, he said:

> There are hundreds of thousands of square miles in Australia, with hardly an inhabitant of any kind.... I am convinced that the I.T.O. might make an experiment in colonization somewhere in Australia.... I would suggest that the Northern Territory would probably be the most suitable locality to make this experiment. The Northern Territory is six or seven times as large as Great Britain and contains vast areas of fertile land.[46]

Arthur took the idea of Jewish settlement in Australia from an article in the *Jewish Chronicle* (London) about agricultural options for Jews there.

He thought that Jewish immigration to Australia and the establishment of a Jewish settlement there could benefit the country and help solve its labor shortage. The Immigration League, founded in 1905, sought to help devise and implement a rational immigration policy. It envisaged four main aims: (1) expanding and strengthening the farming class in Australia; (2) disseminating information about immigration and settlement options in Europe and Australia itself; (3) offering practical assistance and advice to newly arrived immigrants; and (4) assisting those who wished to exchange their urban lifestyle for a rural one. Promotion of Jewish immigration to Australia conformed with the League's aims and Australian government policy.

The Immigration League's activities were part of the general policy of attracting Europeans to Australia and settling them in its outlying regions. At the beginning of the twentieth century, Jewish journalists in London interviewed agents of the Australian provincial governments, who spoke of their government's interest in absorbing Jewish immigrants on condition that they take up farming and not concentrate in the cities.[47] Arthur, who had read in the British press about the ITO's efforts to find a place of refuge for Jews, thought that Jewish immigration would serve Australia's interests and should be promoted and encouraged. He wanted to attract Jewish immigrants to the Northern Territory, which was large enough to absorb many immigrants and was blessed with fertile land and a favorable climate where the Jews could raise "sheep and cattle, wheat and maize, butter and cheese, fruits of every kind, cotton, coffee, sugar-cane, rice and tobacco."[48] Arthur also recommended that a delegation be sent to study the region and investigate the feasibility of the plan. He was convinced that, aided by Jewish capital, hundreds of thousands of immigrants from Russia could be settled on the land and become farmers. He wrote that as president of the Immigration League of Australia he would be happy to cooperate with the ITO, but he stressed that the plan had to be for an agricultural settlement: "There is no place here at present for artisans or middle-men of any kind."[49]

An ITO chapter was established in Australia to promote the territorialist ideology. In November 1905, only three months after the founding of the ITO, Zangwill received an unexpected letter of support from Oscar Bernard, the Jewish mayor of Northam in Western Australia. Bernard expressed his support for Zangwill's split from the Zionist

Organization—something that he and Herzl should have done even earlier—and expressed confidence in the new territorialist organization.[50] Zangwill, delighted by this letter, urged Bernard to set up an ITO branch in Australia and to recruit as many members as possible.[51] Bernard proceeded to establish the first Australian chapter of the ITO in Perth, about 60 miles from Northam, on February 19, 1906. Originally the group was part of the Zionist chapter there; but by March 6 the two sides realized that cooperation between them was impossible, and the Territorialists set up an independent group.[52] They proceeded to elect a president, treasurer, and board. During the course of the year the plenum met ten times and the board twelve, attempts were made to raise funds, territorialist literature in Yiddish and English was distributed, and lectures were given in favor of the territorialist idea.[53]

Arthur's article, published in June 1906, opened a diplomatic channel between the ITO and Australian governing officials, breathed life into the local territorialist branch, and aroused considerable interest among its members. The exchange of letters between Zangwill and Bernard reflected their great interest in the plan and thoughts about ways to advance it in the political sphere.[54] In May 1907, almost a year after the publication of Arthur's essay in the *Hebrew Standard*, the first negotiations about the Northern Territory got under way. Around the same time, the prime minister of Australia, Alfred Deakin, arrived in England to participate in the Imperial Conference in London. Zangwill met with him and his secretary, Attlee Hunt, and tried to persuade them that the plan had advantages not only for the Jewish people but also for Australia. He presented them with a memorandum identical to the one submitted to Lyttelton and Strathcona and attempted to convince them that extensive Jewish settlement was first and foremost in the interests of Australia; not only would it lead to the development of the region, but it would also prevent the intrusion of Japanese and Chinese into the continent.[55]

Zangwill had the impression that the prime minister and his secretary were interested in the plan and were considering it favorably. However, it was made clear to him that the territory would first have to be transferred to the Australian federal government and that the decision on this matter would be made by the end of the year.[56] After the successful meeting with Deakin and his secretary, Zangwill sent a confidential letter asking the prime minister to clarify the conditions in the territory and the chances of settling there.[57] It seems that Zangwill left the meeting with a sense of optimism and proceeded to act simultaneously on the political level with Deakin and on the operative level through the territorialist branch in Perth.

However, the parliamentary debate and decision by the Australian government were delayed time and again. In the meantime, voices of protest were being heard in Australian society, as previously in East Africa, against granting territory to Jews. It appears that most of the members of the Immigration League of Australia did not support their president's position and a majority opposed the admission to Australia of a distinct ethnic group that did not speak English and was not interested in becoming fully integrated into Australian society. Immigration League members were also afraid of competition with the locals, which was liable to lead to a reduction in wages and the standard of living. The delay in the transfer of the Northern Territory to the federal government and hostile public opinion killed the initiative. When the Northern Territory was finally transferred to the federal government, the negotiations were not resumed and the settlement plan was dropped from the agenda of both Australia and the ITO.[58]

## Western Australia

In tandem with the negotiations about the Northern Territory, the ITO tried to advance a plan for Jewish settlement in Western Australia. The plan was initiated by an Australian Territorialist named Alexander Marks, who had once served as the Japanese consul general in Australia. In 1906 Marks applied to the Australian government to acquire an area of about 4,000 square kilometers in Western Australia. Because the ITO took a dim view of contacts between private individuals and governments, Zangwill asked the territorialist branch in Perth to petition the government of Western Australia to allocate territory for Jewish settlement.[59] During April and May 1907 the prime minister of Western Australia, Newton Moore, came to London to promote English immigration to the continent. Zangwill took advantage of this visit to meet with Moore and to explain the details of the plan for an autonomous Jewish settlement, but he discovered that the prime minister opposed it and was afraid of establishing a state within a state in Western Australia.

Moore's response was further proof of the problematic element in the territorialist plan and of the difficulty in persuading diplomats and governments to support the idea of autonomy. In a letter to Moore, Zangwill tried to allay his doubts and noted that Churchill and Lloyd George had supported the territorialist idea. "The danger of a state within a state" wrote Zangwill, "seems to me only real when it is made by emigrants from a country like Germany, with an army and navy, . . . but our emigrants are the only ones in the world behind whom there is no military power and no home-land."[60]

The Australian press expressed interest in the negotiations between the ITO and the prime minister of Western Australia and referred in detail to the plan for Jewish settlement. The ITO archives preserve many press clippings that show that public opinion was against Jewish immigration in dimensions that might endanger the character of the continent in general and of Western Australia in particular. The main argument was that the entry of individual Jews into Australia should be permitted but that any attempt to set up an autonomous settlement should be opposed. The Western Australia plan also reached the territorialist branches in Eastern Europe and created great expectations there. At the beginning of 1911, young Jews from the territorialist chapter in Kovno sent Zangwill a letter of support for the Western Australia plan.

> After a prolonged silence for our cherished idea, the Territorialist idea, we suddenly heard from our center, the Jewish Emigration Society in Kiev, . . . that you are negotiating to obtain a land for our people in Australia and that your work is advancing. This information was like a shining rainbow, like the appearance of the sun on an overcast day, and it has brightened our eyes and cheered our hearts, and will make our hopes soar again like an eagle that our time of deliverance will come, that Israel will one day dwell alone in safety in secure habitations and live an independent and healthy life. . . . If there are only a few today who carry high the flag of Territorialism, this is because it does not yet have anything in sight that can be shown, and we do not have the ordinary soldiers for real activity; but in truth there are tens of thousands of our brethren who conceal their love for it and long in their hearts under a calm front for an independent life. . . . Because all those who are really concerned for the fate of our people are trying with all their spirit and might to obtain a land to which many of our migrants

can go, a place where we can live according to our religion and customs, so with God's help, we may do what we have trained for, and through it develop our abilities so that we may be protected from our enemies who seek our blood.[61]

The letter from the young Kovno Territorialists exposes, first and foremost, the enormous gap between the activists' expectations and the progress of the diplomatic negotiations. The impression received from the letter is that the information that reached the Territorialists in Russia was far from reflecting the diplomatic realities. Zangwill was not in the midst of talks about Western Australia, and the plan's prospects of success, if there ever were any, seemed slight. However, the letter also exposes the Territorialists' longings for an autonomous land where they could live their lives in dignity and safety. The terminology that the members of the territorialist branch in Kovno chose to use did not differ from that of the Zionist pioneers. We merely need to replace the word "Australia" with "Palestine" and the word "Territorialist" with "Zionist" and we would obtain a letter of a Zionist character that represents the Jews' profound desire for a national homeland. The territorialist world of imagery reflected in this letter resembles that of the many Zionists at the beginning of the twentieth century: glad tidings (the shining rainbow), independent life ("a place where we can living according to our religion and customs"), a land of refuge and salvation ("protected from our enemies who seek our blood"), and care for the fate of the Jewish people ("because all those who are really concerned for the fate of our people are trying with all their spirit and might to obtain a land to which many of our migrants can go").

Zangwill and the Territorialists in Perth were unable to allay the government's fears about bringing Jews to the territory on an autonomous basis and not as individuals and about a state within a state on the Australian continent. The local population's hostile attitude toward Jewish immigration did not make it any easier for Zangwill. The plan for Western Australia expired for the same reasons as the plan for Canada did.

## MESOPOTAMIA

The idea of Jewish settlement in Mesopotamia arose for the first time on December 28, 1899, during a meeting between Herzl and the

American ambassador in Constantinople, Oscar Strauss. In his diary Herzl characterized Strauss as a man who was "neither for nor against Zionism" and noted that the ambassador had sworn him to silence about the conversation and the ideas that were raised in it.[62] During that same meeting, which was held in the Imperial Hotel, Constantinople, Strauss told Herzl that he thought Palestine was not within reach. He claimed that the Greek Church and the Catholic Church would not permit the Zionists to receive a charter on Palestine, but on the other hand, Aram Naharaim (Mesopotamia) was obtainable.[63] Strauss told Herzl, "There are no church rivalries there, and it is the original home of Israel." He added, "Abraham came from Mesopotamia, and there we could make use of the mystic elements, too."[64]

The suggestion made by Strauss to Herzl was not fortuitous and was preceded by a dialogue that the ambassador had held with two prominent American Jews, Mayer Sulzberger (1843–1923) and Cyrus Adler (1863–1940). Sulzberger was a jurist who had arrived in the United States from Germany during the second half of the nineteenth century; he had served as a judge in Philadelphia since 1895. Adler was an Orientalist and a mentor of Paul Haupt (1858–1926), a professor in Baltimore who had researched Mesopotamia and neighboring countries. In 1892 Haupt published a memorandum called *Über die Ansiedlung der russischen im Euphart und Tigris-Gebeit: Ein Vorschlag* (On the Settlement of Russian Jews in the Area of the Euphrates and Tigris: A Proposal), and he found adherents to his proposal among leaders of American Jewry, including Adler and Strauss.

Ever since that meeting with Strauss at the end of 1899, Herzl constantly raised the plan for Jewish settlement in Mesopotamia with the sultan and with Jewish bankers, who Herzl hoped would contribute to the Zionist enterprise. Sultan Abdul Hamid II was prepared to open his kingdom to the Jews but set down certain conditions that Herzl could not accept. This is what Herzl wrote in his diary:

> His Excellency the Emperor will allow Jews to migrate to his lands in Asia Minor and Aram Naharaim on condition that the migrants receive permission from their governments to accept Ottoman citizenship. The migrants will be required to accept the Ottoman laws currently in force and to serve in the army. The

## CHAPTER 5

> migration will not be *en masse* nor will settlement be massive, but only in accordance with imperial decisions in the regions to which the migrants will be directed.... In exchange for this, His Imperial Excellency requests that a Jewish financial syndicate be established to assist the government in the regions to which the migrants will be directed.[65]

Herzl politely declined the proposal of the sultan because it did not correspond to his aspirations to receive independence in one of the territories within the realm of the Ottoman Empire. About half a year after the discussions with the sultan, Herzl tried to engage Lord Rothschild in the Mesopotamia settlement plan. In his letter, Herzl mentioned two possible settlement plans, in Cyprus and in El-Arish, and a third plan "that may be carried out at the same time with the first one but separately from it. This is totally confidential. It refers to Aram Naharaim." Herzl told Lord Rothschild that the sultan had offered him "settlement in Aram Naharaim (in February of this year when I went to Constantinople at his invitation). I rejected his proposal because he excluded Palestine from it. I can return to it tomorrow because my relations [with the sultan] remain excellent."[66] Lord Rothschild, who was skeptical about the chances for the success of the plan, rejected the proposal and it was taken off the Zionist agenda.

Toward the end of 1905 a change occurred in the situation of the Jews in Eastern Europe. During the months of October and November 1905, violent pogroms broke out in southern Russia and 3,000 Jews were murdered. In view of the dramatic events in Eastern Europe, the Mesopotamia plan was raised once again on the agenda of the Jewish people.

Otto Warburg (1859–1938), a member of the Inner Actions Committee and from 1911 to 1921 the third president of the Zionist Organization, was the one who tried to advance the Mesopotamia plan in the Zionist movement. He contacted the famous English irrigation engineer, Sir William Willcocks (1852–1932), and asked for his assistance. In his letter to the president of the Zionist Organization, David Wolffsohn (1856–1914), Warburg requested that Wolffsohn study in all seriousness the proposed plan and persuade the Great Powers in its favor.

> If we were not so much in a hurry, and if instead of engaging in political sport and in self-inflicting tactics, we would be engaged

in serious and broad-ranging economic politics, since we surely could now, with the name of Willcocks at the head, obtain from England and America the necessary funds for a large Aram-Naharaim Foundation on a commercial basis. But I am afraid, especially after the experience [at the Brussels Conference] that in the view of our "politicians" this will not be sufficiently political, even though it will be necessary to conduct negotiations of all sorts and with the Sultan. I think that we really must begin with this matter, especially when there is no doubt that the British Government will support us in Constantinople, and certainly the Germans and also the French as well—because of the Baghdad railway line and because of cotton cultivation. The very beginning of this enterprise will already strengthen our status to a great extent.[67]

Willcocks, who is mentioned in Warburg's letter, was considered one of the greatest irrigation engineers of his time. During 1872–1882 he worked in India, and from there he moved to Egypt. He planned the Aswan Dam and oversaw its construction. In 1903 he published his book *The Restoration of the Ancient Irrigation Works on the Tigris or the Re-Creation of Chaldea*. After the Young Turk revolution, the new government invited Willcocks to examine the possibilities of economic development in Mesopotamia. In 1909 he proposed wide-scale plans to utilize the waters of the Euphrates and the Tigris Rivers to make the arid areas flourish by means of a network of irrigation canals and the construction of a railway line running from Baghdad across the desert to the Syrian coast on the Mediterranean.[68] In the framework of this plan he suggested settling Egyptian fellahin, or farmers, from India in Aram Naharaim, without negating the settlement of Jews there.

The appeal by Warburg to Willcocks did not go unanswered, and the English engineer was willing to cooperate with the Zionist Organization.

Now if you are really serious about your irrigation colony or colonies for Jews, and mean to take the matter up thoroughly, I offer my services to your Association and am prepared to thoroughly thresh out the irrigation and agricultural side and try to make them a success. . . . I am free now to take up any work in Asiatic Turkey as it is the ambition of my life to see Mesopotamia on the high way to regain its ancient fertility. In Asiatic Turkey I wish to work and would work gladly for your society as your irrigation and agricultural adviser.[69]

The meeting between Warburg and Willcocks was summed up in a detailed memorandum that was presented to the president of the Zionist Organization, David Wolffsohn, who was asked to act on it and discuss it with the institutions of the Zionist movement. Wolffsohn rejected Warburg's plan and was not prepared to retreat from the "only Palestine" principle, and he thought that Palestine should not be substituted by any other territory, even one that adjoined it. In a meeting of the Zionist Executive Committee held in Paris, he informed Warburg "that they [the members of the Executive Committee] did not agree to accept the Cyprus proposal, and had even less desire to enter into the Aram Naharaim matter; they have no faith in the practical ability of Willcocks to raise the funds, etc.; and generally speaking it was not possible to take on such a great burden without first receiving the required license."[70]

In July 1908, after the Young Turk revolution led to a new government and new political horizons, the Mesopotamia plan began to gain traction. Oscar Strauss, the American ambassador in Constantinople, drew Zangwill's attention to the Mesopotamia plan and informed him that Wilcox was then in Iraq examining the possibilities of an irrigation project for the Turkish government. Zangwill was fascinated by the idea and began promoting it in the ITO institutions. In early February 1909 the ITO Executive Committee decided to push the plan for Jewish settlement in Mesopotamia. It contacted the ICA, which had amassed a great deal of experience in organizing settlements in both Argentina and Palestine, and proposed cooperation between the two groups if and when the plan was put into action.

Unexpected support was received from Ahmed Riza, the former speaker of the Turkish Parliament and leader of the Young Turks in Paris. He was quoted as having told the new chief rabbi in Constantinople, at the beginning of April, that the Ottoman Empire would welcome Jewish immigrants from Russia and Romania. Zangwill quickly sent a letter to Riza in which he presented the aims of the ITO and noted that its directors were prominent Jewish leaders who could take on a settlement project of this scope. Zangwill stressed the contribution that the Jewish settlers could make to Mesopotamia, both in capital and in manpower. However, he wished to make it clear that the final aim of the ITO was to set up a refuge for the Jewish people, so the territory had to be large enough to absorb hundreds of thousands of immigrants every year.

> To his Excellency M. Ahmed Riza Bey,
>
> . . . A speech of your Excellency's has been circulated here purporting to be made by you to the Grand Rabbi Nahum of Turkey, in which you invite the Jews to Mesopotamia. If you really gave such an invitation, then our Organization which is supported by the leading Jews of the world and could undertake to unify all Jewish Organizations in favour of a concrete project, would be willing to go into the matter provided Turkey was ready to set aside definite territory within which the Jews should be able to form the predominant majority. . . . A mere general invitation, however, to the individual emigrant to enter Mesopotamia does not interest our organization which has set itself the task of building up a final land of refuge for those Jews who are unable or unwilling to live in the lands in which they at present live.[71]

Because Mesopotamia was close to Palestine, it was a preferred option for the Territorialists. Zangwill, in his enthusiasm, linked the country with the birthplace of the patriarch Abraham and emphasized that it was located on the borders of the biblical Land of Israel. He regarded Mesopotamia as an uninhabited or sparsely populated territory, without "a known civilization that could influence the Jews to become assimilated." He therefore had no doubt that for the "refugee from Russia it lies across the Black Sea, and when the Baghdad and other railways are finished, it will be a far more convenient centre of refuge than New York."[72]

Max Mandelstamm also spoke in praise of Mesopotamia: "This historic land, once the center of great kingdoms, should not be left desolate and abandoned in the future, too. Given its climate and fertile soil, the land should once again become as great as before and have a strong influence on the future revival of western Asia."[73] Because of the connection between Mesopotamia and Palestine, Zangwill anticipated cooperation with the Zionist Organization, some of whose members had shown an interest in the matter.

> If one cannot rise then it is necessary to descend; one should concede to the other, and if not, then nothing will be done. The ITO and the others as well [the Zionists] have to make concessions! We know that only by unifying our forces can we achieve our goals, and we shall do everything that will bring about our general union. The Jewish people should no longer again face destruction through division and internal disintegration. Its liberation should not and cannot be the work of only one party, but the work of the entire Jewish nation. We hope that all the major Jewish organizations will focus on Mesopotamia, including the Zionist Organization and the ICA. The program of the ITO is: National Unity.[74]

As he had done with the plans for East Africa and Australia and in his attempt to advance the plan for settlement in Mesopotamia, Zangwill tried to take advantage of the fact that the countries of Europe, especially Great Britain, had their own interests in the Ottoman Empire. This was a central motive in his efforts to obtain Mesopotamia; the backwardness of the native population was a good reason to replace them with Russian Jews. "You are aware that the ITO has chosen the ancient land of Mesopotamia to offer it to the Jewish people," Zangwill told his followers in Leeds in the summer of 1909.

> What and where is this Mesopotamia? It is a neglected portion of the Turkish Empire, with few cities and few inhabitants, some settled peacefully, but the majority wild nomads and only nominally under Turkish control.... Unpopulated land, you see, is worth nothing in the market. And who is to cultivate the land of Mesopotamia? Who is to ride on them? Is it the Kurds and the Bedouins? Will they sell their Arab steeds and settle down into farm labourers?[75]

To ensure the plan's success, Zangwill tried to interest the German Jewish banker Jacob Schiff, who was just then involved in the Galveston plan (discussed later in this chapter). At first Schiff showed a certain interest in Mesopotamia, but he soon realized its shortcomings and the enormous sums of money that would be required to turn that land into a place that could absorb settlers. He explained to Zangwill that without government support it would be difficult to carry out the plan for Mesopotamia. The capital required to turn it into a fertile region for settlement exceeded his own resources and those of other financiers in the Jewish world.[76]

Because the ITO did not have the means to bear the expenses alone, its leaders decided to wait and see what would be the position of the ICA on the matter. In October 1909 the ICA decided to send a research expedition to Mesopotamia to examine the possibilities of settlement in it. The members of the expedition began their work in November 1909 and remained in the area until June 1910. Zangwill found himself dependent on the conclusions of an expedition that was unrelated in any way to the ITO, with members who were distant from territorialist ideology, and in the midst of a process for the acquisition of territory over which the ITO had no control. Disconcerted, Zangwill consulted Strauss as to what he should do to quickly activate the Mesopotamia plan. Strauss told him that he had met with Willcocks but what he had heard from him was not particularly encouraging: that the land between the two rivers was not suitable for European settlers.[77] Strauss even offered to send Zangwill Willcocks's full report but asked him to be discreet and not say how he obtained it.[78] However, Strauss urged Zangwill to wait for the ICA report and its conclusions.

> You ask me "What should I do now"; I advise you to cooperate with the [ICA], to wait for the results of their investigation, and not to stand up for the [ITO] Mesopotamia Plan. Even if a small scale settlement there is decided upon, I still recommend that you cooperate with them. Since even large oak trees grow from small acorns. Especially if they are planted in good earth and environment.[79]

The conclusions of the ICA research expedition, which were published at the beginning of 1910, were not positive. The report said that so long as there was no improvement in the security situation in Mesopotamia and so long as the irrigation plan of Willcocks was not launched, it was too early to begin thinking about Jewish settlement. The agronomist Akiva Ettinger (1872–1945), a member of the ICA expedition who went out to examine whether Mesopotamia was suitable for Jewish settlement, summarized his conclusions as follows:

> 1. The north part of Aram Naharaim is destined to be the focal point of a clash between various nations and powers; 2. There is nothing in the region that will attract Jews in particular, and good land also can be found in Russia and in North and South America; 3. Settlement in Aram Naharaim in parallel with Jewish settlement in Palestine will constitute a division of forces and a waste of resources; 4. Aram Naharaim will not arouse national sentiments among Jews; 5. Settlement in Palestine can be more rapid that in Aram Naharaim if efforts were only concentrated in it.[80]

Because it was improbable that these conditions would be met in the foreseeable future, the members of the expedition thought that there was no point in continuing to promote the settlement plan in this region.

> The mission sent by the Jewish Colonization Association to Macedonia visited not only that region, but also Adana, Aleppo, Damascus, Beyrut, and other localities in Asia and Asia Minor. The southern part of Macedonia was found unsuitable for settlement by immigrants from Europe. On the other hand there are tracts in Northern and Central Mesopotamia, which, although very hot, deserve consideration for this object owing to their dryness and salubrious climate. The soil is very fertile, but its cultivation would necessitate a heavy expenditure, as extensive irrigation works would first have to be carried out. Without these preliminary operations and construction of roads, as well as the enforcement of the Constitutional regime, an immigration of Jews, whose number would have to be limited to 10,000, would be impossible.[81]

As soon as it became clear that the ICA would not undertake the settlement enterprise in Mesopotamia, the ITO filed away the plan and took it off its agenda. Zangwill, indefatigable, began searching for other territories for the Jewish people. The last and significant negotiations he conducted were with the Portuguese government over Angola, but this also ended in failure.

## ANGOLA

The interest of the Jews in the possibility of settlement in the Portuguese colonies in Angola had begun in the early twentieth century. The ICA, which was founded by Baron Hirsch in 1891 with its center in Paris, searched for areas for Jewish agricultural settlements and showed interest in Angola. During 1900–1902, the management of the ICA applied to Dr. Alfredo Bensaúde, the Jewish director of the Polytechnion in Lisbon, to find out whether it was possible to send migrants to the Portuguese colonies in Angola. Dr. Bensaúde sent this proposal to the prime minister, Jose Luciano de Castro, but the prime minister responded that because of the religious tendencies of the queen, there was no chance that the proposal would be acceptable.[82]

In 1907 the idea of settling Jews in Angola was raised once again. This time it was proposed by a member of the London branch of the ITO, Meyer Spielman, after he had met with the engineer John Norton-Griffiths, who held the contract to lay the rail line in Benguella plateau. Norton-Griffiths was exposed to the territorialist idea through the speeches of Israel Zangwill that were published in the contemporary press, and he thought that it would be possible to link his dealings on the African continent with the aims of the ITO. From his familiarity with the region, its inhabitants, climate, and personalities in the Portuguese government, Norton-Griffiths was convinced that the ITO would receive a settlement license without any problems because it served both the interests of Portugal, which wanted white settlers in its colonies, and the interests of the ITO, which was searching for a homeland for the Jewish people.[83]

Zangwill, at that time, rejected the proposal because he thought that Angola was not suitable for Jewish settlement and because he was suspicious that Norton-Griffiths's motives were purely for business reasons and not for the benefit of the ITO. Zangwill was also engrossed in negotiations over the Ontario province in Canada, and in addition he claimed that Angola was already inhabited by 4 million people, most of them black, who were liable to make it difficult to carry out the plan.[84] Even the assertions by Norton-Griffiths that there were no more than 200,000 inhabitants and that the designated portion of land was uninhabited did not change Zangwill's negative opinion of Angola because he was suspicious of Norton-Griffiths's hidden motives.[85] The question of Angola was again raised in 1911 by Rabbi M. I. Cohen of Rhodesia, who wrote to Zangwill and recommended Angola as a land of unusual potentialities for the white man.

> During the last couple of years many co-religionists have gone up to the Congo territory, which is enormously rich. As the Rand opened up South Africa, so the Congo will open up the heart of the continent and will be fed both from East and the West. The Lobito bay railway will be completed in a few years' time, and the line will feed enormous market. Now, the Portuguese territory is a beautiful country, healthy, with considerable native population, but practically no whites, and with great agriculture potentialities. Lobito bay will be the route for passenger and trade to the Congo and to South Africa. The possibilities for white colonization are enormous.[86]

After the failure of the negotiations over the Ontario province in Canada and after six years of ceaselessly searching for a territory for the Jewish people, Zangwill tended toward a more positive attitude for the proposal, and it was discussed for the first time by the ITO Executive Committee. The political changes in Portugal also gave him some measure of optimism regarding the chances to set up Jewish settlements in Angola. In October 1910 a revolution broke out in Portugal that deposed the royal family and led to the establishment of a republic. In the first stage, the new government annulled the discriminatory laws and conducted a more liberal and tolerant regime. For the first time Catholic citizens were allowed to leave their religion and adopt another one if they so wished; religious marriages no longer had validity, and church leaders were persecuted by republican loyalists; there was also a real change in diplomatic policy when the young government tried to prevent British and German domination over Angola and at the same time tried to strengthen its hold over its overseas colonies. For this reason the government wanted to encourage the migration of European settlers to Angola and to set up colonies under their patronage.

Against this political and diplomatic background, two prominent Lisbon Jews, Wolf Terló and Alfredo Bensaúde, broached the idea of offering Angola to the Jews. Terló was a Russian-born Zionist who had emigrated to Palestine and studied agriculture at Mikve Yisrael but then settled in Lisbon and became a successful businessman. Bensaúde was of Portuguese Jewish origins and the director of the Lisbon Polytechnic Institute. Both men were intimate with government officials, and their proposals, submitted independently of each other and to different people, fell on attentive ears.[87] Terló drew the attention of the Portuguese economist Jose Relvas to the possibilities latent in the dispatch of Jews to Angola. Bensaúde spoke to Jose d'Almada, a senior official in the Portuguese Colonial Office, and persuaded him that setting up a Jewish colony in Angola would advance the interests of the Portuguese government.[88]

In March 1912 Terló wrote to the territorialist office in Zurich and tried to arouse interest in the possibility of setting up an autonomous Jewish center in Portuguese Africa. Terló was close to the territorialist idea and a reader of the ITO journal, then published in Zurich. It was therefore only natural for him to share with them the idea that had occurred to him after the revolution in Portugal and to draw their attention to the possibilities that Angola presented. His letter set off diplomatic negotiations that were more serious and intensive than any the ITO had ever conducted. "To the Jewish Territorial Organization in Zurich," Terló wrote:

> I read your letter with great pleasure and I shall publish it immediately in the newspapers here. I know the Territorialist Movement. In fact, we aspire to the very same aim—we have to search for radical means to aid our persecuted masses in the various countries. For twenty years I have been following events in the Jewish world with great interest. Eight years ago, when I began working in the department for agricultural affairs of Portugal, I became interested in the question of whether there was any possibility of using my contacts with senior government officials for the benefit of the Jewish people.[89]

## CHAPTER 5

The territorialist office in Zurich forwarded the letter's contents to Zangwill; from that point on the ITO executive worked to promote the plan. A delegation was sent to Lisbon to examine the details more closely. Its members included the president of the territorialist chapter in Sweden, David Jochelman; the chairman of the ITO in Russia, Judge Jacob Teitel; and Nahum Slouschz of Paris. They reported back to Zangwill that the plan was solid and recommended that he come to Lisbon to meet the relevant people. Zangwill arrived in Lisbon on May 12, 1912. Before his departure he held a meeting at the Foreign Office, which supplied him with an informal but sympathetic letter to the English ambassador in Portugal, Arthur Hardinge. In one of his earlier postings, Hardinge had served as governor of the East Africa Protectorate shortly before it was proposed to Herzl.[90]

In Lisbon Zangwill met with the leaders of the Jewish community, d'Almada, and various government officials, from whom he heard further details about the plan and its prospects for success. Zangwill's main efforts were directed toward persuading the Portuguese government to give the ITO a settlement franchise. But the government preferred direct contacts between the colonists and its officials rather than through the mediation of the ITO. This was a difficult matter of principle for both sides in the negotiations. The ITO was interested in a settlement enterprise with a national character, whereas the Portuguese government was afraid of the infringement on its sovereignty.

No decision about this issue was made during Zangwill's visit to Lisbon, but an agreement was reached for a survey expedition to be sent to Angola.[91] From Zangwill's viewpoint these were steps in the right direction and an indication of Portugal's serious intentions. On June 15 the lower house of Parliament passed a bill for Jewish settlement in Angola and sent it on to the Senate. An examination of the bill's text shows that the Portuguese government wanted to control the Jewish colonization of Angola and refused to grant the ITO any management powers. The law stated explicitly that the legal authority to grant a concession for the land rested solely with the government and that the Jewish colonists would become Portuguese citizens. The Senate also empowered the government to grant land to Jewish philanthropic and immigration societies that "were lawfully established in Portugal or abroad, after they demonstrate they possess sufficient capital for the agricultural or industrial exploitation of their respective concessions." These societies would be allowed to set up schools, hospitals, and other public institutions to organize and plan the cities and urban centers in the designated area. The concession would allow each Jewish immigrant to receive an initial land grant of 100–250 hectares, which could be doubled if the settler exploited three-quarters of it. The children would study Portuguese at school, and all the Jewish colony's official correspondence would be conducted in that language.[92]

This was not the law that Zangwill had hoped for. There was no mention of the ITO, no reference to self-government, and the management of immigration to Angola was vested in the Portuguese government and not the ITO. In a letter to Bensaúde, Zangwill noted that "the Jewish colonization law" should guarantee that the government of Portugal "not interfere with our efforts to set up a land of refuge. This is the minimum requirement for autonomy without which the plan is without any value."[93] As the bill stood, he would find it difficult to accept the proposal. However, he hoped that this was not the final text and that it might still be amended. Full of hope and optimism, Zangwill arrived in Vienna for the annual ITO world congress at the end of June 1912.

The territorialist congress was held on June 27–30, with the participation of ITO delegates from Europe and elsewhere. The congress was opened by Dr. Engel, the vice-chairman of the ITO chapter in Vienna. He welcomed the participants and invited Zangwill to the podium to present the Angola plan and discuss its prospects. Zangwill began his speech by lauding the memory of Max Mandelstamm, who had passed away a short while earlier and who had "not been granted the opportunity to see the beginning of the plans for a future land of the Jews which will be discussed at this conference." Zangwill also mentioned Herzl and stressed that the vast majority of those attending the congress had been his disciples. "His memory will not depart from us," said Zangwill, who added that Herzl had believed that "the only solution for the Jewish question was the acquisition of a homeland for the Jewish people." Unfortunately, after his death, "The Palestine faction [of the Zionist Organization] turned the Movement into a caricature, and when the Zionist Congress of 1905 decided to reject the Uganda Plan offered us by the British Government, we founded our own organization—without thinking at first of secession—with the aim of obtaining a territory for the Jewish people."[94]

CHAPTER 5

The annual territorialist conference in Vienna, June 1912. The photograph is of Max Mandelstamm, and Israel Zangwill is seated on the right. (Central Zionist Archives)

After reminding his followers that they were the ones who were continuing on the historical path charted by Herzl, Zangwill said that it was the Zionists who had strayed from the revered leader's path. He referred to the Angola plan and noted the three main reasons that it would succeed:

1. Portugal did not have a large Jewish community that might create problems for the realization of the settlement initiative. Zangwill thought that a Jewish community living under the colonial power that provided the territory might impede or even oppose realization of the plan. But the small Jewish community in Portugal not only was sympathetic to the plan but also actively supported it.
2. Although there were not many Jews in Portugal, it had Jewish blood flowing through it. The Jewish origins of many of the Portuguese created a subconscious sympathy for the Jewish

people. Zangwill also emphasized the moral debt that Portugal owed the Jewish people after the expulsion from Spain in 1492. In his view, granting Angola to the Jews would in some fashion close the circle and atone for its primordial sin.
3. The Angola project was primarily a business initiative and not a sentimental one. The Portuguese government was aware of the fact that it did not have effective control of Angola and that Germany's prominent presence in southwest Africa posed a threat to the Portuguese colony. For this reason, Zangwill thought, a Jewish colony under the Portuguese flag would serve Portugal's interests.[95]

The congress delegates discussed the principles of the Portuguese colonization law of the Portuguese government and rejected it, but they authorized Zangwill to continue the negotiations and approved the dispatch of a survey team, headed by Professor John Walter Gregory, to the Benguella plateau in Angola should this prove necessary.[96]

The delegates were in an enthusiastic mood: The great moment they had so anticipated was finally at hand. As Joseph Kruk, who was at the congress, wrote in his memoirs: "The conference was crowned with great success. After all the various searches and inquiries, after the seven lean years, here at last we had a large and concrete plan that suited our essential national and socialist ideas. What was important above all is that the government contacted us. We decided to accept the offer and to continue with the negotiations, and in case of need to introduce certain amendments as well."[97]

On July 26, 1912, the ITO delegation sailed from Southampton. On August 22, after a stopover in Lisbon, it arrived at the port of Lobito in Angola. The financial difficulties that had plagued the Zionist expedition to East Africa were not repeated; Zangwill had no problem finding Jewish magnates, including Baron Edmond de Rothschild, who were willing to cover its expenses.[98] The delegation was headed by Professor Gregory, a renowned geologist, explorer, and professor of geology at the University of Glasgow in Scotland. Like Alfred St. Hill Gibbons, who had led the expedition to the Guas Ngishu plateau, Gregory was a veteran and experienced professional. He began his career in 1887 as an assistant in the Geology Department of the British Museum, subsequently taught at the University of Melbourne in Australia, and was appointed to the chair in geology in Glasgow in 1904, which he held for a quarter of a century. His research took him on field trips to the Rocky Mountains, East Africa, the Arctic Circle, and Tibet. The fact that Zangwill chose him to head the delegation indicates the great importance he attached to the Angola plan and his desire to receive precise and reliable information about the designated territory.

When Professor Gregory arrived in Lobito, he was warmly received by Edward Robins, the chief engineer of the Angola railway, and his staff. Gregory received much information from them, and on August 24, two days after his arrival, began his study of the interior of the country with the generous help of Robins, who accompanied him with his automobile. Gregory noted in his report that this mode of transportation, as opposed to the train, allowed him to become more closely familiar with the country. Travel by daylight and the many stops they made enabled him to take many samples and to converse with the chief engineer, who knew the country's advantages and disadvantages well. In the town of Lepi Gregory made preparations to continue the expedition on foot. He hired the services of twenty-five local porters and began his trek toward Huambo, about 40 kilometers from Lepi. When he arrived there, he was rejoined by Robins, who took him in his car to Caconda. Gregory left Lobito on September 29 and landed in Southampton on October 17. He had spent five weeks on the Benguella plateau, traveling 1,125 miles by car and 340 miles on foot.[99]

On his return to England, Professor Gregory composed his report and submitted it to Zangwill. A Star of David appeared in the upper third of the front page of the report, the aims of the ITO were stressed, and the purpose of the report was noted in the title: *Report on the Work of the Commission Sent Out by the Jewish Territorial Organization Under the Auspices of the Portuguese Government to Examine the Territory Proposed for the Purpose of a Jewish Settlement in Angola.*

The report consisted of eleven parts: the condition of Angola at the time of the report, a description of the route taken by the expedition, a geographic description of Angola, geological explanations of the region designated for Jewish settlement, the quality of the soil, the clearing of forests, climate, the agricultural character of the region, trade, political issues, and summary and conclusions. Two objectives were defined for the expedition. The first was to examine whether the climate was suitable for Europeans, and the second was to try to understand whether there was any connection between disease and the dearth of population in the Benguella plateau.

> The objects of our expedition to Angola, were, therefore, to inquire, firstly, whether the country is likely to contain a sufficient area of well-watered, fertile, unoccupied land for the ITO colony. Secondly, whether the reported depopulation of the Benguella plateau, if true, is due to diseases which would render the country unsuitable for European colonization.[100]

In this chapter I do not intend to refer to every issue in the report but mainly focus on the way in which the head of the expedition experienced Angola and his attitude toward the local population. The task imposed on Gregory and the negotiations conducted by Zangwill with the senior officials of the Portuguese government are not only a chapter in Jewish national history in modern times but also an inseparable part of European colonialism at the beginning of the twentieth century. The report is an interesting test case that allows us to examine the exploitation of Africa by the European powers. The transfer of the Benguella plateau to the ITO was supposed to serve both sides. On the one hand, the Jews of Eastern Europe would receive a land of refuge, and on the other hand, Portugal would deepen its hold in Africa through white settlers loyal to its government.

Although the journey through the Benguella plateau did not take more than five weeks, it allowed Professor Gregory to conduct a first examination and to determine the settlement potentialities in the designated territory. He reached the conclusion that the climate was favorable and that there were no dangerous or harmful wild animals. Also, many areas were fertile, and the railway line that was being laid could contribute much toward the development of the region.[101] With regard to diseases and the decrease in population, he asserted that

> from the evidence available in London there seemed great reason to fear that the population of the Benguella plateau had been greatly reduced in recent years by disease, and the district might

therefore be unsuitable for a colony; but this fear has proved groundless. The Benguella plateau appears to be remarkably salubrious. Its climate is pleasant as well as healthy, and owing to the beauty of its scenery, the freedom from insect pests, dangerous animals and vermin, the condition of life there are attractive and should easily be made comfortable.[102]

Gregory estimated that the population in the Benguella plateau was about 1,000 Portuguese settlers, most of whom were storekeepers. The number of agricultural families was a few score, and most of them were settled along the railway line. Besides the Portuguese, government officials, and missionaries, some Boer families had also migrated to the Benguella plateau from the Transvaal after its annexation by the British in 1877.[103] Gregory also estimated that the number of natives living on the Benguella plateau was 100,000. With regard to their status in a Jewish autonomy, Gregory determined that "it would be only fair to the natives to insert in any concession provisions securing them the land they already occupy and a reasonable reserve; and that is probably all the natives would expect."[104]

Gregory did not anticipate any problems with the local population and thought that the ITO and the Jewish settlers could achieve coexistence with them without difficulty.

> The natives in Angola would probably place no serious difficulty in the way of occupation of the unoccupied land. Small presents to the chiefs for permission to settle would probably satisfy them. In all probability the natives would retire gradually from the settled country. The Portuguese traders and Boers would very likely do the same, and thus leave the Jewish colonists to the almost continuous occupation of the area wherein they may settle.[105]

However, Gregory noted that the possibilities for settlement by individuals in the designated land were not great and therefore that the involvement of wealthy supporters would be necessary to ease the burden on the settlers.

> As the well-watered, healthy and fertile districts are high, the conditions are those characteristic of the warm temperate rather

than of the tropical zone. It is doubtful whether the country would grow the usual tropical products, and its profitable agriculture development may not be easy. The chances of success for individual colonists, settling there separately, are not hopeful.[106]

This assertion accorded with the decision taken at the Vienna Congress that ruled out settlement by individuals. However, there is a basis for assuming that the last sentence was inserted in the report at Zangwill's request to pressure the Portuguese government to change the law and to allow the ITO to manage the settlement initiative on the Benguella plateau. Gregory's conclusions about the designated land for Jewish settlement was positive, and it was because of the difficult financial situation in Portugal that he thought the ITO had the chance of obtaining a license from the Portuguese government.

> The Benguella plateau is not free from drawbacks, economic and political, but it is owing to them that the land is still vacant, and that a suitable concession might be obtained and developed on the lines desired, for it is owing to the moderate fertility of the land that it could be cheaply cleared and settled. The desert barrier, which must necessarily increase cost of export, has hitherto been an impassable obstacle to satisfactory progress; and that fact that the country belongs to a State which is not sufficiently wealthy to spend much on colonial development renders it possible to secure a concession on terms allowing of great freedom in local self-government.[107]

Not everyone was in agreement with Gregory's conclusions. Harry Johnston, a well-known researcher of Africa and one of the prominent figures of English colonialism on the continent, and Henry Nevinson, who had written on the Second Boer War and reported on the slave trade in Angola at the beginning of the twentieth century, thought that Angola was not suitable for white settlers in general and for East European Jews in particular. Johnston claimed that most of the areas on the plateau were not suitable for settlement and that the only small part of it that was free of disease had already been settled by Boers and Portuguese.[108]

Nevinson, on the other hand, claimed that the Jewish settlers would find it difficult to get laborers to work in their fields, and he regarded

## CHAPTER 5

slavery in Angola as an evil that would affect the Jews living there and the attempt of the East European Jews to settle on the land.

> There are great difficulties in obtaining voluntary labour. All the plantations without exception, are worked by slave labour under the nominal excuse of contract. The whole colony is rotten with slavery. A few mission stations work with free labour, but not for profit. Angola not being a white man's country, the natural tendency is to employ solely black labour for working in the fields.[109]

Nevinson also anticipated a drift of Jews from the colony to the cities and towns of Angola and from there a mass return to Europe. He was pessimistic about Jewish settlement in West Africa and recommended that Zangwill give up the entire idea.

Although Johnston and Nevinson were critical with regard to the Benguella plateau and claimed that it was unsuitable for white settlement for climate reasons, they, like Gregory, also disregarded the native population and did not give any consideration to the system of relations it was expected to have with the new settlers. This sensitive issue was not seriously dealt with in the ITO when its members discussed Angola and other territories, and it seems that the Territorialists thought it could be resolved without any special difficulties.

So long as the expedition was engaged in investigating the designated territory, Zangwill refrained from diplomatic activity regarding the Portuguese government. He waited patiently for its conclusions but was mainly worried about the formulation of the law in its present form. In one of his many letters to Bensaúde, Zangwill wrote that only the common interest of Portugal and the ITO and mutual trust between them could lead to the plan's success. To his regret, there was no section in the law that could prevent the Portuguese government from halting immigration to Angola soon after the settlers arrived. As an emigration land, Angola was far inferior to the United States and many other regions, he wrote. Its only value to Jews would be for group colonization on a great scale. It was not necessary to talk of "autonomy," but it was necessary to obtain guarantees that the Jews' "land of refuge" would have a fair chance of growing and not be destroyed after the foundations had been painfully laid.[110] Yet, despite his criticism, Zangwill was convinced that the ITO and the Portuguese government had a common interest that would eventually induce Portugal to reconsider its proposal: "This little incident of the mouse and the lion is symbolic of the ... one with too much land and too little money and the other with too little land and too much money."[111]

To speed up the negotiations and effect a change in the Portuguese government's position, Zangwill began efforts to persuade Jewish financiers that the Angola plan was going to work. He hung his hopes on the Rothschild family, one of whom, Nathanael, was a member of the ITO Geographical Committee. Rothschild was skeptical about the true intentions of the Portuguese and found it hard to believe that it would grant territory to the Jews. Portugal's display of good will toward the ITO, he asserted, had nothing to do with concern for the Jewish people but stemmed from its desire to obtain a loan to cover its deficit. Zangwill tried to persuade Rothschild that his trip to Lisbon was crucial and would move the negotiations forward. Rothschild did not commit himself to support the Angola plan but was prepared to finance Zangwill's journey to Lisbon. Zangwill interpreted this as a kind of blessing for his journey and perhaps even as an agreement in principle by Lord Rothschild to give favorable consideration to the settlement plan if and when it became a reality.[112]

Despite all the efforts of persuasion by Zangwill and Bensaúde, not only did the government of Portugal refuse to accept their proposals, but also voices began to be heard against the plan itself. Senator Bernardine Roque protested that the ITO committee had rejected the offer of the Portuguese government and the law that was legislated and said that "no one could imagine that on our lands the ancient aspirations of Judaism to rebuild Zion would be realized.... Settlement as Portuguese—yes, but not as national Jews."[113] The support for Jewish settlement in Angola was replaced by doubts and fears that it was the first step toward the loss of the Portuguese colony for Portugal.

The law of Jewish settlement and the stormy debate over it in the Portuguese parliament and in the press opened the eyes of the Portuguese to see the economic and strategic potentialities inherent in Angola. When the law was brought before the Senate on June 29, 1913, it appeared to the senators that even with all its restrictions, the law was still dangerous to the sovereignty of Portugal in Angola. In the arguments and discussions,

## CHAPTER 5

fears were raised that the Jews might use the benefits that the law granted them to set up a state within a state. It was therefore decided to denude the law of its Jewish character and to turn it into a general settlement law. In the end, the law was transferred to the Colonial Committee on behalf of the Parliament for additional clarification and was buried there.[114]

Despite Zangwill's efforts to raise funds for the settlement plan and to persuade the Portuguese government to amend the law, the Angola plan was never realized—and for the same reasons that the plans for East Africa, Canada, and Australia had all failed. The Portuguese government was afraid that the new law might lead to the establishment of a state within a state, undermining the sovereignty of Portugal in general and its control of Angola in particular. Zangwill was again unable to raise the initial capital and faced the same problem as before: No Jewish magnate would pledge funds before the ITO received a promise of a territory, and the Portuguese government wanted to receive financial guarantees before transferring the territory to the ITO. In his letters to Bensaúde, Zangwill thought that money would be the least of his problems and that realization of the plan depended only on the agreement of the Portuguese government. He said that Portuguese assent was the greatest of his problems and that the ITO's financial prospects were limited and that not much could be done without them. Bensaúde also drew his attention to the financing issue and wrote that he had not thought money would be the obstacle, but in view of the situation, he advised Zangwill to file away the plan.[115]

~

To set up Jewish autonomy in Angola, the Territorialists depended on the European colonial powers and tried to take advantage of their interests in territories under their control for the sake of Jewish interests. The Territorialists did not see any contradiction between Jewish migration to Angola and the rights of the native population there. This sensitive issue was given explicit reference in Gregory's report when he asserted that the natives of Angola were satisfied with little and that, by bribing tribal leaders, it would be possible to achieve good neighborly relations and maintain peace between the two sides. However, it should be noted that the main motive of both the Zionists (in relation to the El-Arish and East Africa plans) and the Territorialists was not to dispossess the local population or to exploit the natural resources of Angola. It was to solve the Jewish problem in countries where Jews were in distress (especially in Eastern Europe), in view of the increasing number of pogroms and the fear that the gates of the United States would close. It was a pragmatic attempt to solve a concrete problem of the downtrodden and persecuted East European Jewry.

However, even if this was not an attempt to exploit the local population, the ITO did not think it was necessary to consider the needs and desires of the native population. The approach of Zangwill and his colleagues reflected European interests and attitudes toward Africa and its native population. It expressed the European consensus toward the non-European world in general and Africa in particular and regarded the natives as failed nations and savages who should be reshaped in the Western spirit. According to this approach, the Jews would come in and settle the land and bring progress and money with them, thus transforming the savage African continent so distant from Western advance into a better and more enlightened continent.

The ITO leadership searched the entire globe for an uninhabited territory. When the Angola plan was taken off the territorialist agenda, the organization's members could not avoid feeling deep disappointment and frustration. Doubts began to arise regarding the ITO's justification for existing. For the first time, questions surfaced about its ability to acquire a territory for the Jewish people.

## GALVESTON

The Galveston plan was not part of the ITO's diplomatic efforts to acquire a land of refuge for the Jewish people but was the result of cooperation between Israel Zangwill and the American Jewish banker Jacob Schiff.[116] The plan was first floated in 1901, when Schiff established the Industrial Removal Office, with the aim of reducing the Jewish immigrant population in the cities of the East Coast and dispersing them throughout the United States.[117] As more and more Jews congregated in New York, Boston, and Philadelphia, Schiff was increasingly concerned about the social implications of the poor housing conditions, population density, and destitution in the poverty-stricken neighborhoods where they resided. Any immigrant who was willing to move west received a train ticket from Schiff and assistance in finding a job and integrating into the local Jewish community. Between 1901 and 1905 the Industrial Removal Office supported 25,000 immigrants in this way. Then the mass immigration of Jews reached new and unprecedented peaks. Within ten years (1904–1914), more than 1.7 million Jews arrived in the United States, nearly four times as many as had come in the previous three decades. These numbers overwhelmed the Industrial Removal Office, forcing Schiff to look for a more drastic solution to reduce the pressure on the East Coast cities. Instead of sending Jews westward, perhaps they could be sent directly to other ports of entry. Schiff needed some organization that would handle the travel arrangements, register the immigrants, and send them from their countries of origin to the United States, and he and his staff would see to their dispersal and absorption. The port they selected was Galveston, Texas, on the Gulf of Mexico.

Of all the organizations that were active in Eastern Europe, the ITO was the most natural partner for Schiff's initiative. In the post-Herzl era the Zionist Organization had concentrated its efforts on Palestine, and the ICA, which had been established by Baron Hirsch, became entangled in difficulties in Argentina and avoided new philanthropic adventures. As a young organization established at the height of the mass migration from Eastern Europe westward, the ITO regarded Schiff's initiative as a good opportunity to strengthen its standing in the Jewish street until an appropriate territory could be found. For the enthusiastic territorialist activists who went to work organizing the migration, classifying the migrants, and sending them to Texas, this was good preparation for their role in a future Jewish settlement that would be established if Zangwill obtained a suitable territory.

The connection between Zangwill and Schiff began even before the Galveston plan, when Zangwill tried to persuade Schiff to join the ITO and support the territorialist idea publicly. Schiff politely rejected the request. He praised Zangwill for his readiness to devote his time to solving the Jewish problem in Eastern Europe but was opposed in principle to the territorialist solution: "I have devoted much thought to the question of how the Jewish problem can be solved. I do not believe that Zionism can do this, but even less so can the Territorialist plan." The Zionists, Schiff wrote to Zangwill, "at least have justification based on a glorious historical past." On the other hand, the Territorialists want "to set up a state in the heart of Africa or some other place" detached from the history of the Jewish people, and their failure could have an unfortunate influence. Schiff thought that the solution to the Jewish problem had to be pursued in Russia, not creating autonomies overseas.[118] Zangwill's letters in reply to Schiff and attempts to persuade him to join the ITO did not succeed, but the two men shared feelings of mutual sympathy and esteem.

Because the number of immigrants to the United States had grown dramatically, Schiff realized that he had to take significant steps if he wanted to reduce the number of Jews in the coastal cities in the East. In December 1904 he sent a letter to Paul Nathan, who was then head of the Hilfsverein der Deutschen Juden, and shared his idea of sending the immigrants from Europe directly to Philadelphia, Baltimore, Boston, New Orleans, Charleston, Savannah, and Galveston.[119] This was an idea that had not yet matured into practical terms. By the summer of 1906 Schiff seems to have sketched out the plan in general and reached the conclusion that without cooperation in the immigrants' country of origin, the idea could not be implemented. Schiff needed help in persuading the local Jews to emigrate, in distributing propaganda material that stressed the advantages of Galveston over New York, and in placing a representative in the ports of departure who would negotiate with the shipping companies, concentrate the migrants in the port cities, and send them across the ocean. Given the relations between Schiff and Zangwill, it seemed natural to choose the ITO to play this role.

On August 24, 1906, Schiff sent a letter to Zangwill in which he outlined his project. He described the distress of the Jewish immigrants in the densely populated cities on the East Coast and suggested sending them directly from Europe to New Orleans or Galveston, from which they could be dispersed throughout the interior. He requested the assistance of the ITO, even though he knew that its main aim was finding a territory in which to establish an autonomous settlement for the Jewish people. "Surely," Schiff wrote, "the carrying out of this project will furnish the relief which is so imperatively needed, much more promptly than the creating of a new land of refuge, which at best and even successful, it must take many many years to bring to a condition, where large number of people could enter such a land of refuge with safety to their future well-being."[120] Schiff's arguments that there was not enough time to set up a land of refuge for the masses of Jewish migrants and that the

Galveston plan was the quickest and best solution for their distress were similar to the criticisms that Zangwill had directed against Zionism. However, Schiff stressed that he had no intention of diverting the ITO from its declared goal; he merely wanted to help the Jewish migrants efficiently and without delay; the ITO could continue at the same time in its search for a territory, with no connection to the Galveston plan. He noted that he intended to allocate half a million dollars for the enterprise and to raise another $1.5 million in England, France, and Germany.[121] Zangwill accepted Schiff's proposal in principle but conditioned it on the agreement of the ITO congress, which was due to convene in October 1906.[122] On October 30, the congress agreed to cooperate with Schiff and to handle the arrangements for emigration from Eastern Europe to Galveston.[123]

For the Territorialists the Galveston plan was what the Uganda plan had been for the Zionists: a temporary refuge until a suitable territory could be found to establish a Jewish autonomous region. For them it was a unique opportunity to develop an organizational infrastructure with Schiff's money, which would be used in the first stage to send the immigrants to Galveston but would later be at the ITO's disposal to send migrants to a future Jewish colony. Moreover, the ITO's entry into the field of emigration arrangements reflects the Territorialists' desire to undertake any activity that would relieve the distress of the Jews in the Pale of Settlement, even if it did not advance the immediate aims for which the ITO had been founded. In many ways the Galveston plan resembled the decision taken by the Zionists at the Helsingfors conference in 1906, when they elected to pursue *Gegenwartsarbeit* (work in the present). In other words, although the national problem of the Jewish people could be solved only in Palestine, the Jews in the Diaspora could not be abandoned and their economic and national status had to be bolstered so that they would be able to move to Palestine. The Territorialists thought that arranging transportation to Galveston, registering the emigrants, and meeting with them in the territorialist chapters throughout the Pale of Settlement would help them influence the Jews to recognize the ITO's importance. The contact with the Jewish street would lead to winning hearts and minds, and at the moment of truth the masses would move to the designated territory.

However, Zangwill expected that he would be able to modify the aims of the Galveston plan and channel its resources into a national settlement initiative in the spirit of the ITO. The masses of Jews who arrived in Texas would create a demographic concentration that could not be ignored. In his view, the western part of the United States had a combination of favorable conditions—a relatively sparse population and economic potential—and hundreds of thousands of immigrants could settle there and enjoy a reasonable standard of living.

> Every migrant who arrives in Galveston is doing a double mitzvah. The first is in reducing the chances that the gates of the United States will close. The second is the development of new cities of refuge and new places for our brethren migrating to foreign countries. Every person who sails to Galveston and settles there successfully will increase the Jewish population in the region and pave the way for those coming after him. In this way, a home will be created for our people, one that will be prepared to receive our unfortunate brethren in case of catastrophes in the lands of exile. A home like this is very necessary even if Jews go to Palestine or any other country in which they have their own territory. Even the most enthusiastic Zionist will admit that it is not possible to direct a large wave of Jewish migrants—at least 100,000 each year—to Palestine or any other undeveloped place without creating economic catastrophe and famine. Only a land that is partly developed, like the American West, has the capacity to absorb thousands of immigrants, to support them, and to provide enough possibilities for them to make a living.[124]

Schiff, the plan's originator, never spoke in terms of creating a homeland for the Jewish people. His aspirations were more modest. All he wanted was to bring the Jewish masses to the port of Galveston, to disperse them in small groups throughout the United States, and to avoid as much as possible any demographic concentrations. Zangwill's aspirations, as said before, were completely different. In a "strictly confidential" letter to David Jochelman, the ITO activist overseeing implementation of the Galveston plan in the Pale of Settlement, Zangwill requested that the arrangements be made in the "ITO spirit."[125] Jochelman also wrote about the hidden aims of the Galveston plan. To promote the plan and disseminate it among

## CHAPTER 5

the Jews in the Pale of Settlement, the ITO published a newspaper, *Wohin*, which dealt with matters of Jewish emigration in general and with the Galveston plan in particular. According to Jochelman, the ITO remained loyal to its worldview: "It does not negate the Diaspora with all its joys and sufferings, its fears and hopes"; but it also does not negate "the deep and long-lasting hopes of the Jewish people for its own homeland." With regard to the aims of the Galveston Plan, he wrote:

> Migration is an established fact in the lives of the eternally wandering people and it must be organized. The ITO has begun quietly and energetically not only as a Territorialist Organization, but also as an emigration company that tries to find those new places that can serve as cities of refuge for those who flee their old home. The ITO has set a high aim for itself. Although the working methods [of the emigration company] are meant to help individuals, the main goal it strives for is to benefit everyone.[126]

For Zangwill, Galveston was much more than philanthropic assistance for East European Jewry. Unlike the other territorialist initiatives he had promoted, this time Zangwill refrained from declaring his aims explicitly. American law forbade the entry of immigrants who were members of any kind of ideological movement, especially a national movement. Any expression of a nationalistic coloring would have placed a question mark on the Galveston plan and burdened it with unnecessary difficulties that might even endanger it. One could not possibly expect Zangwill to set aside his nationalistic ideas and promote a plan that was aimed solely at easing the suffering of the immigrants in the cities on the East Coast. The Territorialists agreed to help Schiff realize his plan, but they clearly expected the Galveston plan to break out of its narrow boundaries and lead to the establishment of a homeland for the Jewish people in the western United States. They thought that the demographic situation created in Galveston would be irreversible and would lead necessarily to the official recognition of a Jewish enclave there. Their interpretation of the Galveston plan hardly differed from the arguments of the "practical Zionists" who had claimed that the creation of facts in Palestine was the only way to attain political goals. This idea stood in complete opposition to the aspirations of the Territorialists, who wanted to receive from one of the European powers, by means of a diplomatic process, both a territory and protection for their settlement initiative, as Herzl had defined it in *The Jewish State*.

For this reason the Territorialists preferred to send young migrants in their teens or early 20s to Galveston. According to territorialist doctrine, the pioneers were to lay the groundwork in the designated territory and prepare it for absorbing the masses who would follow them. Indeed, the demographic breakdown of the Galveston immigrants was quite different from that of the migrants who landed in New York. About 77 percent of the Galveston migrants were men, whereas nearly half of those who disembarked at Ellis Island were women. The age distributions were also quite different. A quarter of those who came through Ellis Island were children under the age of 14, whereas the proportion of children who came through Galveston was only 14 percent. About 80 percent of the Galveston immigrants were age 15–44, compared to 70 percent of those who arrived at Ellis Island. The proportions of those over age 45 were similar, however.[127]

The gender and age differences show that the immigrants who came to the western United States under the aegis of the ITO were younger and more able-bodied. Most of them were unmarried and childless. The demographic breakdown is important, because it reveals Zangwill's hidden intentions and desire to take advantage of the plan for his nationalist aims. The plan's overt purpose, as noted, was to bring about a drastic reduction in the number of immigrants landing on the East Coast and staying there. Schiff was not disturbed by the large numbers of energetic young men who arrived in Manhattan every month but by the families with many young children who found it difficult to subsist in the harsh realities of the Lower East Side. Instead of letting men, women, and children into Galveston, the ITO made a careful selection and sent only those who were young, strong, and healthy. The idea was to create an irreversible situation and prepare the groundwork for those who would come after them.

Schiff knew very well that the Territorialists wanted to exploit the Galveston plan to advance their own ideas. In a letter to Judge Mayer Sulzberger—one month after his letter to Zangwill asking for ITO cooperation—he noted that "the aims of Zangwill's plans are above all impractical, and very little will come of them even if they can to some extent ameliorate the present living conditions."[128] However, although Schiff thought that the territorialist idea was not feasible in the United States, it was important for him that the immigrants be aware before they left Eastern Europe that they were not coming as representatives of the ITO but as individuals seeking to become acclimated to and integrated into American society. "I am very clear in my mind," wrote Schiff, "that when immigrants arrive here, they must cease to be under the protection of the ITO or any other society or individual."[129]

It was the ITO that classified the migrants in Eastern Europe and sent them to the United States, but it was Schiff and his agents who received them and dispersed them in small groups throughout the country. In this way the Jewish banker neutralized the influence of the territorialist idea, if it even existed, among the Galveston immigrants. The person greeting the immigrants (Jacob Schiff) had a much greater impact on them than the man who saw them off (Israel Zangwill). A letter to Schiff from Jacob Bilikoff, who was responsible for absorbing the migrants in Kansas City, reflects the extent to which Zangwill's expectations of the Galveston plan were exaggerated and impractical and the accuracy of Schiff's estimations.

> The process of Americanizing, of normalizing the Jewish immigrant begins when he embarks for America. The moment that immigrant enters our night schools, and acquires the rudiment of the English language; the moment he acquires a little competence; the moment he sends his children to school; the moment his boys go to the high school or university, which privileges were denied him and his children in his own country ... that moment all his radicalism evaporates and he becomes a full-fledged and law-abiding member of the community.[130]

In July 1907 the first group of several dozen immigrants landed in Galveston. Only about 8,000 migrants arrived there by the outbreak of World War I. Zangwill's expectations of a migration stream that would create a demographic concentration and produce a turning point in territorialist activities were not realized. Schiff also was displeased. The small number of immigrants who made landfall in Texas did not change the demographic balance in the cities of the East Coast, and Jews continued to live in the overcrowded and impoverished neighborhoods of

New York, Boston, and Philadelphia. Just as the Jewish immigrants were not willing to leave New York after their arrival—even if they received free transportation and the guarantee of a job—they were not prepared to change their original plans, which had been carefully laid out in Eastern Europe, and go to the Gulf of Mexico instead of Ellis Island.

Among all the political initiatives discussed in this chapter, the Galveston plan was the only one that the ITO ever implemented, albeit in limited scope. This was mainly a reflection of its weakness and difficulties in finding an uninhabited territory where it could set up an autonomous colony for the Jewish people under the protection of a European power.

---

When the Territorialists seceded from the Zionist Organization after the Seventh Zionist Congress and set up the ITO, they set themselves the aim of obtaining a territory for the Jewish people on an "autonomous basis for those among Jews who cannot or will not remain in the lands in which they at present live." To obtain such a territory, Zangwill began meeting with a succession of heads of state and government officials and tried to persuade them that granting a territory for an autonomous Jewish colony would primarily serve the interests of their own countries but would also provide a just solution to the Jewish problem. There does not seem to have been a single country on Earth that was not considered and examined for its advantages, disadvantages, and chances of success if and when Jewish settlers arrived there. Territories were examined in the Americas (Ontario, Canada; Nevada, Idaho, and Galveston, Texas, in the United States; Argentina; Bolivia; and Colombia), Africa (Rhodesia, Libya, Angola, and East Africa), Australia (the Federal Territory and the area of Kimberley), and Asia (Mesopotamia).

Among the ideas and possibilities raised over the years, Zangwill conducted negotiations only over East Africa, Canada, Australia, and Angola. All the rest were false hopes that soon came to naught. As time passed, the Territorialists understood that obtaining a territory was not an easy matter. They found it hard to convince their interlocutors that a Jewish autonomous region in one of their overseas colonies was of vital interest for the preservation of their power. Every time Zangwill thought he was on the cusp of a political breakthrough, the negotiations foundered. The reasons were varied: public opinion that reacted with hostility to large-scale immigration by Jews; the fear of ethnic segregation and the establishment of a state within a state; the conditioning of an agreement on guaranteed support of the settlement enterprise by Jewish philanthropists, who in turn would not pledge any funding without an agreement in principle from the European power. Zangwill never found a way out of this vicious circle, and all his negotiations reached a dead end.[131]

The Mesopotamia plan is an interesting test case, because it shows that the Territorialists (like the Zionists) sought historical justification for why Jews were entitled to settle in some place other than the Land of Israel. Zangwill, like the Zionists, enlisted the Bible, the founding father of the Jewish people, Abraham, and the ancient Jewish community in Babylonia. The territorialist attempt to depict Mesopotamia as part of the biblical homeland is evidence that every national movement needs a historical and mythological foundation to mobilize the masses. Both the Territorialists and the Zionists did this.

To obtain some place for the Jews, whether in Mesopotamia or elsewhere, the Territorialists relied on the colonial powers of Europe and endeavored to exploit those countries' interests in the territories under their control on behalf of Jewish interests. The Territorialists' core motive was not dispossessing the natives and exploiting the natural and human resources on behalf of some European power. They wanted to alleviate the Jews' economic and physical distress, mainly in Eastern Europe, and were energized by the escalation of the pogroms and the fear that the United States would shut its doors. Theirs was a pragmatic attempt to solve a concrete problem and did not conceal any complex underlying ideology. Still, even if there was no attempt to dispossess the local population, Zangwill and his associates were not concerned with its needs and preferences. Theirs was a typical European attitude toward the Orient and its inhabitants, expressing the European consensus about the non-European world and perception of non-European peoples as backward and primitive. The East was one vast uncivilized district and light-years removed from Western progress.

Of all the places that Zangwill negotiated for, Angola came the closest to realization. The law to encourage Jewish immigration to migrate to Angola was passed by the Portuguese parliament, and a delegation was sent out to survey the territory. But the high expectations were matched by deep disappointment. The Portuguese government did not accept

Zangwill's demand for autonomy in Angola and removed the settlement plan from its political agenda. On October 5, 1913, shortly before the government of Portugal withdrew its proposal for Jewish settlement in Angola, the ITO Council in London convened to discuss the chances of its success. Zangwill told its members that if this plan was not executed, he could not see any other place on the globe where their settlement program might be carried out.[132] He went on to say that he would be greatly disappointed if no "ITO land" could be found and that there would certainly be those who said that all their work had been a waste of time. But if their results were negative, even negative results have their value. If they did not show the way in which the Jews would go, they would show the ways in which they could not go.[133]

The great hopes of the days following the Uganda plan were exchanged for small ones, despair, and lack of faith. At the ITO meeting held a month after this speech to the ITO Council, the first calls were heard for officially dismantling the organization. World War I made the ITO irrelevant, and its end was only a matter of time.

In January 1914, in the waning days of the ITO, Zangwill gave up and admitted that all the chances of obtaining a territory for the Jewish people had been exhausted.

> It is not true that I no longer believe the Jews have the means to build the ITO state. But I believe less and less that the required territory will be found. This is not a theoretical but a practical question. We have knocked on all the most promising doors and everywhere we received the answer that had been given to the foolish virgins in the poem by Tennyson: "Too late, too late, Ye cannot enter now." The ITO should have been established at least a hundred years ago, when it was still possible to find an empty land with a favorable climate. Our committee will have to decide whether to abandon the ITO plan or to raise another in its place.[134]

# 6

# Swan Song

World War I abruptly and dramatically ended the ITO's diplomatic activity. Europe was drawn into a bloody conflict that lasted more than four years and changed the geopolitical map beyond recognition. The colonial era ended; in the new world order that followed, the ITO had no chance of receiving a territory where the Jewish people could set up an autonomous settlement. The fall of the tsarist empire, the Bolshevik Revolution, the reestablishment of Poland, the quota law that closed the gates to the United States, and the Balfour Declaration—all these made the ITO irrelevant. Its chapters gradually disbanded, and the activists, whose numbers had dwindled over the years, found new political outlets. The ITO became a one-man organization without the wide support of Eastern European Jewry it had enjoyed at the beginning of the twentieth century.

Between the end of World War I and the ITO's official disbanding in 1925, the ITO conducted no diplomatic negotiations and did not engage in any organizational or propaganda activity. The events and the changes, after the war and in the early 1920s, pulled the rug out from under the ITO and Zangwill. But the territorialist idea did not fade away; various Jewish groups still viewed it as a realistic solution for the Jewish problem. The organizational framework was gone, but the concept lingered on.

This chapter is divided into two main sections. In the first section I assess Zangwill's positions toward the Zionist movement in the years from the Balfour Declaration until his death in 1926. I try to understand how Zangwill coped intellectually with the new reality and how he tried to justify his territorialist activity. In the second section I focus on the

New Territorialism that manifested itself during the 1930s, after the Nazis' rise to power. Did the New Territorialists continue the path of the ITO, or did they take a new path that diverged from the territorialist doctrine of the early twentieth century?

## NEW TIMES, OLD SONGS

The outcome of World War I created a new political reality that narrowed the ITO's room to maneuver. In Palestine, though, new political opportunities emerged that provided the Zionist movement with impressive diplomatic achievements. The collapse of the Ottoman Empire and Britain's interest in the Middle East were the basis for long and arduous negotiations between the Zionist leadership and British officials, which culminated on November 2, 1917, in the British government's formal recognition of the Jewish people's right to a national home in Palestine.[1] The Balfour Declaration was the charter that Herzl aspired to receive through his diplomacy and the concession that Zangwill thought could have been obtained after he left the Zionist Organization. It was a diplomatic achievement of the highest importance, enabling the Zionists to regain the Land of Israel and lay the foundations for the Jewish state in the making.

Zangwill greeted the Zionists' feat enthusiastically. This was not surprising; from the first days of World War I Zangwill claimed that Jewish interests should be linked to those of the Allies. In 1915 he suggested that all Jewish soldiers be organized in separate regiments, and when the Zion Mule Corps was established, he expressed his hope that the British would allow this unit to conquer Palestine. He thought that the British should direct the war to the Palestine front, wrest the country from the Ottomans, and hand it over to the Jews, who would guard British interests in the region. In May 1917, six months before the Balfour Declaration was signed, Zangwill published "The Future of Palestine," an article in which he emphasized the natural bond between the Zionist movement and England. Even though the movement's headquarters were in Germany and Austria, England was its true spiritual home. He emphasized that at the start of his diplomatic efforts, Herzl had claimed that only under British sponsorship could the dream of a Jewish state be realized and he had expected that the Zionist movement would continue in this direction.[2]

## CHAPTER 6

So it is not surprising that on December 2, 1917, at the public celebration in London of the Balfour Declaration, Zangwill made a speech in favor of the declaration and congratulated Chaim Weizmann and Nahum Sokolow on their impressive achievement. He noted that the ITO could not object to the Balfour Declaration and would be betraying its own principles if it did so.[3] The purpose of the ITO was "to procure a territory upon an autonomous basis for those Jews who cannot or will not remain in the lands in which they at present live";[4] the Balfour Declaration conditioned the establishment of the national home on the maintenance of the Jews' rights and political status in their countries of residence. From his point of view, this was the other side of the coin and an ideal solution around which the Jewish world should and must unite. On the one hand, Jews who were not interested in coming to live in Palestine would enjoy equal rights; on the other hand, those who were unable or unwilling to remain in their countries of residence would have the option of moving to Palestine and settling there. However, despite the British government's explicit promise, some groups of Jews, especially in England, objected to the declaration and feared it. Zangwill asserted that the ITO's purpose was to serve as a bridge between the Zionists and their opponents.[5] To allay the opponents' concern, Zangwill suggested naming Palestine Judea and calling the Jews who lived there Judeans. Those who did not immigrate would be known as Jews. Thus a clear distinction would be made between the Jews of Palestine and those in the Diaspora who felt threatened by a Jewish state.[6] He concluded his speech with an emotional appeal to the suffering and oppressed nations of the world that they learn from the patience of the Jewish people, that the spirit is stronger than the sword, and "that the seer who foretold his people's resurrection was not less prophetic when he proclaimed also for all peoples the peace of Jerusalem."[7]

Zangwill's speech in favor of the Balfour Declaration reflected the ITO's position toward Zionism during the years of conflict between the two movements before World War I and the Balfour Declaration and shows that this position did not derive from a fundamental objection to Palestine but from the recognition and belief, in those years of pogroms and mass migration, that the Zionists would not achieve anything. In addition, Zangwill claimed that the Ottomans would create problems and would never allow the Zionist enterprise to acquire a substantial foothold in Palestine. But as soon as all the obstacles were removed and the Jewish people's right to a national home was recognized, Zangwill no longer had any reason to continue his search for a territory suitable for Jewish settlement.[8] His support for the Balfour Declaration ended the activities of the ITO. This was reflected by his absence from the Versailles conference in January 1919 and his failure to submit to it an ITO plan regarding the Jewish question. Zangwill left the political arena to the leadership of the Zionist Organization and allowed them to meet with leaders of the Allied powers and discuss the role of Palestine in the new postwar political order.

> The Jewish Territorial Organization did not submit any competing plan to the numerous powers, which gathered in Paris—only to allow a free field of action for the Zionists. After all, the Jewish Territorial Organization was forced to forgo the opportunity which was given to her—to formulate some other demand related to one of the regions under the rule of the British Empire in Canada, Australia, or even America. The demand to improve the state of the Jews was left to the Zionists alone.[9]

Despite his support, Zangwill was critical of the Zionist leadership for how they conducted the negotiations that led to the Balfour Declaration. In his opinion the compromise on the term "national home" instead of "Jewish state" was wrong. Zangwill rejected Weizmann's explanation that the Jews would not get a state if they asked for it. He referred to Weizmann's conduct as "cowardice" and a "forgoing of Zionism."[10] According to Zangwill, any solution that did not lead to the establishment of a Jewish state was unacceptable and should be rejected, because "our eternal aspiration expressed in the Passover Seder is not just 'Next year in Jerusalem.' We always said together with this, 'Next year as a free people.' But if we are to be represented as a minority in the legislative assembly in Palestine, that, as I heard, they are planning to setup in the Holy Land—it will not be freedom."[11]

In the early 1920s Zangwill was the most outspoken (Zionist) critic of Weizmann and the Zionist leadership. When he compared the content of the Balfour Declaration with the British statement on East Africa provided to Herzl in 1903, Zangwill concluded that the Zionist

Organization had been allowed much greater latitude in the Uganda plan. This shows just how much Zionism was reduced when facing Zion. The Balfour Declaration, on which the Zionist leaders tended to rain down "a flood of Messianic manifestos—political, spiritual and financial," was in essence a limited declaration that would make it difficult for the Zionist Organization to win substantial political achievements.[12] Arthur James Balfour, Britain's foreign minister, was "a diplomat who preferred vagueness and avoided any positive definition," and his declaration of November 2, 1917, was a faithful expression of this. "No verbal acrobatics in the words of Mr. Balfour to Lord Rothschild" could endow the declaration with more than it contained. "Nowhere does this document speak of Palestine as the national home of the Jews, but only about a Jewish national home in Palestine."[13]

Because this was the situation, Zangwill claimed, it was not obvious what status the Jews would have in Palestine. Would Jews become citizens of the new British Arab State (or the one now being created) in Palestine? Would their nationality be British, Jewish, or Palestinian?[14] It would seem that they would be "Jewish Palestinian[s]," but, wrote Zangwill, the nations of the world would regard them as British in every matter. This situation might jeopardize the relations between Jews who did not come to Palestine and the majority in the countries where they lived. And because Diaspora Jews would send money to their brethren living in Palestine, they might give the impression that they are pro-British. If hostilities erupted between Britain and other powers with a Jewish community, the local Jews might be tarred with dual loyalty in the best case and as traitors in the worst. Therefore only a Jewish state, meaning a sovereign national identity, could define the Jews' identity in their own state and regularize the relations between the nations of the world and the Jews of the Diaspora.

Zangwill also expressed sharp criticism of the Zionist leadership's blindness to the Arab question. This issue occupied his mind frequently. Even before he quit the Zionist Organization, Zangwill was one of the few Zionist thinkers who paid substantial attention to this urgent question and regarded it as one of the main obstacles for the success of the Zionist enterprise in Palestine.[15] He believed that the Zionist leadership regarded the issue lightly and did not understand that Jewish settlement in Palestine would encounter intense resistance from the local Arabs. The relationship between the Jews and the native population was at the core of territorialist thought. In all the negotiations Zangwill conducted, the first condition was that the proposed territory be uninhabited (or sparsely inhabited). This was the case in the negotiations for the Guas Ngishu plateau in East Africa, for Alberta in western Canada, for the Northern Territory and the Kimberly District in Australia, and for the Benguella plateau in Angola. The Arab population in Palestine was large, so Zangwill viewed the area as a less desirable territory and foretold that it would not yield a real solution for the Jews in distress. The famous statement about "a land without a people for a people without a land," mistakenly attributed to Zangwill, was totally foreign to his thought, and he noted that not he but the philanthropist Lord Shaftesbury had coined it.[16]

In his article "Ha-mediniyut shel ha-hanhagah ha-tsiyonit" (The Policy of the Zionist Leadership), published in February 1919, Zangwill stated that "the Jewish Territorial Organization never used to needle its critics in retribution. We always recognized that if there were a possibility to attain the Land of Israel it would be our obligation to replace our territory with Zion, and we would do so gladly."[17] However, he emphasized, "I cannot understand how we can accomplish even our social and economical ideals within the political conditions that have now been created."[18] The Jews in Palestine were a minority in a mostly Arab society, and this society would not welcome the masses of Jews who would arrive. Therefore, "If a Jewish state must be established through Jewish immigration, they would face an incomparably difficult task—to overcome the existing majority of six to one."[19] The Jews' joy following the Balfour Declaration was equaled by the Arabs' fears. The Arabs, like the Jews, took the declaration seriously and therefore did not "understand—justly—how that tiny territory could provide room for two national homes."[20]

Although Zangwill showed sensitivity to the issue, he did not recognize the Arabs' national rights. He viewed Palestine as the historical homeland of the Jewish people and recognized the Jews' right to settle there, but he refrained from recognizing the Arabs' rights. "Their numerical majority still does not give them the right to the land which they are destroying more than settling." Large parts of the countryside are neglected and unsuitable for settlement. They "were created by the Arabs and Turks who together took the trouble to leave this country desolate."[21] Because the Arabs were responsible for this, they had no right to Palestine. However, their presence in the country was a fact that had to be dealt with.

Given the demographic situation, Zangwill's conclusion was that only one people could live in Palestine; the Jews would have to expel the Arabs: "It seems to me, that if common sense and good will cannot yield a solution—and obviously they should be tried out first—then a single coercive action is better than endless frictions on both sides; it is just like pulling out a sick tooth which is better than an endless toothache." Zangwill advised the Arab leadership to be satisfied with "reviving the glory of Arabia in Hijaz and Damascus" and not to get involved in "a long and tiring conflict with the Jews over one small claim." The Arabs of Palestine should not wait until they become a minority as a result of the expected mass immigration of Jews; he therefore recommended that they gradually emigrate from Palestine, because in any case "the territory is mine and there is no dispute about it."[22]

Although Zangwill viewed Arab emigration as the commonsense solution, he did not believe that either the Jews or the Arabs would adopt it. He characterized Weizmann's leadership as hesitant and viewed him as a leader who "is afraid to hold his needle with a steady hand. He finds it easier to stick it in again and again." Because of this hesitant policy, the Jews (the minority) and the Arabs (the majority) would be condemned to live side by side. The influence of this situation on Jewish society in Palestine "might seriously change Zionism itself." Even the relations between Jewish employers and Arabs workers might create problems that should be considered: "If we give them work, it will be possible to blame us that we do not do the dirty work, as usual, but have instead transformed the Arabs into the hewers of wood and drawers of water, while we stand idly by and profit. If we do not give them work it will be said that we are boycotting them." Another problem Zangwill pointed out was that a Jewish minority could not rule an Arab majority: "This is something unheard of! Therefore it is not unlikely that the English would rule both Jews and Arabs," as in some of their colonies.[23]

Zangwill attached considerable importance to the immediate postwar period and believed that the future of the world would be shaped then, including, perhaps, a resolution of the Jewish problem once and for all. So he was harsh in his criticism of the Zionist leadership for its compromising and hesitant policy and inability to create the political, economic, or demographic conditions that would be favorable to the establishment of a Jewish state. However, his criticism should not be viewed as a continuation of the Territorialists' ideological conflict with the Zionists in the years before World War I. The ITO was not officially disbanded until 1925, but it had been in decline since the failure of the Angola plan. When Zangwill realized that that project could not be realized, he concluded that no territory anywhere on Earth was available that could be given to the Jews. His soldiers defected to the Zionist camp, and he was left a general without troops. The despair and loss of direction that followed the Angola failure were expressed in Zangwill's response to the statement by his rival, Francis Montefiore, during the years of the conflict with the Territorialists, that "an empty territory exists only on the moon." Zangwill disagreed at first, but after the failure in Angola, he changed his mind and added that even on the moon the territorialist idea was infeasible because the Man in the Moon is also no doubt an anti-Semite.[24]

Zangwill first offered to resign as president of the ITO in 1913. The members demurred, but it was only a matter of time until the main territorialist office in London shut down.[25] The outbreak of World War I, the Balfour Declaration, and the closer relations between the Zionist movement and the British government undercut the ITO and made it irrelevant in the new world order. However, precisely the factors that led to the ITO's breakup are the best illustration of the reasons for its birth. In the first half of the 1920s the Zionist movement was marked by an optimism that was the opposite of the spirit that had characterized it in the first decade of the century. The gates of Palestine were open to immigration, and Britain was resolved to implement the Balfour Declaration. The League of Nations granted Britain a mandate over Palestine and recognized the Jewish people's historical connection to the Land of Israel. New settlements were founded in Palestine, and it seemed that the establishment of a Jewish state was only a matter of time. Under these circumstances the territorialist idea was no longer relevant, whereas the Zionist territorial solution in Palestine seemed to be promising.

Territorialism emerged in a time of despair and a climate of existential danger and faded away in the years of hope. When the skies darkened in the late 1920s and early 1930s, doubts about Palestine's ability to absorb thousands of immigrants were heard again. The Nazis' rise to power, the worsening of the world order, the Arab-Jewish conflict, and Britain's retreat from the Balfour Declaration revived the territorialist idea in the Jewish world.

## THE NEW TERRITORIALISM

Two factors favored the revival of the territorialist idea in the early 1930s. The first was the increasing distress of the Jews in Europe, which led to an increase in Jewish emigration. The second was the gradual retreat of the Mandatory authorities from the Balfour Declaration, the institution of a strict immigration policy, and the aggravation of the Arab-Jewish conflict after the riots of 1929. This situation brought both veteran and newly minted Territorialists to the conclusion that the gates of Palestine were closing and that the region could not serve as the home and sanctuary for the hundreds of thousands of Jews destined to flee Europe. An alternative and sparsely populated region had to be found to supplement, but not replace, Palestine.

The second half of the 1920s was overshadowed by the deteriorating situation of East European Jewry. The optimism that prevailed during the Paris Peace Conference and the aspiration for a new world order were replaced by pessimism and the realization that the new political reality in Europe was not only the same as before but was in fact worse. The economic state of the Jews in Poland, the largest Jewish community in Europe, deteriorated; their incomes were reduced by the closure of the Russian market, and the economic plan of the Polish prime minister, Władysław Grabski, despoiled them.[26] Poverty was nothing new for the Jews of Eastern Europe; but in contrast to the beginning of the twentieth century, there was no country willing to absorb masses of Jewish immigrants in the 1920s. In the first half of the 1920s the United States instituted a harsh and selective immigration policy that excluded individuals from Eastern Europe and especially Jews. The Nazis came to power in the 1930s, and the Jews in Central Europe also became the victims of political and economic persecution. The Jewish population of Europe was hard pressed to sustain itself economically and was threatened with a real existential danger.

The only place that admitted Jews who wanted to leave Europe, though in limited numbers, was Palestine. In the 1920s approximately 100,000 Jews arrived there, followed by more than 200,000 in the next decade.[27] The number of Jews in Palestine increased from year to year: 60,000 in 1919, 175,000 in 1929, and 500,000 by 1939. This growth augmented the tension in the triangle of British, Jews, and Arabs. The British began retreating from their promises to the Zionist movement. The Arabs, fearing they would lose their majority in Palestine, resorted to violence to effect a change in British policy. The Arab riots of 1929 changed the situation dramatically and were a watershed in the country's history. The commission of inquiry appointed in their wake blamed immigration and the land acquisition policy. The Shaw Committee report, published in 1930, recommended that restrictions be placed on Jewish immigration and land acquisition. It also proposed the establishment of a legislative council with an Arab majority, an expansion of the Mandatory security forces, and the rescission of the powers that had been granted to the Zionist Organization.[28] The limitations on immigration and land purchases meant a weakening of the Yishuv, a retreat from the Balfour Declaration, and the assurance of an Arab majority in Palestine.

The situation in Europe and in Palestine raised questions about whether the Zionist movement would succeed in establishing the Jewish state in time. The New Territorialists of the early 1930s compared the conditions in Europe and Palestine with those at the start of the century and found many similarities: economic distress in the countries of origin, persecution, barriers to emigration, and doubts about Palestine's ability to absorb the masses of Jews who would arrive there. Against this background, the territorialist idea was revived and discussions of settlement plans outside Palestine were renewed.

A comparison of the causes that favored the growth of Territorialism at the beginning of the twentieth century and those in the 1930s also reveals pronounced and significant differences between the two movements. New Territorialism did not emerge from an internal Zionist conflict, like its precursor in the wake of the Uganda controversy, but from the situation of the Jews in Europe and the political crisis on the continent during the 1930s. Another important difference was that the original Territorialists were part and parcel of the Zionist movement, members of the Zionist Organization, and participants in Zionist activities, whereas the New Territorialists were far removed from the Zionist idea—some even opposed it—and were involved in both European and Jewish political life.

## CHAPTER 6

The nucleus of New Territorialism consisted of Jewish socialists who were disappointed with the Bolshevik Revolution and concerned about rising anti-Semitism in Europe. They no longer believed it possible to integrate into the surrounding society and refused to regard the Zionist solution as the only option. During the 1930s several local territorialist associations were established in Europe, and each in its own way held that the Jews could no longer live in Europe and had to find a territorial solution outside Palestine.

The Shparber Association was established in Vienna in September 1933 by young Jewish socialists who proposed combining socialism with Territorialism.[29] In November of the same year, the Lige far Yiddisher Kolonizatsyie (League for Jewish Colonization) was established in Paris, mainly in response to the flood of German Jews entering France in the wake of Hitler's rise to power.[30] In Poland many Jews subscribed to the territorialist idea. In cooperation with the members of the Shparber Association they founded a territorialist association in Warsaw.[31] In New York, too, Jewish socialists established the Arbeiter Lige farn Alveltkhen Yidishen Kongres with Chaim Zhitlowsky as its chairman.[32] A group with a territorialist outlook also formed in Berlin; its most prominent member was Isaac Nachman Steinberg, editor of the series *Fraye Shriftn farn Yidishen Sotsialistishn Gedank*.[33]

Steinberg was one of the most prominent New Territorialists. Born in Latvia in 1888, he became active in the Socialist Revolutionary Party. In 1907 he was arrested and exiled to Siberia but escaped and made his way to Zurich. In 1910 he completed his doctoral studies in law at the University of Heidelberg and returned to Moscow. After the Bolshevik Revolution Steinberg represented the leftist Socialist Revolutionary Party in the coalition government under Lenin and served as commissar for law.[34] Because he criticized the revolution, which he believed had betrayed the socialist idea, and expressed reservations about its resort to violence, Steinberg was arrested and imprisoned. In 1923 he managed to get out of Russia and settled in Berlin. While living in London from 1933 until 1939, he devoted all his time and effort to promoting the territorialist idea. He spent the first years of World War II in Australia, where he attempted to promote a settlement plan in Kimberley (see later discussion). He lived in New York from 1943 until his death in 1957.[35]

Once several local territorialist associations had been established, it was only a matter of time until a way was found to merge them under a single leader. In his memoirs, *Tahat diglan shel Shalosh Mahapekhot*, Joseph (Yosef) Kruk writes that he was the one who initiated the move. In his published appeal he emphasized that "the new movement must be a free association of people with various viewpoints united around one mission: autonomous and concentrated settlement."[36] This mission, Kruk explained, was the broadest common denominator that would allow "Zionists, socialists, autonomists and Folkists to cooperate."[37]

The First Congress of the Territorialist Associations was held on July 29, 1935, at the Russell Hotel in London and concluded with the establishment of the Freeland League—the league for a free country. Many delegates, mainly from France and Poland, attended the meeting to participate in the founding of the new territorialist organization. Nearly all the speakers at the conference focused on the position of the new league in relation to the Zionist movement. Rabbi Moses Gaster said that "the new movement is the completion of Zionism." The author Alfred Döblin noted that in this period Zionism "illuminates the darkness. It is the continuation of Jewish existence. The Land of Israel is the only land that is sacred for the Jews. But the people are more important than the land."[38]

In the 1930s, as in the early twentieth century, the Territorialists viewed Zionism not as an enemy but chiefly as a movement that was incapable of dealing with the immediate problems. They saw the Freeland League as a direct successor to the ITO, which had been disbanded a decade before. Zangwill was their role model, and during the conference the participants made sure to visit his grave. Kruk was supposed to speak there, but, as he said in his memoirs, "When we reached the site and laid a wreath on his grave we saw that the inscription on the tombstone was very simple, yet highly significant: Israel Zangwill, a fighter for unpopular things. When I saw that, I laid aside the speech I had prepared and spoke of other things."[39]

At the preparatory conference for the congress, the platform of the Freeland League was drafted.

1. The aim of the Freeland League is to create a Jewish agricultural and industrial settlement in a free territory that will

provide a safe haven for social, economic, and national-cultural development.
2. The way to achieve this goal must be based on the wide support of the Jewish masses and on international cooperation.
3. The Freeland League will allow various social groups among the Jewish people to unite under its flag and will be willing to adopt the basic principles of Territorialism as described in the first two paragraphs.[40]

Besides drafting the platform, the conference decided to establish the World Central Organization, which would choose the forty-four members of the World Central Advisory Council, the highest authority in the movement. It was also decided to form the World Central Committee, which would be responsible for territorialist activities, with subcommittees dealing with the political, propaganda, and economic fields and with youth. In addition, local territorialist branches would be set up.[41] The headquarters of the Freeland League would be in London, a fundraising apparatus would be set up, a worldwide public relations campaign would be launched both within Jewish society and outside it, a geographic commission would be organized and would be composed of specialists and interested parties to assess possible settlement plans, and a periodical would be published to give expression to territorialist ideas.[42]

Leopold Kessler was appointed chairman of the Freeland League, and Rabbi Moses Gaster was appointed its honorary president. The choice of these two individuals is especially interesting, given their Zionist activities and their prior objections to the ITO. Kessler was a delegate to the Third Zionist Congress and served as chairman of the Zionist Organization in the Transvaal. In 1900 he moved to England and became an activist in the Zionist Federation there. Kessler headed the El-Arish expedition. From 1899 to 1921 he was a member of the Greater Actions Committee.[43] Moses Gaster was the Sephardic rabbi of London and a member of the Hibbat Zion movement. He helped establish the first colonies of Romanian Jews in Palestine. A supporter of Herzl, he was elected a vice-president of the First Zionist Congress. Gaster was the first president of the Zionist Federation in England and one of the prominent opponents of the Uganda plan. Meir Nathan, a former member of the ITO and treasurer of the territorialist branch in London before World

War I, was appointed treasurer of the Freeland League. Those named to the World Central Committee of the Freeland League included Abraham Rosin (Ben Adir), a Territorialist and member of the Zionist Socialist Party; the attorney Joseph Tschernikhov; Alfred Döblin, author of *Berlin Alexanderplatz*; Joseph Kruk; and Isaac Nachman Steinberg.[44]

Another trigger for the founding of the Freeland League was the declaration by the Soviet Union on February 6, 1928, of a plan to allocate a region for Jewish settlement in Birobidzhan. In 1929 a delegation was sent out on behalf of the Yiddisher Kolonizatsye in Raten Farband to assess the region and the chances of settlement there. It found no special difficulties that could not be overcome by determination and hard work. In May 1934 the Soviet government officially designated Birobidzhan a Jewish autonomous region and closed it to non-Jewish settlement. This was the first time that any government had granted the Jews as a nation, not as individuals, a significant territory of their own.[45] The Freeland League welcomed the Soviet initiative but did not cooperate with it. The Soviet decision to grant the Jews a territory proved to them that it was possible to find a third place, in addition to Palestine and Birobidzhan, for an autonomous settlement for the Jews of Europe.

## THE FREELAND LEAGUE

In October 1935 Steinberg published the article "Far der katastrof" (Before the Catastrophe). Only two years after the Nazis' rise to power and even before the worst persecutions, he detailed the political changes that were taking place in Europe and that he believed would lead to another world war. "These days, none of us knows where and when the catastrophe—a world war—will erupt."

> None of us even knows whether the catastrophe that will erupt will be similar to that of the previous war. But there is no doubt that a catastrophe of this sort is materializing very quickly everywhere. It is possible that at the last moment global developments will be governed by common sense, but we must take into account the current direction, which leads straight to chaos and destruction. Within one year the picture of Europe has fundamentally changed. Terrible acts have begun to occur

in Germany and lately in a prominent way in Europe as well. It has occurred both in submissive and opposing governments. A large part of Europe is influenced by fascism: Germany, Austria, Italy, Hungary, Romania, the Balkans, Latvia, and Turkey. Other countries and nations have been forced to adjust their internal politics to the Hitlerian pressure. Today it is no longer anti-Semitic/chauvinist ideological pressure; today it has already changed into military pressure that cannot be released in a single day but only through war![46]

Steinberg's article, published in *Fraye Shriften* four years before World War II broke out, reflects the reasons for the reawakening of the territorialist idea in the early 1930s. Steinberg and the members of the Freeland League did not predict the annihilation of European Jewry in World War II; nevertheless, because they were deeply involved in European politics and imbued with a deep Jewish national consciousness, their hearts foresaw evil tidings.

In keeping with the decisions of the first congress in London and the meetings that followed, the Freeland League began publishing articles in the Jewish and general press about itself and distributing materials about its aims and the reasons for its establishment. One of the most prominent articles that illuminated the aims of the Freeland League was Steinberg's "Where Are the Jews to Go?" published in *The Jewish Chronicle* in November 1937. Steinberg began by noting two premises that underlay the desire to found a Jewish autonomous region in one of the territories under the control of the British Empire. The first premise was sparse population: Whereas there were 468 people per square mile in Great Britain, there were only 2 per square mile in Australia, 3 in Canada, and 15 in New Zealand. The second premise was that empty and uninhabited regions do not serve British interests and that settling immigrants would strengthen British control of those regions.

Corresponding to the empty regions of the British Empire was the problem of the Jews wanting to flee Europe. So it would be only natural for the Jewish masses to emigrate to one of the empty regions under the control of the British Empire and settle there. Palestine was one solution, Steinberg claimed, but it was certainly not enough: "The Zionist Movement, which has accomplished great things in this line in recent years, is now threatened with rigorous limitations, both geographical and economic. In any case the pressing needs for emigration are out of all proportion to the immediate possibilities of Palestine. Jewry must in these circumstances look for a new large territory in one of the empty areas overseas preferably within the British Empire."[47] According to Steinberg, Australia and New Zealand were the countries most suitable for settlement.

The move from Europe to the designated territory must be en masse and not gradual. Steinberg objected to the idea of absorbing Jewish migrants as individuals. He feared that if Jews migrated as individuals, they would be assimilated into the majority society and would not lay down the infrastructure to absorb those who followed. Only wide-scale settlement could solve the Jewish problem.

> What we must set out to accomplish is colonization, not infiltration of individual Jews into a new territory. Infiltration means the penetration of individuals into an economically organized community. Infiltration of Jews would have the well-known results—drift into the big industrial cities, competition with non-Jews in certain occupations and trades, and the beginning of anti-Semitism. Colonization, however, means taking over of an unpopulated or very sparsely populated area which is still economically undeveloped by groups of properly selected immigrants. We must set out to establish a closed Jewish settlement with its own collective responsibility, modest in the beginning and with the possibilities of further expansion.[48]

Steinberg's distinction between settlement and infiltration and his preference for settlement call to mind Herzl's arguments in *The Jewish State* and, later, Zangwill's arguments.

After the Jewish immigrants arrived, the new colony would base itself on industrialized agriculture, which would develop through the buying and selling agricultural produce among the settlers. The settlers, wrote Steinberg, must be strong and healthy so that they could cope with the harsh living conditions. The industrial centers set up in the designated country must integrate with those already there and not compete with them. In this way Steinberg hoped to minimize the anti-

Semitism that might emerge when the immigrants were absorbed into the designated country. The funds obtained for the settlement program must be distributed according to economic considerations of profit and loss. Steinberg strongly objected to philanthropy and regarded his plan as a business deal in all respects: "There then arises the question of finance. It must be clearly understood that migration on a large scale cannot be conducted by means of charity. Overseas settlement is a business, and like any other business can only succeed if it is well organized and properly financed."[49]

However, the similarity between Herzl's project and Steinberg's territorialist plan also reveals the inherent self-contradictions of the territorialist ideology of the 1930s and 1940s. On one hand, the New Territorialists were looking for a region to alleviate the Jews' immediate distress and provide a rapid solution for their pressing needs. On the other hand, Steinberg, like the Zionists, understood that nonselective mass immigration to a designated territory was apt to end in failure and he consequently proposed to begin with healthy young people who would lay the foundations for absorbing the persecuted and the poor later. His plan was therefore just as gradual as the Zionists' and perhaps even more selective. Gradual construction of the new land and the preference for young and healthy migrants would not provide a quick solution to the current problems of the Jewish people. Moreover, Steinberg's article was written at the peak of a large wave of immigration to Palestine, during which thousands of European Jews (mostly from Poland and Germany) moved there. Given the social structure of the immigration, including the proportion of children and the family structure, it is doubtful that the newcomers to Palestine met the territorialist standards formulated by Steinberg.

Steinberg's article was intended for both Jewish and non-Jewish readers. He tried to convince them that anti-Semitism was not a problem for the Jews alone but for all advocates of peace in Europe. Therefore he called for a general and immediate solution to the Jewish problem. He emphasized that the new movement did not compete with Zionism but complemented it and that Palestine was only one of the many possible territorialist solutions. Steinberg concluded his programmatic article with the hope that it would be possible to draw on the hidden strengths of the Jewish people so that they could escape their misery for a new and more optimistic path. Steinberg emphasized that the Freeland League

> does not compete with Zionism although they both are moving on similar lines, because it would only be to the benefit of Palestine if the high pressure of Jewish emigration could be partly diverted in another direction. Freeland wants to bring a message of new hope and activity to the desperate masses of the Jewish people, to save the self-respect of the wonderful Jewish youth which is seeking feverishly for the fruitful application of its physical and intellectual powers. This inevitable painful process of emigration might be transformed into a positive and creative one. It should not be so much a running away from the old homes as the building up of new homes on free land under a free sky.[50]

The main purpose of the Freeland League, as stated in its platform, was to establish a home in a free unpopulated country for the millions of Jews who were forced to seek a place of refuge and for those Jews who strove toward an autonomous national life in their own home.[51] In a later version the Freeland League was dedicated to the task of finding an undeveloped and unpopulated territory where Jews could be settled peacefully, but it was explicitly noted that, although the settlement would be free of all political aspirations, it would preserve the moral values and the spiritual heritage of the Jews' common past.[52]

There is a certain resemblance between the Freeland League's platform and that of the ITO, formulated thirty years earlier. At the beginning of the twentieth century the ITO wanted to "to procure a territory upon an autonomous basis for those Jews who cannot or will not remain in the lands where they currently live."[53] Zangwill wanted to establish an autonomous Jewish colony with defined national characteristics. The Freeland League had much more modest goals. Steinberg and his colleagues were searching for a land where the Jews could be culturally autonomous without political aspirations. The Jewish settlement would not have the trappings of an independent political community. Its loyalty to the host state would be unquestioned, and the Jews would live under its authority.[54]

An additional point of similarity between the Freeland League and the ITO was the New Territorialists' tolerance for the Zionist idea. The

Territorialists of the early twentieth century did not reject the Zionist idea in principle but thought that Palestine could not absorb a large number of Jewish immigrants. Its economic capacity was limited and 600,000 Arabs already lived there. Already in 1905, immediately after the Seventh Zionist Congress, Hillel Zeitlin had addressed this point: "What all the 'Palestinists' forget, whether accidentally or deliberately, is that Palestine is in the hands of others and is completely inhabited."[55] It was not rejection of the Land of Israel as the land of the Jewish people that led them to the territorialist idea but the simple realization that the Zionist ideal could not be realized there. During the 1930s the Freeland League advanced similar arguments. The needs of the hour were many and the power of the Zionist movement was limited, so some other group had to assume responsibility for the fate of the Jewish people.[56] The New Territorialists, like the old ones, were pessimistic about the Arab-Jewish conflict, which had greatly intensified during the 1930s. For example, after the founding of the Freeland League, Joseph Tschernikhov, a member of its World Central Committee, wrote that "given the size of the country, the density of its Arab population (the reason for the tragic problem of Jewish labor), and the property rights that lead to land speculation, it will not be possible to create mass settlement in the Land of Israel."[57]

The Freeland League and the Zionist movement had different positions regarding their final goals. The Freeland League opposed the Zionists' argument that a Jewish state in Palestine was the full and only solution for the Jewish people and pushed more for cultural autonomy. The New Territorialists asserted that, for the Zionists, a state was the supreme goal, the sum total of all the Zionists' political aspirations, and that the Jewish people's tragedy in the past and present was due first and foremost to their lack of a state. Hence the revival of the Jewish people was possible only if they had a state of their own, just like all other nations. The Freeland League objected to this axiom as a matter of principle. A state for the Jews was not the main issue and did not merit an all-out effort. Indeed, all nations possess states; and World War I gave rise to a number of new ones, Steinberg asserted, but have people become happier as a result? His answer was that patriotism leads to hatred and wars and entrenches countries in their uncompromising positions.[58] Therefore settlement without any political aspirations in any region that might be available was the solution.

The aspiration for cultural autonomy under the patronage of a democratic power made the New Territorialism of the 1930s, in distinction to the original version of the early twentieth century, much closer to Shimon Dubnow's version of Autonomism. Like the Territorialists of the 1930s, Dubnow argued at the beginning of the twentieth century that "in the Diaspora we must demand and obtain a national-cultural autonomy as far as circumstances permit for most of the nation; in Palestine we will achieve it for a minority of the nation."[59] Like the advocates of Dubnowian Autonomism, the Freeland League aspired to cultural autonomy rather than a sovereign state. The difference between them came down to two principles. The first was that the Territorialists, unlike Dubnow, ignored the philosophical and historical aspect of the idea of a state. According to Dubnow, a people's aspiration for a territory is only one stage in their development. The highest stage was their ability to preserve their culture without a territorial link. If a people can retain their culture and not lose their identity after it had been disconnected from their land, Dubnow claimed, "that nation has reached the highest level of cultural-historical individualism and it [will] be immune to extinction, on condition that it continues to hold on to its national will."[60] According to Dubnow, because the Jewish people were at an advanced stage of development, there was no reason for them to retreat. The Territorialists gave no thought to this philosophical issue. The saw obtaining a territory as an impossible mission; cultural autonomy could satisfy their main goal, which was saving the Jews of Europe. The second difference was where this cultural autonomy might be established. The Territorialists were pessimistic with regard to the possibility of establishing it in Europe. Emancipation had failed, and the Jews were being persecuted in Western Europe too. So another region had to be found where the Jews could live their lives without fear.

Therefore three principles were held by the New Territorialism of the mid-1930s: A sparsely populated region had to be chosen; it must be economically undeveloped; and the Jewish autonomy that would eventually be set up would be sponsored by one of the democratic powers, preferably Britain.[61] In the opinion of the Freeland League, a British protectorate was a much more realistic option than the ITO's goal of an independent Jewish state in an unknown region. In both its avatars, the territorialist movement insisted that the essential condition for an autonomous Jewish settlement was that one of the powers recognize it as the national settlement of the Jewish people and not as a means for solving the problem of Jews as individuals. Steinberg's attempt to win the agreement of the powers, mainly Britain, was similar in many aspects to the attempts by Herzl and Zangwill at the end of the nineteenth and beginning of the twentieth century to obtain a charter.

The Freeland League's first diplomatic activity was its participation in the Evian conference in July 1938, at which delegates from thirty-two countries discussed the matter of refugees. The aim was to facilitate emigration from Germany and Austria and to set up a new international organization to devise an overall solution to the refugee problem. The conference was governmental; hence representatives of organizations and of the refugees themselves were allowed to appear only before a subcommittee. When the Freeland League representatives—Charles Zeligman, Leopold Kessler, and Isaac Steinberg—did so, they commended the convening of the conference and expressed their hope that a solution would be found for the problem of Jewish refugees. In a memorandum they submitted to the committee they described the suffering of the Jews of Europe and insisted on the immediate need for a territory for the Jews. "The persecutions of the Jews in our times," the territorialist delegation told the conference participants, "is totally different from those which are well known in the history of the Jewish people."[62] In the past the Jews could escape persecution by conversion or emigration. In 1938, however, the persecution did not spare the young and old, women and children, and its sole aim was to isolate an entire community from the European majority society.

In their memorandum the Freeland League members noted that Jewish organizations had been trying to help the Jewish refugees in two ways. One way was the assistance extended by various Jewish philanthropic organizations to the Jewish refugees, wherever they might be, to relieve their suffering. The other way was that of the Zionist movement, which had gathered a few thousand Jews from Germany and settled them in Palestine. However, it was absolutely clear that these two ways were insufficient and could not offer an overall solution to the refugee problem. The number of refugees increased daily, the Jewish organizations' resources were being depleted, and the Zionist movement, despite its impressive achievements in Palestine, was incapable of coping with the present problems on its own. The natural increase in the Jewish population of Poland was 40,000 per year. Palestine could not absorb migrants in such numbers, either from Poland or anyplace else. Therefore the only viable solution for the refugee problem was a large territory for immediate settlement. According to the Territorialists, there were still empty regions in the British Empire and elsewhere where Jews could be settled.[63] The Freeland League plan for putting an end to this tragedy was presented to the countries at the Evian conference: (1) The area for settlement had to be large enough with broad settlement rights and the possibility for future expansion; (2) The area had to be uninhabited or sparsely inhabited in order to avoid competition with the local population; (3) It had to be completely understood that the Freeland League had no political aspirations; (4) The settlement would be planned so that the livelihood of the community would be based on agriculture, handicrafts, and industry; (5) The settlement would be funded by financial institutions on a business basis. There is no doubt that the Jewish communities would be prepared to offer their assistance in recruiting the necessary funds, but in order to ensure the success of the plan, it would be necessary to obtain an internationally guaranteed loan or financial assistance in another certified form.[64]

At the end of a week of deliberations it became clear, both to the Zionists and to the Territorialists, that the Western democratic countries were not prepared to change their immigration policies and absorb the Jewish refugees. Millions of Jews who wanted to leave Europe were trapped, because no country was willing to accept them. The British delegate declared that the population density of all the lands of the empire was adequate and that many regions were not suitable for European settlers; Australia was not interested in encouraging the arrival of refugees, because it did not have racial problems and did not want to import any.[65] Nevertheless, a few months after the conference, in October 1938, British prime minister Neville Chamberlain, expressed his readiness to allocate 10,000 square kilometers of British New Guinea for Jewish settlement, and it seemed that a certain change for the better was occurring in the attitude toward the Jewish refugees.

Chamberlain's proposal accorded with the principles of the Freeland League, and the Territorialists commended the idea. However, the proposal to settle Jews in British New Guinea was mainly made under

# CHAPTER 6

American pressure and was not the result of Freeland League diplomacy. In early 1939 a survey team went to New Guinea and spent about six weeks there. Its conclusion was that although New Guinea was not an optimal place for refugees, it had settlement potential. It was populated, but the natives would welcome the new European settlers. Despite the favorable report, the British proposal was dropped for the same reasons that Zangwill's attempts at the start of the twentieth century came to naught: the fear of Jewish autonomy; the suspicious attitude of the Jewish organizations, which refused to back the initiative; and the political circumstances on the eve of World War II.[66]

The only direct negotiations that made any headway were those about settlement in the Kimberley region of Australia. The man who initiated the idea, conducted the official talks with the Australian government, and pushed for its realization was Isaac Steinberg, who, at the end of the 1930s, was the most prominent and active member of the Freeland League. The idea of a Jewish colony in Australia was raised after the Evian conference and in the wake of Chamberlain's proposal to settle Jews in British New Guinea. The members of the Freeland League agreed among themselves that the state of Western Australia was large enough—about 1 million square miles—and had a population of only 460,000, half of them in its capital of Perth. It was decided to send Steinberg to Australia to negotiate with the relevant officials and determine whether such an option was at all realistic.

Steinberg arrived in Australia on May 23, 1939. Two days later he met with John Collings Willcock, the prime minister of Western Australia. After explaining the aims of the Freeland League, Steinberg queried Willcock about his position on Jewish settlement in Kimberley. What would be the government's position, and would the Australian people welcome the plan? Willcock's answer surprised Steinberg: "I am not prejudiced against Jewish colonization. But you must go on personally investigate the area with view to avoiding failure."[67] Willcock stressed that measures would have to be taken to ensure that the Jews remained within the borders of the district allotted to them and did not move to the big cities and become a burden on the government. Steinberg heard similar words of enthusiasm from Frank Wise, the minister for lands, who was also an expert on tropical agriculture and predicted a glorious future for a settlement in Kimberley.[68]

The Freeland League was enthusiastic about Willcock and Wise's support, and Steinberg made preparations for examining the land in question. He flew to Perth, looked for a guide who was familiar with the Kimberley District, and collected every scrap of vital information relating to the conditions there and the chances of settlement. At the University of Perth he gave a lecture on the situation of the Jews in Europe, their persecution, and the main aims of the Freeland League and made friends with several professors who showed an interest in the organization. Steinberg noted that the atmosphere in Perth was especially sympathetic and that many people took an interest in the Kimberley settlement plan, including intellectuals, the archbishop of Perth, who was also the head of the Anglican Church in Australia, and, according to the local press, the general public as well. In his encounters with the academic community, Steinberg met a young lecturer, George Melville, who had previously researched the region and found it suitable for settlement. Steinberg was also introduced to a family that owned 700,000 hectares in eastern Kimberley and was willing to help Steinberg during his journey.

On June 8, 1939, Steinberg flew across Western Australia to the port city of Wyndham, which was the jumping-off point for his survey.[69] Steinberg wanted to learn about the natural resources and topography, the climate, the flora, the water sources, and types of soil and the degree to which they were arable.[70] He traveled through Kimberley for three weeks. Although he surveyed only about 750 square miles, he claimed that he had looked at the important part of the region and had been adequately exposed to its advantages and disadvantages. He concluded that the region was suitable for extensive Jewish settlement: "The land is not dead or even barren. It is only an empty land, a slumbering land. Just as in fairy tale, it needs only [a] magic wand to touch its sleeping treasures and bring them to life." The land was good, so "the pioneers will not need to worry about food. Kimberley has always been a cattle country."[71] They could graze tens of thousands of bulls, cows, and sheep on the broad plains; many species of vegetables and tropical fruits grew wild. Irrigation would make it possible to produce abundant harvests of quality fruits and vegetables. Steinberg did not see any insurmountable problems with the water supply. During the four months of summer, from December until March, the region enjoyed ample rainfall, there were no droughts or dry years, and agriculture could flourish and succeed through

# CHAPTER 6

proper irrigation. Two main rivers flowed through Kimberley, the Ord and the Victoria, and smaller streams extended over hundreds of miles. The engineers' main aim would be to exploit the rainwater intelligently for personal needs and for agriculture. The report added that Kimberley had a mixed climate: The months between April and September were dry and cold; the hottest months were October and November; and the warm and rainy season ran from December to March.[72]

Besides the topographic and climatic aspects, Steinberg also considered the extent to which the settlers would be able to settle down and strike roots. "All the people that I met there," he wrote in his book *Australia: The Unpromised Land*, "have spoken of Kimberley with enthusiastic ardour and profound attachment. But all have complained of loneliness, of feeling cut off from current Australian life. The few women there have almost lost their interest in clothes. There is no public to appreciate a pretty frock."[73] Colonization would reduce the loneliness. "The greatest physical and climatic obstacles can be overcome if an organized way of life can be adopted. We know this from Palestine, and it need be no different in Kimberley."[74] Local industry could also be developed. Wyndham, about 50 miles north of the designated territory, was a major port. Goods could be imported through it and exports shipped from it to the entire world, especially to the nearby Asian markets. There was no doubt, Steinberg asserted, that Jews could integrate into the economic life of the region. All that was necessary for the settlement initiative to succeed was young and strong settlers, money, prudent economic planning that would enable the future Jewish settlement to be part of the Australian economy, and, above all, the settlers' determination to create a new life for themselves.[75] The report's conclusion was that Kimberley was suitable for Jewish settlement and could be an appropriate solution to the Jewish distress in Europe.

When Steinberg returned to Perth on July 1, he began writing his report but spent most of his time working to promote the settlement idea. On August 25 he received a letter from the prime minister of Western Australia in which Willcock wrote that he was going to ask the federal government to clarify its position on the plan and make it aware of the plight of the refugees in Europe. Steinberg saw real progress in the basic support for his plan from the government of Western Australia but understood that the Freeland League had to sound out the government in Canberra. For an entire year Steinberg worked to influence Australian public opinion.

He met with many people in Melbourne and Sydney, presenting the main points of his plan and trying to win their sympathy for it. Articles and declarations of support were published in the press in an attempt to persuade the decision makers to back it.[76] In August 1940 Steinberg's memorandum was presented to the Australian prime minister, Robert Menzies, who in turn submitted the proposal to his cabinet for review. However, World War II and the storm in Europe forced postponement of the discussion. In February 1941 Steinberg received a letter that the present government did not believe that the time was appropriate to discuss the matter and had decided to reject his proposal.[77] Steinberg began exploring the possibility of a Jewish settlement in Tasmania, another one of the federal states of Australia. But after the Japanese attack on Pearl Harbor in December 1941, his proposal became moot. The plan for settling Jewish refugees in Kimberley was never carried out.

The Kimberley plan was given special mention by Ze'ev Jabotinsky in a book written in 1940, shortly before his death: *The Jewish War Front*.

> One of the most remarkable features of this scheme is that its advancement is due to the sole effort of one single man, and this man is neither young nor wealthy. Nor is he skilled in the kind of nuisance known as propaganda. His only secret seems to be just calm obstinacy which still wants today what is wanted yesterday. . . . The story is a striking one, for it shows that very important political results can be accomplished single-handed by one quite unofficial person, with little popular backing and no particular credentials, without any use of the witchcraft known as personal magnetism: simply by talking timely common sense.[78]

But Jabotinsky cast doubt on the report's conclusions, especially the readiness of Jewish settlers to settle in the land and cultivate it. In his opinion the Jewish settlers would not put down roots in the rural soil and, as soon as they arrived, would flood the large cities of Australia and aggravate the social problems that already existed there. Ultimately, the only solution for the Jewish people's distress was the Land of Israel.

> The author does not believe in the reality of any "territorialist" project for Jewish settlement outside Palestine; in his opinion,

any research for other suitable areas will be hopeless. But the quest should nevertheless be treated with the fullest respect, even by the most zealous and uncompromising Zionists. Logically, it is in their interest to encourage the closest scrutiny of all non-Palestine schemes.[79]

Steinberg, in *Australia: The Unpromised Land*, disagreed with Jabotinsky's assertions. In the chapter "Kimberley: State or Settlement," he presented his arguments in favor of Jewish settlement in Australia, from which we can learn about the territorialist idea in general. His main contention was that the Land of Israel had always been the cynosure of the Jewish people, but its power of attraction was limited. More than 2 million Jews crossed the sea between the 1880s and World War I, but only a tiny fraction of them reached Palestine.[80] During the 1920s, when immigration to Palestine increased, it was not because of Zionist ideology but because of pogroms in Ukraine and the closure of the gates of the United States. Jewish history during the nineteenth and early twentieth centuries proved that the Jews were indeed able and willing to till the soil if they were given the opportunity to do so. It happened in the time of Alexander I in the early nineteenth century, when Jews settled in southern Russia, and later in the agricultural colonies established in Argentina by Baron Hirsch and in Palestine.

Steinberg argued that there was no reason to assume a priori that Jewish settlement in Kimberley was impossible. However, contrary to the position of the Zionist movement, he thought that a Jewish state in Palestine should not be sought. "I myself doubt the value of a Jewish State, even in Palestine. If in Zionist circles this idea had not been so dominant, the bitter conflict between Jews and Arabs could, I think, have been avoided."[81] Steinberg asserted that a Jewish state necessarily implies a Jewish majority, and because the Arabs of Palestine cannot accept this, suspicion and hatred ensue: "The passion of youth has been focused on a single political aim—the formation of a Jewish State. And such preoccupation may lead to weakening of the universal and moral value of Jewish culture."[82]

There is no reason, wrote Steinberg, to aspire to a Jewish state in Kimberley. The Jewish colony would politically be an organic and inseparable part of the Australian state and not a separate Jewish political entity. The government set up there and the laws enforced would be the same as those in the rest of Australia. There would be no barriers or borders between Australia and Kimberley, and the settlers would be able to devote all their energies to building the new settlement. The schoolchildren would receive an Australian education, along with an emphasis on Jewish content and Jewish culture. The language would be English and the "Jewish language"; it is not clear whether Steinberg meant Yiddish or Hebrew.

The settlers in Kimberley, unlike those in Palestine, would not be forced to devote most of their time to violent conflict in order to justify their existence. Steinberg anticipated that a healthy society would develop with a friendly system of relationships among the settlers themselves and between them and their neighbors.[83] He defined their new identity as "Australian Jewish."

> There is no doubt the European type of Jew would undergo certain changes in Kimberley. For one thing, he would be affected by the new landscape and Nature. It is impossible for a man's body and imagination to remain unchanged in a land of kangaroos, crocodiles and cockatoos, of bottle-trees, man-high grass and fiery sun. The Jew of Europe would see new colors, smell new scents and hear sounds he had never heard before. He would breathe a new air, and the horizon would unfold before him in fresh contours. He would, of course, adapt himself to them no less effectively than he has done in Argentina and in Palestine. But these fundamental changes must deeply affect him and his descendants. Their poets, painters, singers, their jesters and thinkers, would, no doubt, absorb this new natural environment into their creative work.[84]

These lines were written in the first edition of Steinberg's book (1945), in Yiddish, and in the English translation, published in early 1948, shortly before the establishment of Israel. The refugee issue continued to be relevant and the results of World War II were known to everyone. Hence Steinberg thought it was still possible to revive the Kimberley plan and take up the negotiations from the point they had been suspended in February 1941. After the war the Freeland League tried to advance other settlement plans as well, but none of them were as serious and detailed as Steinberg's Kimberley plan.

The Anglo-American Committee of Inquiry on Palestine in 1946 was a good opportunity for the Freeland League to advance its ideas. This committee was set up by the governments of Great Britain and the United States to examine the conditions in Palestine and their influence on Jewish immigration there after World War II. The committee recommended the immediate admission to Palestine of 100,000 survivors, the repeal of the White Paper land law, and the establishment of a UN trusteeship regime until the nature of an independent state was determined.[85] In an attempt to influence the committee's work and conclusions, the Freeland League submitted a memorandum with its demands. It noted that the Freeland League was the historical continuation of the ITO, which had been active at the beginning of the twentieth century under the leadership of Israel Zangwill, and that its main aim was to promote large-scale Jewish settlement in an uninhabited territory outside Palestine.[86] In view of the situation in Europe, the Freeland League requested that the Anglo-American Committee persuade the nations of the world to open their doors to Jewish refugees and allow them to enter not as individuals but as a community that could develop culturally and spiritually. This attempt had already been made in Palestine, but the Freeland League was not of the opinion that the future of the Jewish people should be completely linked to one territory.[87] The Jewish people should therefore be granted a territory where large numbers of refugees could settle. This idea had already been raised in the past, and there was no reason not to raise it again. In 1903 the British government offered Herzl the opportunity to establish a Jewish autonomous region in Uganda. In 1917 Britain promoted the idea of a Jewish homeland in Palestine, and in May 1939 the British government proposed British New Guinea.[88] On the basis of these precedents of the distant and recent past, the Freeland League asked the committee to consider the possibility of settling Jews in Kimberley, Australia, and drew its attention to the plan that Steinberg had formulated on the eve of World War II.

The problem of the refugees after the war and the attempt to find a solution that would help them rebuild their lives revived the efforts of the Freeland League. Steinberg and his colleagues continued the line that had characterized the Territorialists from the start: finding a solution to the problem of European Jewry in Palestine, but not only there. In the situation that emerged after the war, their position in principle was that Palestine could be a land of refuge for the survivors but that it could never in any way be the only solution. In his article "Now Is the Time," Steinberg asserted that one should not hang all one's hopes on the Land of Israel. The Zionists were devoting all their time and energies to establishing a state in Palestine, thereby arousing the enmity and opposition of both the British government and the Arabs: "The new Jewish nation cannot be built only or solely on the foundation of hope for a Jewish majority in the future. Even with such a majority there would be no guarantee of peace throughout the land.... We cannot forget that Palestine Arabs will have the support of the vast majority of their kinsmen in the neighboring countries.... If, therefore, formation of a new state is now imperative let it be neither a Jewish nor an Arab state but, rather, a Palestinian commonwealth."[89] The gates of Palestine must stay open, Steinberg explained, but at the same time he thought that the situation after the war had created an opportunity to set up another home for the Jews outside Europe, in addition to the home in Palestine.[90]

This territorialist view was based on the assumption that a considerable number of the survivors would not want to move to Palestine and start a new life there. Many of them might support the idea of a Jewish state in Palestine in principle, but because of their tragic situation, they might want to rehabilitate their lives elsewhere, not in Palestine. The territorialist press in those years published many letters (and sometimes even photos) of displaced persons (DPs) who wanted to immigrate to Suriname (about which the Territorialists were then conducting negotiations with the Netherlands) or any other possible destination.[91] The many such requests published in the territorialist press do not necessarily reflect the DPs' preferences and may have been more in the nature of Freeland League propaganda. But a comparison of the number of DPs who went to Palestine and other countries indicates that the Territorialists' assumption was correct. Joseph Grodzinsky found that of the 330,000 DPs in the Western zones of occupation, 140,000 (42 percent) immigrated to Palestine and 193,000 (58 percent) immigrated to other countries. The United States admitted 120,000; South America, 20,000; Canada, 15,000; and Australia, 10,000. Another 20,000 remained in Germany, and 8,000 DPs settled in various countries in Western

Europe.[92] But even this attempt to help the DPs find a suitable place for settlement proved to be in vain. The Territorialists had no influence on the postwar political dynamic. Both the Zionists and the international community saw Steinberg and his colleagues as representing only themselves and their arguments as irrelevant.

The establishment of Israel in May 1948 created a different reality for the New Territorialists and left the need for a Freeland League in doubt. In many ways it had to deal with the same questions that the ITO faced in the wake of the Balfour Declaration. Zangwill chose to disband the ITO; Steinberg, by contrast, thought that the Freeland League was more important than ever before and wanted to offer an ideological alternative to the State of Israel.

## THE FREELAND LEAGUE, THE YISHUV, AND THE STATE OF ISRAEL

Just as had been the case with the Uganda plan and the ITO, the Freeland League did have some public support in the Yishuv. But whereas fairly large groups held territorialist positions early in the twentieth century, in the 1930s and 1940s, and then during the first decade of Israeli independence, they were confined to a small though prominent group among the local intellectual elite: the Ihud Association, founded in August 1942.[93] The association's prominent members included Judah L. Magnes, Martin Buber, Samuel Hugo Bergman, Haim Margolis-Kalvaryski, Norman Bentwich, Moshe Smilansky, Rabbi Binyamin (Yehoshua Radler-Feldmann), Nathan Hofshi, and Akiva Ernst Simon. The group opposed Zionist maximalism and promoted the idea of a binational state as the solution to the "Zionist question in the spirit of peace and love for the Arabs."[94] The Ihud Association and the Freeland League were linked by their shared convictions about Zionism and their attitude toward the local Arabs. They agreed that a Jewish majority in Palestine was not a necessary condition for the realization of the Zionist idea and thought that the Zionist leadership's obstinacy on this issue did not serve the best interests of all sections of the Jewish people.[95]

These claims were countered by various figures in the Yishuv and the Zionist establishment in Palestine. Writing in 1934, a short time after the establishment of the Freeland League, Dov Sadan came out against the new territorialist organization and asserted that the Zionist movement had to enter the lists against Territorialism.

> As long as the number of immigrants to Palestine was in the thousands and their influence was nil, one could criticize, doubt, and even mock, but now that immigration has reached forty to fifty thousand a year, when it is not possible to actually describe the spiritual fate of German Jewry without this crutch, when about fifteen to twenty thousand immigrants who come from Poland every year are an enormous economic factor in the desperate lives of the three million Jews of that country, now that the Zionists' prospects have improved and the hopes for the neighboring countries have increased—the attitude toward Zionism in that volume is fraud and childishness.[96]

Zionism, Sadan continued, does not accept the unwritten contract that the Territorialists have drawn up with Zionism, to the effect that "we will not undermine Zionism and Zionism will not challenge us." Sadan recognized that the Zionist movement was alive and breathing and vowed to "fight fiercely against any attempt to divert it even slightly from its path."[97] In 1944 Eliezer Levinstein (Livne), a leader of the Mapai political party, published the small booklet *Ha-territorialism ha-hadashah* (The New Territorialism), in which he tried to demonstrate that the territorialist idea had little chance of success and that the Freeland League was damaging the Zionist movement's efforts to set up a national homeland for the Jews in Palestine. His main thesis was that influential British politicians were liable to exploit territorialist arguments against the Zionist movement and severely undermine the struggle for the Land of Israel.

> If non-Jewish politicians are afraid to subscribe to the plans for their implementation, it should not be inferred that a few of them—in particular the British—will hesitate to make use of the Territorialist slogans for a political maneuver to weaken Jewish claim to Palestine and to divert the attention of the Jewish people and its friends from the fate of the country just at a time when the future of this land is at a decisive point and demands that we focus all our national energies and the full support of

## CHAPTER 6

our friends. If the Territorialists no longer play any constructive colonization role in the lives of the Jews, they may still fill a politically destructive role of the highest degree.[98]

It was not clear to Levinstein why New Territorialists had emerged precisely at such a critical and sensitive period, especially after the Zionist movement had registered such impressive achievements in the fields of immigration and settlement. According to him, during the twenty years of the British Mandate in Palestine, the Territorialists' claim that the country was too small and could not absorb thousands of migrants had been shown to be wrong. The Yishuv, Levinstein wrote, had successfully absorbed the immigrants who arrived in Palestine and much more could have been done had the British not hindered immigration and land acquisition.

Despite the attacks on the Freeland League, the New Territorialists did not constitute a real threat to the Zionist movement; Sadan and Levinstein mistook the shadow for the real thing. Even though Steinberg and his colleagues sought an alternative territory for the Jewish refugees outside Palestine, their actions did not endanger the Zionist enterprise. Nevertheless, some in the Yishuv were still afraid of an increase in the number of Jewish voices directed against Zionism. They feared that such criticism would split and weaken the Zionist movement. The Yishuv was not a sovereign body, and its political regime was voluntary. Hence secession by individuals and groups could undermine the movement's legitimacy as the representative of world Jewry. This was the true reason for the attacks on the Territorialists, even though they were a small group devoid of influence over the Jewish people.

The establishment of Israel created a new reality. The Territorialists had to decide whether the Freeland League should persevere or disband and reconcile itself to the existence of the Jewish state. Unlike Zangwill and his supporters, who had been an integral part of the Zionist movement, the New Territorialists thought that the Freeland League should continue to function; the territorialist idea struck them as all the more relevant after the establishment of the state.

In May 1948, a few days after Israel was born, Steinberg wrote that "we have to be very careful not to deny our Javnian essence, which has been entrenched among us for generations." Contrasting spiritual

Judaism with political or sovereign Judaism, he expressed his fears of the Jewish-Arab conflict and its effects on the young state.

> There are two dangers that lurk for the State of Israel, which has been established in a hostile Arab environment. The danger from without will prod it into being devoted firstly and mostly to the matter of defending itself, to military security. . . . Here the danger is from within as well: the entire life of the people in Israel will be centered on military defense. The youth will become militarized, and education, literature, and all intellectual endeavor and thought will be directed not towards the concerns of mind and spirit but those of defense.[99]

No more than a few score members attended the annual conference of the Freeland League in New York in October 1948. One of its key resolutions held that the State of Israel could not be the sole solution for the Jewish people and that the League should continue to pursue its basic aims. Although

> the Conference appreciates with deep satisfaction the historic importance of the establishment of the State of Israel, thereby officially recognizing the right of the people to its own independent existence, and giving a part of our people the opportunity to lead a free national life, at the same time, it must be stressed that the State of Israel does not solve the problem of Jewish homelessness. Both because of the State's limited area and the hostility of the Arab population, we dare not allow the whole Jewish future to depend solely on Israel.[100]

In the late 1940s and early 1950s the issue of the Jewish refugees was on the agenda of the Jewish and non-Jewish world. Although Israel had been established after a bloody and bitter war, the Territorialists continued to doubt the young state's ability to cope with its immediate problems. They deemed the idea of the ingathering of the exiles impractical and predicted that Israel would not be able to handle the problem of the Jewish refugees and become the home of the entire Jewish people. They accompanied their arguments with illustrations of the security, economic,

## CHAPTER 6

cultural, and demographic aspects. According to the Freelanders, Israel "is situated in a sea of Arab states which can hardly tolerate the Jews and the displacement of 750,000 Arabs from Palestine. As soon as the Middle and Near East become militarized, Israel might be the victim of attack." What is more, Israel had few natural resources and "except for salt, it was devoid of metals, minerals or forests. . . . The agriculture of the land cannot support its inhabitants."[101]

From the cultural viewpoint the Territorialists opposed the imposition of Hebrew language and culture on Diaspora Jewry. Many of them preferred Yiddish. They held that the concentration of Jews in a single territory would be a mistake of the first order, one that would placed the entire Jewish people in danger. The concept of the ingathering of the exiles was in total contradiction to the Jewish history of the last two millennia: "The very dispersion of the Jewish people helped to preserve the continuity of its national entity," because the "annihilation of Jews in one part of the world spared their bulk in other places."[102] In other words, do not put all your eggs (the Jewish people) in one basket (the State of Israel); the Jewish people's strength lies precisely in its dispersion and not in its concentration.

The territorialist criticism of Israel and of the ingathering of exiles seems to embody an inner contradiction that does not accord with the Freeland League's ideology and its search for a land for the Jewish people. The idea of a Jewish cultural autonomy in some territory did not really differ from the Zionist idea of the ingathering of exiles. The Territorialists, like the Zionists, believed that an autonomous Jewish center was the appropriate answer to the Jewish question. They found it hard to explain why a concentration of Jews in Israel was a bad idea but their concentration in any other country was a good and legitimate solution. Another contradiction was the attempt to defend Jewish dispersion and regard it as the main factor in the survival of the Jewish people during its exile. This argument stands in total contradiction to the territorialist assertion from the outset that the solution to the problem of the Jews was their concentration in the Land of Israel or any place they might be given.

This was the core of the difference between the old Territorialists of Zangwill and the New Territorialists of Steinberg. The members of the ITO were an integral part of the Zionist movement; as soon as they realized that obtaining a territory outside Palestine was not within the realm of possibility, they returned to the Zionist Organization and continued with their national activities. On the other hand, not only did the Freelanders avoid a rapprochement with Zionism after the establishment of Israel, they in fact became its harshest critics. The tolerant positions expressed by Gaster and Döblin in the early years of the Freeland League no longer reflected the attitude of its members in later years, who took extreme positions against Israel.

During the 1950s the New Territorialists' criticism of the state grew even harsher because of its aggressive nature, with border incidents and especially the Qibya operation. The State of Israel provided no protection for Jews in the Diaspora and in fact put them in danger. Moreover, Israeli policy reminded Steinberg of the Bolshevik regime after the October Revolution. In both cases the idea and the ideal were shattered as soon as they were realized. The establishment of a state for the Jews in Palestine was the realization of the Zionist ideal, but Israeli policy in its early years, especially the retaliatory raids of the 1950s, turned it, like Bolshevik Russia, into an immoral state that had betrayed the very ideal that had given it life.

> The bloody events of October 14 of this year [1953] on the border between Israel and Jordan [the Qibya raid] are thus a warning symbol to our conscience of our people. The fact that Jews—soldiers or citizens—could in cold calculation murder dozens of innocent men, women, and children in the Arab village of Qibya is itself a hair-raising crime. But far worse is the indifferent or satisfied reaction to this event by Jews in Israel and almost everywhere else in the world. It has been made "kosher' by all possible strategic, political, sentimental arguments—and the moral issue has been completely ignored.[103]

Steinberg claimed that the Israeli diplomatic line was "of course we are sorry but they [the Arabs] are to blame."[104] But in the space between "of course" and "but" the moral sensitivity of the Jewish people, which had guided them throughout the years of exile, vanished.

Steinberg's article "Der Yovel fun an idée" (The Fiftieth Anniversary of an Idea), published in *Oyfen Shvel*, was a harsh indictment of Israel.

# CHAPTER 6

Its aggressive policy, the Territorialists claimed, transformed Jews from persecuted victims into violent attackers. Hence the Freeland League's main goal was no longer merely finding a land for Jewish emigrants and refugees but also preserving "our culture, which is vanishing before our eyes," and the morality of the Jewish people against Israel's violent policies.[105] Fifty years earlier, Steinberg continued, "Our Zionist and Territorialist forbears did not have worries of this kind. Although they saw the poverty of Jewish society, they had no doubt of its spiritual and ethical richness." The current generation, by contrast, "is destined to gaze into the abyss of the Jewish soul and as a result to think deeply [about the future]. This is why the Freeland League is entering a new period, with fewer illusions but with a great sense of responsibility. The goals we must cope with are not just those of the movement but also those of the entire Jewish people."[106] Because the Arab-Jewish conflict was endangering the Jews in the Diaspora, the Freeland League was duty bound to express its position on the issue: "The Arab problem is actually a Jewish problem. We have joint responsibility. We must request, demand, and compel our brethren in the State of Israel to do what is right and just."[107]

In response to the territorialist attack against the morality of Israel, the journalist Judah Gotthelf published an article in *Davar* assaulting the Freeland League and the territorialist idea in general. Gotthelf summed up half a century of the territorialist idea.

> Few social movements have the greatness of spirit to admit their fundamental mistakes or errors and exit the Zionist stage with honor. On the contrary, you generally find movements or their remnants clinging to their errors, and trying in their last impotence to save what remains of their self-respect—at least by belittling their opponents. This is what has happened to the Territorialist movement, or its bungling heirs in the Freeland League, which exists only on paper and recently "celebrated" the fiftieth anniversary of Territorialism. . . . In the eyes of the righteous men of the Freeland League, Israel is to be filled with sins like a pomegranate [has seeds]. It [the State of Israel] is a nest of chauvinism and militarism that has renounced the

fundamental idea of Judaism by promoting violence. The Qibya affair serves them as the writing on the wall.[108]

Gotthelf saw Steinberg and his colleagues as "sworn enemies of Zion" who defamed and leveled false accusations against the Territorialists' rival for the heart of the Jewish people—the State of Israel.

The Freeland League's position on the Arab-Jewish conflict in Palestine bolstered its ties with the Ihud Association, which held similar views. On the tenth anniversary of the Ihud's founding, Steinberg wrote to Ihud members on behalf of the Freeland League and praised their bold stand against the State of Israel and its arrogant policies. He noted that the Territorialists who were "working outside the State of Israel for a free Jewish land were encouraged by every step that you [the Ihud] are taking and every word that you voice, and we will be glad to think that you will also feel encouragement from our activities and our search in every corner of the Jewish world."[109]

In fact, the members of the Ihud Association held the activities of the Freeland League in high regard.[110] Rabbi Binyamin and Nathan Hofshi, pioneers of the Second Aliyah, former members of Brith Shalom, and leaders of the Ihud Association in the 1950s, esteemed Steinberg's public activities. Rabbi Binyamin, for instance, urged the Territorialists to consolidate their forces to realize Herzl's vision. "Herzl had two basic assumptions," Rabbi Binyamin wrote.

> The first was that the Jews had to leave Europe and settle in a place that was not surrounded by enemies. The second was that this had to be done in a decent, moral, ethical manner without illusions. For this purpose he worked and for this he sacrificed his health. Is there any need to say where Zionism stands today from the practical and moral viewpoint? The State of Israel and the Jews are hated by both Christians and Muslims: about 660 million people around the world. And morally, it is better to keep silent.... We must therefore search for new ways (and not those of the Defense Minister) to rescue the State of Israel. We must create Jewish centers in a number of countries. Large centers, not small ones, with their own economy and cultural life.... This is

in my opinion the Freeland movement. This movement is still young and must harness new forces, courage, and ideology.[111]

Hofshi wrote that Israel's aggressive policies had led to a "poisoning of Jewish-Arab relations" and that it was "built on police, army, censorship, blind patriotism, hatred and jealousy, a war against its neighbors, oppression, theft and the shedding of innocent blood." Because it had arisen "in blood and fire, on piles of Israeli and Arab corpses," it was necessary to find a territory "in a more or less quiet corner, where there is no place for war against neighboring nations."[112]

Steinberg and Hofshi never met face to face, but they did conduct a correspondence. Even though both were opposed to the way that the Zionists acquired sovereignty in Palestine, Hofshi was never a proponent of Territorialism. He criticized it on two main accounts. First, he was skeptical about the Freeland League's ability to implement its ideas. Second, he disapproved of the League's rejection of Hebrew. In an April 1950 letter to Steinberg, Hofshi wrote, "I have been and remain a Zionist, from earliest childhood until my present old age, and have endeavored with all my might to express my Zionism in action, in my daily life as a laborer and farmer in our old-new homeland."[113] Hofshi saw the founding of the state as an utter perversion of the concept of Jewish redemption and its appropriate mode of realization. But at the same time he admitted to Steinberg that he had many doubts about the Freeland League: "The fateful question is whether Freeland will be able to create a Jewish community somewhere in the Diaspora with all its Jewish types: merchants, intellectuals, brokers, shopkeepers, peddlers, and urban craftsmen, but they will have to purchase their bread, the fruits and vegetables, the basic commodities of life, entirely or mainly from non-Jews? I am certain that is not your intention."[114] Hofshi's skepticism derived from the fact that the territorialist movement had never included a pioneering elite. "Who will be the pioneers who actually realize the idea, as we were the pioneers and implementers here in the Land of Israel, in the First Aliya, and the Second and Third, in all the difficult and terrible conditions and situations we faced?"[115] Hofshi was particularly disturbed by the motives behind Steinberg's territorialist activities.

What forces that motivate Freeland? Antisemitism, fear of the death camps of Hitler and his ilk, rejection and rejection—you cannot build and create with these, but *only escape from them*. . . . Please understand and believe that I am not saying this to discourage you. My Zionism does not deter me from wholeheartedly wishing you success in your efforts on behalf of Freeland, just as, long ago, it did not deter A. D. Gordon from looking sympathetically at the plan for a Jewish settlement in the Crimea. But a center/refuge for the embittered, for living off air and never putting down roots—Heaven forbid that you should devote your life to that, when the results are liable to be dangerous from every Jewish and human perspective.[116]

Steinberg's campaign for Yiddish and against Hebrew was a recurrent theme in Hofshi's letters to him. "I have read and heard a lot about 'Iddishe sprakh un kultur' [Yiddish language and culture]. Now everyone understands what 'Yiddish language' means. But what is 'Yiddish culture'?!"[117] Hofshi was doubtful that Yiddish culture had the ability to mobilize groups and individuals to drain the swamps and make the desert bloom in whatever land was found and that it could give birth to the new (territorialist) individual: "I very much value and esteem your position, and that of your colleagues, with regard to your love of Yiddish and attachment to Yiddish and wish you success (as long as you do not make war on Hebrew)." But he added:

> In the future, too, I will feel an emotional closeness to I. N. Steinberg the Yiddishist, and will be far removed—as far as is East from West—from Uri Zvi Greenberg, the talented poet with the most successful fascist tongue in Hebrew. That is a tragedy for me, a very great tragedy, but Hebrew has comforted me with Micah and Amos, with Hillel, with Rabbenu Bahya, and with A. D. Gordon. I am not ashamed to confess that I would not have found their like to comfort me in Yiddish. Perhaps I am ignorant, and simply have not discovered such men in Yiddish.[118]

Hofshi rejected Steinberg's assertion that, because most Jews in the Diaspora did not speak Hebrew, the State of Israel's spiritual influence on millions of adult and young people would be poor and insignificant. After the Holocaust, he wrote, the situation was that millions of Jews had no contact with Yiddish language and culture: "I read and was astounded. Not because my opinion differs from yours, but because it simply isn't true! Millions of Jews in Asia, Africa, and the Balkans know nothing of this language called Yiddish. The vast majority of the Jews in America, England, and elsewhere do not know Yiddish, and especially the young people."[119]

However, contrary to the expectations of Rabbi Binyamin and Hofshi, the Freeland League did not continue its activities to create a just and moral Jewish society. After Isaac Nachman Steinberg died in 1957, there was no public figure of his stature who had the strength to adapt the Freeland League to the new situation. Only a handful continued to hold the territorialist idea. The popular Jewish enthusiasm for Territorialism at the start of the twentieth century was replaced by the support of intellectuals and scholars who, other than their criticism of Zionism, were unable to offer an alternative territory for Jewish settlement that could exist alongside the State of Israel. Fifty years after the Uganda controversy, in whose wake Territorialism was transmuted from an abstract idea to a political movement with defined aims and goals, the Freeland League expired and left the scene, taking the last vestiges of Territorialism with it.

# Conclusion

## Zionism Without Zion?

This book began with the Uganda controversy and ends with the story of the Freeland League and its criticism of the State of Israel. By the 1950s only a handful of the thousands who had been drawn to the territorialist ideology in the early twentieth century remained faithful to it. The plan for settlement in East Africa, which had caused an uproar in the Zionist movement and led to the establishment of the ITO, became merely an anecdote in the history of the Zionist movement, and few today are aware of the fateful implications it once had for the Zionist movement and the Jewish people. The attempt to analyze territorialist thought raises sad questions about the history of the Jewish people during the first half of the twentieth century. The state of the Jews, which both Zionists and Territorialists were interested in establishing, whether in Palestine or in some other territory, came into being too late to save the 6 million Jews murdered in the Holocaust. The persecution that began with the Kishinev pogrom increased in geometric proportion and reached its peak during World War II, whereas the national endeavor advanced at a slower arithmetic rate. There is no doubt that the Jewish people lost the race against time.

This assertion does not mean that there is any linear connection between the Kishinev pogrom and the Holocaust, and of course neither the Territorialists nor the Zionists, nor any other ideological movement, could have foreseen what would happen in the years 1939–1945. My claim is otherwise: that after the Balfour Declaration the ITO ceased to exist in principle, although in practice it was officially disbanded only in 1925. The Territorialists returned to the Zionist movement, and some of them held senior positions in it. Their return shows that they abandoned their catastrophic worldview and took part in the national endeavor in Palestine. However, the Kishinev pogrom in many senses was a watershed event in Jewish political life and the starting point for settlement initiatives outside Palestine, the first of which was Herzl's East Africa plan, followed by many others. In other words, Kishinev is a kind of causal ground zero not only of the territorialist idea, which emerged from Pinsker's *Auto-Emancipation*, but also of the territorialist ideology, which advocated the establishment of a Jewish state outside Palestine.

The Uganda controversy was a formative moment in the history of the Zionist movement and the Jewish people. It brought the urgent issue of the need to alleviate the plight of Eastern European Jewry to the top of the agenda. Contrary to popular belief, the Territorialists and the Zionists disagreed not about the Land of Israel but about how much time the Jewish people had to establish a state in accordance with international law. The Territorialists wanted to hasten the redemption, even at the price of giving up the Land of Israel; the Zionists thought that this option was out of the question and that the Zionist enterprise should focus on obtaining the Promised Land. They believed that to forgo the Land of Israel would mean that no state would ever be established, either in Palestine or any place else.

The main reason for the transformation of the territorialist idea into a committed ideology and a mass movement was the physical and economic misery of the Jews in Eastern Europe. The destitution of Jewish society, the pogroms that raged between 1903 and 1905, and the mass emigration from the European continent caused leading figures of the Zionist movement to conclude that it was no longer possible to wait for Palestine and that the needs of the hour required an immediate solution. Their secession from the Zionist Organization in August 1905 was not a denial of the legitimacy of Zionism. Rather, it expressed their different interpretation of the path that should be followed and, most of all, their deep love and concern for the Jewish people, which was greater than their love for the Land of Israel. Unlike Zionism's opponents—Bundists, Communists, Autonomists, Reform Jews, and Orthodox Jews—the Territorialists did not initially propose an alternative ideology to Zionism. Their criticism derived from their pain and deep sympathy for the suffering of the Jews. For this reason their search for a surrogate territory did not imply renunciation of the dream of settlement in the biblical Jewish land. Instead, it was an urgent quest for a land suitable for mass settlement. This open-minded attitude was a product of their realization that they and the Zionists had the same forebears and that the Territorialists were following the historical trail blazed by Pinsker and Herzl. As they saw it, *Auto-Emancipation* and *The Jewish State* expressed the true essence of Zionism.

By contrast, the Zionists were far less tolerant of the Territorialists and saw them as a threat to their existence. As a result, the Seventh Zionist Congress, which struck the Uganda proposal from the Zionist agenda, passed another resolution that barred the future submission of any similar proposals to Zionist institutions. This decision primarily attested to the Zionists' concerns about territorialist tendencies within the movement. Thus they did all they could to remove the Territorialists from their ranks.

My analysis of territorialist thinking reveals that it was a fundamentally pragmatic worldview whose advocates correctly interpreted the realities of the time and consequently set out in search of a dramatic and rapid solution. Their failure to locate a homeland for the Jewish people may cause people to classify Territorialism as a utopian ideology detached from reality and from the life of the Jewish people. In the early twentieth century, however, Zionism itself seemed no less utopian, motivated by a dream and a vision that were even less practical than those of the Territorialists. Palestine was just as difficult to obtain as any other land the Territorialists were investigating, and no world power had yet decided to back the Zionist movement and work to find a solution to the Jewish question. From this perspective the similarities between the rival movements were greater than their differences. Both believed that a territorial solution would solve the Jewish problem in Eastern Europe; both embarked on their national campaign from a complex and problematic starting point and worked against all odds to achieve their goal.

The Territorialists and the Zionists may have diagnosed the problem in the same way, but they were divided over the prognosis. The Territorialists were pessimistic about the future of the Jews in Eastern Europe and had dark forebodings about their physical and economic survival. Their great fear was that the countries that were absorbing immigrants would close their gates and the Jews would find themselves without a suitable alternative. Persecution, suffering, and economic hardship would be their lot, and they would sink into profound and unbroken despair; there would

# CONCLUSION

be no way to rescue them from their tribulations. A territory and a land of refuge were necessary, and the sooner the better. On the other hand, after the Seventh Zionist Congress, the Zionists abandoned the idea of "catastrophic Zionism" that had characterized the period of Pinsker and Herzl and revised their prognosis. Unlike the Territorialists, who thought that current realities would only worsen the Jews' situation, the Zionists were convinced that future political changes would benefit Eastern European Jewry and ease their plight. For this reason they accepted the practical idea of "work in the present" at the 1906 Helsingfors conference. The resolutions passed at this conference led to the Zionist movement's recognition of the existence of Jews in the Diaspora and a commitment to improve the standing of Jewish communities around the world and ensure Jews' rights in the various countries in which they lived.

Here was the essential difference between the Zionist movement and the ITO. The Territorialists regarded themselves primarily as a rescue movement (in the physical sense) and were opposed to the idea inherent in "work in the present" and Ahad Ha'am's "spiritual center." Instead, they invested most of their efforts in the search for a territory for immediate mass settlement. The Zionists, on the other hand, at least until World War I and the British Mandate, saw themselves primarily as a national movement for whom Palestine was the focus but not necessarily a country for the absorption of the Jewish masses fleeing their misery.

A comparison of the territorialist and Zionist prognoses of the existential danger hovering over Eastern European Jewry reveals an interesting and unique resemblance. The territorialist worldview was catastrophic, predicting an ominous future. Economist and demographer Jacob Lestschinsky claimed that Territorialism was "a miserable and tragic movement that contained nine measures of exilic pessimism."[1] The author Yosef Haim Brenner, who briefly entertained territorialist views, eloquently expressed the same idea: "A land! Any land that can be obtained, any land where it will soon be possible to start building our home; a land not for today, which is already lost to us, a land for tomorrow, for the coming generations, for the orphans of Nemirov in twenty years, fifty years, a hundred years."[2] On the other hand, the Zionist movement, at least in its first decades, refused to countenance the territorialist panic and preferred to engage in gradual and judicious national work that was suited to the fragile economic situation in Palestine.

## CONCLUSION

Yet, as we have seen in this book, both the Territorialists and the Zionists were wrong in their prognoses and expectations of the future. The catastrophe that the Territorialists feared and warned against did not occur during their time. Moreover, after the Balfour Declaration was signed, they abandoned the catastrophic ideology that had characterized them, rejoined the Zionist movement, and became active participants in the nationalist enterprise in Palestine. In the Zionist movement, on the other hand, the opposite process occurred. The Zionists discarded their catastrophic predictions and pessimistic interpretations in the early twentieth century, only to resume them in later years. As soon as it became clear that a national catastrophe of unprecedented scope was about to strike the Jewish people, the Zionists began to see the situation in Europe as the Territorialists had in the years following the Seventh Zionist Congress. It was not until the 1930s (and later, after the Holocaust) that the Zionist movement first recognized the dire predicament of the Jews in Europe and the necessity of a rapid solution in Palestine and began using terminology borrowed from the territorialist ideology of the early twentieth century.

The Territorialists' secession from the Zionist Organization, which was due to a fundamental disagreement about how much time the Jews had left to set up a state of their own, sharpened the differences between the two ideologies. But more than that, it made it impossible for the Zionists to pretend that their concern for the Jewish people and their survival in Europe had always been the main element of their ideology. It appears that Zionist rhetoric in the context of the rescue movement and the denial of the Diaspora reveals a little but conceals much more. The Zionists' retrospective claim that they had recognized the existential danger facing the Jews of Europe all along and had made supreme efforts to establish a land of refuge for the masses who wanted to go there is a classic example of twenty-twenty hindsight.

In this regard, the deliberations about Uganda at the Seventh Zionist Congress and the Zionist Organization's decision to reject the British offer and bar any further discussion of settlement outside Palestine were a watershed. At that divisive congress, it was Zangwill, of all people, who said that the Zionist Organization "is not only the parliament of the Zionist Movement" but "a parliament that represented Jews from twenty-three countries."[3] The supporters of the Uganda plan asserted that the

# CONCLUSION

Zionist movement was for the entire Jewish people and that its aim was to save the Jews of the world, whether they wanted it or not, whether they paid their dues or not. The Zionists responded by claiming exactly the opposite: that the Zionist congress was meant to serve only the Zionists; it was not concerned with world Jewry or with anyone who did not pay dues to the Zionist Organization. It seems to me that Shabtai Beit-Zvi was right on the mark when he wrote in his controversial *Post-Uganda Zionism in the Holocaust Crisis* that the debates at the Sixth and Seventh Zionist Congresses were a turning point for the Zionists: They opted for the land and turned their backs on the people. When the Zionists tried to offer help, support, and rescue, it was too little, too late.

Another issue that distinguished the Territorialists from the Zionists was their position toward the Arabs of Palestine. This subject was a major element of the Territorialists' arguments against the Zionists. Two years before Isaac Epstein's "Invisible Question" initiated the controversy about the Arabs for the Zionist movement, the Territorialists had asked similar questions about the future relations between Jews and Arabs in Palestine. They were sensitive to the issue and drew their rivals' attention to the fact that Palestine was home to half a million Arabs and that this demographic situation would lead to an unending blood feud. "How will you expel the half million Arabs living in Palestine? And how will you expel the many Christians residing there?"[4] the Territorialists challenged the Zionists during and after the controversy, but they received no response. In its first forty years, the Zionist movement paid almost no attention to the Arab question, which would later become one of its most central and intractable problems. This was why the Territorialists focused on searching for an uninhabited territory: to prevent friction between the Jews who came to settle the designated land and its native inhabitants. This was the case with the Guas Ngishu plateau in Kenya, with Kimberley and the Northern Territory in Australia, with Canada, and with the Benguella plateau in Angola. As noted, no such territory was ever found.

Despite its precise diagnosis of the Jewish problem and sensitivity to Jewish suffering, the Territorialist movement registered few achievements. Ten years of searching for a territory produced no practical results, and the ITO reached the end of its historical path on the eve of World War II. Six main reasons led to the decline and disappearance of the Territorialist ideology and movement.

# CONCLUSION

1. The Territorialist idea took root in Jewish society in times of crisis and despair. Pinsker published *Auto-Emancipation* in the wake of the pogroms of 1881 and 1882. The Uganda plan was discussed by the Zionist establishment against the background of the Kishinev pogrom. The ITO conducted its negotiations against the background of mass emigration. And the Nazis' rise to power and persecution of the Jews in the 1930s led to the revival of Territorialism and the establishment of the Freeland League. In more quiet and optimistic times, Territorialism lost its attraction for the Jews. Having produced no substantive results, its activists moved on to other political frameworks.

2. The Territorialists wanted to use Jewish emigration from Eastern Europe to advance their political aims. They saw the tens of thousands who left Russia, Galicia, and Romania every year as a reservoir of future colonists and tried to set up a Jewish state by diverting the stream of emigration toward whatever territory they acquired. They believed that it was in their power to intervene in the internal dynamics of Jewish immigration and effect the change they desired. Here I believe that the Territorialists misinterpreted the nature of the migration and overestimated their ability to modify it. The large wave of emigration in the 1920s was prompted primarily by economic distress and the desire to change the existing situation. North America (especially the United States) gave Jewish immigrants the possibility of starting a new life that was completely different from their experience in Eastern Europe. Neither the territorialist nor the Zionist idea could compete with the image of the United States as the land of unlimited opportunity and the hope it inspired in the hearts of millions. Jewish immigrants were hungry for bread and not interested in participating in a socio-ideological experiment; their sole objective was to provide food for their families. This was the reason that, of the 1.5 million migrants, only 8,000 left Europe within the framework of the Galveston plan and under the auspices of the ITO. But as soon as the mass emigration ceased and the Zionist movement received a charter for Palestine, in the form of the Balfour Declaration, the ITO found itself without a political agenda and with no influence over the Jewish people.

3. The ITO's main aim was to secure a territory on an autonomous basis for those Jews who could not or would not remain in the lands in which they presently lived. To that end, Zangwill began his search for a

suitable territory, one that was sparsely populated and capable of absorbing thousands of Jews. His diplomatic efforts involved a close scrutiny of almost every territory on Earth and, in certain cases, official negotiations between the ITO and sovereign governments. All the countries that were approached agreed to receive Jews as individuals, but not as a nation, and rejected any possibility of an autonomous Jewish entity in the territory under their control. Without a territory the ITO could not achieve its one and only goal and thus lost its raison d'être. There was also an inherent problem in territorialist diplomacy. The Territorialists relied on the colonialist impulses of the European powers and tried to exploit the powers' interests in the territories they controlled. Thus there was a moral defect in the ITO's political activities. Although the ITO did not want to accept an inhabited territory, the legitimacy of receiving any territory was dubious. Zangwill never questioned the moral right of the European powers, especially Great Britain, to control extensive territories overseas and sought to exploit their control to meet Jewish needs. But World War I put an end to the age of colonialism, and Zangwill no longer had any chance of finding a common interest between the ITO and one of the European powers.

4. The fourth reason is a corollary of the third. The Zionists believed in the Jewish people's ability to make the nations of the world recognize the justice of the Zionist idea; the Basel plan, which aimed to establish a homeland for the Jewish people in the Land of Israel, secured by international law, expressed this belief. The territorialist diplomatic activities in the years preceding World War I and their failure to persuade national leaders and bureaucrats of the importance of a territorial solution demonstrated that both the Zionists and the Territorialists exaggerated the power of the Jewish people as a collective to influence public opinion. The failure of territorialist diplomacy is above all testimony to the Jewish people's weakness and inability to be an influential player in the international diplomatic arena.

5. The territorialist movement did not have a pioneer elite that could prepare a territory to absorb mass immigration. Doing the groundwork and building the appropriate economic infrastructure would have taken a long time. The Zionist movement had regiments of pioneers who enlisted in its cause, from the time of the First Aliyah until the establishment of the state. Like a relay race in which the tired runner ends his lap and

passes the baton to the next runner, new pioneers replaced their predecessors and continued their Zionist activities. The Zionist engine kept moving ahead and picking up speed, despite all the obstacles. The ITO, on the other hand, never had a pioneer reserve full of motivation and self-sacrifice. Without a territory it was not possible to consolidate a group of outstanding people of the sort that a national movement required, a group that could implement the theoretical idea.

6. In addition to the historical and logical causes for the decline of Territorialism, there is another reason, one that is not necessarily associated with the Jewish predicament or the geopolitical conditions of the early twentieth century. Territorialism analyzed the contemporary situation in a sober manner, without illusions. It saw the persecution of the Jews as posing an existential danger to them; its activities were motivated primarily by the need to save them. But a cold and calculated analysis of the problem was not sufficient to energize a national movement. The Territorialists detached the emotional aspect from their national campaign and assumed that in times of distress the Jews would go anywhere, so long as they could save their lives and families. But dark forebodings were not enough; the people also needed to be inspired with hope and to feel a link to a national enterprise for positive reasons. During times of calm and quiet, the Territorialists found it difficult to continue their activities and convince people that it read the situation correctly. With the same haste of their switch from Zionism to Territorialism, they abandoned the ITO and returned to their former home. Zion could not be separated from Zionism. The ITO's inability to develop into a large and stable mass movement also demonstrates the power of myth in national movements. Without a formative myth the ITO remained the province of a small group of intellectuals, who may have analyzed the situation and the gloomy fate of the Jews of Eastern Europe in cold and calculating terms but did not have the ability to carry out their idea at the crucial hour. In other words, territorialist ideology was a classic failure. The Zionist movement was guided by a national idea based on history and myth, whereas the basis of the ITO was scientific, rational, and intellectual. This was why the failure of the delegations that set out to investigate East Africa, Angola, and Australia was preordained: Research tools and scientific calculations (surveys, statistics, assessment of alternatives) have no power in a national discourse, whose core is premised on myth. This

was the secret strength of the Zionist movement and the main weakness of Territorialism.

~

The second half of the twentieth century was good to the Jewish people. It endowed them with renewed strength and set them on a promising and successful path. In many ways the State of Israel is the center of Jewish life and experience and has assumed the burden of defending the Jewish people against future catastrophes. Should some calamity strike that the State of Israel cannot handle, we might see a reemergence of territorialist ideas, which, like the phoenix, rise from their ashes in times of distress and crisis. I can only add my voice to Eliyahu Benyamini, quoted at the start of this book: "Oy, have mercy!"

# Notes

## Notes to Introduction

1. Pinsker, "Auto-Emancipation," 194.
2. See Ducker, "Jewish Territorialism."
3. See Shimoni, *Zionist Ideology*, xiv.
4. The initialism ITO (rather than JTO) derives from the Yiddish name of the organization, Yidishe (Idishe) Territoryalistishe Organizatsye.
5. Astour, *Geshikhte fun di Frayland Lige*, vii.
6. See Marmur, "Ha-massa u-matan ha-diplomati"; Avni, "Ha-hityashevut"; and Vital, *Zionism*.
7. Pinsker, "Auto-Emancipation," 194.
8. Pinsker, "Auto-Emancipation," 194.
9. Druyanov, *Ketavim le-toledot Hibbat Ziyyon*, 1: 356–57. The Kattowitz conference was the first conference of the Hibbat Zion associations and included representatives from several countries, including Romania.
10. Druyanov, *Ketavim le-toledot Hibbat Ziyyon*, 1: 373.
11. Klausner, *Mi-Katovich ad Basel*, 2: 153.
12. Klausner, *Mi-Katovich ad Basel*, 2: 154.
13. Perlman, "Tsava'ato shel Pinsker," 20.
14. On the Am Olam movement, see Tortel, "Tenuat Am Olam"; Menes, "Am Olam Bavegung"; and Herscher, *Jewish Agricultural Utopias*. See also Frankel, *Prophecy and Politics*, 72–73.
15. Bailey, "Zikhroynes vegen Monye Bokal," 2: 467–68.
16. See Avni, *Argentina*, 65–66. See also Avni, "Ha-hityashevut," 77–79.
17. "Morning and Evening," *Hamelitz* (January 21, 1891): 1.
18. See J. L. Katzenelson, "Letter to the Editor," *Hamelitz* 186 (August 30, 1892): 3.
19. See Klausner, *Mi-Katovich ad Basel*, 2: 149.
20. Herzl, "Jewish State," 222.

21. See Avineri, "Me-inyan hayehudim le-medinat ha-yehudim," 33.
22. Bein, *Theodor Herzl*, 411–52.
23. See Friedman, "Herzl u-fulmus Uganda," esp. 177–78.
24. See Vital, *Zionism*, 265.
25. See Heymann, "Herzl ve-Ziyyonei Rusiya."
26. See Goldstein, *Bein Tsiyonut*, 206.
27. Jacob Lestschinsky, "Z. Latsky-Bartholdy," *Davar* (March 4, 1960): 7.

## Notes to Chapter 1

1. On the building of the railway, see Patterson, *Man Eaters of Tsavo*. See also Huxley, *White Man's Country*; and Eliot, *East Africa Protectorate*, 208–22.
2. See Charles Eliot to Foreign Secretary Lansdowne, November 4, 1903, Central Zionist Archives (CZA), A87, File 365, p. 49.
3. Chamberlain traveled by train to reach the observation post at Lake Victoria. Because of a breakdown on the railway line, he did not arrive at his destination. See Amery, *Life of Joseph Chamberlain*, 4: 290–91.
4. Herzl, *Complete Diaries*, 4: 1473 (April 24, 1903).
5. Copies of the negotiations between Leopold Greenberg and the British Foreign Office were deposited with the Central Zionist Archives. The documents dealing with the issue of Jewish settlement in East Africa were photographed from Public Record Office (PRO), Foreign (FO) file 785, and transferred to CZA, A87, File 365.
6. See "The Jewish Colonization Scheme," CZA, A87, File 365, p. 3.
7. "Jewish Colonization Scheme," 6.
8. "Jewish Colonization Scheme," 6.
9. "Jewish Colonization Scheme," 5
10. "Jewish Colonization Scheme," 9–10.
11. Charles Eliot to Foreign Secretary Lansdowne, November 4, 1903, CZA, A87, File 365, p. 49.
12. Charles Eliot to Foreign Secretary Lansdowne, November 4, 1903.
13. Nahum Wilbush's personal papers include four of Johnston's survey maps of the Guas Ngishu plateau. The maps indicate the quality of the country and its inherent possibilities (CZA, A355, File 49/2).
14. See Eliot, *East Africa Protectorate*, 88. In a letter to his wife, Vera, which was marked "confidential," Chaim Weizmann described his meeting with Harry Johnston. In their conversation the British explorer did not say that conditions in the region were unsuitable for settlement, but he expressed the fear that "large-scale settlement would not

be possible whatever its size might be even after 25 years." He considered the British government's proposal a "mockery of the Jews" and believed that English public opinion was against the initiative. In addition, Johnston warned against the opposition of the white settlers, who would fight against the entry of Jewish strangers into their country. See Weizmann, *Letters and Papers*, 3: 90–91. For further details on this meeting, see Weizmann, *Trial and Error*, 95.

15. Herzl, *Complete Diaries*, 4: 1564 (September 15, 1903).
16. See Heymann, *Minutes*, 2: 124. See also CZA, A87, File 365, pp. 14–15; Medzini, *Ha-mediniyut*, 264–65; and Vital, *Zionism*, 199–205.
17. Heymann, *Minutes*, 2: 125.
18. See Goldstein, *Bein Tsiyonut*, 98–99. See also Maor, *Ha-tenu'ah hatsiyonit be-rusiya*, 220–22.
19. See Tchlenov, *Pirkei hayav u-fe'ulato*, 182. Between congresses the Zionist Organization was formally directed by the so-called Greater Actions Committee; each of the Russian regional leaders was a member, along with representatives of other countries. On a day-to-day basis, affairs were in the hands of Herzl's Vienna-based coterie, organized as the Inner Actions Committee.
20. See Herzl, *Bifnei Am ve-Olam*, 2: 217.
21. Herzl, *Bifnei Am ve-Olam*, 2: 217–18.
22. Tchlenov, *Pirkei hayav u-fe'ulato*, 186.
23. Herzl, *Bifnei Am ve-Olam*, 2: 218.
24. Tchlenov, *Pirkei hayav u-fe'ulato*, 186.
25. See *Stenographisches Protokoll*, 1–10 (Protokol 6); cited from Herzl, *Congress Addresses*, 32–33.
26. Herzl, *Congress Addresses*, 35.
27. Herzl, *Congress Addresses*, 36.
28. *Stenographisches Protokoll*, 9.
29. Herzl, *Congress Addresses*, 37.
30. On David Trietsch's Cyprus plan, see Rabinowicz, *Jewish Cyprus Project*. See also Ben-Artzi, "Jewish Rural Settlement in Cyprus." On the correspondence between Trietsch and the British government, see CZA, K14A, File 61.
31. "Hakongress Hashishi," *Ha-zefirah* 189 (August 27, 1903): 2–3.
32. Nordau, "Ne'um Ba-kongress Ha-shishi," 2: 157.
33. Herzl, *Bifnei Am ve-Olam*, 2: 254.
34. Tchlenov, *Pirkei hayav u-fe'ulato*, 202–3.
35. Vital, *Zionism*, 2: 356.

36. Vital, *Zionism*, 2: 347–56.
37. Herzl, *Bifnei Am ve-Olam*, 2: 265.
38. Herzl, *Complete Diaries*, 4: 1547–48 (August 31, 1903).
39. There are several good in-depth studies of this aspect of the controversy. See, for example, Heymann, "Herzl ve'Ziyyonei Rusiya."
40. Ussishkin to Herzl, in Herzl, *Bifnei Am ve-Olam*, 2: 270.
41. Herzl, *Bifnei Am ve-Olam*, 271.
42. S. P. Rabbinowitz and Isaac Nissenbaum to Ussishkin, 13 Marheshvan 5664 (November 3, 1903), CZA, A24, File 81/2/19 (emphasis in original).
43. Report of the resolutions of the Conference of Representatives of the Zionist Congress in Russia, October 1903, CZA, Arieh Raphaeli Zanzifar Collection, F30, File 20, p. 1.
44. Report of the resolutions, 2.
45. Report of the resolutions, 3.
46. Report of the resolutions, 3–4.
47. Goldstein, *Bein Tsiyonut*, 207–8.
48. Herzl pasted the note into his diary, under the heading, "The solution of the Kharkov riddle: Rosenbaum's résumé." Herzl, *Complete Diaries*, 4: 1589 (January 4, 1904).
49. Herzl, *Bifnei Am ve-Olam*, 2: 317.
50. Weizmann-Lichtenstein, *Be-tsel Koratenu*, 114–15.
51. Weizmann-Lichtenstein, *Be-tsel Koratenu*, 116.
52. Reinharz, *Chaim Weizmann*, 191.
53. Kruk, *Tahat diglan*, 236.
54. Ya'akov Hazan (1899–1992) was an Israeli politician, social activist, and one of the co-founders of the Mapam Party.
55. Y. Hazan, *Yaldut Ne'urim*, 17.
56. Y. Hazan, *Yaldut Ne'urim*, 17.
57. Shmaryahu Levin to Menahem Ussishkin, 13 Nisan 5664 (March 29, 1904), CZA, A24, File 81/2.
58. Borochov to Ussishkin, March 16, 1905, in Mintz, *Iggerot Ber Borochov*, 135.
59. Ussishkin to Borochov, January 14, 1905, in Mintz, *Iggerot Ber Borochov*, 131.
60. Borochov to Ussishkin, February 6, 1905, in Mintz, *Iggerot Ber Borochov*, 129.
61. Medzini, *Ha-mediniyut*, 287.
62. Undated letter, CZA, Z1, File 30.
63. Bialystok, 29 Tevet 5664 (January 17, 1904), CZA, Z1, File 30.
64. Zionist Association in Shaki, 18 Tevet 5664 (January 6, 1904), CZA, Z1, File 30.

65. "A Zionist" to Ussishkin [undated], CZA, A24, File 75.
66. See also Syrkin, *Nachman Syrkin*, 65–66. See also Protokol 6 in *Stenographisches Protokoll*, 178–79.
67. Shmaryahu Levin (Vilna) to Menahem Ussishkin, CZA, A24, File 81/2, p. 1. A few weeks later, Levin wrote another letter in which he again complained that the Zionists were not doing enough in the struggle against the Territorialists: "But there is one scene in which all the Zionists are at present complaining. On the lack of any work or activity. Even here in Vilna silence prevails and no work, and it is impossible to decide whether this is the quiet before the storm or that which comes from despair" (CZA, A24, File 81/2).
68. Dinur, *Be-Olam she-Shaka*, 203–6.
69. Frankel, *Prophecy and Politics*, 366–72. On this political party, see Gotterman, *Ha-miflaga ha-tsiyonit sotsialistit ba-shanim*.
70. See letter to Ussishkin from an unidentified writer (the signature could not be deciphered), 5 Shevat 5665 (January 11, 1905), CZA, A24, File 81/2/2, p. 1.
71. Letter to Ussishkin from unidentified writer (January 11, 1905), 1.
72. "Ha-medinah ha-yehudit," *Hashkafah* (9 Marheshvan 5664 [October 18, 1904]): 1.
73. Nahum Sokolow, "Le-hashiv et ha-ziyyonut le-eitana keneged ha-terotoryalim," *Ha-zefirah* (January 11, 1905): 1.
74. Nahum Sokolow, "Le-hashiv et ha-ziyyonut le-eitana keneged ha-terotoryalim," *Ha-zefirah* (January 24, 1905): 1.
75. See J. Hazan, *Ha-sofrim ha-yehudim ve-hateritoryaliyut*, 1.
76. See J. Hazan, *Ha-sofrim ha-yehudim ve-hateritoryaliyut*, 1; and J. Hazan, *Konstitutsyon*. A notice in *Konstitutsyon* states that the proceeds from its sales are for the benefit of "the family of our gifted friend, the founder of Territorialism among the Jews of Russia and Poland, Judah Hazan of blessed memory." In his memoirs, Judah's son, Ya'akov Hazan, recounts the effect of his father's death on his home life and the assistance received by the family. See Y. Hazan, *Yaldut Ne'urim*, 17–22; and Zahor, *Tenuat hayyim*, 3–8.
77. See J. Hazan, *Ha-sofrim ha-yehudim ve-hateritoryaliyut*, 8–9.
78. See Weizmann, *Trial and Error*, 100. In a letter to Martin Buber, dated October 13, 1903, Weizmann noted that "the Jews of the East End (a mixed population) are seized with Africa fever with the complications of Herzl insanity" (Weizmann, *Letters and Papers*, 3: 87).
79. Herzl, *Complete Diaries*, 4: 1564 (September 15, 1903).

## NOTES TO CHAPTER 1

80. Herzl, *Complete Diaries*, 4: 1563–64 (September 15, 1903).
81. Herzl, *Complete Diaries*, 4: 1568 (October 19, 1903).
82. On the offer made by the South African Zionists to Herzl, see Weisbord, *African Zion*, 200–201.
83. On Samuel Goldreich, see Shimoni, *Jews and Zionism*, 21–23.
84. See Weisbord, *African Zion*, 203–4, esp. n. 15.
85. On the contract and conditions for the commission, see CZA, A14K, File 109, pp. 1–2.
86. Wilbush, *Ha-massa le-Uganda*, 42.
87. See *Report of the Commission* (1905), 4.
88. CZA, K14A, File 109, p. 2.
89. On the commission's journey to East Africa, see Weisbord, *African Zion*. See also Bar-Yosef, "Lama lo Uganda."
90. Wilbush, *Ha-massa le-Uganda*, 45.
91. Wilbush, *Ha-massa le-Uganda*, 48–49.
92. *Report of the Commission* (1905), 5–6.
93. *Report of the Commission* (1905), 6.
94. *Report of the Commission* (1905), 11–12.
95. *Report of the Commission* (1905), 16.
96. *Report of the Commission* (1905), 23–28.
97. *Report of the Commission* (1905), 44.
98. *Report of the Commission* (1905), 51–52.
99. *Report of the Commission* (1905), 56. Elspeth Huxley relates that representatives of the settlers came to see the governor of the British East Africa Protectorate, Charles Eliot, and asked to escort the commission to "help" it in its work. The governor accepted their proposal, saying, "I am sure, sirs, that you can certainly show the members of the commission many things that they would otherwise not have been able to see." According to Huxley, the survey commission was accompanied by a man from the British Foreign Office and a number of British settlers. The commission encountered herds of elephants and threatening natives of the Masai tribe, who frightened them until the terrified commission members took hold of their rifles. In addition, their settler companions told them about cannibal tribes living nearby. Fear did its work, and the survey commission remained in Guas Ngishu for only three days. See Huxley, *White Man's Country*, 17–134. See also Benyamini, *Medinot la-yehudim*, 44. It should be noted that Huxley's story has no factual basis. The survey commission was not accompanied by a Foreign

## NOTES TO CHAPTER 1

Office representative or by white settlers. There is no evidence for this in the official reports. The commission spent four weeks on the Guas Ngishu plateau, not three days as Huxley says. On this matter see also Weisbord, *African Zion*, 211–13.
100. *Report of the Commission* (1905), 56.
101. *Report of the Commission* (1905), 67.
102. *Report of the Commission* (1905), 68–69.
103. *Report of the Commission* (1905), 96.
104. *Report of the Commission* (1905), 16.
105. *Report of the Commission* (1905), 10.
106. *Report of the Commission* (1905), 19.
107. Wilbush, *Ha-massa le-Uganda*, 78.
108. See *Report of the Commission* (1905), 63–65.
109. *Report of the Commission* (1905), 20.
110. See CZA, A355, File 49/2.
111. On the impressions that the Guas Ngishu plateau made on Charles Eliot, see Herzl, *Complete Diaries*, 4: 1564 (September 15, 1903).
112. Herzl, *Complete Diaries*, 4: 1564 (September 15, 1903).
113. Cohen-Reiss, *Mi-zikhronot ish yerushlayim*, 240.
114. See Gibbons, "British East African Plateau Land," 242–43.
115. Gibbons, "British East African Plateau Land," 255–57.
116. The survey commission's report was published in *Die Welt* in weekly installments, beginning with Gibbon's report (*Die Welt*, June 23, 1905). Kaiser's report was published in three parts (June 30 and July 7 and 14), and Wilbush's in two parts (July 7 and July 21). Gibbon's criticism was published on July 21.
117. "Yaffo," *Hashkafah*, 2 Nisan 5665 (April 7, 1905): 5.
118. "Ha-kongress Ha-ziyyoni Ha-shevi'i," *Ha-zefirah* (July 28, 1905): 1. On the proceedings of the Seventh Zionist Congress, see Eliav, *David Wolffsohn*, 31–44. See also Yaffe, "Duah al ha-kongres ha-ziyyoni ha-shevi'i be-bazel (27 July–2 August 1905), in his *Bi-shlihut Am*, 265–324.
119. *Stenographisches Protokoll*, 62 (Protokol 7).
120. *Stenographisches Protokoll*, 67.
121. *Stenographisches Protokoll*, 69.
122. *Stenographisches Protokoll*, 69.
123. *Stenographisches Protokoll*, 71.
124. *Stenographisches Protokoll*, 71.
125. *Stenographisches Protokoll*, 75.
126. *Stenographisches Protokoll*, 75.

127. *Stenographisches Protokoll*, 70.
128. *Stenographisches Protokoll*, 70.
129. "Yeshivot Ha-kongress," *Ha-zefirah* (July 21, 1905): 2. Zangwill was referring to a conversation reported in Herzl's diary. See Herzl, *Complete Diaries*, 4: 1547–48 (August 31, 1903).
130. *Stenographisches Protokoll*, 74–75. See also Yaffe, *Be-shlihut am*, 297.
131. *Stenographisches Protokoll*, 71. See also Yaffe, *Be-shlihut am*, 296.
132. *Stenographisches Protokoll*, 84–88.
133. *Stenographisches Protokoll*, 90.
134. *Stenographisches Protokoll*, 92.
135. *Stenographisches Protokoll*, 93.
136. *Stenographisches Protokoll*, 94.
137. *Stenographisches Protokoll*, 96.
138. Yaffe, *Be-shlihut am*, 306–7.
139. Yaffe, *Be-shlihut am*, 307–8.
140. "Correspondence with the Colonial Office," *Jewish Chronicle* (September 1, 1905): 23.
141. "Correspondence with the Colonial Office," 23.
142. Nordau, *Ketavim*, 3: 17–18.
143. "Di ITO Konferents," *Der Nayer Veg* (August 16, 1906): 1.

## Notes to Chapter 2

1. Leftwich, *Israel Zangwill*, 72–91. See also Rochelson, *Jew in the Public Arena*; and Udelson, *Dreamer of the Ghetto*.
2. On the literary works of Zangwill, see Nahshon, *From the Ghetto*.
3. Herzl, *Complete Diaries*, 1: 276 (November 21, 1895).
4. On Zangwill's national worldview, see Vital, "Zangwill."
5. See Netanyahu, "Hakdama"; and Nordau, *Ketavim*, 1: 35.
6. See Netanyahu, "Hakdama," xxiv–xxv.
7. Zangwill, "Zionism," 4.
8. Zangwill, "Zionism," 4.
9. Zangwill, "Zionism," 4.
10. "Brider Ugandisten un Teritoryalisten," CZA, A36, File 8.
11. "Brider Ugandisten un Teritoryalisten."
12. Kruk, *Tahat diglan*, 243–44.
13. Kruk, *Tahat diglan*, 244.
14. N-B-D, "Ha-kongres shel Ha-territoryalistim," *Hazefira* (August 6, 1905): 2.

## NOTES TO CHAPTER 2

15. See *Protokol pervoi konferenzii Evreiskoi territorialisticheskoi organizazii*.
16. *Protokol pervoi konferenzii Evreiskoi territorialisticheskoi organizazii*, 17.
17. *Protokol pervoi konferenzii Evreiskoi territorialisticheskoi organizazii*, 18. See also Kruk, *Tahat diglan*, 248.
18. *Protokol pervoi konferenzii Evreiskoi territorialisticheskoi organizazii*, 24.
19. *Protokol pervoi konferenzii Evreiskoi territorialisticheskoi organizazii*, 25.
20. Kruk, *Tahat diglan*, 246–47.
21. Jewish Territorial Organization, Circular no. 1, October 1905 (Tishrei 5666), CZA, A36, File 8.
22. On the members in the British Sectional Council, see Cohen, *English Zionists*, 94–95. Among the council members were Mr. Meyer Spielman (respected educator and founder of a reformatory for Jewish boys), Leopold de Rothschild (treasurer of the Jewish Board of Guardians), and Osmond D'Avigdor-Goldsmid (president of both the Board of Deputies and the AJA) (Cohen, *English Zionists*, 95).
23. Constitution of the ITO, CZA, A36, File 1, pp. 1–3.
24. Constitution of the ITO, 4–5.
25. Klausner, *Mi-Katovich ad Basel*, 1: 391–99.
26. Jewish Territorial Organization, Circular nos. 2–3 (September–October 1906), p. 3.
27. Jewish Territorial Organization, Circular nos. 2–3, p. 2.
28. Jewish Territorial Organization, Circular nos. 2–3, pp. 5–6.
29. Klier and Lambroza, *Pogroms*, 228.
30. Klier and Lambroza, *Pogroms*, 231.
31. Klier and Lambroza, *Pogroms*, 228. On the pogroms in Kiev, see also Meir, *Kiev*, 122–30.
32. Waife-Goldberg, *My Father, Sholom Aleichem*, 145.
33. Waife-Goldberg, *My Father, Sholom Aleichem*, 145. The Imperial was the hotel in which the family of Sholem Aleichem spent a few days before the pogrom because they were afraid to continue their normal course of life in the Jewish neighborhood where they had been living.
34. On Rosenblatt, see Rosenblatt, *A Tkufah fun 60 yor*. Rosenblatt was born in 1876 in the town of Briceni in Bessarabia. He settled in Kiev at the beginning of the twentieth century and became the secretary of the Jewish community in the city.
35. Moses Rosenblatt to Israel Zangwill, November 6, 1905, CZA, A36, File 53b, p. 1.
36. Moses Rosenblatt to Israel Zangwill, November 6, 1905, p. 2.

37. Moses Rosenblatt to Israel Zangwill, November 6, 1905, p. 3.
38. Moses Rosenblatt to Israel Zangwill, December 6, 1905, CZA, A36, File 53a, p. 1.
39. Moses Rosenblatt to Israel Zangwill, December 6, 1905, p. 1.
40. On the encounter between Sholem Aleichem and Israel Zangwill, see Berkowitz, *Ha-rishonim kivnei adam*, 299.
41. On the publication of Motzkin's *Die Judenpogrome in Russland*, see Bein, *Sefer Motzkin*, 93–95.
42. See Motzkin, *Die Judenpogrome in Russland*, 2: 339–406.
43. Tamir, *Sefer Kalarash*, 7–8.
44. See CZA, A36, File 53b (n.d.).
45. The committee to Israel Zangwill, (n.d.), CZA, A36, File 53b.
46. Y. H. Brenner, "A Long Letter," in Brenner, *Kol Kitvei*, 2: 29.
47. See Moses Rosenblatt to Israel Zangwill, December 6, 1905, p. 1.
48. Open letter, 20 Tevet 5666 (January 17, 1906), CZA, A36, File 8.
49. Open letter, 20 Tevet 5666.
50. Open letter, 20 Tevet 5666.
51. Open letter, 20 Tevet 5666.
52. Petition (n. d.), CZA, A36, File 44/4.
53. See Meir, *Kiev*, 42–43.
54. Mandelstamm, "Autobiographya."
55. See Slutzky, "Dr. Max Mandelstamm," 58.
56. Mandelstamm, "Autobiographya," 44; See also Nathans, *Beyond the Pale*, 96.
57. Mandelstamm, "Autobiographya."
58. Max Mandelstamm, "Madua Hineni Tsiyoni," *Hashiloah* 6 (1899–1900): 555.
59. Katsovitz, *Shishim Shenot Hayim*, 175.
60. Mandelstamm, "Madua Hineni Tsiyoni," *Hashiloah* 6 (1899–1900): 555.
61. See Slutzky, "Dr. Max Mandelstamm," 45.
62. Mandelstamm, *Mahut Hatsiyonut*, 5.
63. Mandelstamm, *Mahut Hatsiyonut*, 7.
64. Mandelstamm, *Mahut Hatsiyonut*, 8.
65. Mandelstamm, *Mahut Hatsiyonut*, 10.
66. Mandelstamm, *Al ha-Territorialism*, 3.
67. Mandelstamm, *Al ha-Territorialism*, 4.
68. Mandelstamm, *Al ha-Territorialism*, 21.
69. Mandelstamm, *Al ha-Territorialism*, 17.
70. Mandelstamm, *Al ha-Territorialism*, 22

## NOTES TO CHAPTER 2

71. Mandelstamm, *Al ha-Territorialism*, 16. See also p. 38 of the same source.
72. Mandelstamm, *An ofener brief*, 6
73. Mandelstamm, *An ofener brief*, 4
74. Slutzky, "Dr. Max Mandelstamm," 57.
75. "Neumo shel ha-Dr. Mandelstam," *Ha-zeman* 71 (March 31, 1907): 1.
76. Mandelstamm, *How Jews Live*, 607.
77. Mandelstamm, *How Jews Live*, 5.
78. Mandelstamm, *How Jews Live*, 7.
79. Mandelstamm, *How Jews Live*, 8.
80. Mandelstamm, *How Jews Live*, 11.
81. Mandelstamm, "Trachoma i emigratsya v Ameriku," CZA, A3, File 27, p. 94.
82. On the Brussels conference, see Elsberg, "Te'udot al Ve'idat Brisel."
83. Letter, 19 Kislev 5666 (December 17, 1905), CZA, A36, File 53a.
84. Letter, 19 Kislev 5666.
85. Petition (n.d.), CZA, A36, File 44/4.
86. Segall, *Veroeffentlichung*, 64.
87. Hermoni, "Ha-konferatsya ha-briselit," *Ha-zeman* 18 (February 4, 1906): 1.
88. Hermoni, "Ha-konferatsya ha-briselit," 1.
89. Max Mandelstamm, "Matsav ha-yehudim Be-russia," *Ha-zeman* 24 (February 11, 1906): 1.
90. Mandelstamm, "Matsav ha-yehudim Be-russia," 2.
91. Mandelstamm, "Matsav ha-yehudim Be-russia," 2.
92. Mandelstamm, "Matsav ha-yehudim Be-russia," 2.
93. Mandelstamm, "Matsav ha-yehudim Be-russia," 2.
94. Mandelstamm, "Matsav ha-yehudim Be-russia," 2.
95. Mandelstamm, "Matsav ha-yehudim Be-russia," 2.
96. Mandelstamm, "Matsav ha-yehudim Be-russia," 1.
97. Mandelstamm, "Matsav Ha-yehudim Be-russia," 2.
98. Hermoni, "Ha-konferatsya be-briselit," 2.
99. Hermoni, "Ha-konferatsya be-briselit," 2.
100. On the migration from Eastern Europe to the United States, see Sorin, *A Time for Building*.
101. On the troubles encountered by the migrants on their way to the countries of destination, see Nadell, "From Shtetl to Border"; Nadell, "Journey to America"; Nadell, "En Route"; and Alroey, "Out of the Shtetl."
102. "Emigration," CZA, A156, File 26, p. 6.
103. "Emigration," 10.

104. In 1911 there were more than 320 ITO information bureaus. See the list of branches in the Russian Empire at CZA, A36, File 143.
105. "Takanon Ha-hevra ha-yehudit le-hagirah" (May 1909): 3.
106. "Takanon Ha-hevra ha-yehudit le-hagirah," 3–4.
107. "ITO ve JCA," *Ha-zeman* 113 (May 22, 1913): 2.
108. Leftwich, *Israel Zangwill*, 72–91.

## Notes to Chapter 3

1. Constitution of the ITO, n.d., CZA, A36, File 1, p. 1.
2. Constitution of the ITO, 1.
3. "Who We Are and What We Want," n.d., CZA, A36, File 8, p. 1.
4. "Who We Are," 1.
5. "Who We Are," 1–2.
6. Shimoni, *Zionist Ideology*, 85.
7. Raz-Korkotzkin, "Galut betoch ribbonut," 23, 29. See also Daniel Gottwein's critique of Korkotzkin: Gottwein, "Bikkoret shlilat ha-galut."
8. "Who We Are," 1.
9. Beth-Zvi, *Ha-tsiyonut ha-post ugandit be-mashber ha-shoah*, 12 and esp. 146–58.
10. Beth-Zvi, *Ha-tsiyonut ha-post ugandit be-mashber ha-shoah*, 7.
11. Zangwill, *Land of Refuge*, 5.
12. Zangwill, *Land of Refuge*, 5.
13. See J. Hazan, *Ha-sofrim ha-yehudim ve-hateritoryaliyut*, 8.
14. J. Hazan, *Ha-sofrim ha-yehudim ve-hateritoryaliyut*, 8–9.
15. See Israel Zangwill, "The East Africa Offer," in Zangwill, *Speeches*, 210. On Zangwill and his attitude toward the Arabs of Palestine, see Katzburg-Jungman, "Israel Zangwill."
16. Zangwill, "East Africa Offer," 210.
17. On Hillel Zeitlin, see *YIVO Encyclopedia*, 2: 2116–18.
18. See Zeitlin, "Ha-mashber," 259.
19. Zeitlin, "Ha-mashber," 264.
20. Zeitlin, "Ha-mashber," 265.
21. Israel Zangwill, "Ha-mediniyut shel ha-tenua ha-tsiyonit," in Zangwill, *Baderech le-atsma'ut*, 189.
22. This assertion aligns with the conclusion of Stähler, "Constructions of Jewish Identity." Axel Stähler examined the issues of the humor magazine *Schlemiel*, which was published in Berlin between 1903 and 1906, and its treatment of the Uganda affair. See especially p. 272. See also Bar-Yosef, "Lama lo Uganda."

23. See Rochelson, *Jew in the Public Arena*, 162–65.
24. Zangwill, "East Africa Offer," 211. See a similar treatment of this issue in Zangwill, *Land of Refuge*, 6.
25. See Friedman, *She'elat Eretz Israel ba-shanim*, 36–37. On a different approach to the Balfour Declaration, see Levene, "Edge of Darkness."
26. Zangwill, "East Africa Offer," 212.
27. Herzl, "Jewish State," 222.
28. See Zangwill, *Be Fruitful and Multiply*, 15.
29. Zangwill, *Be Fruitful and Multiply*, 15.
30. Herzl, "Jewish State," 220.
31. Zangwill, "East Africa Offer," 227.
32. See J. Hazan, *Ha-sofrim ha-yehudim ve-hateritoryaliyut*, 15.
33. J. Hazan, *Ha-sofrim ha-yehudim ve-hateritoryaliyut*, 16.
34. Ruppin, *Jews of To-Day*, 293.
35. On the immigration policy of the Zionist movement until 1914, see Shilo, "Tovat ha-am ve tovat ha-aretz." See also Alroey, *Immigrantim*, 60–73.
36. Sheinkin to the Odessa Committee, 18 Shvat 5669 (1909), CZA, A25, File 51/2, p. 2.
37. See Alroey, *Immigrantim*, 76.
38. Herzl, "Jewish State," 221.
39. Zangwill, *Be Fruitful and Multiply*, 6.
40. See Alroey, *Ha-mahapekha ha-sheketa*, 115–17.
41. Zangwill, *Be Fruitful and Multiply*, 5.
42. See Zangwill, *Kolonizatsye un emigratsye*, 6, 18.
43. Zangwill, *Be Fruitful and Multiply*, 19.
44. Zangwill, *Kolonizatsye un emigratsye*, 9.
45. Zangwill, "East Africa Offer," 199.
46. Zangwill, *Kolonizatsye un emigratsye*, 9.
47. Israel Zangwill to Alfred Lyttelton, memorandum, December 30, 1905, CZA, A36, File 91a, p. 7.
48. Zangwill to Lyttelton, memorandum, 8.
49. Zangwill to Lyttelton, memorandum, 11.
50. Zangwill, *Kolonizatsye un emigratsye*, 9.
51. "Bendery group" to Israel Zangwill, February 24, 1906, CZA, A36, File 102–103.
52. Mintz, *Iggerot Ber Borochov*, 142.
53. Mintz, *Iggerot Ber Borochov*, 142–43.
54. Zangwill to Lyttelton, memorandum, 22–25.

55. "A Million Jews: Will Australia Take Them?" *Sydney Daily Telegraph*, November 17, 1910, CZA, A36, File 89, pp. 3–4.
56. Israel Zangwill, "Le Yovel Ha-shivim shel Nordau," in Zangwill, *Baderech le-atsma'ut*, 171.
57. "A Million Jews," 2.
58. Israel Zangwill, "A Few Reflections: Is America Forsaking the Ideal of Her Founders?" in Zangwill, *Speeches*, 110.
59. Zangwill, "A Few Reflections," 111.
60. Zangwill, "East Africa Offer," 204.
61. Pinsker, "Autoemancipation," 194.
62. J. Hazan, *Ha-sofrim ha-yehudim ve-hateritoryaliyut*, 13.
63. J. Hazan, *Ha-sofrim ha-yehudim ve-hateritoryaliyut*, 11–12.
64. "Kol Kore shel ha-histadrut ha-teritoryalit ha-yehudit," Warsaw, Tishrei 5666 (September 1906), CZA, A36, File 53a, p. 2.
65. "Kol Kore," 3.
66. Nordau, *Ketavim*, 3: 35.
67. Nordau, *Ketavim*, 3: 35.
68. Ahad Ha'am, "Ha-bokhim," in Ahad Ha'am, *Kol Kitvei*, 337.
69. Ahad Ha'am, "Ha-bokhim," 338.
70. Lestschinsky, "Mi-yamim rishonim," *Niv Hakevutza* 4 (1955): 532.
71. Mintz, *Ber Borochov*, 87.
72. Mintz defined an agitator as "a person who derives his authority from an organizational center and is authorized to act authoritatively in places to which he is sent" (Mintz, *Ber Borochov*, 94).
73. See Mintz, *Iggerot Ber Borochov*, 149.
74. Borochov, "Li-she'elat Ziyyon ve-Territoriya," in Borochov, *Ketavim*, 1: 34.
75. Borochov, "Li-she'elat Ziyyon," 18.
76. Borochov, "Li-she'elat Ziyyon," 19.
77. Territorialist poster 5664 (1904), CZA, A36, File 8, p. 2.
78. Borochov, "Li-she'elat Ziyyon," 19.
79. Borochov, "Li-she'elat Ziyyon," 22.
80. Borochov, "Li-she'elat Ziyyon," 25.
81. Borochov, "Li-she'elat Ziyyon," 25.
82. Borochov, "Li-she'elat Ziyyon," 25.
83. Borochov, "Li-she'elat Ziyyon," 130.
84. Borochov, "Li-she'elat Ziyyon," 132.
85. Borochov, "Li-she'elat Ziyyon," 132.
86. Borochov, "Li-she'elat Ziyyon," 145.
87. Borochov, "Li-she'elat Ziyyon," 132–33.

## NOTES TO CHAPTER 3

88. Borochov, "Li-she'elat Ziyyon," 146.
89. See Katz, *Lone Wolf*, 47–64.
90. Ze'ev Jabotinsky, "Tsiyonut ve-Eretz Israel," in Jabotinsky, *Ketavim*, 115.
91. Jabotinsky, "Tsiyonut ve-Eretz Israel," 115.
92. Jabotinsky, "Tsiyonut ve-Eretz Israel," 117.
93. Jabotinsky, "Tsiyonut ve-Eretz Israel," 123–24.
94. Jabotinsky, "Tsiyonut ve-Eretz Israel," 124.
95. Jabotinsky, "Tsiyonut ve-Eretz Israel," 129.
96. Ze'ev Jabotinsky, "Al ha-territorialism," in Jabotinsky, *Ketavim*, 135.
97. Jabotinsky, "Al ha-territorialism," 141.
98. Jabotinsky, "Al ha-territorialism," 144.
99. Jabotinsky, "Al ha-territorialism," 155–56.
100. Jabotinsky, "Al ha-territorialism," 158.
101. Jabotinsky, "Al ha-territorialism," 158.
102. "Le-verur she'elat Uganda," *Ha-zeman* 1, nos. 1–3 (January–March 1905): 114. Pappus was one of the ten martyrs who sacrificed themselves for the sanctification of God and were put to death during the period of the proscriptions, most of them during the time of Tineius Rufus, the Roman governor of Judea on the eve of the Bar Kochba revolt. By analogy, the Zionists were Pappus and the Territorialists were Tineius Rufus.
103. "Le-verur she'elat Uganda," 117.
104. Bar Yohai, "Pinkas Katan," *Hame'orer* 7–8 (July–August 1906): 70.
105. See Shapira, *Brenner*.
106. Bar Yohai, "Mikhtavim le-Russiya," *Hame'orer* 1 (January 1906): 9.
107. On the establishment of the Mizrachi Party, see I. Klausner, "Bereshit yessud," 343–44.
108. Rabbi Yitzhak Yaakov Reines, "Lifnei Ha-kongress: Ha-tsiyonut u-she'eloteha," *Ha-zeman* 119 (June 6, 1905): 1.
109. Reines, "Lifnei Ha-kongress," 1.
110. Reines, "Lifnei Ha-kongress," 1.
111. Reines, "Lifnei Ha-kongress," 1.
112. Rabbi Y. Y. Reines to Israel Zangwill, 1 Marheshvan 5665, CZA, A36, File 54, p. 1. Reines seems to have misdated the letter and wrote Heshvan 5665 (October 1904) instead of the correct 5666 (October 1905), given that the ITO had not yet been established in 1904 and Zangwill was still a member of the Zionist Organization then.
113. On the rabbis' position on the Jewish mass migration, see Kaplan, *Orthodoxia ba'olam ge-hadash*.
114. Reines to Zangwill, 1 Marheshvan 5665, p. 1.

115. Reines to Zangwill, 1 Marheshvan 5665, p. 2.
116. Reines to Zangwill, 1 Marheshvan 5665, p. 2.
117. Reines to Zangwill, 1 Marheshvan 5665, p. 2.
118. Rabbi Y. Y. Reines to Israel Zangwill, 8 Marheshvan 5666 (1905), CZA, A36, File 54, p. 1.
119. Rabbi Y. Y. Reines to Israel Zangwill, 23 Marheshvan 5666 (1905), CZA, A36, File 54, p. 1.
120. Rabbi Y. Y. Reines to Israel Zangwill, 19 Marheshvan 5666 (1905), CZA, A36, File 54, p. 1.
121. Reines to Zangwill, 19 Marheshvan 5666, p. 1.
122. Reines to Zangwill, 19 Marheshvan 5666, p. 2.
123. On the pogrom in Bialystok, see Lambroza, "Pogroms of 1903–1906," 237. See also Motzkin, *Die Judenpogrome in Russland*, 60–69.
124. Rabbi Y. Y. Reines to Israel Zangwill, 29 Sivan 5666 (1905), CZA, A36, File 54, p. 1.
125. Reines to Zangwill, 29 Sivan 5666, p. 2.
126. Rabbi Y. Y. Reines to Israel Zangwill, 28 Tevet 5668 (1908), CZA, A36, File 54, p. 1.
127. Reines to Zangwill, 28 Tevet 5668, p. 1.
128. Several Mizrachi members to Israel Zangwill, 20 Shevat 5666 (1906), CZA, A36, File 53b, p. 1.
129. Mizrachi members to Zangwill, 20 Shevat 5666, p. 2.
130. Mizrachi members to Zangwill, 20 Shevat 5666, p. 2.

# Notes to Chapter 4

1. See Harel, "Herzl." See also Harel, "Ha-tenu'ah ha-tsiyonit."
2. See Schwartz, "Amadot ha-yishuv."
3. Schwartz, "Amadot ha-yishuv," 9.
4. See Saposnik, *Becoming Hebrew*, 41–63.
5. Ben-Artzi, "Ha-hityashvut ha-yehudit," 2: 346.
6. Ben-Artzi, "Ha-hityashvut ha-yehudit," 2: 349.
7. See Kark, *Yaffo*.
8. Many studies have been written on the First Aliyah. I mention only the two main ones: Eliav, *Sefer Ha-aliyah*; and Aharonson, *Habaron*.
9. Ahad Ha'am, "Emet me-Erets Yisrael," in Ahad Ha'am, *Al Parashat Derakhim*, 26. See also Zipperstein, *Elusive Prophet*, 56–66.
10. See Harel, "Ha-tenu'ah ha-tsiyonit," 394.
11. Herzl, *Complete Diaries*, 2: 742 (October 29, 1898).
12. Zemach, *Shanah Rishonah*, 73.

13. Zemach, *Shanah Rishonah*, 74.
14. Zemach, *Shanah Rishonah*, 76.
15. Zemach, *Shanah Rishonah*, 77–78.
16. Zemach, *Shanah Rishonah*, 74.
17. Zemach, *Shanah Rishonah*, 78.
18. Zemach, *Shanah Rishonah*, 79–80.
19. Zemach, *Shanah Rishonah*, 80–81.
20. See Freiman, *Sefer Ha-yovel*, 14.
21. See Kressel, "Hazon Uganda," 58.
22. See Schwartz, "Amadot ha-yishuv," 143. See also Harel, "Ha-tenu'ah ha-tsiyonit," 401–2.
23. See Schwartz, "Amadot ha-yishuv," 139.
24. David Yudelovich to Dov Lubman, November 1, 1903, Rishon Lezion Archive, File 16, pp. 4–5.
25. Avi Yishai, "Rishon Lezion," *Hashkafah* 84 (11 Tammuz 5665 [1905]): 4–5.
26. Yishai, "Rishon Lezion," 5.
27. Yosef Markovsky to Menahem Ussishkin, 16 Iyyar 1905, CZA, A24, File 81/2, no. 11.
28. Markovsky to Ussishkin, 16 Iyyar 1905.
29. Markovsky to Ussishkin, 16 Iyyar 1905.
30. Yosef Markovsky to Menahem Ussishkin, Rosh Hashanah eve, 5666 (1905).
31. E. Ben Yehuda, "Jerusalem," *Hashkafah* 23 (28 Kislev 5665 [1905]): 8.
32. E. Ben Yehuda, "Jerusalem," 9.
33. Moshe Smilansky, "Ha-matsav ha-nokhehi shel ha-yishuv he-hadash be-Erets Yisrael," *Hashiloah* 1–2 (5665 [1905]): 494.
34. Smilansky, "Ha-matsav ha-nokhehi," 494–95.
35. Smilansky, "Ha-matsav ha-nokhehi," 495.
36. Letter from Yaakov Zvi Zisselman to the editor of *Die Welt*, CZA, Section Z1, File 30.
37. Kressel, "Eliezer Ben Yehuda"; Kressel, "Hazon Uganda," 58–59. See also Lang, "Ittonut Eliezer Ben Yehuda."
38. Lang, *Dabber Ivrit*, 2: 452–587.
39. Lang, *Dabber Ivrit*, 2: 518–19.
40. See Leftwich, *Israel Zangwill*, 50–51. See also Lang, *Dabber Ivrit*, 1: 362.
41. H. Ben Yehuda, *Ben Yehuda u-mifalo*, 179–81.
42. Letter to the Editor, *Hashkafah* 64 (30 Nissan 5665 [1905]): 4. See also the chapters from *The Jewish State* published in the newspaper

# NOTES TO CHAPTER 4

*Ha-zeman* (without the name of the author), "Ben Yehuda on the Uganda Proposal," *Ha-zeman* 28 (February 2, 1905): 2.
43. See Chapter 1.
44. E. Ben Yehuda, *Ha-medinah ha-yehudit*, 5.
45. E. Ben Yehuda, *Ha-medinah ha-yehudit*, 9.
46. E. Ben Yehuda, *Ha-medinah ha-yehudit*, 6–7.
47. E. Ben Yehuda, *Ha-medinah ha-yehudit*, 6–7.
48. E. Ben Yehuda, *Ha-medinah ha-yehudit*, 16, 17.
49. E. Ben Yehuda, *Ha-medinah ha-yehudit*, 11–12.
50. E. Ben Yehuda, *Ha-medinah ha-yehudit*, 7.
51. E. Ben Yehuda, *Ha-medinah ha-yehudit*, 30–31.
52. E. Ben Yehuda, *Ha-medinah ha-yehudit*, 31.
53. Lang, *Dabber Ivrit*, 2: 493 and also 2: 555.
54. Kressel, "Hazon Uganda," 58.
55. Lang, *Dabber Ivrit*, 2: 456.
56. E. Ben Yehuda, "The Pogroms Against the Jews of Kishinev," *Hashkafah* 34 (10 Sivan 5663 [1903]): 262. On Ben Yehuda's apprehensions about the fate of the Jews in Eastern Europe, see also Saposnik, *Becoming Hebrew*, 46–47.
57. E. Ben Yehuda, "Nahamateinu be'onyenu," *Hashkafah* 38 (1 Tammuz 5663 [1903]): 1–2.
58. See Chapter 2.
59. E. Ben Yehuda, "Hapera'ot Be-homel," *Hashkafah* 3 (25 Tishrei, 5664 [1904]): 2.
60. Schwartz, "Amadot ha-yishuv," 84, 87, and see also pp. 139–43.
61. E. Ben Yehuda, "Hasach Hakol," *Hashkafah* 94 (17 Av 5665 [1905]): 2.
62. The secretary of Mizrachi, Yitzhak Moshe Weinberg, to Israel Zangwill, 4 Elul 5665 (1905), CZA, A36, File 61.
63. Weinberg to Zangwill, 4 Elul 5665.
64. Yitzhak Moshe Weinberg to Israel Zangwill, 3 Tishrei 5665 (1905), CZA, A36, File 61.
65. See Manifesto to Israel Zangwill, CZA, A36, File 44.
66. Manifesto to Israel Zangwill.
67. The signatures on the manifesto to Zangwill can be divided into three groups: The first consists of those signatures I could decipher and then find details about the individuals; the second consists of signatures that were deciphered but for which I could not find any information; and the third consists of indecipherable signatures and thus the person could not be identified.

68. "Iggeret la-shanah ha-hadashah," 26 Elul 5666 (1906), CZA, A36, File 61.
69. Avigdor Keleter to Israel Zangwill, September 7, 1911, CZA, A36, File 61.
70. See Yudelovich, *Sefer Rishon Lezion*, 47–48, and see also p. 226.
71. Yudelovich, *Sefer Rishon Lezion*, 94.

# Notes to Chapter 5

1. Leftwich, *What Will Happen to the Jews*, 8.
2. See Marmur, "Ha-masa u-matan hadiplomati," 1: 110.
3. Report by the British Sectional Council to the Geographical Commission, London, 1907, British East Africa, Supplementary Note by the President of the ITO, p. 2 (hereafter British Council Report). The report is a summary that the English Territorialist Council presented to the Geographical Committee, which contained secret reports relating to settlement plans in various territories.
4. Israel Zangwill to Alfred Lyttelton, September 8, 1905, CZA, A36, File 91a.
5. Alfred Lyttelton to Israel Zangwill, September 16, 1905, in *Jewish Territorial Organization: Manifesto and Correspondence* (London, 1907), 5. See also the original document at CZA, A36, File 91a, p. 6.
6. Lyttelton to Zangwill, September 16, 1905, p. 5.
7. Lyttelton to Zangwill, September 16, 1905, p. 5.
8. Israel Zangwill to Alfred Lyttelton, September 20, 1905, CZA, A36, File 91a, p. 6.
9. Joseph Chamberlain to Max Langerman, November 11, 1905, CZA, A36, File 91b, p. 2.
10. Israel Zangwill to Alfred Lyttelton, December 30, 1905, CZA, A36, File 91a, p. 2.
11. Zangwill to Lyttelton, December 30, 1905, pp. 2–3.
12. Zangwill to Lyttelton, December 30, 1905, p. 3.
13. Zangwill to Lyttelton, December 30, 1905, pp. 4–6.
14. Zangwill to Lyttelton, December 30, 1905, pp. 8–11.
15. British Council Report, 19.
16. Zangwill to Lyttelton, December 30, 1905, p. 16.
17. Zangwill to Lyttelton, December 30, 1905, p. 18.
18. British Council Report, 19.
19. Alfred Lyttelton to Israel Zangwill, December 12, 1905, CZA, A36, File 91a.
20. Israel Zangwill to Alfred Lyttelton, December 15, 1905, CZA, A36, File 91a.
21. See Alroey, *Ha-mahapekha ha-sheketah*, 65.
22. Israel Zangwill to the Colonial Office, December 19, 1905, CZA, A36, File 91a.

23. British Council Report, British East Africa Plan, 2. See also CZA, A36, File 91b.
24. British Council Report, British East Africa Plan, 2–3.
25. "Report of the Executive Committee: President's Interview with Lord Elgin of March 26th 1906," CZA, A36, File 91b, pp. 1–2.
26. British Council Report, British East Africa Plan, 2. See also Marmur, "Ha-masa u-matan hadiplomati," 1: 128.
27. See Marmur, "Ha-masa u-matan hadiplomati," 1: 128. See also Adler, *Jacob H. Schiff*, 1: 96–98.
28. See Weisbord, *African Zion*, 237–38.
29. British Council Report, 13.
30. British Council Report, 15–16.
31. Nellie Auerbach to Israel Zangwill, May 18, 1906, CZA, A36, File 23. See also British Council Report, 17.
32. Winston Churchill to Israel Zangwill, July 13, 1906, CZA, A36, File 91b, p. 1.
33. Churchill to Zangwill, July 13, 1906, p. 1.
34. British Council Report, Canada, 2.
35. See Tulchinsky, *Taking Root*, 113–14.
36. Tulchinsky, *Taking Root*, 118.
37. Lambroza, "Pogroms," 237.
38. Israel Zangwill to Lord Strathcona, June 20, 1906, CZA, A36, File 87, p. 1.
39. The memorandum to Lord Strathcona was published in the British Council Report, Canada, 2.
40. British Council Report, Canada, 2–3.
41. British Council Report, Canada, 3.
42. British Council Report, Canada, 3.
43. Israel Zangwill to Lord Strathcona, May 2, 1907, CZA, A36, File 87, p. 1.
44. Zangwill to Lord Strathcona, May 2, 1907, p. 3.
45. Zangwill to Lord Strathcona, May 2, 1907, p. 4. See also Marmur, "Ha-masa u-matan hadiplomati," 1: 131.
46. Richard Arthur, "Australia to the ITO," *Hebrew Standard* (June 29, 1906): 3–4.
47. Marmur, "Ha-masa u-matan hadiplomati," 1: 133.
48. See "Australia for the ITO," CZA, A36, File 89, p. 1.
49. "Australia for the ITO," 1.
50. Oscar Bernard to Israel Zangwill, November 15, 1905, CZA, A36, File 89, p. 1.
51. Israel Zangwill to Oscar Bernard, January 3, 1906, CZA, A36, File 89, p. 1.

## NOTES TO CHAPTER 5

52. See "First Annual Report of the Territorialist Branch in Perth," n.d., CZA, A36, File 89, p. 1.
53. "First Annual Report," 2–3.
54. See, for example, Bernard's letters to Zangwill, August 3 and October 7, 1906, CZA, A36, File 89, p. 1.
55. British Council Report, Australia, 8–9.
56. British Council Report, Australia, 9.
57. Israel Zangwill to Oscar Bernard, May 17, 1906, CZA A36, File 89, p. 1.
58. See Marmur, "Ha-masa u-matan hadiplomati," 1: 135–36.
59. British Council Report, Australia, 10.
60. Israel Zangwill to the Prime Minister of Western Australia, May 24, 1910, CZA, A36, File 89.
61. A group of Territorialists in Kovno to Israel Zangwill, January 18, 1911, CZA, A36, File 53a.
62. Herzl, *Complete Diaries*, 3: 899 (December 29, 1899).
63. The term *Aram Naharaim* is the biblical name for the region, which is usually identified as the land of origin for Abraham and is located in the northern part of Syria near the Turkish border.
64. Herzl, *Complete Diaries*, 3: 899 (December 29, 1899).
65. Herzl, *Inyan hayehudim*, 393.
66. Herzl, *Inyan hayehudim*, 394.
67. See Thon, *Sefer Varburg*, 42.
68. Lyons, "Sir William Willcocks's Survey in Mesopotamia."
69. William Willcocks to Otto Warburg, January 1, 1906, CZA, A12/61.
70. Thon, *Sefer Varburg*, 43.
71. Israel Zangwill to Ahmed Riza, April 30, 1909, CZA, A36, File 64, pp. 1–2.
72. See Zangwill, *Be Fruitful and Multiply*, 10–11.
73. See "Havat da'ato shel ha-professor Mandelstamm al dvar Mesopotamia," *Hed Hazeman* 117 (June 11, 1909): 3.
74. "Zangwill shav el ha-tsiyonut," *Hed Hazeman* 98 (May 18, 1909): 2.
75. Zangwill, *Be Fruitful and Multiply*, 11, 13.
76. See Jacob Schiff to Israel Zangwill, February 3, 1909, and March 11, 1909, CZA, A36, File 41/1.
77. Oscar Strauss to Israel Zangwill, December 1, 1909, CZA, A36, File 64, pp. 1–2.
78. Oscar Strauss to Israel Zangwill, January 10, 1910, CZA, A36, File 64, p. 1.
79. Strauss to Zangwill, January 10, 1910, pp. 3–4.
80. Quoted in Heymann, *Ha-tenu'ah ha-tsiyonit*, 51.
81. "Mesopotamia," CZA, A36, File 64.

82. Alfredo Bensaúde to Israel Zangwill, September 30, 1913, CZA, A36, File 73.
83. Memorandum of Meyer Flieman, December 25, 1907, CZA, A36, File 73/1.
84. Israel Zangwill to Meyer Flieman, December 12, 1907, CZA, A36, File 73/1.
85. *Report of the Commission* (1913), vii.
86. *Report of the Commission* (1913), vii.
87. Marmur, "Ha-masa u-matan hadiplomati," 3: 178.
88. Marmur, "Ha-masa u-matan hadiplomati," 3: 179.
89. Kruk, *Tahat diglan*, 2: 154. At the time, Kruk was a member of the territorialist chapter in Zurich. The letter, which was in his private archives, was published in full in his memoirs.
90. See *Report of the Commission* (1913), viii.
91. *Report of the Commission* (1913), viii–xi.
92. See "The Bill," CZA, A36, File 73/1, pp. 1–4.
93. Israel Zangwill to Alfredo Bensaúde, July 11, 1912, CZA, A36, File 73/5, p. 2.
94. "Ha-ve'ida shel ha-territoryalistim be Vina," *Hazefira* 135 (June 30, 1912): 2.
95. *Report of the Commission* (1913), ix.
96. *Report of the Commission* (1913), x.
97. Kruk, *Tahat diglan*, 2: 160.
98. On Edmond de Rothschild's contribution to the delegation, see Israel Zangwill to Alfredo Bensaúde, August 17, 1912, CZA, A36, File 73/5, p. 1.
99. *Report of the Commission* (1913), 7–10.
100. *Report of the Commission* (1913), 4.
101. *Report of the Commission* (1913), 29.
102. *Report of the Commission* (1913), 29.
103. *Report of the Commission* (1913), 23–24.
104. *Report of the Commission* (1913), 5.
105. *Report of the Commission* (1913), 25.
106. *Report of the Commission* (1913), 29.
107. *Report of the Commission* (1913), 29.
108. Declaration of Harry Johnston, CZA, A36, File 73/1.
109. Declaration of Henry Nevinson, CZA, A36, File 73/1.
110. Israel Zangwill to Alfredo Bensaúde, July 26, 1912, CZA, A36, File 73/5, p. 2.
111. Zangwill to Bensaúde, July 26, 1912, p. 3.
112. Israel Zangwill to Alfredo Bensaúde, August 15, 1912, CZA, A36, File 73/5, pp. 2–3.
113. See Marmor, "Ha-masa u-matan hadiplomati," 3: 183.
114. See Medina and Barromi, "Jewish Colonization Project," 14–16.

115. Alfredo Bensaúde to Israel Zangwill, September 13, 1913, CZA, A36, File 73/5, pp. 2–3.
116. On the Galveston plan, see the comprehensive study by Marinbach, *Galveston*.
117. On the Industrial Removal Office, see Rockaway, *Words of the Uprooted*.
118. Jacob Schiff to Israel Zangwill, October 17, 1905, CZA, A36, File 41/1, pp. 1–2.
119. See Jacob Schiff to Paul Nathan, December 28, 1904, in Adler, *Jacob H. Schiff*, 2: 95–96.
120. Jacob Schiff to Israel Zangwill, August 24, 1906, CZA, A36, File 41/1, p. 1.
121. Schiff to Zangwill, August 24, 1906, p. 4.
122. Israel Zangwill to Jacob Schiff, October 18, 1906, CZA, A36, File 41/1, p. 1.
123. Resolution of the ITO Conference, October 30, 1906, CZA, A36, File 41/1.
124. *Vos hot undz gegeben di Galveston emigratsye*, iv–v. See also the preface to the "Emigration" pamphlet, CZA, A36, File 95b, pp. 3–4.
125. "Strictly Confidential," n.d., CZA, A36, File 53a, p. 1.
126. David Jochelman, "Tsu der geshikhte fun der galvastoner emigratsye," *Wohin* 2 (Tevet 5672 [January 1912]): 2.
127. See Alroey, "Galveston and Palestine."
128. Jacob Schiff to Mayer Sulzberger, September 27, 1906, American Jewish Archives (AJA), Small Collection, SC-3844.
129. Jacob Schiff to Mayer Sulzberger, December 5, 1906, AJA, Small Collection, SC-3844, microfilm, p. 1.
130. Schiff to Sulzberger, December 5, 1906, p. 678.
131. On the financial difficulties, see Cohen, *English Zionists*, 92–93.
132. See Mr. Zangwill's address to the London Council, CZA, A36, File 46, p. 11.
133. Zangwill's address, 14.
134. Israel Zangwill to S. Ginzberg, January 22, 1914, CZA, A36, File 3. See also Avni, "Ha-hityashevut ha-teritoryalistit," 75–76.

## Notes to Chapter 6

1. On the diplomatic maneuvers and the causes that led to the Balfour Declaration, see the comprehensive and scholarly research by Friedman, *She'elat Eretz Yisrael ba-shanim*, 274–365.
2. See Zangwill, *Voice of Jerusalem*, 96.
3. See Israel Zangwill, "The Balfour Declaration," in Zangwill, *Speeches*, 331.
4. Constitution of the ITO, n.d., CZA, A36, File 1, p. 1.
5. Zangwill, "Balfour Declaration," 334.
6. Zangwill, "Balfour Declaration," 334.

7. Zangwill, "Balfour Declaration," 338.
8. See Zangwill, *Voice of Jerusalem*, 100.
9. Israel Zangwill, "Le Yovel Ha-shiv'im shel Nordau," in Zangwill, *Baderech La-atsma'ut*, 178–79. (Here and later, I have translated excerpts from this article from the Hebrew because I have been unable to locate the English originals.)
10. Zangwill, "Le Yovel Ha-shiv'im," 175.
11. Zangwill, "Le Yovel Ha-shiv'im," 175.
12. See Israel Zangwill, "Miksam ha-shav shel ha-medina ha-yehudit," in Zangwill, *Baderech La-atsma'ut*, 223.
13. Zangwill, "Miksam ha-shav," 224.
14. Zangwill, "Miksam ha-shav," 228.
15. On Zangwill and his position regarding the Arabs, see Katzburg-Jungman, "Israel Zangwill."
16. On the meaning of Lord Shaftesbury's phrase, see Garfinkle, "Origin, Meaning."
17. Israel Zangwill, "Ha-mediniyut shel ha-hanhagah ha-tsiyonit," in Zangwill, *Baderech La-atsma'ut*, 184–85.
18. Zangwill, "Ha-mediniyut," 185.
19. Zangwill, "Ha-mediniyut," 187.
20. Zangwill, "Ha-mediniyut," 187.
21. Zangwill, "Ha-mediniyut," 193.
22. Zangwill, "Ha-mediniyut," 189.
23. Zangwill, "Ha-mediniyut," 191.
24. Zangwill's letter to the members of the ITO was not found in the archives of the ITO but is quoted from the biography of Zangwill by Joseph Leftwich, *Israel Zangwill*, 234.
25. Leftwich, *Israel Zangwill*, 234.
26. See Mendelsohn, *Ha-tenu'ah hatsiyonit be-polin*, 231–44. See also Giladi, *Ha-yishuv*, 46.
27. See Gurevitz, *Ha-aliyah*, 56.
28. Merhavia, *Ha-tsiyonut*, 374.
29. See Astour, *Geshikhte fun di Frayland Lige*, 58–60.
30. Astour, *Geshikhte fun di Frayland Lige*, 60–63.
31. Astour notes that there are no documents or letters that can provide information about the association (Astour, *Geshikhte fun di Frayland Lige*, 71).
32. Astour, *Geshikhte fun di Frayland Lige*, 63–65.
33. Astour, *Geshikhte fun di Frayland Lige*, 42–44.

## NOTES TO CHAPTER 6

34. See Enav, *Be-sa'arat ha-hayyim*.
35. See Ravitch, *Isaac N. Steinberg*, 12–13, 42–43. A memorial volume was issued after Steinberg's death; see *Oyfen shvel* 3–4 (March–May 1957). For further information on Steinberg, see Benyamini, *Medinot la-yehudim*, 231; and, more recently, Zuker, "Dr. Isaac Nahman Steinberg."
36. Kruk, *Tahat diglan*, 2: 446.
37. Kruk, *Tahat diglan*, 2: 446.
38. See Kruk, *Tahat diglan*, 2: 461.
39. Kruk, *Tahat diglan*, 2: 462.
40. See "Report of the Preparatory Conference Held in Paris and London, July 18–25, 1935," CZA, A330, File 251, p. 2.
41. "Report of the Preparatory Conference," 7–8.
42. See the protocols of the founding conference of the Freeland League, CZA, A330, File 13. Section 330 in the Central Zionist Archives consists of the papers of Joseph Leftwich, a journalist, author, and biographer of Israel Zangwill. Because Leftwich participated in the meetings and was a Freeland activist, he possessed many documents relating to the League's activities. See also Kruk, *Tahat diglan*, 2: 447.
43. See CZA, A143, for biographical details from the personal archives of Leopold Kessler.
44. See "The Urgent Need of Jewry," CZA, A330, File 622. Joseph Tschernikhov was Michael Astour's father. See Astour, "Joseph Tschernikhov."
45. On the Birobidzhan plan, see Lestschinsky, *Ha-yehudim be-russia*, 172–93. See also the comprehensive study by Levavi, *Ha-hityashvut ha-yehudit be-Birobidzhan*; and Benyamini, *Medinot la-yehudim*, 101–207.
46. See Isaac Nachman Steinberg, "Far der katastrof," *Fraye shriften far yidishen sotsialistishen gedank* 17 (October 1935): 5.
47. Isaac Nachman Steinberg, "Where Are the Jews to Go?" *Jewish Chronicle* (November 11, 1937): 26.
48. Steinberg, "Where Are the Jews to Go?" 26.
49. Steinberg, "Where Are the Jews to Go?" 26.
50. Steinberg, "Where Are the Jews to Go?" 26.
51. See "Aims and Purposes of the Freeland League," n.d. (1941?), CZA, A330, File 622.
52. See Freeland League, *Objective: Freeland*, 2.
53. Constitution of the ITO, n.d., CZA, A36, File 1, p. 1.

54. Steinberg, "Where Are the Jews to Go?"
55. See Hillel Zeitlin, "Ha-Mashber: Reshimot teritoryali," *Ha-Zeman* 3 (July–September 1905): 264.
56. See "The Urgent Need of Jewry," CZA, A330, File 622.
57. See Yosef Tschernikhov, "Der Ruf tsu Frayland," *Freeland* 1–2 (September–October 1934): 9.
58. Steinberg, *Australia*, 115.
59. Dubnow, *Mikhtavim*, 99.
60. Dubnow, *Mikhtavim*, 9. See also Silber, "Dubnow."
61. Steinberg, "Where Are the Jews to Go?" 26.
62. "Memorandum Prepared by the Freeland League for Jewish Territorial Colonization for the Consideration of the Delegates at the International Refugees Conference at Evian" (London, July 1938), 1.
63. "Memorandum Prepared by the Freeland League," 3.
64. "Memorandum Prepared by the Freeland League," 3.
65. "Evian Conference," *Encyclopaedia of the Holocaust*, 454.
66. See Benyamini, *Medinot la-yehudim*, 267–72.
67. Steinberg, *Australia*, 9. Steinberg's book was first published in Yiddish in 1945 as *Gelebt un gekholemt in Australia*. In the English edition Steinberg added another chapter: "How Matters Stand at Present." On Steinberg in Australia, see Gettler, *Unpromised Land*.
68. Steinberg, *Australia*, 14.
69. Steinberg, *Australia*, 15–16.
70. See "Report of the Kimberleys (North-Western Australia)," YIVO, RG 366, Box 1–40, folder 20, p. 1.
71. Steinberg, *Australia*, 22.
72. "Report of the Kimberleys," 2–3.
73. Steinberg, *Australia*, 24.
74. Steinberg, *Australia*, 24.
75. Steinberg, *Australia*, 10, and in a slightly different version, also on p. 22.
76. Steinberg, *Australia*, 146–54.
77. Steinberg, *Australia*, 158.
78. Jabotinsky, *Jewish War Front*, 143, 145.
79. Jabotinsky, *Jewish War Front*, 152–53.
80. Steinberg, *Australia*, 110.
81. Steinberg, *Australia*, 116.
82. Steinberg, *Australia*, 116.
83. Steinberg, *Australia*, 117.
84. Steinberg, *Australia*, 119.

85. See Kokhavi, *Aqurim u-politika bein-leumit*, 73–94.
86. See "Memorandum to the Anglo-American Committee of Inquiry on Palestine from the Freeland League for Jewish Territorial Colonization," January 1946, CZA, A330, File 251, p. 1.
87. "Memorandum to the Anglo-American Committee," 3.
88. "Memorandum to the Anglo-American Committee," 4.
89. I. N. Steinberg, "Now Is the Time," *Freeland* 2 (February 1946): 5.
90. Steinberg, "Now is the Time," 19.
91. On the Suriname plan, see Astour, *Geshikhte fun di Frayland Lige*, 607–33.
92. Grodzinsky, *Homer enoshi tov*, 180.
93. On the Ihud Association, see Heller, *Mi-brith shalom la-Ihud*. See also Gorni, *Zionism and the Arabs*, 358–66; and Margaliyot, "Hakamat Ihud."
94. Rabbi Binyamin, "Kinnus Ihud bi-yerushalayim," *Ner* (August 1956): 2.
95. Nathan Hofshi, "I. N. Steinberg un der Ihud," in Ravitch, *Isaac N. Steinberg*, 305.
96. Sadan, "Al mevakshei moledet," 2: 145.
97. Sadan, "Al mevakshei moledet," 146.
98. Levinstein, *Ha-territorialism*, 28.
99. Isaac Steinberg, "Melukha Yiddishkeit oder Geist Yiddishkeit," *Oyfen shvel* (May 1948): 2–3.
100. Steinberg, "Territorialism," 123–24. See also Isaac Steinberg, "The Place of Freeland in Jewish Life," October 1948, YIVO Archive, RG 366, Box 1–40, folder 20.
101. I. Fruchtbaum, "Israel and Freeland," *Freeland* (February–March 1952): 6.
102. I. Fruchtbaum, "Israel and Freeland," *Freeland* (February–March 1952): 6.
103. See Steinberg, "Melukha Yidishkeit oder Geist-Yidishkeit," 13. For a similar point of view regarding the Arab question, see Myers, *Between Jew and Arab*, 1–19, and especially the chapter on the Arab question. In my humble opinion, Rawidowicz's view should be examined in the context of the activity of the Freeland League.
104. Steinberg, "Melukha Yidishkeit oder Geist-Yidishkeit," 3.
105. Steinberg, "Melukha Yidishkeit oder Geist-Yidishkeit," 3.
106. Steinberg, "Melukha Yidishkeit oder Geist-Yidishkeit," 3.
107. Isaac Steinberg, "Where to Israel?" *Ner* 7 (April 1955): 20.
108. Judah Gotthelf, "Ba likhlal ta'ut—ba kikhlah ka'as: Yovla shel tenuat nefel," *Davar* (March 12, 1954): 2.
109. I. N. Steinberg, "On the Tenth Anniversary of the Yikhud in Israel," *Freeland* (March–April 1953): 4. Steinberg occasionally published pieces from *Ner* that coincided with the Freeland League's outlook. See, for

example, Akiva Ernst Simon, "Where to Israel?" published in *Ner* in May 1954 and in *Freeland* in the June–July 1954 issue.
110. The ties between the leaders of the Ihud Association and the Freeland League are reflected in an exchange of letters saved in Steinberg's private archives in New York. On more than one occasion the members of the Ihud Association applied to Steinberg for moral and monetary assistance from the Jews in the United States. See, for example, Leah Mintz to Isaac Steinberg, May 11, 1954, YIVO Archive, RG 366, Box 1–40, folder 20.
111. On Rabbi Binyamin's letter, see *Freeland* 10 (April–May 1955): 12.
112. Nathan Hofshi, "Be-lev u-nefesh le-zikhro shel Isaac Nahman Steinberg," *Ner* (March–April 1957): 2–3.
113. Nathan Hofshi to I. N. Steinberg, April 19, 1940, in Hofshi, *Heart and Soul*, 243.
114. Hofshi, *Heart and Soul*, 244.
115. Hofshi, *Heart and Soul*, 244.
116. Hofshi, *Heart and Soul*, 244–45 (emphasis in original).
117. Hofshi, *Heart and Soul*, 245.
118. Nathan Hofshi to I. N. Steinberg, early September 1950, in Hofshi, *Heart and Soul*, 261.
119. Hofshi, *Heart and Soul*, 260.

## Notes to Conclusion

1. Jacob Lestschinsky, "Z. Latsky-Bartholdy," *Davar* (March 4, 1960): 7.
2. Bar Yohai, "Mikhtavim le-Russiya," *Hame'orer* 1 (January 1906): 9.
3. *Stenographisches Protokoll*, 70.
4. Zeitlin, "Ha-Mashber," 265.

# Bibliography

Adler, Cyrus. *Jacob H. Schiff: His Life and Letters.* New York, 1928.
Ahad Ha'am. *Kol Kitvei Ahad Ha'am.* Tel Aviv, 1956.
———. *Al Parashat Derachim.* Berlin, 1930.
Aharonson, Ran. *Habaron ve ha-moshavot.* Jerusalem, 1990.
Alroey, Gur. "Galveston and Palestine: Immigration and Ideology in the Early Twentieth Century." *American Jewish Archives* 56, nos. 1–2(2004): 128–50.
———. *Immigrantim: Ha-hagirah ha-yehudit le-Eretz Yisrael be-reshit ha-me'ah ha-esrim.* Jerusalem, 1994.
———. *Ha-mahapekha ha-sheketah: Ha-hagirah me-ha-imperiyah ha-russit, 1875–1925.* Jerusalem, 2008.
———. "Out of the Shtetl: In the Footsteps of Eastern European Jewish Migrants to America, 1900–1914." *Leidschrift* 22, no. 1 (2007): 91–122.
Amery, Julian. *The Life of Joseph Chamberlain,* Vol. 4, *1901–1903.* London, 1951.
Astour, Michael. *Die Geshikhte fun di Frayland Lige.* Buenos Aires, 1967.
———. "Joseph Tschernikhov." *Huliyot* 9 (summer 2005): 313–24.
Avineri, Shlomo. "Me-inyan ha-yehudim le-medinat ha-yehudim." In Theodor Herzl, *Inyan hayehudim: Sifrei yoman,* Vol. 1, *1895–1898,* Shlomo Avineri (ed.), 7–50. Jerusalem, 1998.
Avni, Haim. *Argentina ha'aretz ha-ye'udah: Mifal Ha-hityashvut shel ha-baron Hirsch be-Argentina.* Jerusalem, 1973.
———. "Ha-hityashevut ha-teritoryalistit ve-ha-hityashevut ha-tsiyonit." *Yahadut zemanenu* 1 (1984): 69–87.
Bailey, Shneur. "Zikhroynes vegen Monye Bokal." In Eliyahu Tcherikower (ed.), *Geshikhte fun der Yidisher Arbeter Bavegung in di Faraynikte Shtat'n,* 2: 467–71. New York, 1945.
Baranovsky-Togan, Michail. *Moshavot Sotyalistiyot.* Tel Aviv, 1957.

# BIBLIOGRAPHY

Bar-Yosef, Eitan. "Lama lo Uganda: Ha-mishlahat ha-tsiyonit le-mizrach Africa, 1905." *Teoria u-vikkoret* 28 (spring 2006): 75–100.

Bein, Alex (ed.). *Sefer Motzkin*. Jerusalem, 1939.

———. *Theodor Herzl: Biography*. Tel Aviv, 1961.

Ben-Artzi, Yossi. "Ha-hityashevut ha-yehudit be Eretz Yisrael, 1900–1907: Me'-afyenim geographiyim yeshuviym." In Moshe Lissak (ed.), *Toledot ha-yishuv ha-yehudi be-Erets Yisrael me-az ha-aliyah ha-rishonah: Ha-tekufah ha-othmanit*, 2: 345–413. Jerusalem, 1993.

———. "Jewish Rural Settlement in Cyprus, 1882–1935: A 'Springboard' or Destiny?" *Jewish History* 21, nos. 3–4 (2007): 361–83.

Benyamini, Eliyahu. *Medinot la-yehudim*. Tel Aviv, 1990.

Ben Yehuda, Eliezer. *Ha-medinah ha-yehudit: ma'amarim shonim al dvar hatsa'at Mizrach Africa*. Warsaw, 1905.

Ben Yehuda, Hemda. *Ben Yehuda u-mifalo*. Jerusalem, 1940.

Berkowitz, Dov Yitzhak. *Ha-rishonim kivnei adam*. Tel Aviv, 1938.

Beth-Zvi, Shabtai. *Ha-tsiyonut ha-post ugandit be-mashber ha-sho'ah: Mehkar al gormei mishga'ah shel ha-tenuah ha-tsiyonit ba-shanim 1930–1945*. Tel Aviv, 1977.

Borochov, Ber. *Ketavim*. Tel Aviv, 1955.

Brenner, Y. H. *Kol Kitvei Y. H. Brenner*. Tel Aviv, 1960.

Chabon, Michael. *The Yiddish Policemen's Union*. New York, 2007.

Chlenov, Yehiel. *Pirkei hayav u-fe'ulato*. Tel Aviv, 1937.

Cohen, A Stuart. *English Zionists and British Jews: The Communal Politics of Anglo-Jewry, 1895–1920: the Communal Politics of Anglo-Jewry, 1895–1920*. Princeton, 1982.

Cohen-Reiss, Ephraim. *Mi-zikhronot ish yerushlayim*. Jerusalem, 1967.

Dinur, Ben-Zion. *Be-Olam she-Shaka*. Jerusalem, 1958.

Druyanov, Alter. *Ketavim le-toledot Hibbat Tsiyon*, vol. 1. Odessa, 1919.

Dubnow, Shimon. *Mikhtavim al ha-yahadut ha-yeshanah ve-hahadash*. Tel Aviv, 1937.

Ducker, G. A. "The Jewish Territorialism." *Contemporary Jewish Record* (March–April 1939): 14–30.

Eliav, Mordechai. *David Wolffsohn: Ha-ish ue-Zmano, Ha-tenu'ah ha-ziyyonit ba-shanim 1904–1914*. Jerusalem, 1977.

——— (ed.). *Sefer Ha-aliyah ha-rishonah*. Jerusalem, 1981.

Eliot, Charles. *The East Africa Protectorate*. London: Cass, 1966.

# BIBLIOGRAPHY

Elsberg, Avraham. "Te'udot al ve'idat Brisel, 1906." *Michael: Me'assef le-toledot ha-yehudim ba-tefutsot* 2 (1973): 145–77.

Enav, Moshe. *Bi-sa'arat ha-hayim Isaac Nahman Steinberg, lidmoto vederkh hayav*. Tel Aviv, 1967.

Frankel, Jonathan. *Prophecy and Politics: Socialism, Nationalism, and the Russian Jews, 1862–1917*. Cambridge, UK, 1981.

Freeland League. *Objective: Freeland: The Cross-Examination of a Territorialist*. New York, 1945.

Freiman, Aahron Mordechai. *Sefer Ha-yovel le-korot ha-moshavah Rishon Le-zion me-et hi-vasda 1882 ad shenat 1907*. Jerusalem, 1907.

Friedman, Yeshayahu. "Herzl u-fulmus Uganda." *Iyyunim bi-tekumat Israel* 4 (1994): 175–203.

———. *She'elat Eretz Yisrael ba-shanim 1914–1918*. Jerusalem, 1987.

Garfinkle, Adam. "On the Origin, Meaning, Use, and Abuse of a Phrase." *Middle Eastern Studies* 27, no. 4 (1991): 539–50.

Gettler, Leon. *An Unpromised Land*. South Fremantle, Australia, 1993.

Gibons, Alfred St. Hill. "British East African Plateau Land and Its Economic Conditions." *Geographical Journal* 27, no. 3 (1906): 242–324.

Giladi, Dan. *Ha-yishuv bi-tekufat ha-aliyah ha-revi'it, 1924–1928*. Tel Aviv, 1973.

Goldstein, Yossi. *Bein Tsiyonut medinit le-vein tsiyonut ma'asit: Ha-tenu'ah hatsiyonit be-Russia bereshitah*. Jerusalem, 1991.

Gorni, Yosef. *Zionism and the Arabs*. New York, 1987.

Gotterman, Alexander. *Ha-miflaga ha-tsiyonit sotsialistit ba-shanim 1905–1906*. Tel Aviv, 1985.

Gottwein, Daniel. "Bikkoret shelilat ha-galut ve-hafratat ha-toda'ah ha-yisre'elit." In Eliezer Ben Rafael, Avi Bareli, Meir Hazan, and Ofer Shiff (eds.), *Hayehudim Ba-hoveh: Kinnus u-fizzur*, 201–19. Jerusalem 2009.

Grodzinsky, Yosef. *Homer Enoshi Tov: Yehudim mul Tsiyonim, 1945–1951*. Or Yehuda, Israel, 1998.

Gurevitz, David. *Ha-aliyah ve-hatenu'ah ha-tiv'it shel ha-uchlusia be-Erets Yisrael*. Jerusalem, 1944.

Harel, Haya. "Herzl ve-Ziyyonei Eretz Yisrael." M.A. thesis, Hebrew University, 1980.

## BIBLIOGRAPHY

———. "Ha-tenu'ah ha-tsiyonit ve-hayeihuv be-eretz Yisrael be-shalhei ha-aliyah ha-rishonah." In Mordechai Eliav (ed.), *Sefer Ha-aliyah ha-rishonah*, 303–406. Jerusalem, 1981.

Hazan, Judah. *Konstitutsyon un Teritoryalismus*. Warsaw, 1906.

———. *Ha-sofrim ha-yehudim ve-hateritoryaliyut*. Warsaw, 1907.

———. *Yaldut Ne'urim*. Tel Aviv, 1993.

Hazan, Ya'akov. *Yaldut Ne'urim*. Tel Aviv, 1993.

Heller, Joseph. *Mi-berith shalom la-Ihud: Yeuda Leib Magnes ve-hama'avaq le-medinah du-le'umit*. Jerusalem, 1994.

Herscher, Uri. *Jewish Agricultural Utopias in America, 1880–1910*. Detroit, 1981.

Hertzberg, Arthur (ed.). *The Zionist Idea: A Historical Analysis and Reader*. New York, 1959.

Herzl, Theodor. *The Complete Diaries of Theodor Herzl*, Raphael Patai (ed.), Harry Zohn (trans.). New York, 1960.

———. *The Congress Addresses of Theodor Herzl*, Nellie Straus (trans.). New York, 1917.

———. *Inyan hayehudim: Sifrei yoman*, vol. 1, *1895–1898*. Jerusalem, 1998.

———. "The Jewish State." In Arthur Hertzberg (ed.), *The Zionist Idea*, 204–26. New York, 1959.

———. *Kitvei Herzl, Bifnei Am ve-Olam*, Alex Bain (ed.). Jerusalem, 1961.

Heymann, Michael. "Herzl ve-Ziyyonei Rusiya: Mahaloket ve-haskamah." *Hatsiyonut* 3 (1974): 56–99.

——— (ed.). *The Minutes of the Zionist General Council: The Uganda Controversy*. Tel Aviv, 1977.

———. *Ha-tenu'ah ha-tsiyonit ve-hatokhnit le-yishuv Aram-Naharayim ba-tekufah she-le'ahar Herzl*. Tel Aviv, 1965.

Hofshi, Nathan. *In Heart and Soul: The Struggle for the People and for Man*. Tel Aviv, 1965.

Huxley, Elspeth. *White Man's Country: Lord Delamare and the Making of Kenya*. London, 1935.

Jabotinsky, Ze'ev. *The Jewish War Front*. London, 1940.

———. *Ketavim tsiyonim rishonim*. Jerusalem, 1949.

Kaplan, Kimmy. *Orthodoxia ba'olam he-hadash: Rabbanim ve-darshanim be-America*. Jerusalem, 2002.

# BIBLIOGRAPHY

Kark, Ruth. *Yaffo: Tsmihatah shel ir: 1799–1917*. Jerusalem, 1985.
Katsovitz, Israel. *Shishim shenot Hayim*. Berlin, 1923.
Katz, Shmuel. *Jabo: Biographia shel Ze'ev Jabotinsky*. Tel Aviv, 1995.
———. *Lone Wolf: A Biography of Vladimir Jabotinsky*. New York, 1996.
Katzburg-Jungman, Mira. "Israel Zangwill ve-habe'ya ha-aravit." *Yahadut zemanenu* 8 (1993): 153–76.
Klausner, Israel. "Bereshit yissud ha-mizrahi al yedei ha-rav Yitzhak Yaakov Reines." In Yitzhak Rafael and S. Z. Shragai (eds.), *Sefer ha-tsiyonut ha-datit*, 343–44. Jerusalem, 1977.
Klausner, Yosef. *Herzl be-hazon ha-dor: reshimot, ha'arakhot, zikhronot*. Tel Aviv, 1964.
———. *Mi-Katovich ad Basel*. Jerusalem, 1965.
Klier, D. John, and Shlomo Lambroza. *Pogroms: Anti-Jewish Violence in Modern Russian History*. New York, 1992.
Kokhavi, Arieh. *Aqurim u-politika bein-leumit*. Tel Aviv, 1992.
Kressel, Getzel. "Eliezer Ben Yehuda ve tokhnit Uganda." In G. Kressel and L. Ulitski, *Hol ve-ruah: Me'assef*, 45–72. Holon, Israel, 1964.
———. "Hazon Uganda shel Eliezer Ben Yehudah." *Barkai* (September 1972): 58–59.
Kruk, Yosef. *Tahat diglan shel Shalosh Mahapekhot*. Tel Aviv, 1968.
Lambroza, Shlomo. "The Pogroms of 1903–1906." In John D. Klier and Shlomo Lambroza (eds.), *Pogroms: Anti-Jewish Violence in Modern Russian History*, 195–247. Cambridge, UK, 1992.
Lang, Yosef. *Dabber Ivrit: Hayyei Eliezer Ben Yehudah*. Jerusalem, 2008.
———. "Ittonut Eliezer Ben Yehuda ve-emdoteha be-inyanei ha-yishuv ha-yehudi ve-hatenu'ah ha-le'umit ba-shanim 1884–1914." Ph.D. thesis, Tel Aviv University, 1993.
Leftwich, Joseph. *Israel Zangwill*. New York, 1957.
———. *What Will Happen to the Jews?* London, 1938.
Lestschinsky, Jacob. *Ha-yehudim be-russia*. Tel Aviv, 1943.
Levavi, Jaccob. *Ha-hityashvut ha-yehudit be-Birobidzhan*. Jerusalem, 1965.
Levene, Mark. "Edge of Darkness: The Balfour Declaration and the Great War, 1914–1918." *Jewish Quarterly* 38, no. 3 (1991): 31–36.
Levinstein, Eliezer. *Ha-territorialism hahadashah*. Jerusalem, 1944.
Lyons, H. G. "Sir William Willcocks's Survey in Mesopotamia." *Geographical Journal* 40, no. 5 (November 1912): 501–3.

Mandelstamm, Max. *Al ha-Territorialism*. Bialystok, 1906.
———. *An ofener brief tsu di rusishe tsiyonisten*. Vilna 1905.
———. "Autobiographya." *Ahiasaf: Luah Sifruti ve shimushi* (1900): n.p.
———. *How Jews Live: A Report upon the Physical Condition of the Jews*. Kiev, 1900.
———. *Mahut Hatsiyonut: Michtav Le-viti*. Odessa, 1900.
Maor, Yitzchak. *Ha-tenu'ah hatsiyonit be-rusiya*. Jerusalem, 1986.
Margaliyot, Meir. "Hakamat Ihud u-teguvat ha-yishuv le-nokhah hit'argenutam ha-mehudeshet shel yotsei Brith Shalom." *Hatsiyonut* 20 (1996): 173–51.
Marinbach, Bernard. *Galveston: Ellis Island of the West*. New York, 1982.
Marmur, David Yitzchak. "Ha-masa u-matan hadiplomati shel ha-histadrut ha-teritoryalistit ha-yehudit (ITO) u-mesibot kishlono." *Tsiyon* 1 (1945): 109–140; 3 (1946): 175–208.
Medina, João, and Joel Barromi. "The Jewish Colonization Project in Angola." *Studies in Zionism* 12, no. 1 (1991): 1–16.
Medzini, Moshe. *Ha-mediniyut ha-tsiyonit me-reshitah ve-ad mot Herzl*. Jerusalem, 1934.
Meir, M. Natan. *Kiev, Jewish Metropolis: A History, 1859–1915*. Bloomington, 2010.
Mendelsohn, Ezra. *Ha-tenu'ah hatsiyonit be-polin: Shenot ha-hithavut, 1915–1926*. Jerusalem, 1986.
Mendes-Flohr, Paul, and Jehuda Reinharz (eds.). *The Jew in the Modern World*, 3rd ed. Oxford, 2011.
Menes, Abraham. "Am Olam Bavegung." In Eliyahu Tcherikower (ed.), *Geshikhte fun der Yidisher Arbeter Bavegung in di Faraynikte Shtat'n*, 2: 203–38. New York, 1945.
Merhavia, Hen-Melekh. *Ha-tsiyonut: Otsar ha-te'udot ha-politiyot*. Jerusalem, 1944.
Mintz, Matityahu. *Ber Borochov: Ha-ma'agal harishon, 1900–1906*. Tel Aviv, 1977.
——— (ed.). *Iggerot Ber Borochov*. Tel Aviv, 1989.
Motzkin. Leo. *Die Judenpogrome in Russland*. Cologne and Leipzig, 1910.
Myers, N. David. *Between Jew and Arab: The Lost Voice of Simon Rawidowicz*. Hanover, NH, 2008.
Nadell, Pamela S. "En Route to the Promised Land." In Kerry M. Olitzky (ed.), *We Are Leaving Mother Russia*, 11–24. Cincinnati, 1990.

# BIBLIOGRAPHY

———. "From Shtetl to Border: East European Jewish Emigrants and the Agents System, 1868–1914." In Jacob Rader Marcus and Abraham J. Peck (eds.), *Studies in the American Jewish Archives*, 49–78. Cincinnati, 1984.

———. "The Journey to America by Steam: The Jews of Eastern Europe in Transition." *American Jewish History* 71 (December 1981): 269–84.

Nahshon, Edna. *From the Ghetto to the Melting Pot: Israel Zangwill's Jewish Plays*. Detroit, 2006.

Nathans, Benjamin. *Beyond the Pale: The Jewish Encounter with Late Imperial Russia*. London, 2002.

Netanyahu, Benzion. "Hakdama: Israel Zangwill." In Benzion Netanyahu (ed.), *Ha-derech La-atsmaʾut*, x–lv. Tel Aviv, 1938.

Nordau, Max. *Ketavim*. Jerusalem, 1967.

———. "Neʾum Ba-kongress Ha-shishi." In Benzion Netanyahu (ed.), *Ketavim Tsyiyoniyim*, 2: 149–64. Jerusalem, 1960.

Patterson, Henry John. *Man Eaters of Tsavo and Other East African Adventures*. London, 1914.

Perlman, Moshe. "Tsavaʾato shel Pinsker: Shivʿim shanah mi-yom petirato be-1891." *Bitsaron* 46 (May 1962): 16–22.

Pinsker, Leon. "Auto-Emancipation: An Appeal to His People by a Russian Jew." In Arthur Hertzberg (ed.), *The Zionist Idea*, 179–98. New York, 1959.

*Protokol pervoi konferenzii Evreiskoi territorialisticheskoi organizazii, v Basel, 30–1 Aug. 1905 yy/s predisloviem I. Zangwill*. Geneva, 1905.

Rabinowicz, K. Oskar. *A Jewish Cyprus Project: David Trietsch's Colonization Scheme*. New York, 1962.

Ravitch, Melech (ed.). *Isaac N. Steinberg: Gedank buch*. New York, 1961.

Raz-Korkotzkin, Amnon. "Galut betoch ribbonut: le-vikkoret shelilat ha-galut ba-tarbut ha-yisraelit." *Theoria u-vikkoret* 4 (1993): 23–55.

Reinharz, Jehuda. *Chaim Weizmann: The Making of a Zionist Leader*. New York, 1985.

*Report on the Work of the Commission Sent Out by the Jewish Territorial Organization to Examine the Territory Offered by H.M. Government to the Organization for the Purpose of a Jewish Settlement in British East Africa*. London, May 1905.

*Report on the Work of the Commission Sent Out by the Jewish Territorial Organization Under the Auspices of the Portuguese Government to*

*Examine the Territory Proposed for the Purpose of a Jewish Settlement in Angola.* London, May 1913.

Rochelson, Meri-Jane. *A Jew in the Public Arena: The Career of Israel Zangwill.* Detroit, 2008.

Rockaway, Robert. *Words of the Uprooted: Jewish Immigration in Early Twentieth Century America.* New York, 1998.

Rosenblatt, Moses. *A Tkufah fun 60 yor: A Zamelbuch in Yiddish in Hebreish lichvod dem 60 yorigen yubileum fun harav Moshe Rozenblatt.* New York, 1937.

Rovner, Adam. *In the Shadow of Zion: Promised Lands Before Israel.* New York, 2014.

Ruppin, Arthur. The Jews of To-Day. London, 1913.

Sadan, Dov. "Al mevakshei moledet." In Dov Sadan, *Hadashim ve-gam yeshanim*, 2: 143–46. Tel Aviv, 1987.

Saposnik, Arieh Bruce. *Becoming Hebrew: The Creation of a Jewish National Culture in Ottoman Palestine.* New York, 2008.

Schwartz, Shifra. "Amadot ha-yishuv ha-yehudi be-Erets Yisrael be-yahas le-parashat Uganda ba-shanim 1903–1905." M.A. thesis, Ben Gurion University, 1987.

Segall, Jakob. *Veroeffentlichung des Bureaus für Statistik der Juden.* Internationale Konfessionsstatistik. Berlin, 1914.

Semel, Nava. *IsraIsland.* Tel Aviv, 2005.

Shapira, Anita. *Brenner: Sippur Haim.* Tel Aviv, 2008.

Shilo, Margalit. "Tovat ha-am ve-tovat ha-aretz: Yahasah shel ha-tenu'ah ha-tsiyonit la-aliyah bi-tekufat ha-aliyah ha-sheniya." *Cathedra* 46 (1988): 109–22.

Shimoni, Gideon. *Jews and Zionism: The South Africa Experience (1910–1967).* Cape Town, 1980.

———. *The Zionist Ideology.* Hanover, NH, 1995.

Silber, Marcos. "Dubnow, ra'ayon ha-le'umiyut ha-diasporit u-tefutsato." *Iuyunim bietkumat Yisrael* 15 (1993): 83–101.

Simon, Maurice (ed.). *Speeches, Articles, and Letters of Israel Zangwill.* London, 1937.

Sirkin, Marie. *Avi Nahman Sirkin.* Jerusalem, 1970.

Slouschz, Nahum. *Ha-anusim be-Portugal.* Tel Aviv, 1932.

Slutzky, Yehudah. "Dr. Max Mandelstamm." *He-avar* 4 (Tamuz 1957): 56–57; 5 (Elul 1957): 44–68.

Sorin, Gerald. *A Time for Building: The Third Migration, 1880–1920.* London, 1992.

Stähler, Axel. "Constructions of Jewish Identity and the Spectre of Colonialism: Of White Skin and Black Masks in Early Zionist Discourse." *German Life and Letters* 66, no. 3 (2013): 254–76.

Steinberg, N. Isaac. *Australia, The Unpromised Land: In Search of a Home.* London, 1948.

———. *Gelebt un gekholemt in Australia.* New York, 1945.

———. "Territorialism." In Basil J. Valvianos and Feliks Gross (eds.), *Struggle for Tomorrow*, 111–29. New York, 1954.

*Stenographisches Protokoll der Verhandlungen des Zionisten-Kongresses.* Berlin, 1903.

Syrkin, Marie. *Nachman Syrkin, Socialist Zionist.* New York, 1961.

Tamir, Noah (ed.). *Sefer Kalarash: A Memorial Book for the Jews of Kalarash.* Tel Aviv, 1966.

Tchlenov, Yehiel. *Pirkei hayav u-fe'ulato.* Tel Aviv, 1937.

Thon, Yaakov (ed.). *Sefer Varburg: korot hayav, divrei ha'aracha, michtavim, neumim, ve-ma'amarim.* Herzlia, 1948.

Tortel, Hasia. "Tenuat Am Olam." *He-avar* 10 (1963): 124–43.

Tulchinsky, Gerald. *Taking Root: The Origins of Canadian Jewish Community.* Toronto, 1992.

Udelson H. Joseph. *Dreamer of the Ghetto: The Life and Works of Israel Zangwill.* Tuscaloosa, 1990.

Vital, David. "Zangwill ve-hale'umiyut ha-yehudit ha-modernit." *Zemanim* 25–26 (winter 1987): 62–69.

———. *Zionism: The Formative Years.* Oxford, 1982.

*Vos hot undz gegeben di Galveston emigratsye.* Warsaw, 1910.

Waife-Goldberg, Mary. *My Father, Sholom Aleichem.* New York, 1968.

Weisbord, G. Robert. *African Zion: The Attempt to Establish a Jewish Colony in the East Africa Protectorate, 1903–1905.* Philadelphia, 1968.

Weizmann, Chaim. *The Letters and Papers of Chaim Weizmann*, Barnet Litvinoff (ed.). London, 1972.

———. *Trial and Error: The Autobiography of Chaim Weizmann.* New York, 1949.

Weizmann-Lichtenstein, Haya. *Be-tsel Koratenu.* Tel Aviv, 1948.

Wilbush, Nahum. *Ha-massa le-Uganda.* Jerusalem, 1963.

Yaffe [Jaffe], Leib. *Bi-shlihut am.* Jerusalem, 1968.

Yudelovich, David. *Sefer Rishon LeZion, 1882–1941*. Rishon LeZion, Israel, 1941.

Zahor, Ze'ev. *Tenuat hayyim*. Jerusalem, 1997.

Zangwill, Israel. *Badereck le-atsma'ut*, Ben-Zion Netanyahu (ed.). Tel Aviv, 1938.

———. *Be Fruitful and Multiply*. London, 1909.

———. *Kolonizatsye un emigratsye: Israel Angwill's rede in Pavilion teater, 30.12.1906*. London, 1907.

———. *Land of Refuge*. London, 1907.

———. *Speeches, Articles, and Letters of Israel Zangwill*, Maurice Simon (ed.). London, 1937.

———. *The Voice of Jerusalem*. New York, 1921.

———. "Zionism." *Hatehiya* 10 (October 29, 1899): 4–5.

Zeitlin, Hillel. "Ha-mashber: Reshimot teritoryali." *Ha-Zeman: Yarchon le-Inyanei ha-hayyim, ha-sifrut, ha-Omanut, veha-Mada* 3 (July–September 1905): 258–62.

Zemach, Shlomo. *Shanah rishonah*. Tel Aviv, 1965.

Zipperstein, Steve. *Elusive Prophet: Ahad Ha'am and the Origins of Zionism*. London, 1988.

Zuker, Sheva. "Dr. Isaac Nahman Steinberg: Revolutsyoner un natsyonaler denker." *Oyfen Shvel* 348–49 (2010): 21–31.

Zuta, Haim Arieh. *Bereishit darki*. Jerusalem, 1934.

———. *Darkhei ha-limmud shel ha-tanakh*. Jerusalem, 1935–1937.

———. *Writings of H. A. Zuta*. Jerusalem, 1931.

# Index

Abdul Hamid II (sultan), 221–22
Abramowitz, Grigori ("Zevi Avrahami"), 41
Adler, Cyrus, 221
Ahad Ha'am (Asher Ginsburg), 131, 147–49, 156, 174–75, 179, 184, 189, 298
Aharoni, Yisrael, 197
Ahva Association, 197
AJA (Anglo-Jewish Association), 108, 111
Aleichem, Sholem, 75, 88, 91–92, 313n33
Alexander I (czar), 280
*Algemayne Yedies far di vos villen forn tsu fremde lender* (General Information for Those Wishing to Immigrate to Foreign Countries; ICA manual, 1906), 118–19
Aliens Act 1905 (Great Britain), 139, 205, 208, 213
Alliance Israélite Française, 111
Alroey, Gur: *The Quiet Revolution: Jewish Emigration from Imperial Russia, 1875–1924*, vii; *An Unpromising Land: Jewish Migration to Palestine in the Early Twentieth Century*, vii
Am Olam movement, 7–8, 9, 99
Anglo-American Committee of Inquiry on Palestine (1946), 282

Anglo-Jewish Association (AJA), 108, 111
Anglo-Palestine Company, 28
Angola plan, 229–43; Cohen proposal of 1911, 230; decline of ITO after failure of, 243, 252–53, 261; ICA proposal of 1900–1902, 229; local populations and, 229–30, 237–38, 240, 242–43; Portuguese bill for Jewish settlement, 232–33, 240–42, 252–53; revolution of 1910 in Portugal and, 230–31; Spielman proposal of 1907, 229–30; survey and report, 235–40; Terló/Bensaúde proposal of 1912, 231–33; Vienna ITO Congress of 1912 approving, 233–35, *234*, 239
Arab population of Palestine, 3, 129–32, 154–55, 258–60, 262, 263, 272, 283, 289–91, 300
Arab riots of 1929, 263
Aram Naharaim (Mesopotamia), Jewish settlement in, 139, 198, 220–29
Arbeiter Lige farn Alveltkhen Yidishen Kongres, 264
Argentina, Jewish settlement in, 8–9, 134, 140, 158, 189, 212, 244, 280
El-Arish plan (1902), 11, 17, 24–26, 44, 46, 114, 222, 242, 266

# INDEX

Arthur, Richard, 215–16, 217
Asch, Sholem, 75
assimilation and assimilationism, 77–78, 100–103, 104, 112, 133–34, 163, 250
Astour, Michael, *Geshikhte fun di Frayland Lige* (1967), 3–4
Auerbach, Helena (Nellie), 210–11
Australia, search for a homeland in, 268–69; Immigration League of Australia, 215–16, 218; Kimberley region, 264, 276–82; Northern Territory, 215–18; Western Australia, 218–20
Autonomism, 125
Avni, Haim, 4, 8

Bahya, Rabbenu, 293
Bailey, Shneur (Sidney), 7–8
Balfour, Arthur James, 207
Balfour Declaration, 10, 14, 17, 69, 76, 126, 131, 254–58, 255, 262, 263, 284, 295, 299, 301
Bar Kochba revolt, 319n102
Barzilai, Yehoshua, 190
Basel plan, 11, 24, 29, 34, 57, 68, 80, 124, 194, 302
Bein, Alex, 10
Beit-Zvi, Shabtai, *Post-Uganda Zionism in the Holocaust Crisis* (1977), 300
Belkowsky, Grigori (Zevi), 34–35
Ben Adir (Abraham Rosin), 267
Bendery, Bessarabia, Territorialists of, 142–43
Benguella plateau. *See* Angola plan
Bensaúde, Alfredo, 229, 231, 233, 240, 241, 242
Bentwich, Norman, 284
Benyamini, Eliyahu, *Medinot La-Yehudim* (States for the Jews; 1990), viii, 4, 304

Ben Yehuda, Eliezer, and Uganda plan, 184–93; after Seventh Zionist Congress, 193, 197, 198; compatibility of Ugandist support with Zionism of, 190–93; Hebrew language championed by, 189–90, 191; historical studies of, 172, 184–85, 190–91; *The Jewish State: Various Essays on the East Africa Proposal* (1905), 187–89; Markovsky on, 182; motivation for support for Territorialism, 199; photograph of Ben Yehuda, *185*; pogroms, response to, 191–92; press positions mapped out by, 42; significance of support for Territorialism, 189, 199; Ussishkin and Sokolow criticized by, 184, 188–89; on violent disputes between Zionists, 182–83; Zangwill and, 186, 192, 193; in Zemach's memoir, 176, 178
Ben Yehuda, Hemda, 186, 190, 197, 199
Benzion, Aharon, 45
Bergman, Samuel Hugo, 284
Bernard, Oscar, 216–17
Bernstein, Shlomo Haim (Alter) Shapira, 197
Bernstein-Kogan, Jacob, 24
Beth-Zvi, Shabtai, *Ha-tsiyonut ha-post ugandit be-mashber ha-shoah* (Post-Uganda Zionism in the Holocaust Crisis; 1977), 127–28
Bialik, Chaim Nachman, "In the City of Killing" (1904), 156
Bialystok pogrom, 94, 166–67, 212
Bilikoff, Jacob, 250
Bilu movement, 7–8, 9
Rabbi Binyamin (Yehoshua Radler-Feldmann), 284, 291–92, 294

# INDEX

Birobidzhan Jewish settlement region, Soviet Union, 267
Bnei Moshe Society, 184, 197
Bodenheimer, Max, 24, 175
Bokal, Monye (Michael), 7
Bolshevik regime, 289
Bolshevik revolution, 254, 264
Borochov, Ber: on Territorialist ideology, 149–55, 163, 170–71; therapeutic movement, 143; Uganda plan and, 38–39, 41; Ussishkin and, 38–39, 41, 149, 155, 170, 183
branches, of ITO, 84, 85
Brenner, Yosef Haim, 160–61, 298; "Mikhtav arokh" (A Long Letter), 94–95, 108, 192
Britain. *See* Great Britain
British Sectional Council, ITO, 84–85, 313n22
Brussels Conference (1906), 107–17, 122, 197, 208, 209
Brussels manifesto, 195–97, 322n67
Buber, Martin, 284, 309n78
Buki ben Yogli (Yitzhak Leib Katzenelson), 9
Bundists, 112, 125, 296

Calarasi pogrom, 93
Campbell-Bannerman, Henry, 208
Canada, proposed settlement in, 189, 211–15, 229, 268
Castro, Jose Luciano de, 229
catastrophic Zionism, 298–99
Center of Territorial Associations in Palestine and Syria, 194, 195
Central Zionist Archives, Jerusalem, viii, 203, 306n5, 329n42
Chabon, Michael, *The Yiddish Policemen's Union* (2007), 5
Chamberlain, Joseph: Canadian plan and, 215; East Africa, post-Uganda plan search for homeland in, 205, 209, 211; Uganda plan and, 11, 15, 16–17, 19, 22, 306n3
Chamberlain, Neville, 275–76
Churchill, Winston, 209, 211, 219
Cohen, Menahem, 197
Cohen, Rabbi M. I., 230
Cohen, Yitzhak, 197
Cohen-Bernstein, Jaccob, 111
Cohn-Reiss, Ephraim, 56
colonialism and imperialism of Western Europe, Territorialist hopes to exploit, 129, 207, 237, 302
Committee of Defenders of the Zionist Organization (Va'ad Meginei Hahistadrut), 34, 104
Committee of United Zionist Associations in Palestine, 1950196
Cowen (friend of Herzl, at Sixth Zionist Congress), 30, 63
Cyprus plan, 1, 11, 222, 224

D'Avigdor-Goldsmid, Osmond, 313n22
Deakin, Alfred, 217–18
Delamere, Lord, 211
Democratic Faction, 161
Dinur, Benzion, 41, 104
Diskin, Aharon, 197
displaced persons (DPs) after WWII, 282–84
dissolution of ITO, 14, 80, 254
Döblin, Alfred, 265, 267, 289; *Berlin Alexanderplatz* (1938), 267
DPs (displaced persons) after WWII, 282–84
Dubnow, Shimon, 273

East Africa, post-Uganda plan search for homeland in, 203–11, 242
East Africa survey commission: Angola survey team compared, 235;

345

# INDEX

East Africa survey commission (*continued*)
  composition and activities, 15, 18, 22, 28, 44–50, 66, 310–11n99; Gibbons, Alfred St. Hill, 46, 49, 50–51, 53–59, 66, 70–71, 235, 311n116; Kaiser, Alfred, 46, 47, 49, 50, 51–52, 53–56, 62, 311n116; report and conclusions, 48, 50–58, 59, 66, 70, 311n116. See also Wilbush (Wilbuschewitz), Nahum
Ein Hakoré association, 179
El-Arish plan (1902), 11, 17, 24–26, 44, 46, 114, 222, 242, 266
Elgin, Lord, 69, 208–11
Eliot, Charles, 19–20, 55, 310n99, 311n111
Ellis Island, 249, 251
emigration of Jews from Eastern Europe: Aliens Act 1905 (Great Britain) and, 139, 205, 208; DPs after WWII, 282–84; Evian conference on refugees and, 274–75; France, German Jews fleeing to, 264; ideology of Territorialism and, 135–40; information bureaus for Jewish emigrants, 81, 118–21, 316n104; Jewish Emigration Association (Yudishe Emigratsyone Gezelshaft), 117–21; mass emigrations of 1905 and 1906, 208; New Territorialism and, 262–63; Territorialism as response to, 12–13, 73, 116–17, 296, 301
Engel, Dr. (vice-chairman of Vienna ITO chapter), 233
England. *See* Great Britain
Epstein, Isaac, 300
Epstein, Yitzhak, 131
Eretz Israel Association, 195, 196
Ettinger, Akiva, 227–28
Evian conference (1938), 274–75

Executive Committee, ITO, 84, 224, 230
Exile: emigration as constant spectacle of, 135–36; rejection of, 126–27, 158

Fanarosh, Sarah, 191
Fifth Zionist Congress (1901), 161
Finkelstein, Noah, 187
First Aliyah, 69, 173, 178, 199, 200, 201, 302
First Congress of Territorialist Associations, 265–66
First World War, 198, 250, 253, 254–55, 256, 261, 272, 302
First Zionist Congress (1897), 100
Fourth Zionist Congress (1901), 161
France, German Jews fleeing to, 264
Frankel, Jonathan, *Prophecy and Politics* (1981), 5
*Fraye Shriftn farn Yidishen Sotsialistishn Gedank*, 264, 268
*Der Fraynd*, 42
Freeland League, 265–94; Arab-Jewish conflict in Palestine and, 272, 283, 289–91; articles circulating ideas of, 267–71; Birobidzhan Jewish settlement region, Soviet Union, and, 267; dissolution of, 294; DPs after WWII, 282–84; establishment of, 265–67; at Evian conference, 274–75; ITO and Zionist movement compared, 265, 271–74, 288–89; Kimberley plan, 276–82; platform, 265–66, 271, 329n42; State of Israel, establishment of, 284, 286–94; World Central Organization and World Central Advisory Council, 266, 267; Yishuv and, 284–86, 291–94
Freiman, Aharon, 176, 177–78

# INDEX

Freiman, Moderchai, 201
Friedman, Yeshayahu, 10
fundamental ideology, 1

Galt, Alexander, 212
Galveston plan, 78, 198, 243–51
Gaster, Rabbi Moses, 265, 266, 289
Geographical Committee, ITO, 84, 85, 122, 203, 211, 214, 241
Gepstein family, on Uganda plan, 37–38
Gibbons, Alfred St. Hill, 46, 49, 50–51, 53–59, 66, 70–71, 235, 311n116
Ginsburg, Asher (Ahad Ha'am), 131, 147–49, 156, 174–75, 179, 184, 189, 298
Ginsburg, Baron, 119
Goldberg, Yosef, 197
Goldman, Yaakov, 197
Goldreich, Samuel, 45
Goldstein, Yossi, 11
Gordon, A. D., 293
Gordon, Mrs. E. A., 46
Gotthelf, Judah, 290–91
Grabski, Władysław, 262
Great Britain: Aliens Act 1905, 139, 205, 208, 213; Australia, search for a homeland in, 215–20, 268–69; Balfour Declaration, 10, 14, 17, 69, 76, 126, 131, 254–58, 255, 262, 263, 284, 295, 299, 301; Canada, Jewish settlement in, 189, 211–15, 229, 268; East Africa, post-Uganda plan search for homeland in, 204–11; Freeland League's desire to found Jewish autonomous region in territories under control of, 268–69, 273–74; imperialism and colonialism, Territorialist hopes to exploit, 129, 207; ITO, British Sectional Council, 84–85, 313n22; New Territorialism and British Mandate's retreat from post-WWI promises, 262, 263. *See also* Uganda plan
Greater Actions Committee, 23–24, 29, 30, 34, 35, 38, 66, 67, 71, 266, 307n19
Greenberg, Leopold: East Africa survey commission and, 46, 50, 55; final resolution and rejection of Uganda plan, 68–69; initial negotiations of Uganda plan and, 16–17, 19, 21–22, 132, 306n5; in Rosenblatt's letters from Kiev, 91; Seventh Zionist Congress and, 59; Sixth Zionist Congress and, 27
Greenberg, Uri Zvi, 293
Gregory, Professor (head of Angola survey), 235–40
Grodzinsky, Joseph, 283
Guas Ngishu plateau, Uganda. *See* Uganda plan
Guggenheim, Daniel, 203, 206

Halevy, Yehuda, 101
*Ha-melitz*, 8, 42
*Hame'orer*, 160
Hardinge, Arthur, 232
Harel, Haya, 172
*Hashiloah*, 98, 100, 183
*Hashkafah*, 42, 176, 179, 180, 182, 187
Haupt, Paul, *Über die Ansiedlung der russischen im Euphart und Tigris-Gebeit: Ein Vorschlag* (On the Settlement of Russian Jews in the Area of the Euphrates and Tigris: A Proposal; 1892), 221
Hazan, Judah Haim: Ben Yehuda compared, 187; on exploitation of Western European colonialism and imperialism, 129; ITO, formation of, 80; *Jewish Writers and Territorialism* (1907), 43, 145–46,

# INDEX

Hazan, Judah Haim (*continued*)
187; *Konstitusyon un Teritoryalismus* (1906), 187, 309n76; manifesto of Territorialism published by, 146–47; on Uganda plan, 42–44, 64–66
Hazan, Ya'akov, 38, 308n54, 309n76
*Ha-zefirah*, 42–44, 58, 189
*Ha-zeman*, 42, 121, 130, 160, 162
*Ha-zofeh*, 42
Hebrew language, use of, 103, 189–90, 191, 288, 292–94
*Hebrew Standard*, 215, 217
Heine, Heinrich, 101
Helsingfors conference, 246, 298
Herder, Moses, 7
Herzl, Theodor: *Altneuland* (1902), 144, 170; Balfour Declaration as ultimate aim of, 255; Ben Yehuda's admiration for, 186, 189; Rabbi Binyamin on, 291; catastrophic Zionism and, 298; controversy over Uganda plan and, 29–41, 44; death of, 44, 46, 76; Democratic Faction and, 161; difficult relationship with wife, 82; East Africa survey commission and, 44–45, 46–47, 56; on emigration of Jews, 137–38; as founding father of Zionism, 76; initial presentation and negotiations of Uganda plan, 15, 16–17, 19, 20, 21, 22–23; Jabotinsky and ideas of, 156; *The Jewish State* (1896), 9–10, 11, 75, 134, 135, 249, 269, 297; Mandelstamm and, 100, 103, 104, 113–14; memorialized at Seventh Zionist Congress, 58, 60; Mesopotamia, on Jewish settlement in, 220–22; on Nordau, 76; origins of Territorialism in ideas of, viii, 2, 9–12, 13, 72, 126, 127, 135, 145, 149, 150, 297; Plehve, meetings with, 23–24; Reines and Mizrachi Party, 162; search for homeland after Uganda plan and, 206; Sixth Zionist Congress, presentation of Uganda plan to, 22–31, 35; Steinberg compared, 269, 270, 274; views on Uganda plan, 10–11, 13–14, 35; Yishuv support for, 175, 184, 194, 200; Zangwill and, 75–76, 78–79, 170, 233–34; Zeitlin and, 130; Zionist Congress, offer to resign presidency of, 29–31, 62–63
Heymann, Michael, 11
Hibbat Zion movement, 7, 8, 9, 32, 33, 38, 81, 103, 137, 174–75, 199, 266, 305n9
Hildesheimer, Hirsch, 111, 116
Hilfsverein der Deutschen Juden, 108, 111, 245
Hill, Clement, 22–23, 27
Hirsch, Baron Maurice de, 8–9, 134, 158, 189, 212, 229, 244, 280
Hirsch, Paul, 206
Hitler, Adolf, 264, 268
Hofshi, Nathan, 284, 291–94
Holocaust, 128, 294, 295, 299
Homel pogrom, 192
Hovevei Zion. *See* Hibbat Zion movement
Hurst, Cecil, 19, 22
Huxley, Elspeth, 310–11n99

ICA. *See* Jewish Colonization Association
ideology of Territorialism, 14, 123–46, 170–71; on Arab population of Palestine, 129–32; autonomous safe haven for Jews, establishment of, 123, 124–35; definition of ideology, 1–2; differentiation from Zionism, 125–28, 136–38; on

# INDEX

emigration of Jews from Eastern Europe, 135–40; emotional force, lack of, 303–4; Exile, rejection of, 126–27; on Jews assimilated into other countries, 133–34; "a land for a people, not a people for a land," 127; Palestine, attitude toward, 125–26, 128–29, 146; on process of establishment of Jewish territory, 140–46; on religious component of Jewish state, 144–45; territory, concept of, 128–29; utilitarianism of, 159; Zionist response to (*See* relationship between Zionism and Territorialism)

Idishe Territoryalistishe Organizatsye. *See* Jewish Territorial Organization

Ihud Association, 284, 291–94, 332n110

immigration. *See* emigration of Jews from Eastern Europe

Immigration League of Australia, 215–16, 218

imperialism and colonialism of Western Europe, Territorialist hopes to exploit, 129, 207, 237, 302

Industrial Removal Office, 243–44

information bureaus for Jewish emigrants, 81, 118–21, 316n104

Inner Actions Committee, 28, 32, 34–36, 44, 46, 56, 67, 222, 307n19

International Council, ITO, 84–85

Israel, establishment of State of, 284, 286–94

ITO. *See* Jewish Territorial Organization

Jabotinsky, Ze'ev: as founding father of Zionism, 76; *The Jewish War Front* (1940), 279; on Kimberley plan, 279–80; on Territorialist ideology, 155–60, 163

Jaffe, Leib, 67

Jasinowski, Israel, 24, 34, 81, 104

*Jewish Chronicle*, 215, 268

Jewish Colonial Bank, 28

Jewish Colonial Trust, 17, 22

Jewish Colonization Association (ICA): committees in Pale of Settlement, 9; ideology of Territorialism and, 134–35, 140; ITO, establishment of, 111, 118, 120–21; relationship between Territorialism and Zionism and, 152; search for a Jewish homeland and, 212, 224, 227–29, 244; Uganda Plan and, 45; Yishuv and, 199

Jewish Emigration Association (Yudishe Emigratsyone Gezelshaft), 117–21, 122, 136

Jewish National Fund, 28

Jewish Territorial Organization (ITO), 14, 73–122; Angola plan and decline of, 243, 252–53, 261; Basel congress (1905), 73–74, 79–82; British Sectional Council, 84–85, 313n22; at Brussels Conference (1906), 107–17, 122; dissolution of, 14, 80, 254, 257, 261, 301–2; Executive Committee, 84, 224, 230; formal establishment of, 73–84; fundraising activities, 84; Geographical Committee, 84, 85, 122, 203, 211, 214, 241; incidents leading to establishment of, vii, viii, 2, 5, 10, 11, 73; information bureaus for Jewish emigrants, 120, 121, 316n104; initialism of, 305n4; International Council, 84–85; Jewish Emigration Association, 117–21, 122, 136; London congress (1906), 71, 86; name, settlement of, 80–82; New Territorialism and Freeland

# INDEX

Jewish Territorial Organization (*continued*)
League compared, 263, 265, 271–74, 288–89; organization and structure, 83–87, 122; pogroms and, 14, 87–95, 121; propaganda activities and popular Jewish support for, 83, 87–97, 121–22; records in Central Zionist Archive, viii; Reines and, 162–70; relationship with Zionist Organization, 81, 83, 122, 146, 170; Sectional Councils, 84–85; Uganda plan and founding of, viii, 15, 41, 71–72, 73; Vienna, world congress in (1910), 233–35, *234*, 239; Yishuv support for Zangwill and, 14, 173, 176, 177, 186, 192, 193–98, 200. *See also* ideology of Territorialism; Mandelstamm, Max Emmanuel; search for a homeland; Zangwill, Israel
Jochelman, David, 120, 136, 232, 247–48
Johnston, Harry, 20, 54, 55, 239, 306–7nn13–14
Jüden Territorial Volks Organization (JVTO), 80–82
*Der Jüdische Emigrant*, 119

Kaiser, Alfred, 46, 47, 49, 50, 51–52, 53–56, 62, 311n116
Kattowitz conference (1884), 6, 305n9
Katzenelson, Yitzhak Leib ("Buki ben Yogli"), 9
Keleter, Avigdor, 197–98
Kessler, Leopold, 266, 274
Kharkov conference (against Uganda plan; 1903), 31, 33, 35–36, 40, 104, 184, 193, 308n48
Kiev: pogrom of 1905, 87, 88–92, 192; as stronghold of Territorialist movement, 97

Kimberley region of Australia, 264, 276–82
Kisch, Frederick Hermann, 111, 206
Kishinev pogrom, 23, 24, 25, 87, 108, 110, 155, 191, 192, 295–96, 301
Klausner, Joseph, *Mi-Katovich ad Basel* (From Kattowitz to Basel; 1965), 6
Kovno Territorialists, on settlement in Western Australia, 219–20
Kressel, Getzel, 178, 184–85, 190–91
Kruk, Joseph, *Tahat diglan shel Shalosh Mahapekhot* (1968), 79, 82, 239, 265, 267, 326n89

"A land for a people, not a people for a land," 125, 127, 188, 259, 265
Lang, Yosef, 185, 190
Langermann, Max, 45, 206
Lansdowne, Lord, 19–20, 22, 204
Latzky-Bertholdi, Jacob, 41
Laurier, Wilfrid, 215
League for Jewish Colonization (Lige far Yiddisher Kolonizatsyie), 264
Leftwich, Joseph, 329n42
Lenin, Vladimir Illich, 264
Lestschinsky, Jacob, 13, 41, 298
Levin, Shamaryahu, 38, 41, 309n67
Levinstein, Eliezer (Livne), *Ha-territorialism ha-hadashah* (The New Territorialism; 1944), 285–86
Lige far Yiddisher Kolonizatsyie (League for Jewish Colonization), 264
Lilienblum, Moshe Leib, 6, 156
Litvakov, Moshe ("Nitzotz"), 41
Livne (Levinstein), Eliezer, *Ha-territorialism ha-hadashah* (The New Territorialism; 1944), 285–86
Lloyd George, David, 219
local populations and Jewish settlers: in Angola, 229–30, 237–38,

## INDEX

240, 242–43; Arab population of Palestine, 3, 129–32, 154–55, 258–60, 262, 263, 272, 283, 289–91, 300; Borochov on, 153–55; Christian churches in Palestine, 221; East Africa, post-Uganda plan search for homeland in, 210–11; in Northern Territory of Australia, 218; Uganda plan and, 47, 50, 51, 53, 132
Luban, Haim Zelig, 39
Lubman, Dov, 178–79
Lyttelton, Alfred: East Africa, post-Uganda plan search for homeland in, 204–8, 217; Uganda plan rejection letter sent to, 68–69; Zangwill's letter on emigration process to, 141

Macedonia, ICA expedition to, 228
Magnes, Judah L., 60, 64, 284
Mandelstamm, Ezekiel, 97
Mandelstamm, Max Emmanuel, 97–107; *An ofener brief tsu di rusishe tsiyonisten* (An Open Letter to the Russian Zionists; 1905), 103–4; on assimilationism/Russification, 100–103, 104, 112; biographical information, 97–100; at Brussels Conference, 107, 110–15, 122; establishment of ITO and, 97, 104, 107; Herzl and, 100, 103, 104, 113–14; *How Jews Live: A Report upon the Physical Condition of Jews* (1900), 105–7; Jewish Emigration Organization and, 120, 136; *Mahut Hatsiyonut: Michtav Le-viti* (The Essence of Zionism: A Zionist's Letter to His Daughter; 1900), 100–101; memorialized by Zangwill, 233, *234*; persecution, experience of, 98, 99, 102; photographs, *99*, *234*; search for a homeland, involvement in, 203, 225, 233; Uganda plan and, 34, 103–4, 114, 179
Maori colonization of New Zealand, as model for Jews, 114–15
Mapai Party, 285
Mapam Party, 308n54
Marcus, Mr. (head of Jewish community in Nairobi), 47–49, 51
Margolis-Kalvaryski, Haim, 284
Markovsky, Yosef, 180, 184
Marks, Alexander, 218
Marks, Ellen-Hannah, 74
Marmorek, Oscar, 24, 65, 79
Marmur, Yitzhak, 4
"matter without form," Zionists describing Territorialists as, 148
Medina publishing house, 187
Melville, George, 277
Menzies, Robert, 279
Mesopotamia, Jewish settlement in, 139, 198, 220–29, 252
migration. *See* emigration of Jews from Eastern Europe
Mintz, Matityahu, 149, 318n72
Mizrachi Party, 27, 89, 161–63, 168–69, 193–94
Montagu, Edwin, 133
Moore, Newton, 218–19
Motzkin, Leo, 161; *Die Judenpogrome in Russland* (1910), 92–93
Mozambique plan, 11

Nathan, Meir, 266–67
Nathan, Paul, 111, 112, 203, 206, 245
National Union of Women's Suffrage Societies, 210
natives. *See* local populations and Jewish settlers
*Der Nayer Weg*, 72
Nazis' rise to power, 255, 262, 264, 267, 268, 301

# INDEX

*Ner,* 331n109
Netanyahu, Benzion, 76–77
Nevinson, Henry, 239–40
New Guinea plan, 275–76
New Territorialism, 14, 255, 262–94; Arab-Jewish conflict in Palestine and, 262, 263, 272, 283, 289–91; British Mandate's retreat from post-WWI promises, 262, 263; compared to original Territorialist movement and Zionists, 263, 265, 271–73; DPs after WWII, 282–84; expiration of, 294; First Congress of Territorialist Associations, 265–66; Ihud Association in Palestine, 284, 291–94, 332n110; increased Jewish emigration and, 262–63; members and local associations, 264–65; Nazis' rise to power and, 255, 262, 264, 267, 268, 301; origins and development of, 262–67; relationship to Zionism and ITO, 263, 265, 271–74, 288–89; State of Israel, establishment of, 284, 286–94. *See also* Freeland League
New Zealand: Freeland League and, 268–69; Maori settlement as model for Jews, 114–15
Niger, Samuel, 41
Nissenbaum, Isaac, 32–33
Nitzotz (Moshe Litvakov), 41
Nordau, Max: attempted assassination of, 39; Ben Yehuda and, 186; contributions of, 76; elected president of Zionist Congress, 58; memorialization of Herzl, 58, 60; on relationship between Zionism and Territorialism, 147; on Uganda plan, 27, 30, 39, 58, 59, 67, 70–71; Zangwill and, 75, 79
Northern Territory of Australia, 215–18

Norton-Griffiths, John, 229–30
*Novosti,* 191

Odessa Committee (Society for the Support of Jewish Laborers and Craftsmen in Syria and Palestine in Odessa), 85, 137
operative ideology, 1
Orlans, A. S., 76
Ottoman empire. *See* Turkey
*Oyfen Shvel,* 290–91

Palestine: Arab population of, 3, 129–32, 154–55, 258–60, 262, 263, 272, 283, 289–91, 300; Christian churches of, 221; post-WWI immigration to, 262–63; State of Israel, establishment of, 284, 286–94; Territorialist attitude toward, 125–26, 128–29, 146; Zionist views on emigration to, 136–37. *See also* Rishon Lezion; Yishuv
Palestine Zionist Federation, 172
Pappus, 160, 319n102
Paris Peace Conference, 262
philanthropic assistance for Jewish settlers: ideology of Territorialism and, 140; ITO, establishment of, 96, 110, 111, 113; New Territorialism and, 270; search for a homeland nd, 206, 209–10, 232, 244, 248, 252; Uganda plan and, 25, 26
Pinsker, Leon: *Auto-Emancipation* (1882), 1, 5–6, 7, 8, 9, 99, 145, 174, 296, 297, 301; catastrophic Zionism and, 298; as founding father of Zionism, 76; Jabotinsky and ideas of, 156; origins of Territorialism in ideas of, viii, 2, 5–7, 126, 127, 145, 149, 297
Plehve, Vyacheslav, 23–24
Po'alei Zion, 41, 81, 82

# INDEX

pogroms: of 1880s, 92, 113, 174; of 1903-1906, 2–3, 14, 23, 62, 73, 87–96, *88*, 107–9, 139, 155, 165, 194, 205, 222; Ben Yehuda on, 191–92; Bialystok pogrom, 94, 166–67, 212; Brussels Conference and, 107–10; Calarasi pogrom, 93; Canada, Jewish settlement in, 212–13; East Africa, post-Uganda plan search for homeland in, 205; Homel pogrom, 192; ITO and, 14, 87–95, 121; Kiev pogrom, 87, 88–92, 192; Kishinev pogrom, 23, 24, 25, 87, 108, 110, 155, 191, 192, 295–96, 301; Mesopotamia plan and, 222; Reines on, 165–67; Territorialism as response to, vii, 3, 7–8, 12, 73, 107–8, 139, 165–67, 194, 295–96, 301; Uganda plan, support for, 107–8; Yekaterinoslav pogrom, 87, *88*; Zionism, popular criticism of, 95–96

Poland: post-WWI deterioration of economic condition of Jews in, 262; reestablishment of, 254

Portuguese colonies in Angola. *See* Angola plan

Qibya raid, 289–90

Rabbinowitz, Saul Phinehas ("Shepher"), 32–33, 39
Radler-Feldmann, Yehoshua (Rabbi Binyamin), 284, 291–92, 294
Rawidowicz, Simon, 331n103
Raz-Korkotzkin, Amnon, 127
Reines, Rabbi Isaac Jacob (Yitzhak Yaakov): on Territorialist ideology and ITO, 161–70, 171, 194; on Uganda plan, 27, 179
Reinharz, Jehuda, 37
relationship between Zionism and Territorialism, 2–3, 146–73; Ahad Ha'am on, 147–49; analysis of, 296–300; Borochov on, 149–55, 163, 170–71; Brenner on, 160–61; co-existence, possibility of, 146–47; ideological differentiation, 125–28, 136–38; ITO and Zionist Organization, 81, 83, 122, 146, 170; Jabotinsky on, 155–60, 163; New Territorialists and Freeland League, 263, 265, 271–74, 288–89; Reines and Mirachi Party members on, 161–70, 171; Territorialist responses to Zionist critiques, 160

religion: founding of Mizrachi Party and, 161–62; territorialist federation for religious Jews, Reines's inquiries about, 165; Territorialist ideology on, 144–45

Renan, Ernest, 102

revival of Territorialism. *See* Freeland League; New Territorialism

Rishon Lezion (Palestine): Herzl in, 175; population of, 173; *Sefer Rishon Lezion: 1882–1941* (Book of Rishon Lezion), 200–201; Territorialism, post-Ugandan support for, 197, 199, 200–201; Uganda plan and, 176–80; Zionist associations in, 175, 195

Riza, Ahmed, 224–25
Robins, Edward, 236
Rochelson, Meri-Jane, *A Jew in the Public Arena: The Career of Israel Zangwill* (2008), 4–5, 132
Roque, Bernardine, 241
Rosenbaum, Semyon, 34–35, 308n48
Rosenblatt, Moshe, 89–94, 108, 110, 165, 168, 192, 205, 313n34
Rosin, Abraham (Ben Adir), 267
Rothschild, Edmond de, Baron, 235
Rothschild, Leopold de, 313n22

# INDEX

Rothschild, Lionel Walter, Baron, 140, 174, 203, 210, 222, 241, 258
Rothschild, Nathan, Baron, 174, 199
Rothschild, Nathanael, 241
Rovner, Adam, *In the Shadow of Zion: Promised Lands Before Israel* (2014), 5
Royal Geographical Society, 56–57
Ruppin, Arthur, *The Jews of To-Day* (1913), 136–37
Russia and Russian empire: Bolshevik revolution, 254, 264; hostility to Zionism in, 23–24; insensitivity of Western Jews to sufferings of Jews in, 116; ITO in, 85–87, 206; Jewish settlement in south under Alexander I, 280; territorialist pioneering groups in, 140, 141, 142; Zionist Organization in, 85, 100. *See also* Soviet Union

Sabataeans, 148
Sadan, Dov, 284–85, 286
Salomon, Mordechai, 197
Salomon, Yoel Moshe, 197
Saposnik, Arieh Bruce, *Becoming Hebrew: The Creation of a Jewish National Culture in Ottoman Palestine* (2008), 5, 172–73
Schiff, Jacob, 210, 226–27, 243–50
Schiller, Friedrich, 97, 101
*Schlemiel*, 316n22
Schwartz, Shifra, 172, 178
search for a homeland, 14, 202–53; El-Arish plan (Sinai Peninsula), 11, 17, 24–26, 44, 46, 114, 222, 242, 266; in Canada, 189, 211–15, 229; Cyprus plan, 1, 11, 222, 224; in East Africa, after Uganda plan, 203–11, 242; Galveston plan, 78, 198, 243–51; inherent problems with, 301–2; in Mesopotamia, 139, 198, 220–29, 252; New Guinea plan, 275–76. *See also* Angola plan; Australia, search for a homeland in; local populations and Jewish settlers; Uganda plan
Second Aliyah, 176, 178, 199, 291
Second World War, 128, 153, 264, 268, 276, 279, 281–82, 295, 300
Sectional Councils, ITO, 84–85
Semel, Nava, *IsraIsland* (2005), 5
Seventh Zionist Congress (1905): ITO, establishment of, 5; memorialization of Herzl at, 58, 60; postponement of, 44; program cover, 61; restriction of activities to Palestine, 125–27; Uganda plan removed from Zionist agenda at, 14, 15–16, 58–68, 297
Sforim, Mendele Mocher, 75
Shaarei Zion, 197
Shabbetai Zevi, 148
Shaftesbury, Lord, 259
Shakespeare, William, 101
Sharett, Judah, 148
Shaw Committee report (1930), 263
Sheinkin, Menahem, 137
Shepher (Saul Phinehas Rabbinowitz), 32–33, 39
Shimoni, Gideon, 126; *The Zionist Ideology* (1995), 1–2
Shire, M. (British delegate to Seventh Zionist Congress), 64
Shparber Association, 264
Simmons, Professor (AJA representative at Brussels Conference), 111
Simon, Akiva Ernst, 284
Simon, James, 203, 206
Simon Morris, 77
Sinai Peninsula (El-Arish plan, 1902), 11, 17, 24–26, 44, 46, 114, 222, 242, 266

# INDEX

Sixth Zionist Congress (1903): split between Territorialists and Zionists at, 10; Uganda plan submitted to, 10, 13, 15, 22–31, 35
Slouschz, Nahum, 232
Slutsky, Yehudah, 104
Smilansky, Moshe, 183, 184, 284
Social Democrats, 112
socialism and Zionism: Bolshevik revolution, 254, 264; Mandelstamm on, 112–13; New Territorialism and, 264–65; Shparber Association, 264; Uganda plan and, 40–41, 68; Zionist Socialist Workers' Party, 41, 68, 74
Socialist Revolutionary Party, 112, 264
Social Revisionists, 112
Society for the Support of Jewish Laborers and Craftsmen in Syria and Palestine in Odessa (Odessa Committee), 85, 137
Sokolow, Nahum, 42–44, 188–89, 256
Soviet Union: Birobidzhan Jewish settlement region, 267; Bolshevik regime, 289; Bolshevik revolution, 254, 264. *See also* Russia and Russian empire
Spielman, Meyer, 229–30, 313n22
Stähler, Axel, 316n22
Stein, Menachem, 67, 201
Steinberg, Isaac Nachman: *Australia: The Unpromised Land* (1945/1948), 278, 280–81, 330n67; biographical information, 264; death of, 294; on DPs after WWII, 282–84; at Evian conference, 274; "Far der katastrof" (Before the Catastrophe), 267–71; Ihud Association in Palestine and, 291–94, 332n110; Kimberley plan, 276–82; on State of Israel, 288–94; Yishuv and, 286; "Der Yovel fun an idée" (The Fiftieth Anniversary of an Idea), 289–90
Strathcona, Lord, 212–15, 217
Strauss, Oscar, 203, 206, 221, 224, 227
Sulzberger, Mayer, 203, 206, 221, 249
Suriname, DPs wanting to emigrate to, 283
*Sydney Daily Telegraph,* 144
Syrkin, Nachman, 41, 68, 72, 80

Tchlenov, Yehiel, 6, 24, 28
Teitel, Jacob, 232
Teller, Yisrael Halevi, 197, 199
Terló, Wolf, 231
Territorialism, vii–viii, 1–14, 295–304; Am Olam/Bilu controversy, 7–8, 9; continuation of concept after dissolution of ITO, 254; Herzl and, viii, 2, 9–12, 13 (*See also* Herzl, Theodor); Hirsch's Argentine project, 8–9; as ideology, 1–2; ideology of, 14 (*See also* ideology of Territorialism); ITO, 14, 73–122 (*See also* Jewish Territorial Organization); literature review, 3–5; Pinsker as founding father of, viii, 2, 5–7 (*See also* Pinsker, Leon); pioneer elite, lack of, 302–3; pogroms and emigration, as response to, vii, 3, 7–8, 12–13, 73, 107–8, 116–17, 139, 165–67, 194, 295–96, 301; reasons for decline and disappearance of, 300–304; relationship with Zionism, 2–3, 146–73 (*See also* relationship between Zionism and Territorialism); revival of, 14, 255, 262–94 (*See also* Freeland League; New Territorialism); search for a homeland, 14, 202–53 (*See also* search for a homeland); Uganda plan and, 13–14, 15–72 (*See also*

# INDEX

Territorialism (*continued*)
Uganda Plan); Yishuv and, 14, 172–201 (*See also* Yishuv); Zangwill and (*See* Zangwill, Israel)
therapeutic movement, 143
Third Zionist Congress (1899), 266
Tineius Rufus, 160, 319n102
Tiomkin, Ze'ev, 156
Tolstoy, Leo, 101
Trietsch, David, 27
Tschernikhov, Joseph, 267, 272
Tsippeleshter, Yakov, 93
Turkey (Ottoman empire): collapse of Ottoman empire after WWI, 255; Mesopotamia, Jewish settlement in, 221–29; Palestine, Jewish settlement in, 134–35, 182; Young Turk revolution, 223, 224

Uganda plan (1902-1905), 13–14, 15–72; Balfour Declaration compared to British statement on, 257; completion of construction of Uganda Railway, 16; establishment of ITO and, viii, 15, 41, 71–72; evolution of controversy over, 29–44; final resolution and rejection of, 67–69; as formative moment in Territorialist and Zionist history, 296, 299–300; Holocaust compared, 128; initial proposal and negotiations, 15, 16–23; Jabotinsky on, 156, 157, 158–59; Jewish street reaction to, 31, 36–44; Kharkov conference (1903) against, 31, 33, 35–36, 40, 104, 184, 193, 308n48; land offered for, 19–20, *21*; Mandelstamm and, 34, 103–4, 114, 179; motives of supporters and anti-Ugandists, 69–71; natives of territory and, 47, 50, 51, 53, 132; press on, 40, 42–44;

reconciliation convention, 31, 36; Reines on, 162, 179; Russian Zionists against, 31, 32–36; Saposnik on, 5; in *Schlemiel*, 316n22; Seventh Zionist Congress, removal of plan from Zionist agenda at, 14, 15–16, 58–68, 297; Sixth Zionist Congress, submission of plan to, 10, 13, 15, 22–31, 35; stages of, 15–16; views of Herzl on, 10–11, 13–14, 35 (*See also* Herzl, Theodor); Yishuv on, 175–84. *See also* Ben Yehuda, Eliezer, and Uganda plan; East Africa survey commission

United Kingdom. *See* Great Britain

United States: Am Olam's focus on, 7–8, 99; DPs after WWII immigrating to, 283; economic reasons for Jewish emigration to, 301; Ellis Island, 249, 251; Galveston plan, 78, 198, 243–51; Industrial Removal Office, 243–44; Mandelstamm on eye diseases and Jewish immigration to, 107; proposal to limit Jews entering Germany on way to, 116; quota laws, 254; Reines on Jewish immigration to, 163; Territorialist versus Zionist views on emigration to, 136–39

UN Partition Resolution (November 29, 1947), 10

Ussishkin, Menahem Mendel: archives of, viii; Borochov and, 38–39, 41, 149, 155, 170, 183; ITO opposition to, 74, 82, 146, 147; Jabotinsky and, 156; Mandelstamm on, 103, 104; Palestine Zionist Federation, founding of, 172; Reines and Mizrachi Party, 162, 163; Uganda plan rejected by, 32–36,

# INDEX

38–42, 57, 66–67; vice-presidential candidacy for Seventh Zionist Congress, 58; Yishuv opposition to, 180–82, 183, 184, 188, 193, 200; Zangwill on, 134
utilitarian basis of Territorialist doctrine, 159

Va'ad Meginei Hahistadrut (Committee of Defenders of the Zionist Organization), 34, 104
Versailles Conference (1919), 257
Vienna ITO Congress of 1912 approving Angola plan, 233–35, *234*, 239
Vital, David, 4, 11, 29

Waife-Goldberg, Marie, 88–89
Wallenstein, Yisrael Meir, 197
Warburg, Otto, 46–47, 58–59, 66, 222–24
Weinberg, Yitzhak Moshe, 193–94
Weizmann, Chaim: Balfour Declaration and, 256–57; in Democratic Faction, 161; *Trial and Error* (1949), 44; on Uganda plan, 37, 44, 64, 306–7n14, 309n78; Zangwill on leadership of, 260
Weizmann, Shmuel, 82
Weizmann, Vera, 306n14
Weizmann-Lichtenstein, Chaya, 37
*Die Welt*, 40, 57–58, 66, 108, 178, 179, 180, 311n116
Wertheim, Rabbi Shlomo, 142
Western Australia, 218–20
Western European colonialism and imperialism, Territorialist hopes to exploit, 129, 207, 237
"Who We Are and What We Want" (ITO booklet), 124
Wilbush (Wilbuschewitz), Nahum: appointment to East Africa survey commission, 46, 47; Auerbach in East Africa compared, 210; conclusions reached by, 52–53, 55, 56, 58, 62, 70, 71; in East Africa, 47–50, 56, 58; Gibbons's criticism of, 53–56, 59, 66; map used by, *21*, 55, 306n13; at Seventh Zionist Congress, 59
Willcock, John Collings, 276, 277, 278
Willcocks, Sir William, 222–24, 227; *The Restoration of the Ancient Irrigation Works on the Tigris or the Re-Creation of Chaldea* (1903), 223
Wise, Frank, 276
*Wohin*, 248
Wolff, Lucien, 166, 204, 206
Wolffsohn, David, 56, 107–9, 111–12, 115, 175, 222, 224
Wolfson, Haya, 94
World Central Organization and World Central Advisory Council, 266, 267
World War I, 198, 250, 253, 254–55, 256, 261, 272, 302
World War II, 128, 153, 264, 268, 276, 279, 281–82, 295, 300

Yafo, Pesah, 197
Yanovsky, Shmuel, 119
Yeivin, Israel, 76
Yekaterinoslav pogrom, 87, *88*
Yiddish language, use of, 102–3, 288, 293–94
Yidishe (Idishe) Territoryalistishe Organizatsye. *See* Jewish Territorial Organization
Yishuv, 14, 172–201; Brussels manifesto, 195–97, 322n67; First Aliyah, 69, 173, 178, 199, 200, 201, 302; Freeland League and, 284–86, 291–94; Herzl, support for, 175, 184, 194, 200; historical studies of, 4–5,

# INDEX

Yishuv (*continued*)
172–73; historiography, erasure of Territorialism from, 200–201; Ihud Association, 284, 291–94n33n110; ITO and Zangwill, support for, 14, 173, 176, 177, 186, 192, 193–98, 200; motivations for support for Territorialism, 199–201; numbers, settlements, and demographics, 173–74; Second Aliyah, 176, 178, 199, 291; significance of support for Territorialism, 199; survival of Territorialist idea after defeat of Uganda plan, 173, 193–98; Uganda plan and, 175–84; Ussishkin, opposition to, 180–82, 183, 184, 188, 193, 200; Zionist movement and, 174–75; Zionist preference for wealthier Jews in, 136–37. *See also* Ben Yehuda, Eliezer, and Uganda plan; Rishon Lezion

Young Men's Hebrew Benevolent Society, 212

Young Turk revolution, 223, 224

Yudelovich, David, 176–79, 184, 197, 199, 200–201

Yudishe Emigratsyone Gezelshaft (Jewish Emigration Association), 117–21, 122, 136

Zangwill, Edith Ayrton, 82, *83,* 210

Zangwill, Israel: Angola, search for a homeland in, 229–39, 232–37, 239–43; on Arab population of Palestine, 129–32, 258–60; Australia, search for a homeland in, 215–20; Balfour Declaration and WWI, 255–62; *Be Fruitful and Multiply* (1909), 134, 138, 141; Ben Yehuda and, 186, 192, 193; biographical information, 74–76; Brussels Conference and, 108–10, 115–16; Canada, Jewish settlement in, 212–15; *Children of the Ghetto* (1892), 74–75, 186; concept of Territorialism and, 77–78; contributions of, 76–77; *Dreamers of the Ghetto* (1898), 74–75; East Africa, post-Uganda plan search for homeland in, 204–11; on emigration of Jews, 138–40; Freeland League and, 265, 271; Galveston plan and, 243–50; Herzl and, 75–76, 78–79, 170, 233–34; historical studies of, 4–5; ideology of Territorialism and, 128–34, 138–42, 144–45, 170; ITO, establishment of, 74, 78–82, *83,* 88–94, 96–97, 104, 122; Jewish Emigration Association and, 120, 121; *The King of the Beggars* (1894), 186; Mandelstamm memorialized by, 233, *234; The Melting Pot* (1909), 75, 78; Mesopotamia plan and, 224–28; photographs, *83, 234*; pogroms of 1903-1906 and, 89–94; on process of establishing Jewish territory, 140–42, 144–45; Reines and Mizrachi Party, relationship with, 162–70, 171; relationship between Territorialism and Zionism and, 147, 152, 156, 160, 162–71; search for a homeland by, 202–3, 251–53, 301–2; Steinberg compared, 269, 274; on Uganda plan, 24, 26, 30, 31, 60–64, 312n129; Yishuv support for, 14, 173, 176, 177, 186, 192, 193–98, 200

Zangwill, Lewis, 74

Zangwill, Moshe, 74, 186

Zeitlin, Hillel, 130–31, 272

Zeligman, Charles, 274

Zemach, Shlomo, *Shana rishonah* (The First Year; 1965), 176–81, 184

# INDEX

Zhitlowsky, Chaim, 264

Zionism: on emigration, 136–38; Mandelstamm on, 113; New Territorialism and Freeland League compared, 263, 265, 271–74, 288–89; pogroms and popular criticism of, 95–96; Russian hostility to, 23–24. *See also* relationship between Zionism and Territorialism; socialism and Zionism

Zionist Aid Fund, 92

Zionist Executive Committee, 100

Zionist Organization: Bilu/Am Olam conflict presaging debate within, 8; Brussels conference, 107–8, 110–17; crisis of ideology and principles in, vii, 12; Democratic Faction and founding of Mizrachi Party, 161–62; establishment of, in 1897, 175; Greater Actions Committee, 23–24, 29, 30, 34, 35, 38, 66, 67, 71, 266, 307n19; Inner Actions Committee, 28, 32, 34–36, 44, 46, 56, 67, 222, 307n19; Mesopotamia plan and, 222–24; relationship with ITO, 81, 83, 122, 146, 170; in Russia, 85, 100; secession of Territorialists from, viii, 12, 41, 68. *See also* Uganda plan; *specific Zionist Congresses* (e.g. Sixth Zionist Congress)

Zionist Socialist Workers' Party, 41, 68, 74

Zion Mule Corps (WWI), 255

Zisselman, Yaakov Zvi, 184

Zuta, Haim Arieh, 195, 196–97, 199